Women in Medieval Europe 1200–1500

Second Edition

Women in Medieval Europe explores the key areas of female experience in the later medieval period, from peasant women to queens. It considers the women of the later Middle Ages in the context of their social relationships during a time of changing opportunities and activities, so that by 1500 women were becoming increasingly restricted from the world of work. The chapters are arranged thematically to show the varied roles and lives of women in and out of the home, covering topics such as marriage, religion, family and work.

For the second edition a new chapter draws together recent work on Jewish and Muslim women, as well as those from other ethnic groups, showing the wide-ranging experiences of women from different backgrounds. Particular attention is paid to women at work in the towns, and specifically urban topics such as trade, crafts, health care and prostitution. The latest research on women, gender and masculinity has also been incorporated, along with updated further reading recommendations.

This fully revised new edition is a comprehensive yet accessible introduction to the topic, perfect for all those studying women in Europe in the later Middle Ages.

Jennifer Ward spent much of her career at Goldsmiths College, University of London, where she taught medieval and regional history. Her previous publications include: *English Noblewomen in the Later Middle Ages* (1992), *Women of the English Nobility and Gentry 1066–1500* (1995) and *Women in England in the Middle Ages* (2006).

Women in Medieval Europe 1200–1500

Second Edition

Jennifer Ward

 Routledge
Taylor & Francis Group

LONDON AND NEW YORK

Second edition published 2016
by Routledge
2 Park Square, Milton Park, Abingdon, Oxon OX14 4RN

and by Routledge
711 Third Avenue, New York, NY 10017

Routledge is an imprint of the Taylor & Francis Group, an informa business

© 2016 Jennifer Ward

First edition published 2002 by Pearson Education Limited

British Library Cataloguing-in-Publication Data
A catalogue record for this book is available from the British Library

Library of Congress Cataloging-in-Publication Data
Names: Ward, Jennifer C.
Title: Women in medieval Europe, 1200-1500 / Jennifer Ward.
Description: Second edition. | London : Routledge, 2016. | "First edition published 2002 by Pearson Education Limited"—Title page verso. | Includes bibliographical references and index.
Identifiers: LCCN 2015037828| ISBN 9781138855670 (hardback : alkaline paper) | ISBN 9781138855687 (paperback : alkaline paper) | ISBN 9781315629803 (ebook)
Subjects: LCSH: Women—Europe—History—Middle Ages, 500-1500. | Women—Europe—Social conditions. | Women and religion—Europe—History—To 1500. | Women—Political activity—Europe—History—To 1500. | Europe—Social conditions—T0 1492.
Classification: LCC HQ1147.E85 W37 2016 | DDC 305.4209409/02—dc23
LC record available at http://lccn.loc.gov/2015037828

ISBN: 978-1-138-85567-0 (hbk)
ISBN: 978-1-138-85568-7 (pbk)
ISBN: 978-1-315-62980-3 (ebk)

Typeset in Sabon
by Keystroke, Station Road, Codsall, Wolverhampton

Printed and bound in the United States of America by
Edwards Brothers Malloy on sustainably sourced paper

In memory of John

Contents

Preface

Over the past twenty years, interest in women's history has continued unabated, and research is throwing new light on women's activities, interests and beliefs. History is not the only discipline contributing to this upsurge. Literary, social, cultural and religious studies have all made great contributions to the story of women in the past. Archaeological excavations and work on architecture and art history enable us to reconstruct women's houses, daily lives and relationships to family and children. Women in Europe had and have a common inheritance, and in many ways in the Middle Ages their lives were similar wherever they lived. Yet recent work is also pointing to strong regional differences, some of which can still be traced in the modern world. Aspects of the Middle Ages are still alive in the Europe of today.

In writing this book, I have incurred a number of debts. I would like to thank Patricia Skinner, one of the editors of the series, and Heather McCallum and her colleagues at Pearson Education for their help, and Philip Broadhead, Paul Fouracre, Kay Lacey and Kate Lowe for their advice on particular parts of the book. Any remaining mistakes are mine. I would also like to thank family and friends for visiting with me numerous sites associated with medieval women and discussing their implications.

Jennifer Ward
March 2002

Preface to the second edition

For the second edition a new chapter, 'Ethnic minorities: Jews, Muslims and slaves', has been included. 'Women and the work they do' has now been divided between a rural and an urban chapter. I would like to thank Laura Pilsworth and Catherine Aitken for their help with the revisions.

Jennifer Ward, September 2015

Abbreviations

Introduction

Women, the Church and the law

Few women of the later Middle Ages, apart possibly from Joan of Arc, are known by name to people in the twenty-first century. Joan of Arc was herself exceptional in taking on the male role of a soldier and raising the siege of Orleans in 1429. More is heard of kings, popes, philosophers and scholars than of queens and women mystics and writers. Partly this is due to the subordination of medieval women and the way in which they were viewed by the Church and the law, partly it is due to traditions in historical writing until recent times. However, the continuing interest in social history and gender from the second half of the twentieth century to the present day has resulted in women becoming more noticed.

During this time, the historian's tools for analysis have become more refined. Women's history became more prominent as a result of the feminist movement. About forty years ago, historians wanted to open up knowledge of medieval women by using new methodologies of analysing sources, and this concern is ongoing. Sources which had previously been used were re-examined from fresh viewpoints. More recently, work on gender studies as an effective tool of analysis has opened up new understandings of medieval society. Gender is essentially a social and cultural construction of human relationships, whether in the home, workplace or community.[1] The present study of masculinity is an essential part of this, and, as a result, the picture of human relations has become more complex and nuanced, as rigid, polarised identities of men and women have been undermined by deeper analysis.

This approach to gender gives rise to studies in difference set in the contexts of place and time, since people differ in numerous ways – in sexuality, ethnicity, religion, status, age, occupations, authority and power. Understanding of the complexity of sexualities has grown, and this has a bearing on relationships and needs to be set against the rigid definitions of sexuality in the medieval world and the emphasis on male authority and control.[2] Gender entails an understanding of place since men's and women's relationships varied considerably from region to region in medieval Europe, and changes took place in societies and culture during the later Middle Ages. Gender has to be looked at from more than the biological point of view. Although most women had common experience as mothers, the social construction of status highlights their different experiences over place and time.

It is a truism that women were regarded as inferior and subordinate in the later Middle Ages, and to understand this it is essential to go back to the classical past. The Greeks believed that all matter in the universe, including mankind, was made up of four elements – earth, air, fire and water – in varying combinations. These elements corresponded in the human body to the four humours: choler or yellow bile was associated with fire; phlegm with water; black bile with earth; and blood with air. Each element had its own characteristics: fire was hot and dry; air hot and wet; water cold and wet; and earth cold and dry. Good health was ensured by keeping a balance between the humours, but one or two were usually predominant, giving the personality and appearance their main traits – an individual might be choleric, phlegmatic, melancholic (through an excess of black bile) or sanguine, if blood was the dominant humour.

More significant from the point of view of women was the opinion that in them the cold and moist elements were uppermost. This idea was emphasised by Aristotle, as when he claimed that women matured and aged earlier than men because they were weaker and colder by nature; they were inferior to men who had the heat to grow more slowly. For Aristotle, a woman was an imperfect man. The same point was made in the second century A.D. by the physician Galen who asserted that man was more perfect than woman because of the element of heat.[3]

The imperfect nature of women was apparent in their sexual organs. Both Aristotle and Galen believed that men's and women's sexual organs were mirror images of each other. As Galen put it, the organs were formed inside the woman when she was a foetus in the womb and because of her lack of heat could not emerge on the outside of the body; however, he considered this an advantage for humanity, since women were essential for procreation, and the Creator would not have made women imperfect unless there had been good reason for this. Aristotle and Galen differed on the question of the woman's role in procreation. Aristotle distinguished between the man as active and the woman as passive partner, the man providing the form and the woman matter, as befitted the weaker creature. The woman produced menstrual fluid, not semen. The male semen implanted itself in the womb and developed into a foetus, the woman simply providing the site for this development to take place. Galen, however, was aware of the presence of the ovaries, which he regarded as small testes, and saw women's semen as having a role in procreation; at the same time he pointed out that the semen of the male had a more important part to play. Both theories are found during the Middle Ages. The recovery of Aristotle's works in the twelfth and early thirteenth centuries led to his having great influence on medical science as on other forms of learning. St Thomas Aquinas subscribed to his belief in matter and form, arguing that the foetus received its form from the power of the father's semen.[4]

Menstruation was a further sign of women's imperfection, and for Aristotle this explained why women did not produce semen. Menstrual blood was regarded as unclean and polluting in classical and medieval times. Yet it was believed that menstrual blood nourished the foetus in the womb and that the breast-milk which fed the baby after birth was a form of menstrual blood. The girl-baby was disadvantaged even in the womb; boys, it was believed, developed on the right side of the womb, while girls on the left suffered from a colder environment from the time of conception.[5]

These scientific views have to be set against the religious ideas of the Middle Ages. According to the Church, mankind fell from the state of grace through the action of Eve who, according to the story in the Bible in the Book of Genesis, was tempted by the devil to pick the fruit of the tree of the knowledge of good and evil growing in the middle of the Garden of Eden. God had forbidden Adam and Eve to touch this fruit, but Eve ate it and gave it to her husband. As a result, God drove Adam and Eve out of the Garden and condemned them to a life of toil and suffering.[6] Eve's weakness in succumbing to temptation underlay much of the misogynistic writing of the Middle Ages. Although St Paul stressed the obligations of marital partners towards each other, he saw the wife as a person lacking in authority and subject to her husband.[7] The Fall, taken together with the influence of classical writings and the long tradition of women's subordination, largely explains the Church's deep distrust of women. The idealising of virginity by the Church led to the opinion that marriage was second best. Yet gender analysis shows some variety among churchmen's views, as is apparent in the pastoral manuals of practical advice to parish priests, written from *c.* 1200 onwards. Although Thomas of Chobham saw husband and wife as having a good influence on each other, the wife was certainly subordinate to her husband, whereas Robert Grosseteste saw the marital relationship on a more equal footing of reciprocal support and partnership.[8]

Women's vices were a popular subject for preachers, writers and poets in the later Middle Ages. Jacques de Vitry (d. 1240) was a prominent churchman and crusader, well known for his support of the beguines, the religious women of the Low Countries, and in particular of Mary of Oignies whom he regarded as his inspiration. He was also a prolific preacher and fully aware of women's shortcomings. He expected wives to obey their husbands; Eve was created from Adam's rib, not from his head, in order to reduce women's arrogance. Women were self-willed, quarrelsome, disobedient, weak, deceitful and untrustworthy.[9] Two traits were particularly emphasised by churchmen: women were lustful and had an insatiable sexual appetite, and they lacked reason and therefore needed to be subject to a man's guidance.

The antithesis of Eve was the Virgin Mary, the woman who obeyed God's call to become the mother of his Son, Jesus Christ, who redeemed the world through his death on the cross and his resurrection. She epitomised obedience to God's will, whereas Eve stood for disobedience. The cult of the Virgin became more prominent from the later eleventh century, and carvings and paintings of her increased as the Gothic style took hold in Europe. Depictions of the Coronation of the Virgin of the late twelfth century put her on the same level as Christ, but subsequent images show her in an attitude of submission to her Son. Later medieval depictions of the Virgin and Child emphasised her human qualities as a mother, and these human qualities come out in the visions of women mystics. However, this concern with the Virgin's humanity did not give rise to a more positive view of women, because Mary was the outstanding exception to women's general nature – she was not only mother but virgin, a status impossible for any other woman to achieve.[10] Mary inspired deep devotion, was regarded as a model of the Christian life, was called upon as intercessor, and adopted as patron by cities and churches, but she did not alter the way in which women were viewed by the Church in the later Middle Ages.

Preachers and writers were bound to speak in general terms in order to make their point. The reverence for authorities, whether classical philosophers or Church Fathers, meant that it was highly unlikely that views on women's status and imperfections would be overturned. These views permeated social attitudes, but do not give the whole story as to how women were regarded. One thirteenth-century woman disagreed with the traditional interpretation of the Fall. She argued that Adam disliked the original Eve whom God had created and killed her, whereupon God created a second Eve out of Adam's rib. She was loved excessively by her husband and this passion became more important to him than God's commands. This writer saw Adam as responsible for the Fall.[11] Christine de Pizan argued vigorously in the early fifteenth century that women possessed both intelligence and strength of character. She based her views on her own experience and on classical myths and the lives of the saints. She accepted the concept of obedience to one's husband, but regarded women as rational beings and expected them to act independently if the need arose.[12]

As with Church writings, the law emphasised women's subordination. The laws in later medieval Europe varied widely, with customary law usual in the North and Roman law increasingly adopted in the South, and with state law, promulgated in both city-state and kingdom, coming to play a more significant role between the thirteenth and fifteenth centuries. Yet despite the differences, all types of law regarded women as inferior to men and treated them as daughters, wives and widows rather than as individuals in their own right. They were widely regarded as irrational and incapable, and in the interests of social order needed to be kept under male control. These ideas underlay and supported patriarchal society.

Many women lacked legal identity. It was usual all over Europe for minors to be represented by father or guardian and for the wife to be represented by her husband. In areas of customary law, however, women who were described as *femmes soles* had the right to their own legal identity and might conduct business on their own and bring cases in the courts, although gender prejudice against women was often apparent. These women might be the wives of townsmen who were working independently of their husbands, or sometimes the wives of nobles. Most *femmes soles* were widows and were frequently to be found in northern France, the Low Countries and England. In parts of Italy, however, no woman enjoyed independent legal status during her father's lifetime, unless she had been emancipated from his control, and even the widow needed a *mundualdus*, or male legal guardian, to conclude deeds and contracts. This applied in Florence and a number of other cities, and although the *mundualdus* appears on occasion to have been bypassed, the underlying assumption remained that women were incapable of acting independently in law.[13]

Women's inferior status was particularly marked in relation to property. The growing emphasis on primogeniture and agnatic lineage (or patrilineage) restricted women's rights of inheritance and, in certain parts of Europe, of dower. From the eleventh or twelfth centuries, descent in the male line became increasingly the norm, with the largest share of the inheritance passing to the eldest son. It was accepted that daughters had a right to a share in the family property, and in many areas the dowry came to be regarded as the daughter's share; Castilian brides in the fifteenth century, for instance, were sometimes asked to renounce in writing all rights to the family inheritance. Patrilineage was increasing in importance at about the same time as the provision of a dowry became essential for marriage. By the thirteenth century, the dowry had largely taken the place of brideprice or bridewealth, given by the husband or his family on his marriage. Moreover, women's rights to dower, the money or property provided by the husband to support his widow, became more limited and women's rights to dispose of property more circumscribed.[14] These changes had a direct bearing on women's position in the family and society, and might well reduce their authority and powers of agency in society, the economy and politics.

Considerable regional differences existed as to the laws on women's inheritance and dower. In areas such as England, Scotland, France and the Low Countries in the thirteenth century, landholding by women, whether as heiresses or widows, was accepted. The dowry constituted the woman's contribution to the marriage and, if she was widowed, she received one-third or one-half of her husband's property as her dower. Moreover, in the absence of sons, it was usual for a daughter or daughters to inherit from their father, although in certain regions such as Occitania, Burgundy and the Limousin, where the dowry comprised the daughter's share of the inheritance, she had to surrender her dowry before receiving a part of the family lands. Similar customs applied among Frankish immigrants in the Latin empire of Constantinople, established in 1204.[15]

The importance of women landholders is illustrated in the roll of fiefs of 1252 from the *bailliage* of Troyes in Champagne where the main holdings were in the hands of 213 men and 66 women, the latter comprising 23.7 per cent of the total. Some of these women were holding land in the absence of their husbands in the East or as guardians of minor sons, while others held by right of inheritance or dower. For the thirteenth century it has been calculated that about 20 per cent of fief-holders were women.[16] The significance of prominent noblewomen in north-west Europe in the later Middle Ages is reflected in the wealth and influence of women such as Jeanne and Margaret, Countesses of Flanders, Mahaut, Countess of Artois, and Margaret de Brotherton, Duchess of Norfolk.

Such a situation was not, however, universal. In Germany and parts of Lorraine, it was usual to divide the inheritance among the male members of the family. Rights of heiresses were accepted only occasionally and not necessarily without question, as when Simon III's daughter Mahaut succeeded to the county of Saarbrücken, a move said to be contrary to the custom of Germany and of the church of Metz. Some lordships were trans-ferred to new families as a result of marriage, as when the counts of Mark succeeded to Cleves in 1368.[17]

Towns had their own customs. In London, a woman had the right to inherit property in the absence of a male heir and to receive dower from her husband if widowed. Her dower comprised the right to continue living in her husband's house until she remarried or died, and to have a life interest in one-third of her husband's property, or one-half if there were no children. She was also entitled by the custom known as *legitim* to one-third (or one-half) of her husband's goods and was allowed to dispose of these as she liked. In Ghent, sons and daughters benefited from the system of partible family inheritance. On her husband's death, the widow received as her own half of the common property she had held with her husband and a life interest in one-quarter of the property as her dower – property common to husband and wife dated from the time of their marriage. Her dowry remained her own property during as well as after the marriage. In Douai, the position of widows declined as a result of legal changes precipitated by plague, the decline of the textile industry and commercial change. During the thirteenth century, on the death of the husband, his widow became responsible for the whole of the household property. Later changes saw the widow replaced by a patrilineal system of inheritance, and she only retained the property she had brought to the marriage as her dower. In Bohemian towns, it is possible to trace an improvement in the wife's position during the fourteenth and fifteenth centuries. In a system where the right of inheritance lay with sons or male kin, the widow was entitled to only the return of her dowry, but husbands increasingly left property to their wives, either in their own right or jointly with their children.[18]

Male inheritance was the norm in southern Europe where it was seen as perpetuating the power of the lineage. It was usual for the eldest son to inherit the principal house and a large share of the property, the rest being divided among younger sons, the girls receiving their dowry.[19] In this situation, women were at a disadvantage compared with north-west Europe, and changes concerning dowry and dower also weakened their position. Dowries increased markedly in the late Middle Ages and were essential for the woman's maintenance as a widow. The husband's family was bound to return her dowry to the widow after her husband's death, together with any bequest from the husband and any property which he had settled on her at the time of the marriage. However, such a dower settlement was steadily whittled down from the twelfth century onwards. The earliest legislation is found at Genoa in 1143 where the husband's contribution in future was not to exceed half the amount of the dowry or a maximum of 100 Genoese lire. By 1200, the husband's contribution had virtually vanished at Padua, Bologna, Siena and Lucca, and restrictions were imposed during the thirteenth century at Milan and Florence. Such moves meant that wives became virtually dependent on their dowries during widowhood.[20]

Similar developments came about more slowly in Spain. At Barcelona, the emphasis on a single male heir inheriting most of the family property was becoming more marked by the early thirteenth century, although daughters continued to receive bequests from their parents in addition to their dowries. The dowry was regarded as the wife's property, although usually administered by the husband. The importance of the dowry increased in comparison with dower, but the latter, in the form of a counter-gift from the husband, continued to exist. By the mid-thirteenth century, the dowry was often twice the amount of the husband's contribution. The widow therefore became more dependent on her dowry, although not to the same extent as in some of the Italian cities.[21]

During the fourteenth and fifteenth centuries, moves were afoot to strengthen male inheritance in both northern and southern Europe. These moves were particularly marked among the nobility and reinforced the vision of a family as a dynastic lineage, centred on a male head and rooted in chivalry and the heroism of its ancestors. The entail proved to be an effective means of reinforcing the patrilineage.[22] By this means, the succession to the estate was legally settled during the father's lifetime, usually on the eldest son, and could not be overturned after his death. In Andalusia and Estremadura, the entail was used with royal consent in the fourteenth and fifteenth centuries to preserve the unity of the patrimony; in some cases, the daughter could pass on her rights to her son, although she could not inherit herself.

Members of the higher nobility in England created entails to ensure male succession, such as John de Vere, Earl of Oxford (d. 1360), and Thomas Beauchamp, Earl of Warwick (d. 1369). Male heirs were favoured in Ireland where the Rochefort family of Ikeathy in County Kildare laid down in 1299 that the barony should never pass to daughters. Male entails were also to be found in Scotland, although in view of the number of sons born to the higher nobility in the late Middle Ages, they were rarely needed.[23] In southern France, there was increasing concern to secure the unity of the patrimony, the Albret family manipulating local custom in order to achieve this. Others used their wills to stress the importance of the eldest son, Armand VII of Polignac going so far in 1343 as to assert that the establishment of the heir was the most important element in his will.[24]

The laws on dowry, dower and inheritance thought of women as enclosed within the family and saw them primarily as brides, wives and mothers, and as widows. The main concern of the laws lay with property and the ways in which it could be maintained and expanded in the interests of the family; the planned marriage has to be seen in this context. Land and urban property were a valuable but finite resource, and this helps to explain the growing tendency in the thirteenth century and later for dowries to be paid in money and for restrictions to be placed on dower. The changes in law and practice concerning dowry, dower and inheritance reduced women's powers of agency. A widow with landed wealth was able to exercise agency over her family, dependants and tenants, and sometimes able to wield political power. With the changes in the later Middle Ages, patriarchy became more deeply embedded in society.

The failure to see women as individuals and the desire to secure both public order and property lay behind other aspects of medieval law, notably the law on rape. Although the Emperor Constantine made rape a public crime punishable by death, this was regarded as too harsh a penalty in later medieval Europe. Rape was often regarded as a crime against male property, in line with the view that the woman usually lived under the protection of father, guardian or husband. This comes out clearly in changes to the law of rape in England. Whereas the treatise of the late 1180s attributed to Glanvill classed rape as a felony punishable by death and stressed the element of violent assault, 'Bracton's' treatise about forty years later put the emphasis on loss of virginity. Bearing in mind the importance attached to the concept of the virgin bride, and the view that a girl who had lost her virginity might not be regarded as marriageable, the concern with the woman as property is evident. Moreover, although 'Bracton' asserted that the man, if convicted, should be blinded and castrated, this punishment was extremely rare. By the late thirteenth century, in the statute of Westminster II of 1285, rape had been absorbed into the felony of abduction, and the idea that the crime was committed against the family rather than the woman was paramount. This concept was taken further in the statute of 1382 when fathers and husbands were allowed to bring in an appeal for rape, and couples who had eloped were counted as dead for purposes of inheritance.[25]

The language used in rape cases in Venice has been described as 'distant and antiseptic' and penalties were on the whole lenient. Although cases involving children attracted heavier punishments, the state does not appear to have been much concerned with the victimisation of women, although rape among the upper class was treated more seriously. With children, the fear that the rape might make them unmarriageable led to the investment of fines levied on the rapist for the girl's dowry, as in a 1467 case when a man raped his adopted daughter and 100 ducats of the 150 ducat fine was invested for her dowry. On the whole, however, rape was not regarded as a serious crime and there was little idea of protection for the raped woman.[26]

In both Germany and northern France rape was punishable by death, although again sentences were usually much more lenient in practice. As in Venice and England, the protection of a woman's sexuality was hardly a concern, although the rape of children was taken more seriously. In adult cases, the woman might well find that she was fined more heavily than the man. The number of prosecuted cases was relatively few. In the register of the Officiality of Cerisy of 1314–1457, covering part of Normandy, there were twelve cases of rape and attempted rape; all concerned virgins and women of higher status, and it can be assumed that many cases went unreported. A woman needed the backing of a powerful network to bring a prosecution and secure a conviction. The register of criminal cases of St-Martin-des-Champs at Paris between 1332 and 1357 contains six instances of rape, and the court's main concern centred on urban violence rather than rape itself. The general attitude can be summed up in a case of 1391 from Cerisy when a man was fined 5 sous for breaking into the house and raping Alice, widow of Jean Hoquet, while Alice was fined 15 sous for allowing sex to take place.[27]

The situation concerning rape emphasises the subordination of women. The concept of woman as property rather than as a person in her own right was dominant, and the family unit under the control of her father or husband was all-important. Legal practice was in line with classical and ecclesiastical views of women as weak, emotional and irrational. Sumptuary legislation, aiming to control material consumption, was also intended to keep women in their rightful place in society and the state. Again, the underlying assumption was that women were weak, extravagant and pleasure-loving, and that their vices, unless checked, would undermine both family and the state.

Sumptuary legislation was issued in Italian communes from the mid-thirteenth century, but became more general in Europe in the fourteenth and fifteenth centuries. Its apparent ineffectiveness did not stop its promulgation. Although the laws paid increasing attention to clothes and fashion, they also sometimes included furnishings and celebrations such as weddings and funerals. In the kingdoms of England and France, Philip IV's regulations of 1294 and Edward III's of 1363 were concerned with maintaining the hierarchical ordering of society, ensuring that each social order wore appropriate clothes and, in 1294, had appropriate furnishings. To take just one of the English provisions, craftsmen and yeomen and their wives and daughters were not to wear cloth costing more than 40 shillings per cloth; the women were not to wear silk veils, and for furs were allowed only lamb, rabbit, cat and fox.[28]

The fifteenth-century legislation of the north and central Italian cities was particularly critical of fashion and extravagance in women's clothing.

Women's clothes were expected to identify them with the group to which they belonged, not set them apart as individuals. The sumptuary law at Bologna of 1474 allowed the wives and daughters of knights to wear cloth of gold, those of notaries and bankers to have gold sleeves, and those of important artisans to wear crimson. Wives and daughters of humbler crafts-men were permitted to have crimson sleeves. The desire to maintain a proper social order is apparent in this legislation. There was also a desire to limit expense; the 1398 law at Bologna gave the reasons for the legislation as the desire to curb expenditure which husbands could not afford, and the wish to have a strong community and to please God; excess in clothing was regarded by the Church as a manifestation of the sin of pride.[29]

The views of the Church and the provisions of the law influenced the lives and activities of women throughout the later Middle Ages, and women lived and worked within these parameters. Yet anyone looking round them at society would have been aware of the sheer variety existing among men and women. The prologue and stories in Chaucer's *Canterbury Tales* describe a number of women who were highly individual. Some like Constance and Griselda were idealised, but women like the prioress and the wife of Bath were to be found in late fourteenth-century towns. There was far more to medieval women than the traits highlighted by the preachers and legislators.

In order to discover women's actual experience, we need to look at as wide a range of sources as possible. Women appear comparatively rarely in the chronicles describing wars and great political events. Other records, however, proliferated in the later Middle Ages, as kings, lords, towns and Church developed their jurisdictional and governmental powers, and a written bureaucratic culture became the norm.[30] Documents were needed to record legal proceedings, levies of military forces and taxation, economic and social regulations, and religious grants and dispensations. Accounts were kept to record receipts and expenditure not only in the state but in households and manors. Although references to women in most of these sources are few, since the documents were mainly concerned with their husbands as heads of the family, a detailed picture of women's lives, responsibilities and activities emerges when all the available information is put together.

Occasionally, the women's own voices can be heard in wills and letters which provide an insight into social and religious attitudes and family relationships. Although most women lacked education, some of their writings are outstanding, notably the mystical works of the thirteenth and fourteenth centuries. Inevitably, the records provide more infor-mation on women of the elite and on the religious life than on labourers and the poor, although even here a considerable amount can be gleaned. Problems arise for the historian when assumptions made in the records result in particular groups being overlooked. Because marriage for women was taken for granted, it can, for instance, prove difficult to detect women who never married, even though they were probably numerous in the towns.[31]

The women of the later Middle Ages have to be set in the context of their social relationships in order to see how far and in what ways they could exercise agency despite the limitations imposed by the Church and the law. Both men's and women's activities were affected by the ideas current in the society around them, and by the political, economic and social conditions of time and place. The wife who was dependent on her husband would have a degree of agency within her household and in her responsibility for husband and children. Possibly she also had agency through her social networks and paid work, although practice varied as to what was regarded as acceptable and suitable, whether women worked at home or elsewhere, or whether they embarked on businesses on their own account. It was far more usual to find women working in the crafts in the towns of northern Europe than in Italy. Yet even in northern Europe, opportunities for women became more limited at the end of the Middle Ages. Customs varied from town to town; the women's guilds of Paris and Cologne were not found in London, and the Paris guilds of the late thirteenth century disappeared before the end of the Middle Ages.

Women, like men, have to be seen in the context of their place in the social hierarchy. Status was determined not only by wealth; in fact there were wide variations of wealth within particular social groups. A family's social order prescribed its lifestyle, privileges and obligations. Those of the lowest social groups found that they were restricted not just by poverty but by the demands of lords and masters and by the lack of free legal status. These people included serfs, who were declining in numbers in the later Middle Ages, and slaves, who were to be found mainly in the towns and ports of the Mediterranean region. Social groupings overlapped and it was possible to move both upwards and downwards on the social scale. On the whole, however, men and women were expected to conform to the attitudes of their own order. The social context of women's lives overlapped with the religious, and they were influenced to a greater or lesser extent by the Church's doctrines and practice. The sacraments of the Church, such as baptism and marriage, marked important rites of passage. Religious worship focused on Mass. Some women adopted the religious life, as nuns, beguines or members of the third orders. Lay women's piety centred on worship, pilgrimage and charity, and their religious practice overlapped with their household responsibilities.[32]

Disaster and conflict often made life difficult for the men and women of the later Middle Ages. Their lives were inevitably affected by the demands of the state for armies and money, and warfare, devastation or siege led to loss of kin and livelihood, malnutrition or famine. Little is known about what happened to countless displaced people. Life was always uncertain, and from 1347 recurrent outbreaks of plague made early death more frequent than before. It was against a background of conflict and uncertainty, as well as in the context of religious, social and legal ideas and practices, that later medieval women lived their lives.

Notes

1 M. Schaus (ed.), *Women and Gender in Medieval Europe. An Encyclopedia* (London, 2006), pp. 308–15; J.M. Bennett and R.M. Karras (eds), *The Oxford Handbook of Women and Gender in Medieval Europe* (Oxford, 2013), pp. 2–5. D.M. Hadley (ed.), *Masculinity in Medieval Europe* (London, 1999), pp. 1–8.

2 K.M. Phillips, *Medieval Maidens. Young Women and Gender in England, 1270–1540* (Manchester, 2003), p. 11; M.K. McIntosh, *Working Women in English Society 1300–1620* (Cambridge, 2005), p. 35.

3 G. Duby and M. Perrot (eds), *A History of Women in the West*, 5 vols (Cambridge, Massachusetts, 1992–4), II, C. Klapisch-Zuber (ed.), *Silences of the Middle Ages*, pp. 49–50; C. Rawcliffe, *Medicine and Society in Later Medieval England* (Stroud, 1995), pp. 32–5; A. Blamires (ed.), *Woman Defamed and Woman Defended* (Oxford, 1992), p. 41.

4 Blamires (ed.), *Woman Defamed*, pp. 39–42, 47.

5 Klapisch-Zuber (ed.), *Silences of the Middle Ages*, pp. 51–5, 58–9; Rawcliffe, *Medicine and Society*, pp. 172–5.

6 *Genesis*, chapter 2, verse 8–chapter 3, verse 24.

7 St Paul, *Letter to the Ephesians*, chapter 5, verses 22–33; *First Letter to Timothy*, chapter 2, verses 11–15; Blamires (ed.), *Woman Defamed*, pp. 37, 63–74.

8 Both men were writing in the first third of the thirteenth century; J. Murray, 'Thinking about gender: the diversity of medieval perspectives', in J. Carpenter and S-B Maclean, *Power of the Weak. Studies on Medieval Women* (Urbana and Chicago, 1995), pp. 9–16.

9 Blamires (ed.), *Woman Defamed*, pp. 144–7.

10 P.S. Gold, *The Lady and the Virgin. Image, Attitude and Experience in Twelfth-Century France* (Chicago, 1985), pp. 43–75.

11 J. Beer, 'Woman, authority and the book in the Middle Ages', in L. Smith and J.H.M. Taylor (eds), *Woman, the Book and the Worldly* (Woodbridge, 1995), pp. 64–7.

12 These views were forcefully expressed in Christine de Pizan, *The Book of the City of Ladies*, (trans.) R. Brown-Grant (Harmondsworth, 1999); and in Christine de Pisan, *The Treasure of the City of Ladies or The Book of the Three Virtues*, (trans.) S. Lawson (Harmondsworth, 1985).

13 T. Kuehn, '*Cum consensu mundualdi*: legal guardianship of women in quattrocento Florence' *Viator* 13 (1982), 309–33; reprinted in T. Kuehn, *Law, Family and Women: Towards a Legal Anthropology of Renaissance Italy* (Chicago, 1991), pp. 212–37.

14 D.O. Hughes, 'From brideprice to dowry', *JFH* 3 (1978), pp. 276–85; D. Herlihy, *Medieval Households* (Cambridge, Massachusetts, 1985), pp. 77–8, 82–103; M-C. Gerbet, *La noblesse dans le royaume de Castille. Etude sur ses structures sociales en Estrémadure, 1454–1516* (Paris, 1979), pp. 170, 182.

15 R. Hajdu, 'The position of noblewomen in the *pays des coutumes*, 1100–1300', *JFH* 5 (1980), pp. 122–44; R. Hajdu, 'Family and feudal ties in Poitou, 1100–1300', *Journal of Interdisciplinary History* 8 (1977–8), pp. 117–39; R.L. Wolff, 'Baldwin of Flanders and Hainaut, first Latin emperor of Constantinople: his life, death and resurrection, 1172–1225', *Speculum* 27 (1952), p. 284; J. Hudson, *Land, Law and Lordship in Anglo-Norman England* (Oxford, 1994), pp. 108–18; G.W.S. Barrow, *Kingship and Unity. Scotland 1000–1306* (London, 1981), pp. 43–59; M-T. Caron, *La noblesse dans le duché de Bourgogne*

1315–1477 (Lille, 1987), pp. 194–201, 216–18; J. Verdon, 'Notes sur la femme en Limousin vers 1300', *Annales du Midi* 90 (1978), pp. 319–29; J. Smith, 'Unfamiliar territory: women, land and law in Occitania, 1130–1250', in N.J. Menuge (ed.), *Medieval Women and the Law* (Woodbridge, 2000), p. 31; P. Lock, *The Franks in the Aegean* (London, 1995), pp. 302–5.

16 T. Evergates, *Feudal Society in the Bailliage of Troyes under the Counts of Champagne* (Baltimore, 1975), pp. 69–71.

17 B. Arnold, *Princes and Territories in Medieval Germany* (Cambridge, 1991), pp. 151, 239, 242; M. Parisse, *Noblesse et chevalerie en Lorraine médiévale* (Nancy, 1982), p. 186; F.L. Carsten, *Princes and Parliaments in Germany from the Fifteenth to the Eighteenth Century* (Oxford, 1959), p. 261; E. Ennen, *The Medieval Woman*, (trans.) E. Jephcott (Oxford, 1989), pp. 239–40.

18 C.M. Barron and A.F. Sutton (eds), *Medieval London Widows 1300–1500* (London, 1994), pp. xvii–xxi; D. Nicholas, *The Domestic Life of a Medieval City: Women, Children and the Family in Fourteenth-Century Ghent* (Lincoln, Nebraska, 1985), pp. 25–8; J. Klassen, 'The development of the conjugal bond in late medieval Bohemia', *JMH* 13 (1987), pp. 161–78; M.C. Howell, *The Marriage Exchange. Property, Social Place and Gender in Cities of the Low Countries, 1300–1550* (Chicago, 1998), pp. 1–26.

19 Gerbet, *Noblesse*, pp. 206–10; J. Larner, *Italy in the Age of Dante and Petrarch, 1216–1380* (London, 1980), pp. 66–7; D. Nicholas, *The Growth of the Medieval City* (London, 1997), pp. 197, 247–8.

20 C.E. Meek, 'Women, dowries and the family in late medieval Italian cities', in C.E. Meek and M.K. Simms (eds), *'The Fragility of her Sex'? Medieval Irishwomen in their European Context* (Dublin, 1996), pp. 138–9.

21 S.P. Bensch, *Barcelona and its Rulers, 1096–1291* (Cambridge, 1995), pp. 256–7, 268–72.

22 J.C. Ward, 'Noblewomen, family and identity in later medieval Europe', in A. Duggan (ed.), *Nobles and Nobility in Medieval Europe* (Woodbridge, 2000), pp. 249–54. In England, however, joint tenure of property, found from the late thirteenth century among all social groups, strengthened the position of the married woman; J.C. Ward, *English Noblewomen in the Later Middle Ages* (London, 1992), pp. 26, 36; R.M. Smith, 'Coping with uncertainty: women's tenure of customary land in England *c.* 1370–1430', in J. Kermode (ed.), *Enterprise and Individuals in Fifteenth-Century England* (Stroud, 1991), p. 45.

23 Gerbet, *Noblesse*, pp. 197, 206–10, 213–26; G.A. Holmes, *The Estates of the Higher Nobility in Fourteenth-Century England* (Cambridge, 1957), pp. 47–9; C. Given-Wilson, *The English Nobility in the Late Middle Ages* (London, 1987), pp. 140–4; R. Frame, 'Power and society in the lordship of Ireland 1272–1377', *PandP* 76 (1977), pp. 25– 6; J. Wormald, *Lords and Men in Scotland: Bonds of Manrent, 1442–1603* (Edinburgh, 1985), p. 79.

24 R. Boutruche, *La crise d'une Société. Seigneurs et paysans du Bordelais pendant la guerre de cent ans* (Paris, 1947), pp. 386–8; A. Jacotin, *Preuves de la Maison de Polignac*, 5 vols (Paris, 1898–1906), II, pp. 1–11.

25 K. Gravdal, *Ravishing Maidens. Writing Rape in Medieval French Literature and Law* (Philadelphia, 1991), pp. 6–9; K.M. Phillips, 'Written on the body: reading rape from the twelfth to fifteenth centuries', in Menuge (ed.), *Medieval Women and the Law*, pp. 128–42; J.B. Post, 'Ravishment of women and the statutes of Westminster', in J.H. Baker (ed.), *Legal Records and the Historian* (London, 1978), pp. 150–64; J.B. Post, 'Sir Thomas West and the statute of rapes, 1382', *BIHR* 53 (1980), pp. 24–30.

26 G. Ruggiero, *The Boundaries of Eros. Sex, Crime and Sexuality in Renaissance Venice* (Oxford, 1985), pp. 89–108; the quotation is taken from p. 90.

27 Gravdal, *Ravishing Maidens*, pp. 123–31; W. Prevenier, 'Violence against women in a medieval metropolis: Paris around 1400', in B.S. Bachrach and D. Nicholas (eds), *Law, Custom and the Social Fabric in Medieval Europe. Essays in honor of Bryce Lyon* (Kalamazoo, Michigan, 1990), pp. 262–84.
28 A.R. Myers (ed.), *English Historical Documents 1327–1485* (London, 1969), p. 1154.
29 D.O. Hughes, 'Sumptuary law and social relations in Renaissance Italy', in J. Bossy (ed.), *Disputes and Settlements. Law and Human Relations in the West* (Cambridge, 1983), pp. 69–99; T. Dean (ed. and trans.), *The Towns of Italy in the Later Middle Ages* (Manchester, 2000), p. 203.
30 For England, this development is analysed in M.T. Clanchy, *From Memory to Written Record. England 1066–1307* (Oxford, 1993).
31 This area of research is now being tackled, as in J.M. Bennett and A.M. Froide (eds), *Singlewomen in the European Past 1250–1800* (Philadelphia, 1999).
32 The majority of men and women in later medieval Europe were Christian, following the doctrines and practices of the Church centred on the pope at Rome. Jews, Muslims and other ethnic groups will be considered in Chapter 7 ('Ethnic minorities: Jews, Muslims and slaves').

1 Upbringing

Upbringing and education, in the widest sense of the terms, were designed to fit children for their adult lives. This was the basic premise for all social groups, although there were inevitably considerable differences between them, depending on the status and expectations of the children's families. More emphasis was put on the training of boys in both treatises and practice, but girls were not neglected. There was considerable discussion in the treatises as to how to instil feminine virtues and to fit the girl for her future life as wife and mother, or as a nun. In accordance with contemporary ideas on gender, girls came to accept that women were subordinate and that they were expected to be quiet, peace-loving and obedient. Parents provided their daughters with religious and moral training and this was reinforced by parish priests, friars' sermons and by godparents, neighbours and friends. Socialisation by the community was a vital element in children's upbringing. Parents were also concerned to provide the practical training that a girl needed. Although many girls of the elite were taught to read, the main emphasis was put on housekeeping and social accomplishments. Daughters of peasants and artisans learned the skills of the housewife as well as ways in which they could earn money; their training was predominantly practical. The girls who were in most danger of neglect were bastards and orphans, especially among the poor, but steps were taken in various parts of Europe to make some provision for them.

The views of Philippe Ariès that childhood was a discovery of the eighteenth century and that medieval children were regarded with indifference by their parents has come under strong criticism from medieval historians. Ariès considered that in an age of high infant mortality parents sought to safeguard themselves against the possible death of a child, a view attacked by Shulamith Shahar in her book titled *Childhood in the Middle Ages* in which she argued for the strong bond existing between parent and child, and by Joel Rosenthal, emphasising the concern and affection for children in an age when life was often tough.[1] Both artistic and documentary evidence bears out the emotional involvement of parents with their children. The emphasis on the human qualities of the Virgin and Child and the growing importance attached to St Joseph led to the depiction of the Holy

Family in human terms, and showed the importance attached to the relationship between parent and child.[2] A painting of the Virgin and Child, dating from about 1435 from the workshop of Robert Campin, showed the Virgin at home playing with her Child; a fire blazed in the hearth, the baby's bath stood ready, and there was a basket of clean nappies on the floor. Such scenes had their counterpart in real life. Parents rejoiced at the birth of their children, nurtured them with care and grieved when they died. A young mother at Châteauverdun found it almost impossible to tear herself away from her baby when she left home to rejoin the Cathars. Alessandra Strozzi described how the death of her son caused her the greatest pain that she had ever felt.[3] Such expressions of emotion are rare. Parents' bequests to children in their wills were expressed in formal language, but show a caring attitude in the desire that the child should have some provision for the future.

Didactic treatises proliferated from the thirteenth century, sometimes prompted by the parents themselves and highlighting the overall importance of the mother's role in upbringing. Vincent of Beauvais wrote *De eruditione filiorum nobilium* at the end of the 1240s at the request of Queen Margaret of France, in order to meet the educational needs of the queen's son Louis and probably also of her daughter Isabelle. The knight of La Tour-Landry compiled his book for his daughters in 1371–2, considering it as a substitute for his personal guidance during his inevitable absences. Giovanni Dominici wrote for an upper-class Florentine mother in the early fifteenth century. The thirteenth-century treatise of Walter de Bibbesworth was specifically designed to help the English noblewoman, Denise de Montchesney, to teach her children French. At least one mother, Elizabeth of Bosnia, queen of Hungary (d. 1382), composed her own book of instruction for her daughters, but this has not survived.[4] For people lower down the social scale, advice was dispensed in sermons, pastoral handbooks and vernacular poems. Many of the treatises circulated widely. The work of Vincent of Beauvais continued to be read in the fifteenth century, while *De regimine principum* by Giles of Rome was translated into English in the fourteenth century by John Trevisa.[5] The book of the knight of La Tour-Landry was translated into English by Caxton at the request of 'a noble lady with many noble and fair daughters'; possibly this was Queen Elizabeth Woodville who had five daughters. Although many of these works paid more attention to boys than to girls, they took the upbringing of girls seriously, realising that adult life required serious preparation.

Childhood was divided into distinct stages of which the first two, infancy between birth and the age of seven, and childhood between the ages of seven and fourteen, were of particular relevance for girls. By the third stage of adolescence, envisaged as lasting from the age of about fourteen or puberty to at least twenty-one, most girls were at work or married. During infancy, it was the mother who was primarily responsible for the child, although in elite families she would not carry out physical care and would have a wet-nurse to breastfeed the baby. By the age of two, the child would have been weaned and the greatest risk of infant mortality was over, although death remained an ever-present threat in medieval families. During infancy, writers put their emphasis on both physical care and the beginnings of moral and religious training. For Giles of Rome, the diet of milk was to be followed by one of soft food, and wine was forbidden; the child was to be kept from crying, to get used to cold, and to play in moderation; the telling of stories to the child was encouraged. Vincent of Beauvais and Bartholomew the Englishman were equally concerned with the care of the child, Vincent stressing the need to develop harmony between soul and body, and Bartholomew urging the need to give attention to the child, especially early on.[6]

Children's toys have been found in excavations, although it can be difficult to identify particular objects as toys. Certainly children had rattles, tops, dolls and toy animals, and a finger puppet was found in a London excavation. Some of the dolls were used for religious instruction as well as play and were owned by grown-ups as well as children. As children grew older, their toys imitated adult life, and the miniature jugs and plates which have been discovered were probably the property of girls beginning to learn housekeeping skills. Children generally enjoyed games and could make toys out of all sorts of objects. The avoidance of games by young children was regarded as one of the signs of a potential saint.[7]

From the age of about seven, the education of boys and girls began to diverge. Mothers continued to be responsible for their daughters, although among the nobility a mistress might be put in charge. It was the duty of the mother or mistress to instil the moral precepts and manners which girls needed for the adult world. The recommendations in the didactic treatises applied particularly to girls of the elite. Vincent of Beauvais considered that parents should keep their daughters at home and maintain a close watch in order to preserve their chastity. Girls were to be instructed in modesty, humility and silence; gossip and personal adornment were to be discouraged, and the company a girl kept was to be carefully vetted. Similar recommendations were made by Giles of Rome, as well as by preachers who extended the clerical message to a much wider circle of families; Guibert of Tournai emphasised chastity and modesty, and an absence of make-up for older girls.[8] The importance of manners is also found in vernacular literature, such as the poem 'How the Goodwife Taught her Daughter', dating from the mid-fourteenth century and probably written by a cleric. The poem depicts the mother teaching her daughter, as she had previously been taught by her mother, and urging her to be mild and true, wise and of good reputation. The poem may also have been used by women who were training servants and apprentices.[9]

This teaching was very much in line with late medieval clerical views of women. The knight of La Tour-Landry drew on biblical and ecclesiastical sources and was helped by two priests and two clerks of his household. The examples which he used were designed to teach his daughters Christian morals and good manners; he wanted them to possess the virtues of chastity, modesty, humility, obedience and courtesy. His stories were vividly expressed. In speaking of courtesy, he drew a comparison with the sparrowhawk which, he said, would come to the hand if it was called courteously, but would never come if the owner was rude or cruel. The knight was especially hostile to new fashions and warned his daughters not to wear make-up or to be proud of their beauty. He cited a bishop who in a sermon deplored the new fashion of horned head-dresses and described women as horned snails with the devil living between the horns. According to the bishop, Noah's flood was caused partly by women wearing indecent clothing.[10] One wonders about the reaction of the knight's daughters to such teaching.

Advice varied as to whether girls should be taught to read. The Florentine, Paolo da Certaldo, was adamant in opposing this unless the girls were to become nuns.[11] Pierre Dubois went to the other extreme in recommending that girls should receive the same education as boys, studying Latin, an eastern language, grammar, logic, religion, natural science, surgery and medicine. Pierre was thinking primarily of the reconquest of the Holy Land; he thought that some girls would marry physicians and surgeons and use their education in the care of the sick, while others would marry wealthy Muslims and convert them to Christianity.[12] Other writers considered reading as a useful occupation to prevent idleness, although some expressed anxiety about the effect of romances on young girls. Giles of Rome coupled reading with the spinning and weaving of silk as a way of preventing evil thoughts, while Vincent of Beauvais saw supervised reading, especially of the Bible, and the arts of sewing and weaving as enabling girls to avoid the vanities of the flesh. The knight of La Tour-Landry was less grudging in his attitude and believed that it was good for women to read. He cited the prophetess Deborah, who lived a good life and persuaded her wicked lord to rule his people justly, and St Catherine of Alexandria, who through her wisdom and learning overcame the wisest men of all Greece and converted them to her faith.[13] In practice, reading was a useful skill for women who in adult life might find themselves taking over estate and business responsibilities in town and country; daughters of German merchants were also taught writing and numbers. In the case of Christine de Pizan, her father's insistence on a good education stood her in good stead when, as a widow, she supported her family by her writing; her mother could not see the point of education and wanted to see Christine spinning like other girls.[14]

The examples used by the knight underline the medieval view that the whole education in manners, morals and reading was rooted in religion. The virtues inculcated were regarded as fostering the girl's Christian development. Religious practice was to be an integral part of her life. Humbert de Romans considered that girls should know how to recite the psalter, the hours and the office of the dead, together with other prayers.

The knight of La Tour-Landry set his daughters' day in a religious framework, wishing them to say matins and the hours devoutly before breakfast and to attend all the masses that they could. He also urged them to carry out good works and almsgiving, and to care for orphans and poor children. The Goodwife's daughter was to go to church when she could, even in the rain, and to be charitable to the poor and sick.[15] The love of God, as expressed in prayer, was coupled with love of one's neighbour. Parents in all social groups agreed with the writers and preachers on the importance of religion, morality and social behaviour, and children learned from parental example as well as from their attendance at church. Jean Gerson recorded how his parents taught him to pray for the things which he wanted, like apples and nuts, and then dropped the objects in front of him.[16]

For many of the better-off, religious education was probably supplemented by reading and the mother probably had the responsibility of choosing reading matter as well as often teaching her daughters to read. The images of St Anne teaching her daughter, the Virgin Mary, to read, and of the Virgin Mary herself reading at the Annunciation may well have mirrored practice in wealthier households. Lives of the virgin martyrs constituted popular role models for adolescent girls, although mothers would not want their daughters to imitate the martyrs' resistance to parental or public authority. Books of Hours presented teaching material; the Bolton Hours contained the alphabet, Pater Noster, Ave Maria and the creed, and may have been used by Margaret Blackburn of York to teach her daughters.[17]

Although many girls of the elite were educated within the household, some urban schools were open to girls as well as boys, providing them with an elementary education. Giovanni Villani estimated that between 8,000 and 10,000 boys and girls were being educated in Florence before the Black Death; if this estimate was accurate, it would imply that 60 per cent of children were at school between the ages of six and thirteen. There are incidental references to schools for girls in late medieval London, and the licensing of grammar school mistresses in Paris shows that some girls were probably receiving more than an elementary education. Schools for girls existed in the towns of the Low Countries, Germany and Switzerland in the fourteenth and fifteenth centuries.[18] Noble girls all over Europe were sometimes sent to nunneries for their education, some of them remaining there to become nuns. In the early fifteenth century, Katherine, Countess of Suffolk, was having her daughter and granddaughter educated in a nunnery while a younger son was at grammar school, the family being reunited at home for the holidays.[19]

In practice, the education of girls of the elite was very much along similar lines to the treatises, but these underestimated the important part played by the community in girls' socialisation, and parents placed greater emphasis on social and practical skills than the writers did. Sewing and embroidery were widely regarded as useful and a suitable occupation for girls, but were not the only accomplishments to be learned. Girls needed to be able to run a household. In Spain, girls learned to weave silk and ribbons as well as to spin, and it is probable that many girls all over Europe were taught to sew clothes, wash and cook, as recommended by Giovanni Dominici and Paolo da Certaldo. The niece of the knight of La Tour-Landry came out to greet him with dough on her hands. The lives of the virgin martyrs served as exemplars, and the skills of St Catherine of Alexandria in running a household were brought out in the accounts of her life in late medieval English household books.[20] Social skills to be learned included singing and dancing, riding and hunting. As well as her mother's teaching, a girl must have learned much from observation of her own or other households. In addition to social gatherings, English girls of the gentry and nobility were placed in other noble households, giving them an opportunity to develop their social skills and enlarge their contacts. In the late fifteenth century, Anne de Beaujeu, daughter of Louis XI, planned to send her daughter to court or to another noble household. John the Fearless, Duke of Burgundy, realised the importance of social contacts for his children, sending his son and four of his daughters to Burgundy in 1408 to benefit from the healthy air and to get to know the nobles of the duchy.[21]

Wherever they were living, girls would be closely supervised and disciplined if it was thought necessary; this included physical punishment. Parents regarded discipline as an integral part of upbringing. Although faced on occasion with teenage rebellion, they expected to be obeyed. Agnes Paston chastised her daughter Elizabeth who made a late marriage after several unsuccessful attempts to secure a husband. Some teenagers were successful in their opposition to their parents. Clare of Assisi achieved her desire to enter the religious life; Margery Paston secured her wish to marry the family bailiff, Richard Calle, but at the price of being disowned by her mother.[22]

Margery Paston's marriage raises the question of attitudes towards love. Romance literature was popular, and many girls and older women must have enjoyed the lovers' adventures in the Arthurian and other stories.[23] Parents, like the writers of didactic treatises, were concerned to guard girls' chastity until marriage, but their daughters must have come into contact with courtly love romances through conversation, reading and listening to stories. The knight of La Tour-Landry tackled the question by staging a debate on courtly love with his wife. He argued that there were times when the lady or girl might have lovers; he praised the true lover, and thought that the lover-knight received great encouragement to excel in arms through his love. His wife was much more cautious; she thought that lords were insincere when they spoke of love. She saw them as false and faithless, and considered that a woman in love was tempted into danger and neglected her duty to God. The knight then changed his ground and asked his wife about a hypothetical case of a knight who had set his heart on their daughter and married her – why should she not love him? His wife replied that men differ. She did not want her daughter to set her heart on a man of lower status because she would lose the respect of her parents and friends, nor to enjoy the company of a man of high estate who would pay court to her but not marry her. She set her face firmly against paramours, asserting that she had evaded men's protestations of love in the past and pointing out that she was the one who had charge of their daughters and had the duty of disciplining them.[24] Although the debate can be regarded as a literary device setting out the views of the knight as a youth and as an older man, the caution expressed by his wife reflects the care which mothers took to supervise their daughters. Girls probably realised early in their lives that, although they might dream of love, marriage was a matter of family business. The knight and his wife probably rejoiced when their three daughters contracted suitable marriages.[25]

The role of the mother and of the community in upbringing was equally important in humbler families, both in town and country, but here the emphasis was usually placed on the acquisition of skills to enable the girl to run her future household and to earn money for that household's support. Moreover, the need to earn a dowry took some girls away from their natal family and saw them completing their training elsewhere. As with the households of the elite, mothers were expected to instil the norms of good behaviour, and much was learned from observation and practice. Children began to do small jobs from an early age and girls had specific responsibilities which continued throughout their lives: caring for younger children, looking after animals and helping with the housework. These activities were usually documented only when accident or disaster occurred. Coroners' rolls for England describe girls fetching water and wood, babysitting and begging; they also show how some suffered injury, rape or even death as they went about their jobs. Although the rolls have to be used with care, their accounts of girls' work reflect household practice in the later Middle Ages.[26]

The practice of sending children away from home for work and training varied. Where this happened, children spent much of their adolescence away from parents and siblings and sometimes at a distance from their home village or town. They were forced to become self-reliant and their contact with their natal families might well be minimal for the rest of their lives. In many parts of Europe, it was customary to employ adult women as servants, but girls were engaged in domestic service in England, Germany and southern Europe and used this as the means of acquiring a dowry. Girls from the age of eight entered Florentine and Venetian families as servants, the employer often agreeing to provide a dowry when they reached marriageable age; he might also be responsible for choosing the husband. At Arles, instances are found of girls between the ages of three and thirteen working as servants, the master providing their dowry at the end of their term, and girls were earning wages, often as servants, under the age of twelve in fourteenth-century Marseilles. Girls worked as servants in Valencia for anything up to ten years, receiving at the end of their term clothing and a sum of money, presumably used as their trousseau and dowry.[27] At a time when dowries were rising in amount, this method of securing one must have appealed to poorer families. Service was not without its dangers, however, as girls suffered sexual abuse and rape. Bernardo Machiavelli found that his servant was pregnant by a member of his family; with a group of men he decided that the servant should be cared for until the baby was born and should then be married off. In Paris in 1333, Jacqueline la Cyrière was said to have lured a ten-year-old girl into her home to do housework, where she was raped by a Lombard; the Lombard disappeared, and Jacqueline was sentenced to be burnt at the stake, a reflection on the age of the child and the seriousness of her injuries.[28]

In England and Germany after the Black Death, teenage girls migrated to towns to work for several years before marriage, presumably to accumulate their dowry as well as to learn skills. The girls might well have had relatives or contacts within the towns, or have been hired at markets or fairs; in fifteenth-century Germany, employment agents found jobs for those who had no contacts. It is known that there was a high proportion of servants in the towns – the 1377 poll tax for York described 31.9 per cent of the population over the age of fourteen as servants. This figure included apprentices, mostly boys, but the number of female servants in the late fourteenth and fifteenth centuries is corroborated by wills and by the proceedings of the church courts.[29] The acquisition of skills might be supplemented by a bequest from an employer, as when Agnes de Kyrketon of York left 10 silver marks to little Margaret, her maid, if she lived to adulthood, and Thomas Wood of Hull bequeathed an amount of Spanish iron to his maid in 1491.[30]

Servanthood overlapped with apprenticeship. Although the majority of apprentices were boys, girls in a number of European towns were entitled to become apprentices. At Orleans, 336 out of 376 apprenticeship contracts between 1380 and 1450 were for boys and 40 for girls, the girls mostly being apprenticed to the textile trades; out of 208 contracts at Montpellier between 1293 and 1348, 30 were for girls, who were mostly trained in the textile and food trades, and in mercery and silkwork.[31] The silk industries in Paris, Cologne and London also took female apprentices, the industry in the first two towns being regulated by women's guilds. Girls were also apprenticed to the textile trades in southern Spain and in Barcelona and Valencia; the girl apprentice at Seville whose master was bound to deliver a loom at the end of her contract so that she could set up in business had a valuable addition to her dowry.[32] The length of contract varied; at Montpellier it lasted for between two and ten years. Restrictions on women increased as a result of guild regulation in the late Middle Ages; several Paris guilds allowed only the daughters of masters to become apprentices.[33] In this situation, it is likely that most girls learned their skills within their families or as servants. It was widely accepted that the wife would help her husband in his work, and that the father would teach his children. This enabled many women to have craft skills.

Although the master or mistress of servants and apprentices stood in the place of parents, it is possible that teenagers were less closely supervised than they would have been at home. The combination in England of late age for marriage and economic independence gave young men and women what has been described as considerable freedom in their social contacts and the choice of marriage partners.[34] The poem 'The Servant Girl's Holiday' describes the maid as looking forward to her day off with glee, enjoying her time with her boyfriend, and becoming worried only afterwards when she realised that she was pregnant.[35] The detailed statements in the York Cause Papers also point to freedom of association between couples. Yet at least some masters kept an eye on their apprentices and servants. John Bown, a cordwainer of York, found his apprentice John Waryngton with Margaret Barker in the hayloft of his house and strongly suspected them of having a sexual relationship. He was at first inclined to have John put in prison, but then gave him the chance of making amends by marrying Margaret, a step which John agreed to somewhat unwillingly.[36]

Even at home it could prove difficult to supervise teenagers. J-L. Flandrin considers that girls in the countryside were reasonably free to meet boys.[37] In England, the evidence of leyrwite fines, levied on girls or their fathers in the event of fornication or pregnancy, is a probable indication of social freedom which allowed young people to associate with each other and perhaps choose their marriage partners. In some cases there is a link in the manorial court rolls between leyrwite and marriage fines, with the court possibly enforcing a clandestine marriage. Much depended on the strength of the manorial authority as to whether the fines could be levied, and it is likely that much illicit sexual activity went on undetected.[38]

The likelihood that a parent would die suddenly in childbirth or accident or through disease meant that orphans were numerous, and family structures became complex as the surviving parent remarried and step-relationships developed. There is no means of calculating the number of illegitimate and abandoned children among the poorer groups in society. The children in all these categories were vulnerable, especially among the poor. Children from propertied families were usually cared for, although some suffered from exploitation and loss of land or livelihood. The degree of personal trauma among orphans and abandoned children cannot be assessed for the Middle Ages.

In the event of the death of the father in feudal society, the wardship and marriage of the heir came into the hands of the lord. The mother was often granted guardianship during the later Middle Ages, although not in Normandy where the lord was regarded as a more trustworthy protector of the heir. This position was mirrored in the literature of the time where a number of stories turned on the defrauding of the heir by mother and step-father.[39] In the case of an heiress, the lord was guided by political and financial considerations in choosing her husband. Families were aware of the danger that this posed to their existing strategies and this explains why they often arranged the marriage early in the girl's life, during her father's lifetime. The girl was brought up to accept the concept of an arranged marriage and it may have made little difference to her whether her husband was chosen by her father or her lord.

Major towns often supervised orphans' guardians and there was a widespread desire to ensure that step-parents did not interfere with orphans' property. In London, the mayor's court took responsibility for the orphans of citizens, deciding who should be responsible for their upbringing and property; the court kept an eye on orphans' progress, had a say in their apprenticeship and marriage, and prosecuted in the event of neglect. Mothers were favoured as guardians and often remarried, but the court's supervisory role appears to have prevented the occurrence of major abuses. The town authorities in fourteenth-century Ghent exercised a general supervision over orphans; while the child usually remained in the care of the surviving parent, the latter was not normally the legal guardian, the extended family nominating the most suitable man for the task. According to David Nicholas, many step-fathers were conscientious and sometimes affectionate in their relationship with orphans. In Florence, rights of guardianship rested with the male members of the family, although widows are found taking responsibility for upbringing.[40]

The emphasis placed by the Church on marriage as a sacrament meant that illegitimate children did not necessarily have a legal position in society, and a bastard girl was even more vulnerable than a boy. Attitudes varied, but on occasion the secular law was harsher than that set down by the Church; whereas the Church took the line that children born out of wedlock were legitimised by a subsequent marriage between the parents, the law of England denied these children any right of inheritance. In contrast, although a social stigma attached to bastardy in northern Italy, children born of long-term concubinage had some rights of inheritance and were legitimised by their parents' marriage. In the event of having no legitimate son, some Florentines preferred to legitimise a bastard rather than risk inheritance by daughters or distant kin.[41] When bastardy occurred, everything depended on the readiness of the father to acknowledge his offspring and to make some provision for mother and child. Alternatively, the mother had to manage as best she could. At the top of society, if bastards were recognised, boys had the chance of a successful career and girls might make splendid marriages, as in the case of the children of John of Gaunt and Katherine Swynford. Further down the social scale, prospects were much bleaker, although it was possibly easier to absorb bastards in small communities, especially if, as at Montaillou, mistresses as well as wives were accepted by local society.

The abandonment of destitute children was probably widespread in the later Middle Ages. Many towns had their own orphanages, such as St Katherine's hospital in London which catered for abandoned children. Pope Innocent III founded the hospital of Santo Spirito in Rome because, he asserted, so many women were throwing their babies into the River Tiber.[42] In Florence, the hospitals of Santa Maria della Scala and San Gallo were taking in abandoned children from the late thirteenth century. The increasing problem over foundlings, especially in times of war and famine, led to the decision in 1419 to establish the hospital of the Innocenti which opened in 1445. It is significant that larger numbers of girls were abandoned than boys; according to the catasto or tax survey of 1427, Santa Maria della Scala had ninety-eight girls and forty-one boys in its care, and of 708 children admitted to the Innocenti between 1445 and 1453, 58.9 per cent were girls. A large proportion of the children were illegitimate. Of the first one hundred foundlings to enter the Innocenti, ninety-nine were bastards, with about one-third of the mothers slaves; about half the fathers were patricians and about half professionals or artisans. There was little future for these children. Mortality levels at the Innocenti, and presumably at other foundling hospitals, were high, particularly so among children sent out to wet-nurses. A girl who survived childhood would go into service, but there was little chance of marriage without a dowry. Santa Maria della Scala is said to have provided dowries, otherwise there was a very real danger that the girls would become prostitutes.[43]

There was a huge gulf between the daughters of the knight of La Tour-Landry and the girls growing up at the Innocenti. Yet there was a common factor: upbringing was firmly focused on the needs of adult life and on the moral and social qualities and skills which it entailed. For most girls, the goal was marriage and the establishment of their own households. It is likely that the five principles laid down by Vincent of Beauvais, who wanted them to be taught before a girl left her parents, were firmly inculcated by the girl's teenage years: love and honour for her husband's relatives, including her mother-in-law; love and obedience to her husband, putting up patiently with his faults, looking after his house and offering hospitality; avoidance of jealousy; rejection of make-up; love for her family, teaching her sons, daughters and servants; and running her household according to God's law.[44] These precepts represented an ideal, but could be adapted to any type of household.

One other common factor stands out. By modern standards, the girl embarked on her adult life before she was out of childhood. Childhood and adult life overlapped, as child labour, inside or outside the home, was the norm for all girls except the elite. Many girls were married while their brothers were still at school or in apprenticeship – the Church allowed marriage from the age of twelve – and some girls were mothers at thirteen. Parents loved and cared for their children, did their best to train and educate them, but were anxious to see them started on the next stage of their lives.

Notes

1 P. Ariès, *L'Enfant et la vie familiale sous l'Ancien Régime* (Paris, 1960), pp. 23–8; S. Shahar, *Childhood in the Middle Ages* (London, 1990), pp. 1–5; J.T. Rosenthal (ed.), *Essays on Medieval Childhood* (Donington, 2007), pp. 19–22.

2 A. Burton, 'Looking forward from Ariès? Pictorial and material evidence for the history of childhood and family life', *Continuity and Change* 2 (1989), p. 211.

3 E. Le Roy Ladurie, *Montaillou, village occitan de 1294 à 1324* (Paris, 1982), p. 311; C. Guasti (ed.), *Lettere di una gentildonna fiorentina del secolo XV ai figliuoli esuli* (Florence, 1877), pp. 177–83; G. Brucker (ed.), *The Society of Renaissance Florence. A Documentary Study* (New York, 1971), pp. 47–9.

4 Vincent of Beauvais, *De Eruditione Filiorum Nobilium*, (ed.) A. Steiner (Cambridge, Mass. 1938); A.L. Gabriel, *The Educational Ideas of Vincent of Beauvais* (Notre Dame, Indiana, 1962), p. 20; W. Caxton, *The Book of the Knight of the Tower*, M.Y. Offord (ed.), (EETS, Supplementary Series 2, 1971), pp. 3–4, 195; C. Klapisch-Zuber, *Women, Family and Ritual in Renaissance Italy*, (trans.) L.G. Cochrane (Chicago, 1985), pp. 115, 320–1; Annie Owen (ed.), *Le traité de Walter de Bibbesworth sur la langue française* (Paris, 1929), p. 43.

5 D.C. Fowler, C.F. Briggs and P.G. Remley (eds), *The Governance of Kings and Princes. John Trevisa's Middle English Translation of the De Regimine Principum of Aegidius Romanus* (New York, 1997).

6 Ibid., pp. 237–9; Gabriel, *Educational Ideas*, p. 17; Shahar, *Childhood*, p. 23.

7 D. Alexandre-Bidon and M. Closson, *L'enfant à l'ombre des cathédrales* (Lyon, 1985), pp. 174–81; G. Egan, *The Medieval Household. Daily Living c. 1150–c. 1450* (London, 1998), pp. 7, 281–3; M. Goodich, 'Childhood and adolescence among the thirteenth-century saints', *History of Childhood Quarterly*, 1 (1973–4), pp. 287–8; Klapisch-Zuber, *Women, Family and Ritual*, pp. 310–29; N. Orme, 'The culture of children in medieval England', *PandP* 148 (1995), pp. 51–4; F. Piponnier, 'Les objets de l'enfance', *Annales de Démographie Historique* (1973), pp. 69–71; R. Gilchrist, *Medieval Life. Archaeology and the Life Course* (Woodbridge, 2012), pp. 148–151.

8 Vincent of Beauvais, *De Eruditione*, pp. 172–94; Fowler, Briggs and Remley (eds), *Governance*, pp. 219–20, 245–9; J. Swanson, 'Childhood and childrearing in *ad status* sermons by later thirteenth century friars', *JMH* 16 (1990), p. 322.

9 P.J.P. Goldberg (ed.), *Women in England c. 1275–1525* (Manchester, 1995), pp. 97– 103; T.F. Mustanoja (ed.), *The Good Wife Taught her Daughter; the Good Wyfe Wold a Pylgremage; The Thewis of Gud Women* (Helsinki, 1948), pp. 158–72; F. Riddy, 'Mother knows best: reading social change in a courtesy text', *Speculum*, 71 (1996), p. 83; K.M. Phillips, *Medieval Maidens. Young Women and Gender in England, 1270–1540* (Manchester, 2003), p. 92.

10 Caxton, *The Book of the Knight of the Tower*, pp. xxxviii–xlii, 13, 23–4, 38–40, 70–1, 78, 107.

11 T. Dean (ed.), *The Towns of Italy in the Later Middle Ages* (Manchester, 2000), pp. 194– 5.

12 C-V. Langlois (ed.), *De Recuperatione Terre Sancte. Traité de politique générale par Pierre Dubois* (Paris, 1891), pp. 49–71; D. Herlihy, *Opera Muliebria. Women and Work in Medieval Europe* (New York, 1990), pp. 107–10.

13 Fowler, Briggs and Remley (eds), *Governance*, p. 248; Vincent of Beauvais, *De Eruditione*, pp. 172–6; Caxton, *The Book of the Knight of the Tower*, pp. 121–2.

14 M.E. Wiesner, *Working Women in Renaissance Germany* (New Brunswick, New Jersey, 1986), p. 79; Christine de Pizan, *The Book of the City of Ladies*, (trans.) R. Brown-Grant (Harmondsworth, 1999), p. 141.

15 Swanson, 'Childhood and childrearing', p. 324; Caxton, *The Book of the Knight of the Tower*, pp. 16–17, 38; Goldberg, *Women in England*, p. 97; Mustanoja (ed.), *The Good Wife*, pp. 168–9.

16 F. Bonney, 'Jean Gerson: un nouveau regard sur l'enfance', *Annales de Démographie Historique* (1973), pp. 138–9.

17 M. Clanchy, 'Did mothers teach their daughters to read?', in C. Leyser and L. Smith (eds), *Motherhood, Religion and Society in Medieval Europe, 400–1400. Essays presented to Henrietta Leyser* (Farnham, 2011), pp. 129–53; Phillips, *Medieval Maidens*, pp. 77–81; P. Cullum and P.J.P. Goldberg, 'How Margaret Blackburn taught her daughters: reading devotional instruction in a Book of Hours', in J. Wogan-Browne, R. Voaden, A. Diamond, A. Hutchison, C. Meale and L. Johnson (eds), *Medieval Women: Texts and Contexts in Late Medieval Britain. Essays for Felicity Riddy* (Turnhout, 2000), pp. 217–36.

18 Shahar, *Childhood*, p. 225; Klapisch-Zuber, *Women, Family and Ritual*, pp. 108–9; C.M. Barron, 'The education and training of girls in fifteenth-century London', in D.E.S. Dunn (ed.), *Courts, Counties and the Capital in the Later Middle Ages* (Stroud, 1996), pp. 141–3; E. Uitz, *Women in the Medieval Town*, (trans.) S. Marnie (London, 1990), pp. 71–2, 97–8; Wiesner, *Working Women*, p. 79.

19 British Library, London, Egerton Roll 8776, m. 4, 5; J.C. Ward (ed.), *Women of the English Nobility and Gentry 1066–1500* (Manchester, 1995), pp. 76–7.

20 D. Alexandre-Bidon and D. Lett, *Les enfants au moyen âge* (Paris, 1997), pp. 147, 151–2, 207–8; Dean (ed.), *Towns of Italy*, p. 196; Caxton, *The Book of the Knight of the Tower*, pp. 158–60; K.J. Lewis, 'Model girls? Virgin-martyrs and the training of young women in late medieval England', in K.J. Lewis, N.J. Menuge and K.M. Phillips (eds), *Young Medieval Women* (Stroud, 1999), p. 35.

21 N. Orme, *From Childhood to Chivalry. The Education of the English Kings and Aristocracy 1066–1530* (London, 1984), pp. 58–60; P. Contamine, *La noblesse au royaume de France de Philippe le Bel à Louis XII* (Paris, 1997), pp. 188, 323.

22 N. Davis (ed.), *Paston Letters and Papers of the Fifteenth Century*, 2 vols (Oxford, 1971, 1976), I, pp. 82, 341–4; II, pp. 31–3, 498–500.

23 K.M. Phillips, 'Bodily walls, windows and doors: the politics of gesture in late fifteenth-century English books for women', in J. Wogan-Browne *et al.* (eds), *Medieval Women*, pp. 185–98.

24 Caxton, *The Book of the Knight of the Tower*, pp. 163–76.

25 Ibid., p. xxxvii.

26 Goldberg, *Women in England*, pp. 81–3; B.A. Hanawalt, *The Ties that Bound. Peasant Families in Medieval England* (Oxford, 1986), pp. 158–62; C. Smith, 'Medieval coroners' rolls: legal fiction or historical fact?', in Dunn (ed.), *Courts, Counties and the Capital*, pp. 93–115; J.C. Ward, 'Community', in L.J. Wilkinson (ed.), *A Cultural History of Childhood and Family in the Middle Ages* (New York, 2010), pp. 41–55.

27 Klapisch-Zuber, *Women, Family and Ritual*, pp. 106–7, 173–4; D. Romano, *Housecraft and Statecraft. Domestic Service in Renaissance Venice, 1400–1600* (Baltimore, 1996), pp. 152–3; J. Guiral-Hadziiossif, *Valence, port méditerranéen au quinzième siècle* (Paris, 1986). p. 450; L. Stouff, *Arles à la fin du moyen âge*, 2 vols (Aix-en-Provence, 1986), I, p. 127; F. Michaud, 'From apprentice to wage-earner: child labour before and after the Black Death', in Rosenthal (ed.), *Essays on Medieval Childhood*, pp. 75–88.

28 Brucker (ed.), *Society of Renaissance Florence*, pp. 218–22; T. Kuehn, *Law, Family and Women. Towards a Legal Anthropology of Renaissance Italy* (Chicago, 1991), pp. 83–8; K. Gravdal, *Ravishing Maidens. Writing Rape in Medieval French Literature and Law* (Philadelphia, 1991), p. 128.

29 Wiesner, *Working Women*, p. 83; P.J.P. Goldberg, 'Female labour, service and marriage in northern towns during the later Middle Ages', *Northern History*, 22 (1986), pp. 18– 25; P.J.P. Goldberg, 'Marriage, migration, servanthood and life-cycle in Yorkshire towns in the later Middle Ages: some York cause paper evidence', *Continuity and Change*, 1 (1986), pp. 141–69; P.J.P. Goldberg,

Women, Work and Life Cycle in a Medieval Economy. Women in York and Yorkshire c. 1300–1520 (Oxford, 1992), pp. 158–202.

30 Goldberg, *Women in England*, p. 88; *Testamenta Eboracensia*, J. Raine (ed.), 6 vols (Surtees Society, 1836–1902), IV, p. 60.

31 D. Nicholas, 'Child and adolescent labour in the late medieval city: a Flemish model in regional perspective', *EHR* 110 (1995), p. 1109; F. Michaud-Frejaville, 'Contrats d'apprentissage en Orleanais. Les enfants au travail (1380–1450)', in *L'Enfant au Moyen Age* (Aix-en-Provence, 1980), pp. 63–71; K.L. Reyerson, 'The adolescent apprentice/worker in medieval Montpellier', *JFH* 17 (1992), pp. 354–7. In 63 per cent of the Orleans contracts, the children apprenticed were orphans.

32 Nicholas, 'Child and adolescent labour', pp. 1108–9, 1113–14; M. Wensky, 'Women's guilds in Cologne in the later Middle Ages', *Journal of European Economic History* 11 (1982), pp. 641–2; Barron, 'Education and training of girls', pp. 144–6; A.F. Sutton, 'Alice Claver, silkwoman (d. 1489)', in C.M. Barron and A.F. Sutton (eds), *Medieval London Widows 1300–1500* (London, 1994), p. 130; K.E. Lacey, 'Women and work in fourteenth and fifteenth century London', in L. Charles and L. Duffin (eds), *Women and Work in Pre-industrial England* (London, 1985), pp. 46–8; Alexandre-Bidon and Lett, *Enfants au moyen âge*, p. 164; Guiral-Hadziiossif, *Valence*, p. 456; *L'Artisan dans la Péninsule Ibérique* (no editor; Nice, 1993), p. 106.

33 Nicholas, 'Child and adolescent labour', p. 1113.

34 Goldberg, *Women, Work and Life Cycle*, pp. 339–40.

35 R.H. Robbins (ed.), *Secular Lyrics of the Fourteenth and Fifteenth Centuries* (Oxford, 1952), pp. 24–5.

36 Goldberg, *Women in England*, pp. 110–15.

37 J-L. Flandrin, 'Repression and change in the sexual life of young people in medieval and early modern times', *JFH* 2 (1977), p. 199.

38 Leyrwite was also paid by married women for offences of adultery. E.D. Jones, 'The medieval leyrwite: a historical note on female fornication', *EHR* 107 (1992), pp. 945–9; T. North, 'Legerwite in the thirteenth and fourteenth centuries', *PandP* 111 (1986), pp. 7–15.

39 N.J. Menuge, 'A few home truths: the medieval mother as guardian in romance and law', in N.J. Menuge (ed.), *Medieval Women and the Law* (Woodbridge, 2000), pp. 77–103.

40 B.A. Hanawalt, *Growing Up in Medieval London. The Experience of Childhood in History* (Oxford, 1993), pp. 89–104; D. Nicholas, *The Domestic Life of a Medieval City: Women, Children and Family in Fourteenth-Century Ghent* (Lincoln, Nebraska, 1985), pp. 109–17; Klapisch-Zuber, *Women, Family and Ritual*, pp. 121–9.

41 S.L. Waugh, 'Marriage, class and royal lordship in England under Henry III', *Viator* 16 (1985), p. 190; T. Kuehn, *Law, Family and Women*, pp. 160–2, 177–93.

42 Hanawalt, *Ties that Bound*, p. 251; B. Bolton, 'Received in His name: Rome's busy baby box', in D. Wood (ed.), *The Church and Childhood* (Studies in Church History 31, Oxford, 1994) and reprinted in B. Bolton, *Innocent III: Studies on Papal Authority and Pastoral Care* (Aldershot, 1995), pp. 153–67.

43 Klapisch-Zuber, *Women, Family and Ritual*, p. 104; R.C. Trexler, 'Infanticide in Florence: new sources and first results', *History of Childhood Quarterly* 1 (1973–4), pp. 99–101; R.C. Trexler, 'The foundlings of Florence 1395–1455', ibid. pp. 261–74.

44 Vincent of Beauvais, *De Eruditione*, pp. 197–206; Gabriel, *Educational Ideas*, p. 43.

2 Marriage

Marriage for a young couple marked the rite of passage from childhood to adult life, entailing not only the marriage itself but also in many cases the establishment of a new independent household. Marriage was the occasion for celebration, whatever one's social status and wherever one lived in medieval Europe. A royal or noble marriage was marked by feasting and tournaments; similarly, eating and drinking were an integral part of a peasant marriage. These celebrations underlined the public and in the eyes of the Church the sacramental nature of the wedding; family and friends gathered to witness the marriage ceremony in which the couple pledged themselves and gave their consent to marriage for life. The bride and bridegroom and their families were at the centre of attention. Yet marriage at all social levels also involved the institutions of both Church and state, the frequent intervention of king and lord, and the regulation of both canon and secular law. Marriage was often the culmination of a long period of negotiation.

In addition to personal, religious and cultural factors, general economic developments had a significant influence on marriage. The expansion of settlement and colonisation of new land, and the growth of towns and markets in the twelfth and thirteenth centuries, made for a more mobile population, and migration, particularly into large towns such as Paris and Florence, continued throughout the later Middle Ages.[1] Sometimes, migration was forced on people as a result of war and devastation; more often they moved in order to find work and in the hope of bettering their position. With women, migration also occurred as a result of marriage. Even if people chose to remain in their villages, the practice of going to markets and fairs and travelling on pilgrimage led to their having a circle of contacts extending beyond the place where they lived.

Migration and movement made for a greater choice of marriage partners. Although endogamy, the practice of marrying within a close circle of families, is found in all parts of society, exogamy, or the custom of marrying outside this circle, was widespread. Certainly among the nobility and urban patricians endogamy is found where families were primarily concerned with consolidating property and power. Similarly, close relationships were generated as a result of marriage within the village community. Yet it cannot be taken for granted that marriage would be endogamous. In England, the evidence of merchet payments (when women married outside the manor) points to a considerable degree of mobility; an examination of merchet payments on the Ramsey abbey estates showed that women marrying outside the manor usually married within a fifteen-mile radius and did not necessarily marry a man from a village held by the abbey.[2] Girls who moved away from their homes to work as servants probably married in their new place of settlement and this may well have given them a freer choice of marriage partner.[3]

Some men who migrated into the towns looked to their place of birth for a wife. Immigrants to Genoa from Liguria in the twelfth and thirteenth centuries often returned to their original villages to find a wife or married women whose parents originated from the same places as themselves.[4] An analysis of the marriage patterns of the labouring classes of Florence between 1343 and 1383, and between 1450 and 1530, shows that about one-third of the marriages were between people of the same parish; the number of those marrying outside Florence went up from 12 to 16 per cent. A large number of German men and women migrated to Florence in the fifteenth century to work in the textile industry and over half the men chose German wives. In the Florentine contado, the area round the city ruled by Florence, one-third of those living in the plains married within their own parish and 14 per cent made long-distance marriages; people living in the mountains were far less likely to make a local marriage, and over one-third travelled in search of a partner, sometimes going into other city-states.[5]

A minority of marriages crossed linguistic boundaries, mainly among overseas merchants who sometimes chose to marry in the area where they were doing business. The Genoese citizen Geronimo di Loreto married Violantina Lulo, niece of a canon of Famagusta in Cyprus, around 1450. Moreto de Domino was born in Pavia of Lombard parents and worked in Pisa and Florence for three years before going to Valencia in Spain, where he married a Florentine girl who travelled to Valencia to join him; after her death he married the daughter of a local knight. By the mid-fifteenth century when the details were recorded, he was a naturalised citizen of Valencia. Alternatively, merchants were found living with a concubine, sometimes in a long-term relationship. Another fifteenth-century Italian merchant, Clemento de Sumaya, was born and married in Avignon; he and his wife had at least two daughters. Subsequently, Clemento went to Aragon where he divided his time between Barcelona and Valencia, where he had a slave with whom he had children.[6]

Concern with alliance, property and status shows that far more was involved in marriage than a personal decision by the parties. Before marriage could take place, the parties had to be able to support a family and household, and this economic consideration largely determined the age at which marriage took place. The Church approved of betrothal at the age of seven and marriage at puberty, at the age of twelve for girls and fourteen for boys.

Marriage tended to take place at a young age among the nobility – concern for the continuity of the lineage coupled with often short life expectancies encouraged parents to plan marriage strategies for their children early on. Lack of source material makes it much more difficult to elucidate age at marriage for the peasantry, although for England calculations of possible ages have been made from manorial court rolls. In his analysis of the court rolls of Halesowen in the West Midlands, Zvi Razi has suggested that peasants married in their late teens or early twenties, and the same pattern may have been true of Brigstock in Northamptonshire.[7] Yet calculating ages for marriage from court rolls involves making a number of assumptions and the results have to be regarded as possibilities rather than certainties. What is clear is that for marriage to take place, the couple had to have access to land in order to ensure their livelihood.

For the period after the Black Death, there appears to have been a strong contrast in ages at marriage between England and Northern Italy, and again this can be linked to economic considerations. Using cause papers, poll tax data and wills, Jeremy Goldberg has suggested for England that men and women married in their mid to late twenties, although the age was falling by the late fifteenth century.[8] Men had to complete apprenticeships and women accumulate their dowries before marriage could be embarked on, and the English evidence appears to conform to the north-west European pattern of the early modern period.[9]

In northern Italy, economic and cultural factors combined to produce a late age for men and an early one for women. Men were not expected to marry until apprenticeship and training had been completed, and this usually meant in their late twenties or early thirties. On the other hand, the desire for purity and virginity in the bride led to a preference for girls who were still in their teens. Ages in individual towns varied. At Florence, the evidence from the Monte delle Doti (dowry fund) for 1425 to 1442 shows that the average age of girls at the time of the dowry payment was eighteen years three months, so they had probably married just before the age of eighteen. The catasto of 1427 shows that the bridegroom was on average thirteen years older than his bride; the age gap was narrower in the country-side of the contado, but even there it was likely to be six or seven years. The girls married later at Verona than at Florence, and in 1425 there was a seven-year average age difference between the couples. In that year, 84.3 per cent of Florentine girls between the ages of eighteen and twenty-two were married, as against 39.9 per cent at Verona; of the men aged between twenty-three and twenty-seven, 50 per cent of the Veronese were married and 23.1 per cent of the Florentines. The pattern of marriage for girls in their teens or very early twenties is found in other parts of the Mediterranean region, as in the towns of south-east France, and at Toulouse and Valencia; at Ragusa the age gap between bride and groom may have been greater than at Florence, with the bride being betrothed at the average age of eighteen and the groom at thirty-three.[10]

Didactic treatises provided advice as to the choice of a wife. Alberti, in his treatise on *The Family*, advised a man to marry at the age of twenty-five when he had reached maturity. He proposed that the man's mother and female relatives should draw up a list of the well-born girls of good reputation in the neighbourhood from which he should make his choice with care. He should take into consideration the girl's beauty, family and wealth. Beauty applied to body, manners and mind; the girl should be young, modest and virtuous, fit to be the mother of his children and his companion. Her potential for motherhood was particularly emphasised, as the birth of fine children was the main reason for marriage. As far as the dowry was concerned, a medium-sized one which was paid was preferable to a large one which was not.[11]

These views can be compared with those of Alessandra Strozzi when she was on the lookout for marriages for her exiled sons in the mid-fifteenth century. She even made sure that she stood next to a prospective bride in church so as to have a good look at her. Alessandra was practical and realistic in her approach. She and her sons were looking for a bride from an old, distinguished and wealthy Florentine family; in view of the Strozzi exile, they wanted a family with secure political connections. They expected the girl to be good-looking and to enjoy good health, this last point being particularly important in view of the desire for an heir to maintain the continuity of the lineage. The Paston family of Norfolk went into less detail but were equally practical, wealth being the main criterion discussed in their letters.[12]

The choice of a suitable candidate was only the first step in the long process of negotiating and celebrating a marriage. In this process, parents and Church participated, together with friends and relations, possibly a marriage broker as was to be found at Florence, and other interested parties, notably king and lord. The arrangements made had to be in accordance with law, comprising canon law and the law of kingdom, state or town, as well as local custom. In order to elucidate the various strands, the Church's position will be discussed first, as this constituted the essence of marriage as it was understood in the later Middle Ages. The roles of parents, king and lord will then be examined, with reference to the nature of the alliances preferred, and the financial means by which marriage was effected.

The Church and the formation of marriage

The Church saw the ideal life for a woman as one of perpetual virginity, but it realised that marriage was essential in human society for the procreation of children and the avoidance of sin; the Church considered that all sexual activity should take place within the context of marriage. During the eleventh and twelfth centuries, marriage came to be regarded as one of the seven sacraments, as the nature of marriage as an indissoluble bond was emphasised and rules devised as to its formation. Gratian, in the *Decretum* of around 1140, stressed both consent and consummation as the constituents of valid marriage in the eyes of the Church. However, Peter Lombard considered that it was present consent (consent *de presenti*) which validated a marriage – that is, consent expressed by the couple in the present tense at the time of the marriage. He distinguished between future (consent *de futuro*) and present consent, the former implying betrothal or a promise to marry at a future time. In his view, consummation was not essential to creating a marriage.[13]

This standpoint with its stress on present consent was adopted by both Popes Alexander III and Innocent III and became the basis for marriage within the Roman Church, as laid down by the Third Lateran Council of 1179 and the Fourth of 1215. The expression of present consent constituted an indissoluble marriage, while future consent followed by intercourse also came to be regarded as establishing marriage. In the event of early betrothal, present consent had to be given when the parties reached puberty, the age sanctioned for marriage by the Church. Forced marriages were condemned, the couple being expected to give their consent freely. The Fourth Lateran Council was also concerned to stress the public nature of marriage and laid down that banns of marriage were to be published during parish Mass, a practice already adopted in England and northern France. Priests were forbidden to take part in clandestine marriages. However, the Church always insisted that clandestine marriages (without banns or witnesses) were valid, provided that the partners had consented to marry each other in the present tense and without conditions; it was not until the Council of Trent in 1563 that a religious service became essential for a valid marriage in Catholic Europe.[14]

The Church had long been concerned to prevent marriage between relatives, but the ban on marriage within seven degrees of consanguinity was regarded as too extreme. In 1215, marriage was forbidden within four degrees, but this applied not only to one's natal kin but to relatives by marriage (affinity) and also to spiritual kindred such as godparents. There were various ways of calculating degrees of relationship, but normally the four degrees went back to great-great-grandparents. A couple with a common ancestor had to obtain a dispensation from bishop or pope before the marriage took place and this became common practice among nobles and urban patricians whose families frequently intermarried.[15] Those who were less knowledgeable about their ancestors or lacked the money to secure a dispensation could but hope that no relationship came to light after marriage.

Looking at the Church's provisions from the viewpoint of lay society, it is clear that they contain some surprising omissions. The Church seems to have taken the consummation of marriage for granted; however, non-consummation, due to the impotence of the husband, was one of the few reasons for divorce. Alarming, from the parental point of view, was the lack of reference to the couple's families, let alone the lord and ruler, and there is no doubt that all three continued to play a major role in many marriages. The laws of many Italian cities insisted on parental consent to marriage. Yet the Church's pronouncements were far-reaching and a determined effort was made to enforce the decisions of 1179 and 1215 through synodal legislation, the marriage liturgy and the work of the Church courts. Although the legislation was widely enforced, some parts of Europe, such as Scandinavia, were slow in adopting its decisions, possibly due to late conversion to Christianity. The Church continued to face problems over clandestine marriages, and long-term concubinage remained a socially acceptable relationship in Spain, Sicily and Ireland.[16]

The half-century after the Fourth Lateran Council saw a spate of local legislation on marriage. Provincial and diocesan synods in England were concerned to legislate on marriage from early on. The Council of Westminster of 1200 laid down regulations on marital and spiritual relationships and ordered the publication of banns and the public celebration of marriage in the presence of a priest. Certain aspects of the papal decrees created parti-cular problems, such as why marriage should be prevented because of a spiritual relationship. Constant concern over banns in the later Middle Ages indicates that this provision was particularly difficult to enforce. During the fourteenth century, Archbishop Thoresby of York stressed that parish priests should explain the rules concerning banns to their congrega-tions in the vernacular, and banns also continued to cause problems in both France and Florence.[17] The banns made it essential for the local community to know about the wedding so that it could comment on any impediments, but it is likely that many families continued to regard marriage as a private contract, of interest only to those immediately concerned.

Ideally, the marriage took place at the church door in the presence of family and witnesses. Diocesan statutes saw the parish church as the proper setting for the wedding; consent was to be exchanged at the church door, the wedding probably taking place before noon on a Sunday morning before Mass, although not in Advent or Lent. From at least 1215, teaching on mar-riage was reinforced by sermons and handbooks for parish priests.[18] Marriage liturgies also set the wedding at the church. The appearance of such liturgies in England, France and Italy in the eleventh and twelfth cen-turies testifies to the Church's concern over the celebration of marriage. The rite at the church door before Mass included the exchange of consent, the handing over of the bride to the bridegroom, the blessing and giving of the ring, and the husband's gift to his wife of dower and money. After further prayers the couple were taken into church by the priest for the nuptial Mass which included the blessing of the couple; any children born before the marriage were declared legitimate. Regional variations in the liturgy existed and in some rites the bride's father was given an active role; in an early thirteenth-century pontifical of the kingdom of Naples, he was asked if he was willing to give his daughter in marriage, an element which is also found elsewhere. The liturgy did not end with the Mass – the nuptial chamber, bed and the couple themselves were blessed before the consummation of the marriage.[19]

The medieval Church was powerless to insist that all marriages should take place in a church. In Tuscany it was the notary who was present at the bride's house when consent was exchanged and the ring given. Usually soon after, a further public ceremony took place when the bride was taken to her husband's house, where a feast was held and the marriage consummated.[20] The ceremonies here were held in public, but without reference to the Church. All over Europe, clandestine marriages took place, with no reference to banns or priest, and the proceedings of the church courts show that the words of consent had not necessarily been expressed in the proper form so as to make the marriage valid. Marriage litigation came before the Church courts and was dealt with under canon law, although in certain parts of Europe, such as England, Sicily and Italian city-states, marriage cases might also come before the secular courts. Much of the Church court material comes from England and northern France, and procedural differences make it difficult for the historian to draw comparisons. The subject matter of the cases also differed, the French material being far more concerned with *de futuro* and the English with *de presenti* consent.

It was the actual formation of marriage which brought the parties before the Church courts. In his analysis of the evidence from the consistory court of Ely between 1374 and 1382, Michael Sheehan found that the 122 marriage cases comprised about one-quarter of the court's business, and of these eighty-nine involved a clandestine union; the cases apply to all social groups, although the well-off were probably under-represented. In deciding whether a marriage was valid, much depended on the words used, whether *de futuro* or *de presenti*. Further difficulties arose in cases where the contract had been conditional or when two men or two women claimed to have a valid contract to the same partner; it was the prior marriage which counted as valid. The parties showed a knowledge of the canon law on marriage formation, but did not always realise how precise the words of present consent needed to be.

In England, the number of suits to enforce marriage contracts declined in the second half of the fifteenth century and this may point to a better understanding in society of the Church's rules over marriage formation. This development may have occurred earlier in France and the Low Countries. The material from northern France concerning *de futuro* consent possibly reflects a growing desire by parents to control the marriage choices of their children, since parents could dissolve a *de futuro* contract but not a *de presenti* one; certainly in the sixteenth century marriages in France came to need parental authorisation.[21]

In spite of problems of enforcement, the Church's role was crucial in establishing the nature of later medieval marriage. It had made its point about the nature of consent; had it not done so, there would not have been the number of cases in its courts turning on the words *de presenti* and *de futuro*. Clandestine marriages continued into the early modern period, but it is likely that a growing number of couples were married at the church door by the end of the Middle Ages. At the same time, parents and others continued to have a major influence on marriage formation.

Parents and the formation of marriage

In his discussion of marriage in the twelfth century, Georges Duby set the ecclesiastical model against the aristocratic, with the nobility primarily concerned with the continuity of their lineage and the maintenance of the social order which was strengthened by suitable marriage alliances between families. The need for a legitimate heir, born of a monogamous marriage, was crucial, and therefore the aristocracy accepted licit sexual relations within a lifelong marriage.[22] Yet although they accepted the role of consent at the time of the wedding, they set this in the framework of the arranged marriage. For them, the consent of the couple was not sufficient on its own for a marriage; the consent of parents and family was an essential part of the arrangements. The arranged marriage was the norm across medieval Europe. This was especially true among elites, but it is likely that parents had a substantial say in the marriage of their children at lower social levels as well. In the event of the death of the father in feudal society, his lord or the king would take over the arrangements for marriage; among townspeople and the peasantry, responsibility for the children's marriage lay with their guardians, and with the town authorities or lord.

Parents evolved their own marriage strategies and did not necessarily plan marriage for all their children. Among the nobility and urban patricians, the cost of dowries might prevent marriage for some of the daughters; boys were also affected by parental plans for ecclesiastical careers. The situation varied according to region and over time. In the Lyonnais in eastern France between 1300 and 1500, 23 per cent of sons and 31 per cent of daughters of noble testators entered the Church or became nuns; the figure for daughters dropped during the period from 64 per cent between 1300 and 1350, before the Black Death, to 40 per cent between 1351 and 1400, 29 per cent between 1401 and 1450, and 14 per cent between 1451 and 1500. Seventy-six per cent of the girls who became nuns belonged to families with five or more children.[23] Among the seventeen children of Pierre d'Amboise and Anne de Bueil in the fifteenth century, six boys went into the Church, five of them becoming archbishops or bishops, and one the Grand Master of the Hospital of St John of Jerusalem; three girls became nuns, one becoming abbess of Sainte-Menous, one the prioress of Poissy, while the third was a nun at Fontevrault. Of the four daughters of Bernard-Ezi II, lord of Albret (d. 1358), the two youngest became Poor Clares. Urban patrician families also put their daughters into nunneries and, as dowries rose in Florence in the fifteenth century, nunneries expanded rapidly.[24] It cost less to raise a dowry for the religious life than for marriage.

Information is much more sparse as far as artisan and peasant families are concerned. Some girls did not marry, but it is not clear whether this was due to parental policy, poverty or lack of suitors. The aristocratic nature of nunneries meant that opportunities in the religious life were limited. Single women worked as servants, craftswomen and labourers, and often seem to have migrated to the towns. While the labour market was buoyant after the Black Death, some may have chosen not to marry, an option rarely open to noble and patrician women. Families may have found it most difficult to find marriages for illegitimate children.[25]

On the whole, European parents agreed with the criteria laid down by Alessandra Strozzi in her choice of a bride. Political considerations mainly affected members of the elite, but the importance of good family, wealth and property was understood by all social groups to a greater or lesser degree, as is apparent in marriage agreements. In an age when death struck suddenly, marriage agreements were realistic in substituting one son or daughter for another in the event of death. The attractiveness of the bride was much more rarely mentioned, although it was probably taken into consideration. In the agreement for a double marriage between the families of Richard FitzAlan, Earl of Arundel, and William de Bohun, Earl of Northampton, each father picked the daughter he preferred and may well have been looking for beauty, good health and a pleasant personality.[26]

Quite apart from personal factors, parents were on the lookout for a marriage which would enhance the standing of the family, preferably by increasing its wealth and property or by creating an alliance from which, it was hoped, it would reap advantages in the future. Families normally married within their own social group, but these groups were often fluid and contained considerable variations of wealth and status. The prospect of upward social mobility was attractive to both noble and peasant, as it was to the townsman, lawyer or administrator anxious to move up into the aristocracy, although this was often achieved over more than one generation. Luis de Sentangel of Valencia made his money as a merchant. His two sons went into royal service, one marrying a townswoman, but the other marrying into the family of the counts of Oliva.[27]

Social mobility, however, has to be set in context. Much depended on circumstances, both political and economic. Marriage alliances between rich townspeople and landowners occurred widely; in times of economic difficulty, for instance, the marriage of a rich townswoman to a noble would be welcome to both the noble family who would benefit financially and the urban family whose status would be more highly regarded. Noble parents expected the lawyer or administrator to have established his career and built up wealth before they would countenance a marriage; in such a case, royal or noble service provided the primary avenue to upward mobility, with marriage setting the seal on the rise in status. Ambitious men in Andalusia,

France, England and elsewhere needed to combine royal service with
well-planned and successful marriage alliances if they were to reach the top
of lay society.

Parents were ambitious but at the same time realistic in their expectations.
Most couples and their families hoped for an advantageous alliance but
were well aware that misfortunes might occur. The desired upward mobility
might not materialise for a whole host of reasons: the early death of one
of the partners, the childlessness of the marriage, economic or political
disaster or war. Any of these factors might result in downward mobility.
Moreover, a woman and her family might well find that she had to accept a
lower rank or not get married at all; with the nobility in Estremadura,
although marriages took place within the same social group, some girls were
married to nobles of lower rank.[28]

The prospects of gaining an heiress in marriage varied widely, not only
because of demographic factors but also because of the law of the region. As
seen in the Introduction, sons were preferred as the heirs to the family property and the emphasis on patrilineal succession became more marked
between the thirteenth and fifteenth centuries. Yet in areas where the daughter had the right to inherit property and not just to receive a dowry,
marriage was a means by which established families increased their power
and 'new men' secured land and rank. Competition for heiresses was keen
in all social groups among parents, guardians and overlords. The danger to
the heiress lay in her being used as a pawn in the game of family politics.

Parents made the most of daughters who were heiresses and some of
the marriages among rulers and nobility had long-term implications for
European history. This is evident in the marriages of the four daughters
of Count Raymond-Berengar of Provence who married into four ruling
families as a result of parental and Capetian manipulation. In order of age,
Margaret married Louis IX of France, Eleanor Henry III of England, Sancia
his younger brother Richard of Cornwall, claimant to the Holy Roman
Empire, and Beatrice Charles of Anjou, the youngest brother of Louis IX,
who later conquered the kingdom of Sicily. The decision that the whole
inheritance should pass to Beatrice sparked long-lasting resentment,
especially with her eldest sister, Margaret.[29]

Marriage to heiresses was equally welcome to families of the lesser
nobility and gentry, townspeople and peasants. Yet in most cases an heiress
was unavailable and many parents thought in terms of an alliance which
would strengthen the family's standing in society; and as good a dowry as
they could secure. This desire for alliance explains the close interrelation-
ships which existed among the higher nobility in kingdoms such as England,
Portugal and France, and the endogamous patrician marriages in cities such
as Florence and Venice. Such a policy was taken to great lengths at Ragusa
(Dubrovnik) where only a few exogamous marriages took place to nobles in
Venice or Dalmatian ports, and where it was rare to find a non-noble
marriage. This policy concentrated wealth within Ragusa itself, preventing

its dissipation outside the town when Ragusa was hit by plague in the second half of the fourteenth and the early fifteenth century.[30] In many towns, an exogamous marriage was designed as a way of making an alliance with a successful new family and absorbing it into the patriciate. In thirteenth-century Barcelona, Bernat Marquet (d. 1257) started out as the co-owner of a galley, married the daughter of a rich entrepreneur and landowner in 1236 and was able to use her dowry to purchase valuable land at a time when property was booming.[31]

Some alliances had the more specific aim of creating peace between warring parties. They were particularly to be found among rulers as a means of sealing a treaty, as in the marriage of Katherine, daughter of Charles VI of France, to Henry V. Nobles made similar agreements, as when William de Bohun, Earl of Northampton, married Elizabeth de Badelesmere, widow of Edmund Mortimer, in order to lessen the enmity between their families. William had played a prominent role in seizing Edmund's father, Earl Roger, in the coup which brought Edward III to power in 1330. Such attempts at peace-making did not always work.[32] The marriage alliance was also designed to secure useful contacts with men of influence who could provide support in disputes and litigation. Such marriages had advantages for both retainer and patron. The late medieval gentry of an English county found it useful to be on good terms with the local nobility and such ties were often underpinned by marriage.[33] In Genoa in the thirteenth and early fourteenth centuries, patrician neighbourhoods were held together by marriage as well as business connections, and the poor relations of the patrician were married to inhabitants of the enclave.[34]

In the towns, marriage alliances and business concerns often went together and reinforced horizontal occupational relationships. In Cordoba and Seville, between 15 and 20 per cent of the daughters of masters married artisans in the same craft, and the same was true of the silk industry in Valencia.[35] In many cases, marriage enabled a man to set up in business. Willem Ruweel, an immigrant in Bruges, secured his financial exchange through his mid-fourteenth century marriage to Margaret van Ruuslede, a member of the merchant elite, whose family had had the exchange since at least the early fourteenth century, and her dowry provided Willem with capital for investment.[36] These horizontal and vertical relationships were as useful in the village as in the town and probably underlay many peasant marriages. In view of the economic and tenurial variety among the peasantry, it is unlikely that marriage would be restricted to those of one's own condition. At Brigstock and Iver before the Black Death, about one-third of the marriages were between a party of higher and a party of lower rank.[37]

Kings, lords and the formation of marriage

All these considerations over alliance occupied parents' minds in the negotiation of marriage, but for orphaned children of the feudal nobility and for certain children among the peasantry, the king and the lord had a vital role to play. Seigneurial rights of wardship and marriage gave both kings and lords a source of patronage and finance. Marriage to an heiress enabled king or lord to reward a courtier, official or retainer at no cost to himself and, in the event of wards choosing their own marriage partners, the king or lord benefited from the fine paid.[38] From the point of view of the king especially, the right of marriage enabled him to exercise some control over baronial families and inheritance, and augment the power of the Crown. In England, Henry III used marriage as a means of promoting his Savoyard and Lusignan relatives, a policy which intruded on the barons' own arrangements for their estates and which caused grievance and ultimately rebellion in 1258. Edward I made use of his right to determine matters of baronial inheritance to enhance his power and provide for his family.[39] This policy was similar to that pursued by the thirteenth-century Capetian kings who used their rights as feudal overlords to increase their hold over French lordships. Even if the ruler had no feudal rights, he might still exercise patronage over marriage. Lorenzo de' Medici was concerned to encourage patrician marriages for which he sometimes provided the dowry; these weddings often took place in his presence at the Medici palace.[40]

Marriage was also an instrument of royal policy. Charles of Anjou engineered strategic marriage alliances in his planned expansion into the Balkans. Once he had received William de Villehardouin's surrender of his principality of Achaia in 1267, it was decided that most of the lands should pass to Charles's second son Philip, who was married to William's daughter Isabelle. William died in 1278 and the Morea, in southern Greece, came under Charles's rule. Isabelle, by then a widow, remained in Naples. In order to placate the barons of the Morea, she was given the title of princess of Morea in 1289 and married to Florent of Hainault, with the promise that the succession should pass to their heirs, although no daughter was to marry without Charles's agreement. Isabelle continued to rule the Morea in her own right after Florent's death eight years later; she was subsequently married to Philip of Savoy, but their claim to the Morea was terminated by Charles II in 1306–7.[41] For much of her life, Isabelle appears as little more than a pawn in Angevin politics.

The rights of the lord to have a say in and receive payments for peasant marriage varied according to local custom. In many parts of Europe, such as England, France and the Low Countries, food renders were payable to the lord. In Germany, the lord often had the right to forbid marriages between peasants of two different lordships. Marriage dues were payable to the lord in various parts of Germany, and on certain estates, such as Weitenau in the Black Forest in 1344, he had the right to insist on peasants getting married. Marriage dues were originally payable to the lord in France, but with the growth of leaseholding and peasant emancipation in the twelfth and thirteenth centuries these payments tended to disappear. *Formariage*, the fine on those who married outside the manor, was regarded as a servile charge in the mid-thirteenth century, but by the beginning of the fourteenth century serfdom had virtually disappeared round Paris and Orleans, and the desire to get rid of servile obligations was widespread. Changes in Italy as a result of the growth of sharecropping and townsmen taking over village land meant that many former obligations disappeared.[42]

In England, merchet was regarded as a mark of serfdom in the thirteenth century; it was payable on marriage, although customs varied from manor to manor. This payment was probably linked to the transfer of the dowry from father to husband and signified the lord's acceptance of the marriage and of the change in ownership of chattels and land. There is some evidence that lords put pressure on parties to marry. Evidence from Norfolk manors before the Black Death shows tenants being ordered to marry, with partners being chosen by a village jury; most paid fines rather than marrying the partner nominated. By no means all villein marriages paid merchet and it appears that the women who made the payment were drawn from the better-off in village society. After the Black Death, merchet payments gradually disappeared, although efficient lords, such as the abbot of Ramsey, continued to levy them into the fifteenth century.[43]

Dowry

Financial and property considerations were integral to marriage formation. At all levels of society, both families were expected to make provision in money or land, and the changing balance between the woman's and the man's contribution reflects the growth of patriarchy in the later Middle Ages. The concept that no marriage could be finalised without a dowry, whether that dowry was paid by the family or by the girl herself, held true across Europe. The dowry came to be regarded as increasingly important in establishing and maintaining a new household and, especially in southern Europe, in safeguarding the bride's future if she were to be widowed. Marriage had to have this economic foundation; Margery Brewes was thoroughly realistic in thinking that her love for John Paston III would come to nothing if her father failed to secure the settlement he desired.[44] Lack of a dowry posed serious problems for the poor, so there were attempts to provide one through bequests in wills and by employers for servants.[45]

The eleventh and twelfth centuries were a time of crucial change in the economic contributions to marriage. The dowry had been an integral part of marriage in the classical world, but in the early Middle Ages the husband's contribution of the *morgengabe*, or morning-gift, given on the morning after the consummation of the marriage, gave the wife substantial rights in her husband's property, amounting to a quarter in Lombard Italy, and one-third according to Frankish and Burgundian custom. However, the dowry reappeared in Italy, southern France and Catalonia in the eleventh century and spread all over Europe in the next 200 years; for many girls, dowry came to constitute their share of the family inheritance. At the same time, the morning-gift declined and the husband's payment in southern Europe comprised only a small proportion of the dowry. Further north, it continued to be customary for women to be assigned a share of their husbands' land as dower.[46]

Dowries varied in amount according to the family's rank and wealth and also within families and over time. Bernard-Ezi II, lord of Albret, was willing to pay a higher dowry for his eldest daughter than for his second; this was also usual practice at Barcelona. Alessandra Strozzi paid out modest dowries for her daughters in order to preserve family property for her sons. At Chartres in the late Middle Ages, a noble might provide a dowry of 900 *livres tournois*, merchant dowries ranged from between 150 and 250 *livres tournois* for the richest to between 20 and 60 *livres tournois* for the poorest, while weavers' daughters received only a few *livres* (pounds). Artisan dowries in the silk industry at Valencia ranged from 20 to 200 *livres*, with the majority amounting to 100 *livres*; women marrying notaries and lawyers, however, needed a dowry of between 300 and 350 *livres*. The diversity of wealth among commoners was also apparent at Venice where cobblers' dowries, for instance, ranged from 13 to 130 ducats.[47]

The importance of the dowry is borne out by the experiences of Giucardino, son of Guglielmo de Matarana, in the mid-thirteenth century. At the age of fifteen, in 1260, he made a year's work contract in Ventimiglia with Jacopo the tailor, and the contract was renewed in 1261 for a further year. By the age of seventeen Giucardino was ready to marry into another tailor's family and, accompanied by Jacopo as adviser, he agreed to marry Raimundina, daughter of Nicola and Adalasia Testa de Porco. Raimundina's dowry amounted to £20, to be paid over five years, and Giucardino promised an equivalent amount as his marriage gift. It was agreed, again with Jacopo as adviser, that Giucardino and his wife should form a four-year partnership with Raimundina's parents, living and working together, taking their living expenses out of the business and sharing the profits at the end. Nicola and his wife put all their resources into the partnership, while the young couple invested £10.[48] Without the dowry it is unlikely that this arrangement would have been feasible. Many artisan husbands must have used the dowry to set up a workshop and provide the capital for a new business.

Although dowries came increasingly to be paid in money, they could also be made up of property and goods, the goods comprising personal items or household furnishings. At Brigstock, Beatrice Helkok's dowry consisted of cash, a cow and clothing, and her husband later had to sue for delivery of the goods.[49] Peasant dowries varied in size according to the wealth and circumstances of the family. In 1330, in one village of Upper Provence, one peasant dowered his daughter with 75 *livres* in money, a chest, two sets of bedding and a fur-trimmed robe of Ypres cloth and a tunic of Chalons cloth, while another managed only two pieces of cloth and a coverlet. Some peasants in the village were rich enough to be virtually petty nobles and gave their daughters a dowry of 50 gold florins.[50] Thirteenth-century noble dowries in France consisted of land and money; in the marriage contract of 1245 between Heracle de Montlor and Agnes, daughter of Pons *Vicomte* de Polignac, Pons arranged for a dowry comprising the castle of Prades and 400 marks of silver. The danger of diminishing the family patrimony came to be realised during the thirteenth century, and increasingly noble dowries consisted of money; the 1373 contract for the marriage of Agne II, lord of Olliergues, and Beatrice de Chalançon specified a dowry of 3,500 gold francs.[51]

Money dowries had gone up substantially by the end of the Middle Ages, posing considerable problems for fathers with a large number of daughters. Certain Mediterranean cities tried to set maximum limits for dowries. At Ragusa, a law of 1235 set the maximum dowry at 200 *hyperpera*, an amount which was increased to 1,600 *hyperpera* in 1423. The 1235 law was obviously a dead letter by 1280–2 when there seems to have been a customary limit of 400 *hyperpera*, plus a sum of gold and a personal slave, and the majority of dowries had risen to 1,000 *hyperpera* and a sum of gold by the time of the Black Death. The later law seems to have been more readily obeyed.[52] Venetian patrician dowries averaged about 650 ducats in the mid-fourteenth century, but rose steeply thereafter. A ceiling of 1,600 ducats was set in 1420, of which two-thirds comprised the dowry and one-third the *corredo*, originally the trousseau but by the early fifteenth century a gift to the husband which was retained by his family when the dowry was returned to the widow. This limit was ineffective and the amount was raised to 3,000 ducats in 1505.[53] Florence tackled the problem by establishing the Monte delle Doti, or dowry fund, in 1425, partly to cope with the city's financial crisis resulting from the war against Milan, but also to enable fathers to invest money for their daughters' dowries and so to encourage marriage. Although initially unsuccessful in attracting investors, changes in 1433, including a lower model deposit of 60 florins, a greater variety of investment terms, increased interest rates and repayment of the deposit on the death of a daughter, resulted in a marked improvement; four years later, a refund was allowed if the girl became a nun. Although this did not provide a complete solution to Florence's dowry problems, dowries were funded for 1,814 girls between 1425 and 1442.[54]

Usually the dowry was paid by the father. Evidence from the Monte delle Doti between 1425 and 1442 shows that 662 of the 898 known depositors were fathers, 68 were mothers and 70 were uncles.[55] The father who died before his daughter's marriage generally made provision for the dowry in his will, as Leone Morosini of Venice did in 1342, leaving his daughter Lucia a dowry of 576 ducats and a trousseau worth 346 ducats. In the absence of the father, the son took responsibility for his sisters' marriages if he was old enough, otherwise male relatives, usually on the paternal side, took over. At Venice a wide family circle is found contributing to the dowry, with the mother making provision if the father were too poor, and grandparents, aunts and uncles helping to augment the sum. Similar practice is found in England, and at Toulouse and Montpellier.[56] With marriage depending on the dowry, and its size reflecting the standing of the whole family, it was important for relatives to make a contribution if the parents had difficulty in raising a respectable sum. The dowry was normally paid in instalments, and failure to pay led on occasion to marital problems. The marriage of Perchta Rožmberk and John of Lichtenstejn ran into difficulties partly because her father delayed the payment of her dowry for a number of years.[57]

The dowry and the bride's trousseau were supplemented by gifts from the husband and his family. When Mary de Bohun married Henry Bolingbroke in 1381, she received ruby and diamond rings, and her two sisters-in-law each gave her a silver-gilt goblet and ewer. At Florence, the trousseau was delivered to the bride's new home on the wedding day or the day after, while the husband furnished the conjugal chamber and provided clothes and jewels. He was allowed to spend up to two-thirds of the amount of the dowry, but had the right to take the gifts back and dispose of them later. In addition, the female members of his family presented the bride with rings which they had received themselves on entering the family.[58]

The discussion of property, finance and political advantage makes the process of medieval marriage formation appear cold-blooded and legalistic. Certainly there were instances where boys and girls were used as pawns in the marriage market and pressure was brought to bear on them to give their consent. Many parents, however, may well have tried to combine family interest with what they thought would be best for their children personally. Margery Brewes' love for John Paston III was realised by her mother and future mother-in-law who jointly did their best to secure the necessary property settlement.[59] The problem for the historian lies in the nature of much of the evidence; it is rare to have letters providing personal and emotional detail, and the extant marriage contracts and legal and financial documents inevitably limited their concerns to the business side of the match. What goes unrecorded is the degree of acquaintance or liking between the parties. It is probable that, among the peasantry and young people away from home, there was a considerable degree of freedom in the choice of partner. This did not necessarily preclude parental involvement in any property arrangements, however. The presence of young people at social gatherings, at all social levels, may well have led to mutual attraction which in turn may have resulted in parental agreement to negotiate marriage. What parents were unwilling to countenance was elopement, although they might subsequently have to accept the marriage; in Spain, the daughter who eloped was disinherited and her husband outlawed.[60] Few girls insisted on marrying for love, as did Margery Paston who gave up her gentry status as the wife of Richard Calle.[61]

Elopements and abductions were relatively rare. Assuming that parental consent was given, the financial and property business successfully concluded and any necessary dispensation for consanguinity secured from the

Church, the marriage went ahead. The banns were issued, and the couple gave their consent to the marriage in the present tense in the presence of witnesses and amid family celebration and feasting. The couple then embarked on their married lives.

Notes

1 D. Herlihy, *Opera Muliebria. Women and Work in Medieval Europe* (New York, 1990), pp. 136–42; D. Herlihy and C. Klapisch-Zuber, *Tuscans and their Families. A Study of the Florentine Catasto of 1427* (New Haven, Connecticut, 1985), pp. 112–15.

2 J.M. Bennett, 'Medieval peasant marriage: an examination of marriage licence fines in *Liber Gersumarum*', in J.A. Raftis (ed.), *Pathways to Medieval Peasants* (Toronto, 1981), pp. 219–21; R. Smith, 'Moving to marry among the customary tenants of late thirteenth- and early fourteenth-century England', in P. Horden (ed.), *Freedom of Movement in the Middle Ages. Proceedings of the 2003 Harlaxton Symposium* (Donington, 2007), pp. 169–85.

3 P.J.P. Goldberg, 'Marriage, migration and servanthood: the York Cause Paper evidence', in P.J.P. Goldberg (ed.), *Women in Medieval English Society* (Stroud, 1997), pp. 10–12.

4 D.O. Hughes, 'Kinsmen and neighbors in medieval Genoa', in H.A. Miskimin, D. Herlihy and A.L. Udovitch (eds), *The Medieval City* (New Haven, Connecticut, 1977), p. 104.

5 S.K. Cohn, Jr., *The Laboring Classes of Renaissance Florence* (New York, 1980), pp. 17, 38–9, 102–11; S.K. Cohn, Jr., 'Marriage in the mountains: the Florentine territorial state, 1348–1500', in T. Dean and K.J.P. Lowe (eds), *Marriage in Italy, 1300–1650* (Cambridge, 1998), pp. 190–4.

6 L. Balletto, 'Ethnic groups, cross-social and cross-cultural contacts in fifteenth-century Cyprus', in B. Arbel (ed.), *Intercultural Contacts in the Medieval Mediterranean* (London, 1996), p. 46; Guiral-Hadziiossif, *Valence*, pp. 402–3.

7 Z. Razi, *Life, Marriage and Death in a Medieval Parish. Economy, Society and Demography in Halesowen 1270–1400* (Cambridge, 1980), pp. 60–4; C. Howell, *Land, Family and Inheritance in Transition. Kibworth Harcourt 1280–1700* (Cambridge, 1983), pp. 221–5; J.M. Bennett, *Women in the Medieval English Countryside. Gender and Household in Brigstock before the Plague* (Oxford, 1987), p. 72.

8 P.J.P. Goldberg, *Women, Work and Life Cycle in a Medieval Economy. Women in York and Yorkshire c. 1300–1520* (Oxford, 1992), pp. 225–32.

9 J. Hajnal, 'European marriage patterns in perspective', in D.V. Glass and D.E.V. Eversley (eds), *Population in History: Essays in Historical Demography* (London, 1965), pp. 101–43; R.M. Smith, 'Some reflections on the evidence for the origins of the European marriage pattern in England', in C. Harris (ed.), *The Sociology of the Family: New Directions for Britain* (Keele, 1979), pp. 74–112; R.M. Smith, 'The people of Tuscany and their families in the fifteenth century: medieval or Mediterranean?', *JFH* 6 (1981), pp. 107–28; R.M. Smith, 'Hypothèses sur la nuptialité en Angleterre aux treizième et quatorzième siècles', *Annales ESC* 38 (1983), pp. 107–36.

10 J. Kirshner and A. Molho, 'The dowry fund and the marriage market in early *quattrocento* Florence', *Journal of Modern History* 50 (1978), pp. 413, 420–2; Herlihy and Klapisch-Zuber, *Tuscans and their Families*, pp. 202–11; D. Herlihy, 'The population of Verona in the first century of Venetian rule', in J.R. Hale (ed.), *Renaissance Venice* (London, 1973), p. 113; D.B. Rheubottom, '"Sisters first": betrothal order and age at marriage in fifteenth-century Ragusa', *JFH* 13

(1988), pp. 362–3; Guiral-Hadziiossif, *Valence*, p. 451; G. Laribière, 'Le mariage à Toulouse aux quatorzième et quinzième siècles', *Annales du Midi* 79 (1967), p. 350; J. Rossiaud, 'Prostitution, jeunesse et société dans les villes du Sud-Est au quinzième siècle', *Annales ESC* 31 (1976), pp. 294–6.

11   R.N. Watkins (ed.), *The Family in Renaissance Florence* (Columbia, South Carolina, 1969), pp. 114–20.

12   L. Martines, 'A way of looking at women in Renaissance Florence', *Journal of Medieval and Renaissance Studies* 4 (1974), pp. 26–7; C. Guasti, *Lettere di una gentildonna Florentina del secolo xv ai figliuoli esuli* (Florence, 1877), pp. 547–52; N. Davis (ed.), *Paston Letters and Papers of the Fifteenth Century*, 2 vols (Oxford, 1971, 1976), I, pp. 82, 155–6.

13   M.M. Sheehan, 'Choice of marriage partner in the Middle Ages', *Studies in Medieval and Renaissance History*, new series 1 (1978), pp. 1–16; J. Murray (ed.), *Love, Marriage and Family in the Middle Ages* (Peterborough, Ontario, 2001), pp. 170–81; C. McCarthy (ed.), *Love, Sex and Marriage in the Middle Ages. A Sourcebook* (London, 2004), p. 63.

14   C.N.L. Brooke, *The Medieval Idea of Marriage* (Oxford, 1989), pp. 130–42; C. Donahue, Jr., 'The canon law on the formation of marriage and social practice in the later Middle Ages', *JFH* 8 (1983), pp. 144–7; J.D. Mansi, *Sacrorum Conciliorum Nova et Amplissima Collectio*, 55 vols, XXII (Graz, 1961), columns 251–2, 254, 256, 267, 1035–9; D. d'Avray, 'Marriage ceremonies and the Church in Italy after 1215', in Dean and Lowe (eds), *Marriage in Italy*, pp. 107–15; Murray (ed.), *Love, Marriage and Family*, pp. 202–5; McCarthy (ed.), *Love, Sex and Marriage*, pp. 68–72.

15   Brooke, *Medieval Idea of Marriage*, pp. 134–6; J. Goody, *The Development of the Family and Marriage in Europe* (Cambridge, 1983), pp. 134–46, 262–78; E. Champeaux, 'Ius sanguinis' *Revue Historique de Droit Français et Etranger*, fourth series 12 (1933), pp. 275–6; Murray (ed.), *Love, Marriage and Family*, pp. 212–14. The papal dispensation for the marriage of John de Hastings Earl of Pembroke and Anne Mauny in 1368 is given in translation in J.C. Ward (ed.), *Women of the English Nobility and Gentry 1066–1500* (Manchester, 1995), pp. 35–7.

16   J.M. Jochens, 'The politics of reproduction: medieval Norwegian kingship', *AHR* 92 (1987), p. 332; H. Dillard, *Daughters of the Reconquest. Women in Castilian Town Society 1100–1300* (Cambridge, 1984), pp. 127–8; Bresc, *Un monde méditerranéen*, II, pp. 697–701; A. Cosgrove (ed.), *Marriage in Ireland* (Dublin, 1985), pp. 29–30; T. Dean, 'Fathers and daughters: marriage laws and marriage disputes in Bologna and Italy, 1200–1500', in Dean and Lowe (eds), *Marriage in Italy*, pp. 89–90.

17   M.M. Sheehan, 'Marriage theory and practice in the conciliar legislation and diocesan statutes of medieval England', *Mediaeval Studies* 40 (1978), pp. 408–60; F. Pedersen, 'Did the medieval laity know the canon law rules on marriage? Some evidence from fourteenth-century York Cause Papers', *Mediaeval Studies* 56 (1994), pp. 147–8; P. Adam, *La vie paroissiale en France au quatorzième siècle* (Paris, 1964), p. 111; R.C. Trexler, *Synodal Law in Florence and Fiesole, 1306–1518* (Rome, 1971), pp. 68, 124–5.

18   Sheehan, 'Marriage theory and practice', pp. 443–4; Murray (ed.), *Love, Marriage and Family*, pp. 307–29.

19   J-B. Molin and P. Mutembe, *Le rituel du mariage en France du douzième au seizième siècle* (Paris, 1974), pp. 32–8, 43–4, 67–70, 79–94, 100–12, 130, 142, 172–4, 207–8, 233, 257–64. The marriage liturgy of the Sarum use in England is given in Murray (ed.), *Love, Marriage and Family*, pp. 261–70.

20   C. Klapisch-Zuber, *Women, Family and Ritual in Renaissance Italy*, (trans.) L.G. Cochrane (Chicago, 1985), pp. 185–6, 193–4.

21 Donahue, 'Canon law on the formation of marriage', pp. 147–56; A.J. Finch, 'Parental authority and the problem of clandestine marriage in the later Middle Ages', *Law and History Review* 8 (1990), pp. 190–201; C. Donahue, Jr., 'Clandestine marriage in the late Middle Ages: a reply', *Law and History Review* 10 (1992), pp. 316–22; Pedersen, 'Did the medieval laity know?', pp. 115–17, 140; M.M. Sheehan, 'The formation and stability of marriage in fourteenth-century England: evidence of an Ely register', *Mediaeval Studies* 33 (1971), pp. 234, 249–50; R.H. Helmholz, *Marriage Litigation in Medieval England* (Cambridge, 1974), pp. 33–40, 47–50, 57–66, 165–7.

22 G. Duby, *Medieval Marriage. Two Models from Twelfth-Century France*, (trans.) E. Forster (Baltimore, 1978), pp. 2–3, 9–12, 16–17; G. Duby, *The Knight, the Lady and the Priest. The Making of Modern Marriage in Medieval France*, (trans.) B. Bray (Harmondsworth, 1983), pp. 189–209.

23 M-T. Lorcin, *Vivre et mourir en Lyonnais à la fin du moyen âge* (Paris, 1981), pp. 75–83; M-T. Lorcin, 'Retraite des veuves et filles au couvent. Quelques aspects de la condition féminine à la fin du Moyen Age', *Annales de Démographie Historique* (1975), p. 199; P. Contamine, *La noblesse au royaume de France de Philippe le Bel à Louis XII* (Paris, 1997), p. 246.

24 Contamine, *Noblesse*, p. 245; Boutruche, *Crise d'une société*, p. 515; R.C. Trexler, 'Le célibat à la fin du Moyen Age: les religieuses de Florence', *Annales ESC* 27 (1972), pp. 1333–4.

25 G. Brucker (ed.), *The Society of Renaissance Florence. A Documentary Study* (New York, 1971), pp. 40–2; I. Del Badia and G. Volpi, *La Cronica Domestica di Messer Donato Velluti* (Florence, 1914), pp. 147–50. Donato recounted his difficulties in finding a marriage for his illegitimate niece whom he had taken into his household after his brother's death.

26 *Calendar of Entries in the Papal Registers relating to Great Britain and Ireland. Papal Letters, 1342–62* (London, 1897), p. 606.

27 Guiral-Hadziiossif, *Valence*, p. 452.

28 M-C. Gerbet, *La noblesse dans le royaume de Castille. Etude sur ses structures sociales en Estrémadure 1454–1516* (Paris, 1979), pp. 172–4.

29 E.M. Hallam, *Capetian France 987–1328* (London, 1980), pp. 211, 215, 225, 256; J. Dunbabin, *Charles I of Anjou. Power, Kingship and State-making in Thirteenth-Century Europe* (London, 1998), pp. 13, 15, 42–3; M. Howell, *Eleanor of Provence. Queenship in Thirteenth-Century England* (Oxford, 1998), pp. 8–14. See later, pp. 131–3 for information on royal marriages.

30 M.J.V. Branco, 'The nobility of medieval Portugal (eleventh to fourteenth centuries)', in A. Duggan (ed.), *Nobles and Nobility in Medieval Europe* (Woodbridge, 2000), pp. 236–9; S.M. Stuard, *A State of Deference: Ragusa/Dubrovnik in the Medieval Centuries* (Philadelphia, 1992), pp. 61–9.

31 S.P. Bensch, *Barcelona and its Rulers, 1096–1291* (Cambridge, 1995), pp. 336–7, 348–55.

32 *Calendar of Entries in the Papal Registers relating to Great Britain and Ireland. Papal Letters, 1305–42* (London, 1895), p. 527; D.O. Hughes, 'Urban growth and family structure in medieval Genoa', *PandP* 66 (1975), pp. 12–13.

33 For example, C. Carpenter, 'The Beauchamp affinity: a study of bastard feudalism at work', *EHR* 95 (1980), pp. 514–28.

34 Hughes, 'Kinsmen and neighbors', pp. 100–2.

35 R. Córdoba de la Llave, 'La femme dans l'artisanat de la péninsule ibérique', in *L'Artisan dans la Péninsule Ibérique* (no editor; Nice, 1993), p. 105; G. Navarro, 'L'artisanat de la soie à Valence à la fin du Moyen Age', in ibid., p. 170.

36 J.M. Murray, 'Family, marriage and moneychanging in medieval Bruges', *JMH* 14 (1988), pp. 115–18.

37 Bennett, *Women in the Medieval English Countryside*, p. 97.

38 S.S. Walker, 'Free consent and the marriage of feudal wards in medieval England', *JMH* 8 (1982), pp. 123–34.

39 S.L. Waugh, 'Marriage, class and royal lordship in England under Henry III', *Viator* 16 (1985), pp. 181–207; K.B. McFarlane, 'Had Edward I a "policy" towards the earls?', *History* 50 (1965), pp. 145–59, and reprinted in K.B. McFarlane, *The Nobility of Later Medieval England* (Oxford, 1973), pp. 248–67.

40 Cohn, *Laboring Classes*, p. 53.

41 C. Perrat and J. Longnon (eds), *Actes relatifs à la Principauté de Morée 1289–1300* (Paris, 1967), pp. 21–9; K.M. Setton (ed.), *A History of the Crusades*, 6 vols (Madison, Wisconsin, 1955–89), II, R.L. Wolff and H.W. Hazard (eds), *The Later Crusades, 1189–1311*, pp. 262–8; P. Lock, *The Franks in the Aegean 1204–1500* (London, 1995), pp. 84–6, 90–7, 102–3, 108.

42 R. Faith, 'Seigneurial control of women's marriage', *PandP* 99 (1983), pp. 138–9; W. Rösener, *Peasants in the Middle Ages*, (trans.) A. Stützer (Cambridge, 1992), pp. 181–2; R. Fossier, *Peasant Life in the Medieval West*, (trans.) J. Vale (Oxford, 1988), pp. 136, 142–6, 192; G. Fourquin, *Les campagnes de la région Parisienne à la fin du moyen âge, du milieu du treizième siècle au début du seizième* (Paris, 1962), pp. 166–9; G. Duby, *Rural Economy and Country Life in the Medieval West*, (trans.) C. Postan (London, 1968), pp. 243, 513–14.

43 J. Scammell, 'Freedom and marriage in medieval England', *Economic History Review*, second series 27 (1974), pp. 523–37; E. Searle, 'Seigneurial control of women's marriage: the antecedents and function of merchet in England', *PandP* 82 (1979), pp. 3–43; P.A. Brand, P.R. Hyams, R. Faith and E. Searle, 'Debate. Seigneurial control of women's marriage', *PandP* 99 (1983), pp. 123–60; R.M. Smith, 'Women's property rights under customary law: some developments in the thirteenth and fourteenth centuries', *TRHS* fifth series 36 (1986), pp. 169–72; Bennett, 'Medieval peasant marriage', pp. 193–246; E. Clark, 'The decision to marry in thirteenth- and early fourteenth-century Norfolk', *Mediaeval Studies* 49 (1987), pp. 499–502.

44 Davis (ed.), *Paston Letters and Papers*, I, pp. 662–3.

45 P. Skinner and E. Van Houts (trans. and eds), *Medieval Writings on Secular Women* (London, 2011), pp. 91–3, 133–6.

46 D.O. Hughes, 'From brideprice to dowry', *JFH* 3 (1978), pp. 262–96.

47 Boutruche, *Crise d'une société*, pp. 492, 515; C. Billot, *Chartres à la fin du moyen âge* (Paris, 1987), p. 253; Navarro, 'Artisanat de la soie', p. 169; C. Batlle, 'Le travail à Barcelone vers 1300: les métiers', in C. Dolan (ed.), *Travail et travailleurs en Europe au moyen âge et au début des temps modernes* (Toronto, 1991), p. 92; D. Romano, *Patricians and Popolani. The Social Foundations of the Venetian Renaissance State* (Baltimore, 1987), pp. 34–6; Martines, 'A way of looking at women', p. 20.

48 S.A. Epstein, *Wage Labor and Guilds in Medieval Europe* (Chapel Hill, North Carolina, 1991), pp. 121–2.

49 Bennett, *Women in the Medieval English Countryside*, p. 93; the parents of Beatrice's husband promised that he would inherit half a virgate.

50 Duby, *Rural Economy and Country Life*, pp. 283–4.

51 A. Jacotin, *Preuves de la Maison de Polignac*, 5 vols (Paris, 1898–1906), I, p. 180; II, pp. 62–3.

52 S.M. Stuard, 'Dowry inflation and increments in wealth in medieval Ragusa (Dubrovnik)', *Journal of Economic History* 41 (1981), pp. 799, 803–4.

53 S. Chojnacki, 'Dowries and kinsmen in early Renaissance Venice', *Journal of Interdisciplinary History* 5 (1974–5), pp. 571–2; S. Chojnacki, 'Nobility, women and the state: marriage regulation in Venice, 1420–1535', in Dean and Lowe (eds), *Marriage in Italy*, pp. 128–34.

54 J. Kirshner and A. Molho, 'The dowry fund and the marriage market in early *quattrocento* Florence', *Journal of Modern History* 50 (1978), pp. 403–12.

55 Ibid., pp. 412–13.

56 Chojnacki, 'Dowries and kinsmen', pp. 576–9; Ward, *Women of the English Nobility and Gentry*, pp. 34–5; N.H. Nicolas, *Testamenta Vetusta*, 2 vols (London, 1826), I, p. 127; Laribière, 'Mariage à Toulouse', p. 345; J. Hilaire, *Le régime des biens entre époux dans la région de Montpellier du début du treizième siècle à la fin du seizième siècle* (Paris, 1957), pp. 28, 44, 48–51.

57 J.M. Klassen (ed.), *The Letters of the Rožmberk Sisters: Noblewomen in Fifteenth Century Bohemia* (Woodbridge, 2001), pp. 4–6, 35–45.

58 E.C. Lodge and R. Somerville (eds), *John of Gaunt's Register, 1379–83*, 2 vols (Camden Society, third series 56–7, 1937), I, pp. 178–9; Klapisch-Zuber, *Women, Family and Ritual*, pp. 218–28.

59 Davis (ed.), *Paston Letters and Papers*, I, pp. 378, 605–8.

60 Dillard, *Daughters of the Reconquest*, p. 41.

61 Davis (ed.), *Paston Letters and Papers*, I, p. 351; II, pp. 498–500.

3   Women and family

At marriage the woman passed from the authority of her father to that of her husband and her identity was henceforth associated with her marital rather than her natal family. In the parts of Europe where the nuclear family (comprising husband, wife and children) was the norm, marriage entailed the establishment of a new household. Medieval views on patriarchy took it for granted that the husband was the head of the household, responsible for its well-being, carrying out public duties and controlling its members. As a *femme covert*, the English wife's legal personality was subsumed into her husband's and he owned the property she brought to the marriage; this custom was known as *coverture*. Elsewhere, in northern France, Scandinavia and the Low Countries, community of property operated between husband and wife, with the husband controlling, not owning, his wife's property and representing her at law.[1] In practice, relations between husband and wife varied according to their ages and personalities. For the wife, marriage led to new duties with household, work and children. Her degree of agency would be greater if her husband's occupation or obligations took him away from home; wives of nobles, merchants, fishermen and sailors all had to be prepared to take over as head of the household from time to time. Over time, the household fluctuated in size as children were born, grew up and left home, as servants came and went, and as members of the family died. Relationships with kindred might strengthen or weaken as the family's circumstances changed.

Recent research has brought out the complexity of household structures in the later Middle Ages, and in several regions nuclear and extended families are found alongside each other. Both complex and nuclear households existed in southern Italy about 1500, and there were a few multiple and three-generation households in Palermo in 1480.[2] Even in regions where there was a strong sense of lineage, joint households were not necessarily established. In both Venice and Genoa artisan families tended to be nuclear, although the joint patriarchal family was to be found among the nobility, with, in Genoa, aristocratic enclaves where the family established its centre of power.[3] The most detailed examination of household structure has been made for Tuscany, with the analysis of the Florentine catasto of 1427.

Although nuclear families existed in Tuscany, there was a preponderance of extended households, with 52.5 per cent of the population living in households of at least six people. In the cities, there was a definite link between wealth and the size of the household, with the largest households being the richest, and in Florence their heads were often members of the major guilds, while the minor guildsmen mostly had households of four or five people. Wealth also affected size of household in the contado. Many sharecroppers had households of over six members; these families were sometimes groups of married brothers, or three-generation families with the father and one or more married sons. The largest group comprised ten conjugal families, with forty-seven members extending over four generations.[4]

Joint family households were found among the peasantry of central Europe in the Middle Ages, extending from the Baltic south to the Balkans, as well as in Switzerland, Bavaria and north-west Germany, although certain regions such as Macedonia had a preponderance of nuclear households.[5] Although it has been considered that the general line of development was from the joint household to the nuclear, in certain parts of Europe the extended family re-emerged in the late Middle Ages. At Montaillou in the Pyrenees, nuclear families were in the majority around 1300, although there were some three-generation families, and people kept in touch with their kindred. However, in Languedoc, Gascony and Auvergne in the aftermath of the Hundred Years War, owing to the need for labour, extended families were established. Such households were sometimes set up as a result of marriage, as when two or three brothers married into a family of sisters. At Montplaisant in Perigord, the deserted village was repopulated after 1453 by immigrants who came in as extended families.[6]

The nuclear family was to be found in the later Middle Ages in the villages and towns of northern France, west Germany, the Low Countries and England, as well as in towns in parts of eastern Europe such as Bohemia. This did not preclude contact with more distant relations. In Ghent the extended family intervened at times of death or marital separation to protect widows and orphans and also settled disputes and matters of inheritance.[7] However, in the event of migration, contact with kindred could be lost and was replaced by occupational and neighbourhood ties. Evidence from the English peasantry points to the growing prevalence of nuclear families by the end of the Middle Ages. Zvi Razi has found that in the West Midlands nuclear families were in the majority before the Black Death, although extended families were quite common, and nuclear families made use of their extended kindred ties. Extended kinship networks were less common in East Anglia, however, probably because of fragmentation of holdings and the nature of the land market. After the Black Death, the situation changed in the West Midlands, especially in the fifteenth century, as a result of the drastic fall in population, and this explains the prevalence of the nuclear family in the early modern period.[8]

Wives and husbands

The blessing of the marriage bed prior to the consummation of the marriage was included in the Sarum liturgy of the first half of the thirteenth century,[9] and husband and wife were expected to meet the conjugal debt at the request of the other. The Church's attitude to sex was ambivalent, and canon law imposed restrictions on sexual activity, limiting sexual relations to married couples with the intention of procreating children. Sex for pleasure, even between husband and wife, was regarded as sinful and husbands were criticised for loving their wives passionately. Sexual relations were forbidden during menstruation and during pregnancy when it was considered dangerous to the foetus, as well as during the seasons of Advent, Lent and Pentecost, on Sundays and feast days, and on Wednesdays and Fridays which were days of fasting.[10]

Although medieval records rarely commented on the relationship of husband and wife unless it had broken down, enough evidence survives to show every imaginable type of marital relationship, from passionate love to hatred. Alteration of feelings during the marriage is difficult to trace, however. Romantic love was frowned on as the basis for marriage, but for some couples love already featured at the time of the wedding, while for others it developed after the marriage had taken place. A number of didactic treatises stressed that the wife should love her husband, Francesco Barbaro arguing in the early fifteenth century that love led to obedience. Husbands loved their wives and were desolated when they died; Luca di Matteo da Panzano described his intense grief when he lost his wife after a twenty-year marriage.

Christine de Pizan did not agree with marrying for love and emphasised the wifely virtues of loyalty and obedience. Her marriage to the court notary Estienne de Castel was a very happy one and she could not have wished for a better husband; she thought that he was kinder, gentler and more loving and loyal than all other men, and she never ceased mourning his death. But she was aware that she was lucky and that many men and women were much less fortunate in their marriage partners. Another woman who regarded herself as fortunate was Margery Brewes, who was in love with John Paston III before their marriage and lamented his absence afterwards. Love and affection were also found among the peasantry. At Montaillou, the marriage of Bernard Clergue and Raymonde Belot has been described as a love match, and the priest Pierre Clergue laughed at his brother because he was so passionately in love. Jean Maury fell in love and married a Catalan girl.[11] It is likely that mutual attraction and love existed when young people had a say in the choice of their marriage partners.

The companionate element may most often have been present when the husband and wife were of much the same age. The teenage bride may have had respect rather than love for her much older husband. The description of Giannozzo's marriage in Alberti's treatise on *The Family* emphasised the husband's dominance over his wife, although Giannozzo saw the welfare of the family as being in his wife's hands as well as in his own.[12] In an age when most women had to put up with their husbands, whatever they were like, it is probable that they hoped for economic security and a working partnership with their husbands. As many types of work were gender-specific, the best prospect for economic success, or even survival, was for a couple to pool their resources, skills and energy. Husbands were expected to be the main breadwinner; wives took responsibility for household and children, and in many occupations worked alongside their husbands or deputised for them when necessary. The urban practice of wives working independently helped to support family aspirations and may well have facilitated their children's training and marriages.

Certain preachers such as Jacques de Vitry and Guibert of Tournai saw husbands and wives as partners, and the tendency of men in certain parts of Europe to appoint their wives as executors of their wills points to mutual trust and knowledge of business affairs. At Genoa between 1150 and 1250, about half the male testators chose their wives as executors. Although the position of Italian women often worsened as a result of the emphasis on the patrilineage in the later Middle Ages, there was a growing tendency for Venetian husbands in the fifteenth century to name their wives as executors, a few even making them the sole executor, and wives were more frequently described in affectionate terms. Occasionally a Florentine husband gave his wife control over his property until his heir came of age. The use of the wife as executor in English wills was common practice.[13] Occasionally, a statement in a will is particularly revealing. The merchant Johan Marti of Valencia left a sum of money to his wife Na Francescha because she had helped him to earn what he had and had worked well in the house. William, Duke of Suffolk, made his wife Alice the sole executor of his will since he trusted her more than anyone else on earth.[14]

Yet in spite of evidence of love and partnership, there was never any doubt over the wife's duty of obedience and the husband's right to give orders to his wife and to chastise her. Disobedient wives who turned the tables on their husbands made them a laughing stock. Wife and child beating was accepted in European society, and it is likely that the violence reported represented only a tiny proportion of what actually took place. Domestic violence occurred in all social groups, from the nobility to the poor. Usually it was the wife who suffered violence, although there are cases of wives allegedly trying to murder their husbands. A London mother had a miscarriage and lost her baby because of a beating by her husband in the late fifteenth century. During a marital quarrel in Ireland, the husband threw a knife which missed his wife but wounded his daughter in the head. Beligno Signolo, a Venetian nobleman, prompted, as he claimed, by the devil, mutilated his wife by cutting off her nose and lips and the four fingers of her right hand. Some wives returned home only to face more violence; another Venetian case reported that when Moreta returned to her husband, Stefano the tailor, he beat her up again.[15] Marital separation was sanctioned by the courts only when the violence was deemed excessive, and it is likely that many poorer women were forced to return home, the alternative being destitution for themselves and their children.

Separation and divorce were normally dealt with by the Church courts, but a number of Italian cities, such as Bologna and Venice, exercised this jurisdiction, considering that the regulation of marriage was a matter of social order. Separation was allowed on the grounds of adultery, apostasy, heresy or violence, or when both parties wished to live the religious life. This was referred to as divorce *a mensa et thoro* (from board and bed) and did not put an end to the bond of marriage. Maintenance was assigned to the woman, but not in cases where she had committed adultery. Thus, at the court of Cerisy in Normandy, Mathieu Evrart claimed that the two sons born to his wife Jennet were not his and was awarded a separation, the children remaining with their mother. Church courts dealt with numerous cases of adultery, often punishing the woman more harshly than the man.[16] As with the cases of violence, it is likely that many couples stayed together in spite of adultery, for economic if not for personal reasons, and illegitimate children were absorbed into the household. Where children had been born before the marriage took place, they were often legitimised at the subsequent marriage ceremony. Some wives found that they were expected to bring up their husbands' bastards, and the Florentine patrician household often included the master's children by servants or slaves. Adultery with servants was a Europe-wide problem.

Annulment (divorce *a vinculo*, or from the marriage bond) was permitted in canon law in cases of impotence, bigamy, consanguinity and where compulsion had been used to secure present consent at the wedding. Annulments were comparatively rare in the later Middle Ages, comprising just over 10 per cent (ten out of ninety-eight) of the cases at Canterbury between 1372 and 1375, and for those at the top of the social scale political pressure was sometimes brought to bear to secure them. The low number may be partly explained by couples splitting up without reference to the courts. The marriage had to be proved invalid before it was annulled. In cases of impotence, a group of mature women was used, first in England and later in other parts of Europe, to try to excite the man sexually and prove the case one way or the other; instances of annulment on grounds of impotence are found at the court of Cerisy. The existence of a prior marriage invalidated a present one and provided grounds for divorce. In the case between Peter Southchurch and Eva Lovecot, Peter asserted that he was originally married to Matilda Peyfrere, but repudiated her some years later and married Eva through fear of his parents. He left Eva after his father's death and his succession to the inheritance. Matilda died before the lawsuit. Peter was granted his divorce because he and Eva did not pledge themselves again by present consent after Matilda's death.[17]

Some cases throw into high relief the human tragedy lying behind an annulment. The case of Agnes Herford, daughter of a Dublin butcher, was heard in 1440. Agnes had married John Hert at Kilmainham fourteen years before, and five or six years later married William Beg at Drogheda. John may have deserted her; at the time of the case he was living in Calais with the wife of a man from Sandwich. Agnes's and William's marriage was annulled, but the court considered that he had acted in good faith, so he was allowed to marry again and his and Agnes's children were declared legitimate.[18]

Mothers and children

The main reason for marriage, as expressed by both the Church and lay society, was the procreation of children. It is often assumed that women's married lives were dominated by frequent pregnancy, and this was certainly the case for many. The birth of a son and heir was eagerly anticipated among all ranks of society. Yet not all couples had children and many had only daughters. Childlessness was normally blamed on the wife, but the infertility or early death of the husband, or the incompatibility or ages of the couple, might all prevent the birth of children. The wife's failure to conceive could lead to pressures building up inside the marriage, as in that of Francesco and Margherita Datini; the difficulties were probably augmented by the birth of Francesco's illegitimate children, one of whom Margherita brought up as his daughter. Miscarriages or injury to the wife during childbirth, as apparently happened to Margaret Beaufort during the birth of Henry VII, might prevent further conception.[19] Moreover, infant mortality drastically reduced the number of children in a family, and there are strong indications that the number of deaths was highest among the poor. This was especially the case after the Black Death, since young people appear to have been particularly vulnerable to plague. Calculations of the levels of infant mortality are bound to be speculative for the Middle Ages. Shulamith Shahar has suggested that between 200 and 300 out of every 1,000 babies died in their first year, and only 500 reached the age of five; mortality continued to be high until the age of ten, and after that young people, and their parents, might die in epidemics, famine or war. In Forez between 1470 and 1517, 214 children were baptised, but 66.25 per cent died before their first birthday.[20]

Among the elite, families varied very much in size. Alessandra Macinghi, born in 1407, married Matteo di Simone Strozzi at the age of fifteen and had a child almost every year between 1426 and her husband's death ten years later; at her death in 1471, four children survived her. Lapo di Giovanni Niccolini dei Sirigatti, also of Florence, had seven children with his first wife and six with his second, of whom ten survived to adulthood. According to his first will of 1341, Bernard-Ezi II, Lord of Albret, had seven sons and five daughters; five sons and four daughters were mentioned in his last will of 1358, although some children may have been omitted. Ralph Neville, first Earl of Westmorland, had twenty-two children in the course of two marriages, but Humphrey de Bohun, Earl of Hereford, Essex and Northampton, left only two daughters at his death in 1373.[21]

Frequent pregnancy and infant mortality are both highlighted by families at Arles. Catherine, wife of Bertran Boysset, had eleven children in a little over twenty-two years, between 1372 and 1393. Three of the children did not survive childhood, and Catherine's will of 1428 mentioned none of her children, her only heir being a grandson. All her children seem to have predeceased her. Johan Meyriani, a notary, married an eleven-year-old bride in 1430. Their first babies were twins and were stillborn. They had seven more children before September 1452, of whom a daughter died at the age of twelve and two sons at five months and two years. Four out of nine children survived childhood.[22]

The size of poorer families has been reconstructed from the Florentine catasto of 1427 and from English manorial court rolls. The evidence from Florence points to wealth having an effect on the size of the family and to variations within the Florentine state. The country round Pistoia comprised the fertile plain and the poorer, mountainous area of the Apennines. Women in both town and country made up just under 21 per cent of the recorded population, but whereas children under the age of four constituted 18.71 per cent of the population in the city of Pistoia, the figures for the mountains and plain were 18.1 and 21.96 per cent respectively. In Florence, the percentage of children under four in families with less than 100 florins was 13.77 per cent, in families with between 101 and 200 florins 14.64 per cent, and in families with over 401 florins 15.89 per cent.[23] The numbers of children in the catasto represent minimum figures; births were under-reported, although the rich were more conscientious than the poor in making their returns.

In his analysis of peasant families at Halesowen between 1270 and 1349, Zvi Razi calculated the mean number of children over the age of twelve as 3.6 in rich families, 2.2 in middling families and 1.6 in poor families; the mean number of sons was 2.5, 1.5 and 0.9 respectively. Over three-quarters of the poor families had one or two children over twelve; only two families had five children, and two had six. In comparison, nearly one-quarter of rich families had one or two children, and over half had three or four; nine families had six children, three had seven and three eight. The Black Death ushered in greater change for the rich and middling families than for the poor; the mean number of offspring over the age of twelve amounted to 2.1 for the rich, 1.5 for middling and 1.1 for the poor. There were no families with more than five children and only two of the rich families reached this figure. It is clear that many families were not reproducing themselves.[24] The court rolls do not give total numbers of children, as those under twelve and many daughters over twelve would have no occasion to figure in court proceedings; moreover, the poor generally had less business before the court than the rich. However, the figures provide useful illustration of general trends.

It is likely that some couples tried to limit the size of their families, and contraception, abortion and infanticide were all practised in the medieval period, although they have left little trace in the records. The discussion of contraception and abortion by university scholars such as Jean Gerson, and their denunciation by preachers like St Bernardino of Siena, point to the fact that they were known about and used. Although it has been argued that this knowledge was used only among prostitutes, contemporary evidence points to its use by married couples. Particular attention was paid to the subject by pastoral manuals in the early fourteenth century, the time when the medieval population had reached its peak and there was widespread famine. Writing in Paris, Peter de Palude from Savoy commented on the man who engaged in *coitus interruptus* so as to avoid having children he could not feed. Some leeway was allowed by the Church, in that it was thought that God did not give the foetus its soul until up to eighty days into the pregnancy. Church punishments for using contraception varied and were more lenient when a poor woman already had many children.[25]

A number of techniques were used for contraception, none of them completely effective. *Coitus interruptus* was probably fairly widespread in Europe. It is likely that many women had recourse to herbal concoctions for both contraception and abortion, and that knowledge of these was spread and perpetuated by local wise-women. Some of the potions were dangerous and the woman might die. It is significant that apothecaries in Paris and Basel were forbidden to sell abortifacients without medical authorisation.[26] Various plants in different parts of Europe have contraceptive and abortifacient properties, such as pomegranate, rue, juniper and Queen Anne's Lace. Many were known to classical medicine, but the medieval period made its own additions, such as tansy. Some women resorted to hard exercise or violence to abort a foetus, as revealed by fifteenth-century evidence from Canterbury.[27]

Infanticide, or the killing of a baby under the age of one, engaged the attention of both canon lawyers and the authors of pastoral manuals, but it was often very difficult to prove. Accusations were certainly made in England and elsewhere in Europe that babies were drowned, exposed or burnt at birth, many referring to illegitimate births, while the abandonment of children led to the establishment of foundling hospitals at Rome, Florence and elsewhere.[28] Deliberate attempts at infanticide were probably caused by a mixture of shame, poverty and sheer desperation. Infanticide also occurred as a result of negligence or accident, and English Church legislation and manuals were particularly concerned with this.[29] Parental negligence leading to the baby's death is hard to assess; many deaths were probably accidental, but the circumstances are usually not known. There was widespread concern over the suffocation of babies who were in bed with their parents. This was the subject of the largest number of fifteenth-century prosecutions in the province of Canterbury; men and women were not accused of intention to kill, but were answerable for negligence, a charge which many contested. Those found guilty were sentenced to public penance. The legislation ordering that the child should be placed in a cradle and not in the same bed as the parents appears to have been widely ignored.[30]

Although some people tried, with varying degrees of success, to limit the size of their families, many women spent their fertile years bearing and bringing up children. It was recognised that a woman needed care during pregnancy, but most women probably found that there was a deep gulf between what was recommended and the realities of everyday life. With the amount of work required in child-care and running the household, there was little prospect of rest, especially for poorer women, and accidents might also occur. According to a story told by Peter the Chanter, a priest out hunting knocked a woman against a wall and she fell. However, she went home and continued carrying goods to market. After three weeks, she miscarried. Pastoral manuals recommended parish priests to urge pregnant women not to do heavy work because of the danger of a miscarriage.[31]

German village customs made special concessions to pregnant women. They had the right to pick fruit if they hankered after it. They were free to fish, provided that they had the agreement of the local fisherman or were supervised by witnesses. The payment of chicken rents was often relaxed and they were allowed extra firewood after the birth of the child. Labour services were also relaxed.[32] German cities were also aware of the need to protect pregnant women; the Nuremberg authorities allowed them special alms in 1461, and in 1478 permitted them to beg in front of the churches, wearing a special badge. It was widely held that pregnant women should be kept from seeing monstrosities, and at Nuremberg in the same year beggars were ordered to keep their deformed limbs out of sight.[33]

The recommendations of medical treatises, such as *Li Livres dou Sante* written in French in 1256 for Beatrice of Savoy, Countess of Provence, by Aldobrandino of Siena, were really applicable only to wealthy women, his advice on refraining from work and from beatings being unrealistic for most. Aldobrandino thought that the most risky times for the pregnant woman were early on, during the first, second and third months, and when childbirth was near. He gave detailed recommendations on diet, thinking it best to eat little and often, having meat like chicken, partridge, blackbird, kid and mutton, and drinking wine mixed with water. Pears, pomegranates and sour apples stimulated the appetite. Salty food was to be avoided or the baby might be born without nails and hair. Electuaries strengthened the body, although only the rich could have afforded these, the recipe including ground pearls, ginger, cinnamon bark, nutmeg and pepper. Mood and attitude were also important. Especially at the beginning and end of pregnancy, a joyful and contented outlook was to be cultivated, and anger, fear and trauma were to be banished from the mind. It was not a good idea to bathe too often or to stay too long in the sun, and clothing should be clean and fresh.[34]

The whole of society was aware of the dangers of childbirth. Bartholomew the Englishman regarded certain women as being particularly at risk, namely young girls, fat women and those whose baby had grown very big. Women were urged to put themselves into God's hands. Many women, like the mother of Clare of Assisi, must have prayed for an easy delivery. The risks explain the widespread recourse to charms and relics, and certain saints, such as St Margaret of Antioch, were especially invoked at childbirth. Some women went on pilgrimage beforehand, such as Cecily Neville, Duchess of York, who had difficult confinements and who visited the famous shrine of the Virgin Mary at Walsingham in Norfolk.[35]

With wealthy women, care was taken over the preparation of the room where the delivery would take place. Noble chambers were sumptuously decorated, green being the colour chosen by the French royal family in the first half of the fifteenth century. Special images and furnishings were chosen. Childbirth for the majority of women took place at home, but certain urban hospitals made special provision, the Hôtel-Dieu at Paris having a separate lying-in room.[36] Childbirth was essentially the concern of women and although the medical treatises included details on childbirth, it was rare for a male doctor to be present. Occasionally, in the case of wealthy families, a doctor was summoned in the event of prolonged labour or complications, as when a servant was sent to Norwich in 1322 to find a doctor for Lady Joan Basset. James II of Aragon was concerned to secure a court physician before the birth of his queen's first son in 1296. As medicine developed as a learned profession in the later Middle Ages, the university-trained physician became more important in treating female conditions.[37]

Normally, the birth was handled by a midwife who mainly learned her skills by observation and experience, although later medieval midwives in France and Germany were expected to serve an apprenticeship. During the fourteenth and fifteenth centuries, German and French towns appointed municipal midwives, one of the earliest being Frankfurt-am-Main in 1302. Regensburg had a system of licensing midwives in 1452, although more attention appears to have been paid to their morals than to their skills. Midwives became sworn city officials at Nuremberg in 1417, when they numbered sixteen, and from 1463 they were supervised by a group of patrician women.[38]

Much of the information about childbirth in the treatises derived from classical texts, notably from the work on gynaecology by Soranus of Ephesus of the early second century C.E. During the eleventh and twelfth centuries, Salerno was the major centre for advances in medical knowledge, combining earlier texts with translations of new Arabic material into Latin and with empirical practices. The most popular treatise, known as the Trotula, dates from the late twelfth century and takes its name from Trota of Salerno who contributed to the section on empirical cures but was not the author of the entire work. The Trotula comprises three treatises: the Book on the Conditions of Women; Treatments for Women; and Women's Cosmetics. The Book on the Conditions of Women made use of classical and Arabic texts, and its discussion of gynaecology treated the subject from the conception of the foetus, through pregnancy and childbirth to the care of the infant. The Treatments for Women comprised a collection of empirical cures associated with the women of Salerno, including Trota. Women's Cosmetics was also empirical in its approach. By the fifteenth century, the Trotula had been translated into most West European languages, and this increased gynaecological knowledge. Aldobrandino's work was written in French, and more vernacular treatises were produced in the fourteenth and fifteenth centuries, but it is not known how far they were consulted by midwives. At least one author, Anthonius Guainerius, made use of midwives' treatments in his *Tractatus de Matricibus*.[39]

The treatises recommended bathing, anointing and massage as the time of childbirth drew near; Soranus recommended the stretching of the vagina, and massaging the stomach was thought to hasten delivery. The treatises paid particular attention to difficult births. Manipulation had to be carried out by the midwife in the event of a false presentation, if the baby was emerging feet first, and details were given for expelling a dead foetus and the afterbirth. A Caesarian operation was carried out only if the mother was dead, but the child was unlikely to survive it. Even when the child was born safely, the mother was still at risk, especially from puerperal fever or from infections caused by lack of hygiene. Post-natal depression certainly occurred, as with Margery Kempe.[40] In the long run, the mother might have been damaged during the birth and might never conceive again.

After the birth, Aldobrandino recommended bathing and good food for the mother, but most attention at this stage had to be lavished on the baby. Once a first cry had been uttered and the umbilical cord cut, the baby was bathed in warm water, the limbs were massaged and the baby was then dried in the sun or by the fire. Even at this stage, there was a differentiation between boy and girl. According to Bartholomew the Englishman, the boy's limbs were rubbed harder than the girl's because of the labour he would have to do in the future. The baby was swaddled in order to support the limbs and, according to the medical theory of the time, to prevent loss of moisture from the body.[41]

After all this had been completed, the celebrations began. The immediate essential was for the baby to be baptised. This was done by the midwife straight after birth if the baby was unlikely to survive; otherwise, the baby was taken to church by the godparents when he or she was a few days old.[42] It was envisaged that the mother would stay in bed for about a fortnight after the birth, although this must have been impossible for poorer women. Visitors arrived with presents, and Christine de Pizan was scathing about the extravagance displayed by the Paris bourgeoisie for their reception; the lying-in chamber of the wife of a Paris grocer had its dresser with golden dishes, the bed its gold bedspread and fine curtains, while the mother was clothed in crimson silk and lying back on silk pillows. It is possible that Christine was exaggerating, but her description is borne out by a painting of the birth of Alexander the Great which depicts a queue of women visiting the mother and having a good look at the baby on the nurse's lap.[43] German and Swiss cities in the fifteenth century, however, encouraged economising on child-bed visits, as Constance did in 1436.[44] After about two weeks, the mother underwent the religious ritual of churching, or purification, and usually a feast was held. John de Grey's great banquet at Rotherfield Greys in 1321 was well remembered twenty-one years later because abbots, priors and almost all the other good men of the neighbourhood were present.[45]

Peasant and labouring women breastfed their babies. Thomas of Chobham, writing in the early thirteenth century, was bitterly critical of women who refused to breastfeed; he regarded this as a form of infanticide and described the mother concerned as more cruel than a beast.[46] Yet wet-nursing was widespread among the better-off in medieval Europe. It was usual to breastfeed the child for between eighteen months and two years, a crucial time in the infant's life. The subject of wet-nursing was given careful consideration in the treatises. The Trotula recommended a young and clean nurse, with a pink and white complexion, well-built, and with full breasts. She should have given birth not long before. Detailed recommendations were made on her diet and above all she was to avoid garlic. Aldobrandino was also concerned over the nurse's character and urged that she should be cheerful and good-tempered and should not terrify the child. He also thought it better if the nurse's own child had been a son. At the age of two, he thought that the child should be weaned on a pap of bread, honey and milk to which a little wine might be added, the nurse softening the bread by chewing it herself.[47]

Many of these recommendations were put into practice. Much is known of the wet-nurses in Florence where the baby was either sent away to the nurse or breastfed at home by a specially engaged nurse or a domestic slave; it was more usual to keep boys at home than girls. Wet-nursing was found among craftsmen and professional families as well as the elite. It was assumed that the nurse would feed only one baby and send her own child to another nurse. The arrangements and salary were made by the baby's father and the nurse's husband, the father having to make alternative plans if the nurse became pregnant or the child failed to make progress. Wet-nursing could also be cut short by financial considerations, as when Tribaldo dei Rossi, in about 1500, could afford for his last daughter to be nursed for only twelve months as against the period of between seventeen and twenty months adopted for her siblings.[48] It is likely that children often bonded with their nurses and that it took time for them to bond with their families on their return home as toddlers.

Once the child had been weaned, the mother took responsibility for upbringing in the early years and after that continued to educate and train her daughters. Mothers were accused of favouritism, but this was not always for their sons. Salimbene alleged that his mother rescued his two sisters during an earthquake at Parma and forgot about him. Children might be neglected by their parents because of disability.[49] In view of the greater attention paid to boys in the treatises, the question arises as to whether they received better food and care. It is quite likely that in a poor family the best food available went to husband and sons. At times, mothers found their children exasperating, like Margaret Paston who had no patience with her daughter Margery when she fell in love with the family bailiff. Evidence given by poor adolescent girls in Bologna indicates that they were regarded as of little interest to their families, especially if they rebelled against social conventions.[50]

Once children moved away from home, or set up their own households, contact might well be lost, but examples from the elite point to the relationship between mother and child continuing into adult life. Mahaut, Countess of Artois and Burgundy, had one son and two daughters, a second son dying as a baby. She was widowed in 1303 while the children were still under age. Although her son Robert had his own household the following year, Mahaut continued to act on his behalf from time to time. Her two daughters, Jeanne and Blanche, married the younger sons of Philip the Fair and were involved in scandal when accusations of adultery were brought in 1314 against them. Blanche was found guilty and spent the rest of her life at the abbey of Maubuisson; her offence was so great that there is no further reference to contact between her and her mother. Jeanne, however, was proved innocent and continued to be entertained frequently in her mother's household.[51] The letters of both Margaret Paston and Alessandra Strozzi show that they remained in touch with their adult children, and both women's caring attitude comes through the hard-headed business details. Wills testify to the fact that women remembered their children and wanted to be remembered by them. In her will of 1473, Amédée de Saluces, *Vicomtesse* de Polignac, left 100 gold écus to each of her five sons and six daughters, describing them all as beloved, although her eldest son was described as beloved and most dear.[52] In many of these wills, the feelings of motherhood combined with those of family and lineage.

Widows

Many women found that their husbands predeceased them. In spite of the dangers of childbirth, women on the whole lived to an older age than men, and in marriages where there was a considerable age gap it was always likely that the husband would die first. For some women, in England for instance, widowhood was a time of greater independence as *femmes soles*, having their own legal identity and making their own business decisions. Others, such as those in Florence, remained dependent on their marital or natal families. All had to try to ensure that they had sufficient financial support for themselves and often for their children and had to face the question of possible remarriage. Husbands dictated their views on these questions through their wills, and natal and marital families also brought pressure to bear.

Every woman was provided at marriage with her future support as a widow. In southern Europe, the woman's dowry was returned to her at the death of her husband. Although the practice of the husband providing dower from his own resources for his wife had declined, husbands might make extra provision for their wives' support in their wills. However, this provision might be conditional on the widow remaining with the marital family and not remarrying. In feudal society, the wife generally received one-third or one-half of her husband's lands as dower, and special customs applied to dower in the towns. These provisions did not always work out satisfactorily for women. Many families were too poor to provide for widows, and on occasion among both rich and poor it proved difficult to raise and return the dowry and to allocate dower. Women often found themselves in straitened circumstances, especially if they had young children.

Remarriage might therefore appear the obvious option for the widow. Yet while the widower's right to remarry was generally accepted, the remarriage of widows was often looked on askance. Moreover, the widow might be unable to attract a second husband if she had little money or property, and many children. Whereas the widows of London and Ghent merchants who remarried did so quickly, it is likely that poorer women found this much more difficult.[53] Both noble and peasant women with what was regarded as valuable dower often had the chance to remarry; some were able to make their own choice of husband, while others found that pressure was brought to bear by king or lord. English noblewomen had to secure royal consent to remarriage, but usually made their own choice, some of them selecting a husband of lower social rank, as when Edward I's daughter, Joan of Acre, married Ralph de Monthermer, a squire in her first husband's retinue. The desirability of peasant widows depended not only on their dower but on the demographic situation. In Cottenham, Cambridgeshire, high payments were made to the lord in about 1300 for the right to marry a widow, but there was a definite decline in the number of these marriages after the Black Death.[54]

A woman who was faced with loss of resources if she remarried needed to think carefully; she might well be torn between a wish to remarry and the desire to remain as guardian of her children. In his first will of 1341, Bernard-Ezi II, Lord of Albret, provided for his wife, Marthe of Armagnac, to be the guardian of their children and to have the usufruct of his goods as long as she did not remarry; if she did so, she lost the guardianship to Jean Count of Armagnac and to her brother-in-law. Once the children were of age, if she wanted to be independent, he gave her property for her to enjoy as long as she remained a widow; if she remarried, this was to revert to her eldest son, who was named his father's universal heir. However, if she chose to marry again, she was to have 5,000 *livres bordelaises* as a return for the pleasant services and profits which she had brought to her husband during their marriage. At the other end of the social scale, Andrea di Feo, a stonemason of Florence, left his wife her dowry, together with a bequest if she remained a widow.[55]

The dilemma for widows can be seen particularly clearly at Florence. Widowhood, like marriage, was subject to family strategies, and dominated by financial and property considerations. Dying husbands left money to their wives on condition that they remained with the marital family; they were not to remarry or to exercise the right of *tornata*, or take refuge with their natal family. By remaining with her husband's family, the widow stayed with her children and the family did not have to return her dowry; the 'cruel mother' was the woman who withdrew, with her dowry, to her natal family. However, if she stayed, she might over the years come increasingly to be regarded as an outsider since, unlike her children, she was not a member of the patriarchal lineage. Alessandra Strozzi chose to remain with her children and her close relations with them continued until her death in spite of the circumstances of the Strozzi exile. On the other hand, on the death of Matteo di Bernardo Parenti in 1426, his widow remarried, leaving four children under the age of four in the care of their great-uncles.[56]

A woman who was widowed very young might well wish to remarry and her natal family might have an advantageous alliance in view. The pressure brought to bear by both marital and natal families was considerable. According to certain jurists, the father continued to have authority (*patria potestas*) over his married daughter. It has been calculated from family memoirs that two-thirds of the widows under the age of twenty remarried and one-third of those in their twenties. The Florentine preference for young wives meant that only 11 per cent of widows in their thirties married again.[57]

The position of the widow depended on her social status and resources, and on local law and custom. Women who were well off among the nobility and in towns in Germany, France, the Low Countries and England could enjoy an active and fulfilling life after their husbands' deaths, running their households and estates, engaging in trade and industry, and promoting the fortunes of their families. They might choose to adopt a religious way of life, either at home or in a religious community. Grandmothers might continue to play an active role in the family, defending rights to property, as did Agnes Paston, and keeping an eye on orphaned grandchildren, as well as maintaining social contacts; in the early 1420s, Elizabeth Clifford joined forces with her daughter-in-law to secure the custody of the lands and castles of her grandson who had come as a minor into the king's wardship. Bequests in grandmothers' wills increased dowries and passed on treasured family possessions; Cecily Neville, Duchess of York, singled out her grandchildren in her will.[58] In so doing, grandmothers fostered the links of children and grandchildren with their own ancestors as well as with those of their husbands.

However, many European households were headed by widows who were poor, and it is likely that they had a difficult old age, especially if their children were alienated or living elsewhere and unable to provide for them. Much depended on the community where they lived and on support received from kindred, neighbours and friends. The Church's encouragement of charity to widows underlined a real need in the later medieval world. The provisions for dowry and dower sound good in theory, but have to be placed in the overall context of widows' lives.

The family, whatever its structure, was the setting for most women's lives. Brought up in her natal family subject to her father's authority, the woman moved into the family of her husband and was subject to him. The years of marriage were usually a time of frequent pregnancies and of child-care. This biological framework has to be set against the universal laws of the Church concerning married life and against local custom and family structures which made for varying relationships in different parts of Europe. Doubtless there were innumerable gradations in the relationship between husband and wife and parents and children which come to light only rarely. Economic and demographic pressures also have to be taken into account, especially the effects of the Black Death which had a devastating impact on the size of families. Marriage and family life were regarded in a down-to-earth and practical way, and medieval people were unsentimental in their attitudes. For women, the care of husband and children constituted the most important aspect of their married lives, but they were also responsible for running their households and earning extra money for the family, duties which gave them a heavy workload.

Notes

1 C. Beattie and M.F. Stevens (eds), *Married Women and the Law in Premodern North-West Europe* (Woodbridge, 2013), pp. 1–10.
2 F. Benigno, 'The southern Italian family in the early modern period: a discussion of co-residence patterns', *Continuity and Change* 4 (1989), pp. 165–94; H. Bresc, 'L'Europe des villes et des campagnes', in A. Burguière, C. Klapisch-Zuber, M. Segulen and F. Zonabend (eds), *Histoire de la famille*, 2 vols (Paris, 1986), I, p. 396.
3 D. Romano, *Patricians and Popolani. The Social Foundations of the Venetian Renaissance State* (Baltimore, 1987), pp. 56–7; D. Romano, *Housecraft and Statecraft. Domestic Service in Renaissance Venice, 1400–1600* (Baltimore, 1996), pp. 85–91; J. Heers, *Family Clans in the Middle Ages*, (trans.) B. Herbert (Amsterdam, 1977), pp. 40–1; D.O. Hughes, 'Urban growth and family structure in medieval Genoa', *PandP* 66 (1975), pp. 10–13, 16, 20; D.O. Hughes, 'Kinsmen and neighbors in medieval Genoa', in H.A. Miskimin, D. Herlihy and A.L. Udovitch (eds), *The Medieval City* (New Haven, Connecticut, 1977), pp. 98–101.
4 D. Herlihy and C. Klapisch-Zuber, *Tuscans and their Families. A Study of the Florentine Catasto of 1427* (New Haven, Connecticut, 1985), pp. 283, 286, 288–92, 294, 296–8; C. Klapisch-Zuber, *Women, Family and Ritual in Renaissance Italy*, (trans.) L.G. Cochrane (Chicago, 1985), pp. 36–67. The catasto understated the wealth of the sharecroppers.
5 R. Wheaton, 'Family and kinship in Western Europe: the problem of the joint family household', *Journal of Interdisciplinary History* 5 (1974–5), pp. 601–28; W. Rösener, *Peasants in the Middle Ages*, (trans.) A. Stützer (Cambridge, 1992), pp. 187–9; M. Mitterauer and R. Sieder, *The European Family. Patriarchy to Partnership from the Middle Ages to the Present*, (trans.) K. Oosterveen and M. Horzinger (Oxford, 1982), pp. viii–xi; Bresc, 'L'Europe des villes et des

campagnes', p. 397; E.A. Hammel, 'Household structure in fourteenth-century Macedonia', *JFH* 5 (1980), pp. 242–73.

6 Bresc, 'L'Europe des villes et des campagnes', pp. 397–8; E. Le Roy Ladurie, *The French Peasantry 1450–1660*, (trans.) A. Sheridan (Aldershot, 1987), pp. 83–5; E. Le Roy Ladurie, *Montaillou, village occitan de 1294 à 1324* (Paris, 1978), pp. 53, 59; R. Boutruche, *La crise d'une société. seigneurs et paysans du Bordelais pendant la guerre de cent ans* (Paris, 1947), pp. 119–21.

7 Rösener, *Peasants in the Middle Ages*, p. 177; D. Nicholas, *The Domestic Life of a Medieval City: Women, Children and the Family in Fourteenth-Century Ghent* (Lincoln, Nebraska, 1985), pp. 176–7; J. Klassen, 'Household composition in medieval Bohemia', *JMH* 16 (1990), pp. 55–75.

8 Z. Razi, 'The myth of the immutable English family', *PandP* 140 (1993), pp. 3–44; R.M. Smith (ed.), *Land, Kinship and Life-Cycle* (Cambridge, 1984), pp. 17–21, 57–9.

9 J. Murray (ed.), *Love, Marriage and Family in the Middle Ages* (Peterborough, Ontario, 2001), pp. 261–70.

10 M. Schaus (ed.), *Women and Gender in Medieval Europe. An Encyclopedia* (London, 2006), pp. 755–6; Murray (ed.), *Love, Marriage and Family*, pp. 304–6; F Broomfield (ed.), *Thomae de Chobham Summa Confessorum* (Analecta Mediaevalia Namurensia 25, Louvain and Paris, 1963), p. 362; E.M. Makowski, 'The Conjugal Debt and Medieval Canon Law', *JMH*3 (1977), pp. 99–114; J.A. Brundage, *Law, Sex and Christian Society in Medieval Europe* (Chicago, 1987), pp. 91–2, 155–61, 242, 255, 285, 415; J-L. Flandrin, *Sex in the Western World* (trans. S. Collins), (Chur, 1991), p. 108.

11 Romano, *Housecraft and Statecraft*, pp. 10–12; G. Brucker (ed.), *The Society of Renaissance Florence. A Documentary Study* (New York, 1971), pp. 44–5; C. de Pizan, *The Book of the City of Ladies*, (ed.) R. Brown-Grant (Harmondsworth, 1999), pp. xxv, 109–10; B. Gottlieb, 'The problem of feminism in the fifteenth century', in J. Kirshner and S.F. Wemple (eds), *Women of the Medieval World* (Oxford, 1985), pp. 349–53; N. Davis (ed.), *Paston Letters and Papers*, 2 vols (Oxford, 1971, 1976), I, pp. 662–5; Ladurie, *Montaillou*, pp. 262, 269–70.

12 R.N. Watkins (ed.), *The Family in Renaissance Florence* (Columbia, South Carolina, 1969), pp. 207–11.

13 D.L. d'Avray and M. Tausche, 'Marriage sermons in *ad status* collections of the central Middle Ages', in N. Bériou and D.L. d'Avray (eds), *Modern Questions about Medieval Sermons. Essays on Marriage, Death, History and Sanctity* (Spoleto, 1974), pp. 118–21; E.G. Rosenthal, 'The position of women in Renaissance Florence: neither autonomy nor subjection', in P. Denley and C. Elam (eds), *Florence and Italy. Renaissance Studies in honour of Nicolai Rubinstein* (London, 1988), p. 373; S. Epstein, *Wills and Wealth in Medieval Genoa, 1150–1250* (Cambridge, Massachusetts, 1984), p. 223; S. Chojnacki, 'The power of love: wives and husbands in late medieval Venice', in M. Erler and M. Kowaleski (eds), *Women and Power in the Middle Ages* (Athens, Georgia, 1988), pp. 126–8, 132–5; R.E. Archer and B.E. Ferme, 'Testamentary procedure with special reference to the executrix', in *Medieval Women in Southern England* (*Reading Medieval Studies* 15, 1989), p. 4.

14 Archer and Ferme, 'Testamentary procedure', p. 4; J. Guiral-Hadziiossif, *Valence, port méditerranéen au quinzième siècle* (Paris, 1986), p. 462.

15 Rösener, *Peasants in the Middle Ages*, p. 184; Guildhall Library, London, MS 9064/2, fo. 179r; A. Cosgrove (ed.), *Marriage in Ireland* (Dublin, 1985), pp. 36–7, 43–4, 47; L. Guzzetti, 'Separations and separated couples in fourteenth-century Venice', in T. Dean and K.J.P. Lowe (eds), *Marriage in Italy, 1300–1650* (Cambridge, 1998), pp. 258–9, 265–6.

16 Guzzetti, 'Separations', pp. 252, 257; A. Finch, '*Repulsa uxore sua*: marital difficulties and separation in the later Middle Ages', *Continuity and Change* 8 (1993), pp. 15–16; A.J. Finch, 'Sexual morality and canon law: the evidence of the Rochester consistory court', *JMH* 20 (1994), pp. 265–6, 269–73; S.L. Parker and L.R. Poos, 'A consistory court from the diocese of Rochester, 1363–4', *EHR* 106 (1991), pp. 652–65; R.H. Helmholz, *Marriage Litigation in Medieval England* (Cambridge, 1974), pp. 100–7.

17 Helmholz, *Marriage Litigation*, pp. 74–100; J.C. Ward, *English Noblewomen in the Later Middle Ages* (London, 1992), p. 31; J. Murray, 'On the origins and role of "wise women" in causes for annulment on the grounds of male impotence', *JMH* 16 (1990), pp. 235–49.

18 Cosgrove (ed.), *Marriage in Ireland*, pp. 41–2.

19 S. Shahar, *Childhood in the Middle Ages* (London, 1990), pp. 36–7; M-T. Lorcin, *Vivre et mourir en Lyonnais* (Paris, 1981), p. 15; M.K. Jones and M.G. Underwood, *The King's Mother. Lady Margaret Beaufort, Countess of Richmond and Derby* (Cambridge, 1992), p. 40; I. Origo, *The Merchant of Prato* (Harmondsworth, 1962), pp. 161–3, 167–72.

20 R. Horrox (ed.), *The Black Death* (Manchester, 1994), p. 85; Shahar, *Childhood in the Middle Ages*, pp. 149–50; Bresc, 'L'Europe des villes et des campagnes', p. 411.

21 L. Martines, 'A way of looking at women in Renaissance Florence', *Journal of Medieval and Renaissance Studies* 4 (1974), p. 19; Klapisch-Zuber, *Women, Family and Ritual*, p. 72; Boutruche, *Crise d'une société*, pp. 386–7, 492–516; *Calendar of Inquisitions Post Mortem*, XIII (London, 1954), p. 130; J.R. Lander, 'Marriage and politics in the fifteenth century: the Nevilles and the Wydevilles', *BIHR* 36 (1963), p. 120.

22 L. Stouff, *Arles à la fin du moyen âge*, 2 vols (Aix-en-Provence, 1986), I, p. 128; II, pp. 690–1.

23 Herlihy and Klapisch-Zuber, *Tuscans and their Families*, pp. 239–41.

24 Z. Razi, *Life, Marriage and Death in a Medieval Parish. Economy, Society and Demography in Halesowen 1270–1400* (Cambridge, 1980), pp. 84, 142.

25 J.T. Noonan, Jr., *Contraception. A History of its Treatment by the Catholic Theologians and Canonists* (Cambridge, Massachusetts, 1966), pp. 199–230, 237, 269–70, 274; Flandrin, *Sex in the Western World*, pp. 100, 106–7; D. Herlihy, *Medieval Households* (Cambridge, Massachusetts, 1985), pp. 145–8; Herlihy and Klapisch-Zuber, *Tuscans and their Families*, pp. 251–4; C. Rawcliffe, *Medicine and Society in Later Medieval England* (Stroud, 1995), p. 203; P. Biller, 'Birth-control in the West in the thirteenth and early fourteenth centuries', *PandP* 94 (1982), pp. 20–35; P. Biller, 'Marriage patterns and women's lives: a sketch of the pastoral geography', in P.J.P. Goldberg (ed.), *Women in Medieval English Society* (Stroud, 1997), pp. 70–5.

26 L. Reutter de Rosemont, *Histoire de la pharmacie à travers les âges*, 2 vols (Paris, 1931), I, pp. 210, 307.

27 Biller, 'Birth-control in the West', p. 20; Rawcliffe, *Medicine and Society*, pp. 177, 203–4; J.M. Riddle, 'Oral contraceptives and early-term abortifacients during classical antiquity and the Middle Ages', *PandP* 132 (1991), pp. 5–27; J.M. Riddle, 'Contraception and early abortion in the Middle Ages', in V.L. Bullough and J.A. Brundage (eds), *Handbook of Medieval Sexuality* (New York, 1996), pp. 261–77; R.H. Helmholz, 'Infanticide in the province of Canterbury during the fifteenth century', *History of Childhood Quarterly* 2 (1974–5), pp. 380–1, and reprinted in R.H. Helmholz, *Canon Law and the Law of England* (London, 1987), pp. 159–60.

28 Rawcliffe, *Medicine and Society*, pp. 203–4; Biller, 'Marriage patterns', pp. 76–81; Helmholz, 'Infanticide', p. 380; R.C. Trexler, 'Infanticide in Florence:

new sources and first results', *History of Childhood Quarterly* 1 (1973–4), p. 99.

29 Biller, 'Marriage patterns', pp. 78–80.

30 Helmholz, 'Infanticide', pp. 381–5.

31 W.A. Pantin, *The English Church in the Fourteenth Century* (Cambridge, 1955), p. 197; Biller, 'Marriage patterns', pp. 79, 81.

32 Rösener, *Peasants in the Middle Ages*, p. 83.

33 U. Rublack, 'Pregnancy, childbirth and the female body in early modern Germany', *PandP* 150 (1996), pp. 88, 96.

34 L. Landouzy and R. Pépin (eds), *Le régime du corps de maître Aldebrandin de Sienne* (Paris, 1911), pp. 71–2.

35 D. Alexandre-Bidon and M. Closson, *L'enfant à l'ombre des cathédrales* (Lyon, 1985), pp. 38–41; Rawcliffe, *Medicine and Society*, pp. 95–8, 179; J. Carnandet (ed.), *Acta Sanctorum*, editio novissima, 69 vols, August II (Paris and Rome, 1867), p. 755; C. Rawcliffe, 'Richard, Duke of York, the king's "obeisant liegeman": a new source for the protectorates of 1454 and 1455', *Historical Research* 60 (1987), pp. 233, 237.

36 Alexandre-Bidon and Closson, *L'enfant à l'ombre des cathédrales*, pp. 54–5; B. Geremek, *The Margins of Society in Late Medieval Paris*, (trans.) J. Birrell (Paris and Cambridge, 1987), pp. 170–1. The confinements of Caterina, wife of Girolamo da Colle, as seen through her husband's account books, are described in J.M. Musacchio, *The Art and Ritual of Childbirth in Renaissance Italy* (New Haven, Connecticut, 1999), pp. 35–57.

37 The National Archives, London, C134/72/1; J.C. Ward (ed. and trans.), *Women of the English Nobility and Gentry 1066–1500* (Manchester, 1995), p. 70; M.R. McVaugh, *Medicine before the Plague. Practitioners and their Patients in the Crown of Aragon, 1285–1345* (Cambridge, 1993), p. 5; M.H. Green, *Making Women's Medicine Masculine. The Rise of Male Authority in Premodern Gynaecology* (Oxford, 2008), pp. 4–21.

38 M. Green, 'Women's medical practice and health care in medieval Europe', *Signs* 14 (1988–9), pp. 449–50, 461; M. Salvat, 'L'accouchement dans la littérature scientifique mediévale', in *L'enfant au moyen âge* (Aix-en-Provence, 1980), p. 92; D. Jacquart, *Le milieu médical en France du douzième au quinzième siècle* (Geneva, 1981), pp. 48–9; M.E. Wiesner, 'Early modern midwifery: a case study', in B.A. Hanawalt (ed.), *Women and Work in Preindustrial Europe* (Bloomington, Indiana, 1986), pp. 95–6.

39 O. Temkin (ed. and trans.), *Soranus Gynecology* (Baltimore, 1956); M.H. Green (ed. and trans.), *Trotula. A Medieval Compendium of Women's Medicine*, (Philadelphia, 2001), pp. 2–51, 70–111; J.F. Benton, 'Trotula, women's problems, and the professionalization of medicine in the Middle Ages', *Bulletin of the History of Medicine*, 59 (1985), pp. 44–9; B. Rowland, *Medieval Woman's Guide to Health. The First English Gynaecological Handbook* (London, 1981); M-R. Hallaert (ed.), *The 'Sekenesse of Wymmen'. A Middle English Treatise on Diseases in Women* (Brussels, 1982); H.R. Lemay, 'Anthonius Guainerius and Medieval Gynaecology', in Kirshner and Wemple (eds), *Women of the Medieval World*, pp. 326–7.

40 Temkin (ed. and trans.), *Soranus' Gynecology*, pp. 69–79; Green (ed. and trans.), *Trotula*, pp. 98–107; E. Amt (ed.), *Women's Lives in Medieval Europe. A Sourcebook* (New York and London, 1993), pp. 102–5; S.B. Meech and H.E. Allen (eds), *The Book of Margery Kempe* (EETS 212, 1940), pp. 6–7.

41 Green (ed. and trans.), *Trotula*, pp. 106–11; Landouzy and Pépin, *Le régime du corps*, pp. 73–8; Rawcliffe, *Medicine and Society*, p. 201; Alexandre-Bidon and Closson, *L'enfant à l'ombre des cathédrales*, pp. 62–7.

42 K. Taglia, 'Delivering a Christian identity: midwives in northern French synodal legislation, *c.* 1200–1500', in P. Biller and J. Ziegler (eds), *Religion and Medicine in the Middle Ages* (Woodbridge, 2001), pp. 77–90. Ralph Basset was baptised when he was two days old; Ward, *Women of the English Nobility and Gentry*, p. 70.

43 Alexandre-Bidon and Closson, *L'enfant à l'ombre des cathédrales*, pp. 70–6; Christine de Pisan, *The Treasure of the City of Ladies or the Book of the Three Virtues*, (trans.) S. Lawson (Harmondsworth, 1985), p. 154. The birth of Alexander the Great is depicted in British Library, London, Royal MS 20 CIII, fo. 15r, and reproduced in Rawcliffe, *Medicine and Society*, p. 178.

44 Rublack, 'Pregnancy, childbirth and the female body', p. 102.

45 The National Archives, London, C134/72/1; Ward, *Women of the English Nobility and Gentry*, p. 71.

46 Broomfield (ed.), *Thomae de Chobham Summa Confessorum*, p. 465.

47 Green (ed. and trans.), *Trotula*, pp. 110–11; Amt, *Women's Lives*, p. 105; Landouzy and Pépin, *Le régime du corps*, pp. 76–8.

48 Klapisch-Zuber, *Women, Family and Ritual*, pp. 132–58, 163–4.

49 M. Goodich, 'Childhood and adolescence among the thirteenth century saints', *History of Childhood Quarterly* 1 (1973–4), pp. 291–2, 295–6.

50 C. Lansing, 'Girls in trouble in late medieval Bologna', in K. Eisenbichler (ed.) *The Premodern Teenager. Youth in Society, 1150–1650* (Toronto, 2002), pp. 293–309.

51 J-M. Richard, *Mahaut comtesse d'Artois et de Bourgogne* (Paris, 1887), pp. 5–15.

52 A. Jacotin, *Preuves de la maison de Polignac*, 5 vols (Paris, 1898–1906), II, p. 319.

53 B.A. Hanawalt, *Growing Up in Medieval London. The Experience of Childhood in History* (Oxford, 1993), pp. 96–7; Nicholas, *Domestic Life of a Medieval City*, p. 27.

54 R.M. Smith, 'Hypothèses sur la nuptialité en Angleterre aux treizième et quatorzième siècles', *Annales ESC* 38 (1983), pp. 125–7.

55 Boutruche, *Crise d'une société*, pp. 507–10; Brucker, *Society of Renaissance Florence*, pp. 56–9.

56 Klapisch-Zuber, *Women, Family and Ritual*, pp. 117–31; Rosenthal, 'The position of women in Renaissance Florence', p. 371.

57 Klapisch-Zuber, *Women, Family and Ritual*, pp. 120, 125–7; T. Kuehn, *Law, Family and Women. Towards a Legal Anthropology of Renaissance Italy* (Chicago, 1991), pp. 200–3.

58 Davis, *Paston Letters and Papers*, I, pp. 284–5, 288, 341–3, 350, 374, 524, 538; *Calendar of Fine Rolls, 1413–22* (London, 1934), p. 433; ibid. *1422–30* (London, 1935), p. 28; J.G. Nichols and J. Bruce (eds), *Wills from Doctors' Commons* (Camden Society old series 83, 1863), pp. 1–8; J.T. Rosenthal, 'Looking for grandmother: the Pastons and their counterparts in late medieval England', in J.C. Parsons and B. Wheeler (eds), *Medieval Mothering* (New York, 1996), pp. 259–77.

4 The house and household

Household and family overlapped in the Middle Ages, and husbands and wives were responsible for servants and apprentices as well as for their children and sometimes members of their kindred. The household served as a social, economic and religious unit, as residence and workplace, and also as the place where religious faith was taught and practised. It was subject to constant change, as children were born, grew up, married or died, servants, apprentices and possibly lodgers came and went, and husband or wife died or remarried. It was the wife's responsibility to ensure that the household ran smoothly. The Ménagier of Paris, writing in the 1390s, expected his wife to keep him comfortable, pointing out that the three things which drive a husband from home are a leaking roof, a smoking chimney and a bad-tempered wife.[1] The wife's duties were arduous and time-consuming, whether she had servants or not, even though her husband did not necessarily believe her tales of an unceasing round of work.[2]

In theory, there was a line of demarcation between the wife's private role and the public sphere occupied by her husband. This was especially apparent among the north Italian patricians, as brought out vividly in Alberti's treatise on *The Family*, written in the 1430s. One of the participants in the dialogue, Giannozzo, described how he trained his young wife in household management.[3] A few days after his marriage, he took his wife over the house, even showing her his treasures, but there was one room she was not allowed to enter: his study, where he kept his books and family records. Although his wife could not read, she was told that if ever she came across anything in Giannozzo's handwriting, she was to hand it over to him at once. Giannozzo expected his wife to see that the household was well organised. He ridiculed her first suggestions on its management, but she overcame her early fears of giving orders to the servants and came to rule the household wisely. Giannozzo's only criticism was that she sometimes took on tasks which were beneath her dignity. Giannozzo obviously drew a clear distinction between his public role outside the house and his wife's private role inside. The Ménagier of Paris made the same distinction, but in more down-to-earth terms. Like Giannozzo, he saw men as responsible for affairs outside the home and these entailed journeying in rain, wind, snow and hail, and putting up with poor meals, cold rooms and uncomfortable beds. He looked forward to the blazing fire, clean clothes and good meal provided by his wife on his return, and also to her company.[4]

In view of the early age of marriage for many girls and the gap in ages between husband and wife, especially in southern Europe, it is likely that other husbands taught their wives the housekeeping skills which they expected. This probably happened less often when brides were older or when husband and wife were of much the same age. It can be assumed that Giannozzo had married a teenage bride, and Alberti refers to her home-sickness for her mother and natal family immediately after her wedding. Her mother had taught her to spin and sew, but not the details of daily housekeeping.[5] The Ménagier was an elderly husband, writing his treatise soon after his marriage for his fifteen-year-old wife. She was an orphan from outside Paris and asked him for instruction soon after their wedding, when they were in bed one night. Paternal and practical in his attitude, he wanted her to be a credit to her second husband after his death. Both these writers belonged to the elite; the Ménagier has been identified as Guy de Montigny, a knight in the service of the duke of Berry.[6] Further down the social scale, it is likely that most girls learned their housekeeping skills from their mothers; certainly they were expected to help their mothers in the home. Girls also had the opportunity to learn during their time as servants or apprentices and through observation of what went on around them.

The houses for which wives were responsible ranged from the one-roomed cottage to the castle, the common factor being the lack of privacy in which women carried out their work. Although the building of chambers and lodgings in the later fourteenth and fifteenth centuries provided more comfort and privacy for the well-off, their lives continued to be overlooked by servants, retainers and visitors.[7] Among the poorer members of society, neighbours were curious and usually well informed as to what went on. In southern Europe, much activity was carried on outdoors. Over the past fifty years, archaeological excavations have provided a much fuller picture of what houses were like and the artefacts women used. This information can be supplemented by details in court cases and by household accounts, and wills and inventories, often for the better-off.

Houses for the majority were small, not comprising more than two or three rooms, and were often rebuilt, not necessarily on the same site or alignment. In southern Europe, it was usual to find two-storey houses, especially in the hilltop villages of Provence and Italy. The hilltop settlement at Rougiers, occupied between the late twelfth century and about 1400, contained two-storey houses, six to eight metres high, close-packed and with few open spaces. The houses had two or three rooms, and most of the hearths were outside the house. These hearths were used for cooking and evidence of meals has been found around them. Houses at Montaillou had one room which served as kitchen and bedroom, and sometimes addi-tional rooms. Richer houses had a first floor over the kitchen. Animals shared the house, although there might be buildings for livestock round the farmyard.[8]

In England, regional patterns of housing are apparent. At the deserted village of Wharram Percy in Yorkshire, houses were usually built and rebuilt within an enclosure; the houses were rectangular and of a single storey, with livestock housed at one end and people at the other. The household had one or two rooms, the main room having a central hearth. In the West Midlands, it was usual to have a two- or three-room dwelling, with a separate building for livestock and sometimes a separate kitchen. By the end of the Middle Ages wealthy peasants had substantial buildings. The rectangular house of one or two rooms has also been found in France and Germany, as in the Forez in the fourteenth century, and at Hohenrode in the Harz mountains and at Königshagen between the twelfth and fourteenth centuries. At Hohenrode, some enclosures had a separate kitchen and storehouses as well as the dwelling-house. In the late Middle Ages, some farms were planned round a courtyard, and examples have been found at Königshagen and at Gomeldon in Wiltshire. Chimneys were uncommon before the end of the Middle Ages, although ovens, and later stoves, are found in villages in eastern Europe.[9] Town houses were similar in size, although as they were built on a narrow frontage since space was at a premium, they were likely to be of more than one storey. They often contained a shop or workshop.

The furnishings which the housewife was expected to look after varied according to the family's resources. Those used by peasants and labourers were basic; little has survived since bedsteads, chests, benches and tables were made of wood, and when they ceased to serve as furniture, the wood was reused or chopped up for the fire. Bedclothes, pots and pans and tools were probably used until they wore out. A fifteenth-century Worcestershire peasant who was not particularly well off had his bed, comprising three bed boards, a mattress, sheet, four pillows and three worn coverlets, a trestle table, chair and form, and three chests; for utensils he had a vat, a barrel, a two-gallon brass pan, three buckets, a tub, eight trenchers and a bottle; for tools he owned a spade, shovel, axe, auger and a spinning-wheel. It was only the wealthy members of society, particularly in the towns, who were able to afford tapestries, rich hangings and covers for beds, elaborate clothes and jewellery, and silver plate, although less well-off townsmen bought status symbols such as cushions and silver spoons. Peasants were more likely to invest spare cash in land, livestock and tools.[10]

During the later Middle Ages, rich merchants and townsmen, as for instance in England and the Low Countries, were building large town houses in which they could enjoy greater privacy, more of a home life, and a higher level of material culture and comfort. The phenomenon has been described as a bourgeois ideology of domesticity and has been studied particularly at York where surviving houses of the urban elite stand in contrast to the small houses or renters of poorer people. The elite house still contained the workshop, shop and storehouse, but the family enjoyed greater space than earlier in the Middle Ages and richer furnishings. The chamber was the room particularly belonging to the wife who may well have been responsible for the choice of furnishings.[11]

Whatever possessions the household owned, the housewife had to ensure that they were well looked after and not lost or mislaid. In an age in which people's goods reflected their status, the use and display of possessions affected the way in which the family was thought of among neighbours and in the community as a whole. The wife contributed to her husband's public reputation by showing furnishings off to the best advantage as well as through her exercise of hospitality. Husband and wife worked as partners in building up the family's standing. Women's wills show that they took pride in their possessions. In England, women of varying degrees of wealth concentrated on bequeathing their personal possessions, whether these were clothes, jewels, or household furnishings or utensils.[12] These items were not simply private possessions; they marked out the status of the woman, her family and household.

'The Ballad of a Tyrannical Husband' paints a bleak picture of the wife with no servant who had more than she could cope with in looking after the house as well as her numerous small children.[13] Her husband was angry when he came home to find that dinner was not ready. He accused her of spending her time gossiping to the neighbours. She retorted that she got little sleep because of looking after a fretting child. She had to get up before him, milk the cows and drive them to the field, make butter and cheese, feed all the poultry, bake, brew, clean flax, and card and spin wool, weave linen and woollen cloth for clothes, and feed the livestock and the family. Whatever her husband said or thought, all these tasks were carried out by the peasant housewife, and many of them also applied to townswomen. The wife could have added to her list, cleaning the house, fetching water from the well and looking after the garden. All these jobs can be corroborated in legal and other evidence. They were undoubtedly tiring and time-consuming and bring out the importance of the wife's contribution to a peasant or artisan partnership. Wives of better-off men in the country found themselves with responsibility for livestock as well as for house and children; the Ménagier's housekeeper took charge of the animals, but he gave his wife a method for killing wolves, and instructed her in the use of cats, ratcatchers and poison for killing rats.[14]

Looking after the house itself was something that many medieval women took seriously. One English archaeologist has complained that floors of peasant houses were so well swept that there is often little left to excavate.[15] The Ménagier recommended cleaning the entrances of the house and the hall early in the day, shaking out the coverings and cushions on the benches, then cleaning and tidying the other rooms ready for the day. He was anxious that there should be no flies, mosquitoes and fleas in the house, and gave his wife six ways of catching fleas, such as spreading alder leaves in the room, using a piece of bread spread with glue or turpentine with a candle in the centre, using a rough cloth or sheepskins on which they would show up, or packing items tightly in a chest so as presumably to squash them. Sheets, coverlets, robes and furs had to be aired and beaten, and grease spots and stains removed. The real problem here came from moth damage and from damp; damp furs became hard and had to be restored to suppleness.[16]

The provision of meals was one of the housewife's main duties, yet for the majority facilities for cooking were limited and open fires had their dangers. Diet varied in amount according to the family's economic circumstances. For the poor, famine was a real threat in the period before the Black Death, and many families must have suffered from malnutrition, especially in the spring and summer months before the next harvest was gathered in. Types of food and drink varied in different parts of Europe according to climate and geographical situation which determined whether the household drank wine, ale, milk or water, and made use of either animal fat or olive oil. All Europeans, however, relied on a cereal-based diet. For bread, many households had to use communal ovens or purchase from the baker, since not all houses had an oven of their own. The grain used depended on what was grown in the locality, such as spelt in south-west Germany and rye in central Europe. Studies of maintenance agreements for old people in England, mostly before the Black Death, indicate that types of grain varied over comparatively small areas, with wheat, for instance, predominating in Essex, Surrey and Somerset, and rye and barley in Norfolk. Pottage – consisting of grains, pulses (peas, beans, lentils), salt and water, which were mixed and then boiled – was also consumed.

Meat and fish consumption was small among the poorer members of society, although the pig was probably highly valued by the housewife, since the whole animal could be used and some of the meat preserved as bacon. Poaching probably brought in the occasional deer or rabbit. Otherwise, it is unlikely that the peasant would slaughter livestock until it was of no use for anything else; sheep and cattle were kept for their milk and wool, for traction, and for reproduction, and would not be killed until they were past these uses. There must have been many tough stews. High meat and fish consumption marked out the rich, who could rear livestock on their estates and afford to make large purchases. Vegetables and fruit appear to have been consumed in relatively small quantities by all members of society. In the years after the Black Death, patterns of diet were similar to the earlier period, but meat consumption by peasants and artisans increased in England, Germany, southern France and Sicily. In Sicily, for instance, agricultural workers were eating meat three times a week in the fifteenth century, the price having dropped appreciably in the hundred years after 1350.[17]

Although diet and cooking methods were simple, they entailed much work for the housewife and took a considerable amount of time. The whole process, and not just the act of cooking, has to be taken into account. Bread-making started with grinding the flour; then the bread had to be mixed, kneaded, left to rise and taken to the oven for baking.[18] Ingredients for pottage had to be prepared. Wine-making and killing the pig and curing bacon may have been done by husband and wife together, but it is likely that women were responsible for making butter and cheese. Some housewives may have preferred to purchase bread, meat or fish either in the village or at the nearest market. In England, women often took charge of brewing and it was usual for the better-off to brew ale for their own consumption and to sell the surplus. Such purchases, however, were not affordable for the poorest families, and there were times when even substantial peasants would not be able to make them.

Another alternative, more usual in the town than in the country, was to buy ready-cooked meals. Fast food was not an invention of the twentieth century. In his description of London of about 1180, William fitz Stephen gave an account of the public cookshop on the bank of the Thames which sold a wide range of meat and fish dishes. There were a large number of cookshops in London and other English towns, and probably also in Paris, and it is likely that these were mostly patronised by the poor, possibly by single-person households where the man or woman could afford only a cheap lodging with rudimentary or no cooking facilities; it is equally possible that poor families lived in similar accommodation. The wealthy preferred to avoid cookshops, which had an unhygienic reputation, but it was only in such places that many of the poor were able to obtain hot food.[19] Even so, it is unlikely that they would have been able to afford this very often.

The wealthy housewife in town or country had a supervisory role over meals and may have been responsible for making certain dishes herself. The Ménagier of Paris included food and shopping in his treatise, telling his wife how to recognise the quality of food; plaice, for instance, was soft to the touch, while dabs should feel hard. He gave an account of the Paris meat markets and commented on food served in very rich households, such as swan, heron and peacock, although he pointed out that these were not suitable for his establishment. He was concerned in his recipes that fresh ingredients should be used, and included a wide range of meat, fish and egg dishes, sauces, sweets and preserves. His inclusion of twenty-four menus and his description of the arrangements for several feasts indicate that he wanted his wife to be able to choose what would be appropriate for particular occasions.[20] In the greatest households, this choice was probably made by the top servants.

Sewing was a skill learned during a girl's upbringing. While the wealthy were occupied with embroidery, many women were engaged in making or mending clothes for their families, often using undyed white or grey woollen cloth. Sumptuary laws indicate that poorer people aspired to imitating their betters, but according to the Peace of Bavaria of 1244, peasants were to wear cheap grey cloth and plain leather shoes, and their hair was to be worn short.[21] This clothing was probably worn until it fell to bits; children's clothes could be passed down from one child to another. Making and mending clothes did not take as much time as cooking and cleaning, but were tasks which had to be done.

The garden needed particular attention at planting and harvest time, but also had to be weeded, watered and kept tidy. The Ménagier of Paris included a section on gardening and expected his wife to have enough knowledge to supervise the gardener; he told her that he was pleased that she tended the roses herself. His practical knowledge comes out in his comments on grafting and planting, and he was well aware of the effects of dry weather and rain. He expected the garden to be useful as well as ornamental, and saw it as a place to spend one's leisure. Besides the roses, he mentioned violets, pinks, peonies and lilies. A wide range of vegetables was listed, including various varieties of cabbage, leeks, beans and peas, spinach, lettuce, radishes, pumpkins, beet, turnips and parsnips. Herbs were important in cooking and for medicines as well as for ornament, and his list included lavender, marjoram, sage, mint and hyssop.[22] It was important to cultivate medicinal plants, as the housewife was expected to be able to prepare the medicines and ointments needed in her household, and to look after husband, children and servants when sick; the Ménagier urged his wife to take trouble over the care of servants when they were ill.[23] His remarks about gardening applied to most housewives, from the wealthy to the poor. English peasant gardens supplied cabbage, garlic, onions and leeks, together with apples and pears; peas, beans and turnips, and plums, cherries and strawberries were also grown.[24]

Although women of the nobility were not expected to carry out household tasks, the majority of married women spent much of their time cleaning, cooking, sewing and gardening, working either on their own or with servants. Even a rich woman who could afford servants, or in the Mediterranean region slaves, did not lead a life of leisure. Margherita Datini of Prato, the wife of a wealthy merchant, found that her time was fully occupied with supervising the house, carrying out her husband's orders and sending foodstuffs to him at Florence. He was often critical of her efforts, as when he thought that she had let water leak into the cellar or had lost household linen. In the early years of her life at Prato, three servants were employed, a man, a woman and a girl of twelve.[25]

Even quite humble households could afford a servant. In Coventry in the early sixteenth century, 13.4 per cent of the households in the lowest rental category of between 1 and 6 shillings employed at least one servant, and 28.2 per cent of the households paying a rent of between 6 shillings and 8 pence and 12 shillings had one or two servants. Numbers of servants were obviously greater in wealthier households; in the rental category of 70 shillings or more, 90 per cent had six or seven servants.[26] In comparison, between a quarter and a third of Florentine families employed at least one servant, but the number of servants in Italian patrician households was relatively small. In Venice in 1505, Francesco Priuli and his wife and two children had four servants: a man, a woman and two wet-nurses, costing a total of 48 ducats. Simone da Sancasciano of Pisa was the head of a household of twenty people in 1428–9, including his children and grandchildren; he employed a male and a female slave and a woman servant aged thirty-six.[27] It was only among the higher nobility and at the courts of rulers that very large numbers of servants were found.

Many housewives needed the skills of directing and working alongside servants, and it was a subject on which the Ménagier gave careful instructions.[28] He already had Master Jehan le Dispensier in charge of the household and Dame Agnes the Beguine as housekeeper and companion to his wife. House-servants were engaged by the year and lived in the household, a practice also found in England.[29] In addition, the household from time to time needed to engage workers for particular jobs, such as the tailors and shoemakers paid by piecework and the reapers hired by the day or for the harvest season. Master Jehan was to engage these men, as they could be rough. Dame Agnes chose the domestic servants, since the Ménagier's wife lacked experience. The Ménagier considered that references were essential to check on servants' character and ability to work. Because his wife was, under him, the mistress of the house, the maids had to obey her, and not quarrel, slander, lie or swear. She and Dame Agnes set the servants to work and told them in advance what they would be doing the next day. They received two meals a day and had plenty of plain food. The Ménagier's account makes it clear how the household with servants worked in practice. He showed awareness of the difficulties which could arise with servants, but did not touch on the problems servants encountered with their masters and mistresses through suspicion, excessive work, failure to pay wages and demands for sexual relationships.

The Ménagier's wife and her contemporaries were directly involved in running their households; they had time for leisure and amusement once the house was cleaned, the kitchen and garden supervised and provisions secured. These tasks, together with child-care, must often have taken up much of the day. For women at the top of society, the question arises as to how far they were really involved in overall supervision of household and servants. Women were named as head of the household only if they were widows, but many women of the elite were virtually in charge in the absence of their husbands on business or in the service of king or city-state. Although many decisions were probably taken by the principal servants, letters and household accounts make it clear that difficult questions were referred to the lady and the final decision rested with her. It is likely that it was the lady who specified what she wanted by way of tapestries, furnishings and plate.[30] Active supervision was in the best interests of both family and household.

The overall responsibility of the lady is strongly brought out in the treatise written by Robert Grosseteste, Bishop of Lincoln, for the widowed Countess of Lincoln about 1241. He advised her that servants should be obedient, faithful and honest, that the household should be peaceful, guests well received and meals served in the hall with propriety; he also gave instruction over her residence and purchases.[31] Cecily Neville, Duchess of York, reserved the hour after dinner for business. Her household rules laid down detailed regulations as to meals and the payment of wages and fees, and proclamation was made four times a year in the market towns round her residence at Berkhamsted in Hertfordshire to find out whether her supplies had been paid for; if not, payment was to be made immediately.[32]

Noblewomen's involvement with their servants is apparent in wills which show a concern for their well-being as well as a desire to be remembered. In her will of 1414, Elizabeth, Countess of Salisbury, made bequests to her servants in their hierarchical order, from the chaplains down to the grooms, and commented on the long service of several; her chief lady-in-waiting, Agnes Grene, was bequeathed 100 marks and the countess's two best robes furred with trimmed minever.[33] Similar concern for servants was shown in royal wills, as in that of Blanche of Navarre (d. 1398), widow of Philip VI of France. Jehanne de Rouieres, one of her ladies, was bequeathed one of the queen's robes, religious and medical books and a breviary, a house or a sum of money, and furniture, linen and pewter to enable her to set up her household.[34] Neither noblewoman nor queen can be regarded as divorced from her household – she had responsibility for its inmates and smooth organisation, while the household enabled her to play her part in society.

Family and household comprised the two main responsibilities of the medieval wife and widow. Many women, however, had more to do. With marriage regarded as an economic partnership as well as a sexual relationship, the working wife at several levels of society, in both town and country, was a reality in the later Middle Ages. This might involve helping the husband with his work or undertaking paid work inside or outside the home. Customs varied as to the types of work which were regarded as suitable for women. The nature of women's paid work and the extent of regional and chronological variation will be examined in the next three chapters.

Notes

1 G.E. Brereton and J.M. Ferrier (eds), *Le Ménagier de Paris* (Oxford, 1981), pp. 99–100; E. Power (trans.), *The Goodman of Paris* (London, 1928), p. 172.
2 For example, 'The Ballad of a Tyrannical Husband', in T. Wright and J.O. Halliwell (eds), *Reliquae Antiquae*, 2 vols (London, 1843), II, pp. 196–9; in modern English in P.J.P. Goldberg (ed. and trans.), *Women in England c. 1275–1525* (Manchester, 1995), pp. 169–70.
3 R.N. Watkins, *The Family in Renaissance Florence* (Columbia, South Carolina, 1969), pp. 207–12, 227–9.
4 Brereton and Ferrier (eds), *Ménagier*, p. 99; Power (trans.), *Goodman*, p. 172.
5 Watkins, *The Family in Renaissance Florence*, pp. 208, 212.
6 Brereton and Ferrier (eds), *Ménagier*, pp. 1–2; Power (trans.), *Goodman*, pp. 41–3; N. Crossley-Holland, *Living and Dining in Medieval Paris* (Cardiff, 1996), pp. 7–8.

7 M. Girouard, *Life in the French Country House* (London, 2000), pp. 52–4; C.M. Woolgar, *The Great Household in Late Medieval England* (New Haven, Connecticut, 1999), pp. 48–50, 59–63.

8 J. Chapelot and R. Fossier, *The Village and House in the Middle Ages*, (trans.) H. Cleese (London, 1985), pp. 183–95, 241; E. Le Roy Ladurie, *Montaillou. Village occitan de 1294 à 1324* (Paris, 1978), pp. 69–73.

9 Chapelot and Fossier, *Village and House*, pp. 197–217, 220–3, 239–44; J.M. Steane, *The Archaeology of Medieval England and Wales* (Beckenham, 1985), pp. 148–9, 186–93; W. Rösener, *Peasants in the Middle Ages*, (trans.) A. Stützer (Cambridge, 1992), pp. 57–60, 70–82; C. Dyer, 'English peasant buildings in the later Middle Ages (1200–1500)', *Medieval Archaeology* 30 (1986), pp. 22–30.

10 C. Dyer, *Standards of Living in the Later Middle Ages* (Cambridge, 1989), pp. 170–1. For contrast, the inventory of Richard Toky, a London grocer, is given in A.R. Myers (ed.), *English Historical Documents 1327–1485* (London, 1969), pp. 1068–71; P.J.P. Goldberg, 'The fashioning of medieval domesticity in later medieval England: a material culture perspective', in M. Kowaleski and P.J.P. Goldberg (eds), *Medieval Domesticity. Home, Housing and Household in Medieval England* (Cambridge, 2008), pp. 124–44.

11 R. Gilchrist, *Medieval Life. Archaeology and the Life Course* (Woodbridge, 2012), pp. 114–15, 119–20; F. Riddy, '"Burgeis" domesticity in late medieval England', in Kowaleski and Goldberg (eds), *Medieval Domesticity*, pp. 14–36; S. Rees Jones, 'Women's influence on the design of urban homes', in M.C. Erler and M. Kowaleski (eds), *Gendering the Master Narrative. Women and Power in the Middle Ages* (Ithaca and London, 2003), pp. 190–211; F. Riddy, 'Looking closely: authority and intimacy in the late medieval urban home', in Erler and Kowaleski (eds), ibid. pp. 212–28; Kowaleski and Goldberg (eds), *Medieval Domesticity*, p. 8.

12 Such close attention to personal possessions is not found in men's wills; K.J. Lewis, 'Women, testamentary discourse and life-writing in later medieval England', in N.J. Menuge (ed.), *Medieval Women and the Law* (Woodbridge, 2000), pp. 69–74. The will of Beatrice Lady Roos gives a large number of bequests of possessions; Borthwick Institute of Historical Research, York, archiepiscopal register 18, fos 357v–358v; translated in J.C. Ward (ed. and trans.), *Women of the English Nobility and Gentry 1066–1500* (Manchester, 1995), pp. 227–30.

13 Wright and Halliwell (eds), *Reliquae Antiquae*, II, pp. 196–9; in modern English in Goldberg (ed. and trans.), *Women in England c. 1275–1525*, pp. 169–70.

14 Brereton and Ferrier (eds), *Ménagier*, pp. 131–2; Power (trans.), *Goodman*, pp. 211–13.

15 Steane, *Archaeology*, p. 185.

16 Brereton and Ferrier (eds), *Ménagier*, pp. 101–2, 129–30, 132–3; Power (trans.), *Goodman*, pp. 173–6, 210–11, 214–15.

17 Rösener, *Peasants in the Middle Ages*, pp. 95–101; C. Dyer, 'English diet in the later Middle Ages', in T.H. Aston, P.R. Coss, C. Dyer and J. Thirsk (eds), *Social Relations and Ideas. Essays in honour of R.H. Hilton* (Cambridge, 1983), pp. 191–216; Dyer, *Standards of Living*, pp. 151–60; E. Le Roy Ladurie, *The French Peasantry 1450–1660*, (trans.) A. Sheridan (Aldershot, 1987), pp. 68–76; W. Abel, *Agricultural Fluctuations in Europe*, (trans.) O. Ordish (London, 1980), p. 71; M. Aymard and H. Bresc, 'Nourritures et consommation en Sicile entre le quatorzième et le dix-huitième siècle', *Annales ESC* 30 (1975), pp. 593–4.

18 Dyer, *Standards of Living*, p. 173, comments that many English inventories included a hand-mill in the kitchen.

19 D.C. Douglas and G.W. Greenaway (eds), *English Historical Documents 1042–1189* (London, 1953), p. 958; M. Carlin, 'Fast food and urban living standards in medieval England', in M. Carlin and J.T. Rosenthal (eds), *Food and Eating in Medieval Europe* (London, 1998), pp. 27–51; A. Franklin, *Dictionnaire historique des arts, métiers et professions exercés dans Paris depuis le treizième siècle* (Paris, 1906), pp. 242–3, 359–60, 528, 552.

20 Brereton and Ferrier (eds), *Ménagier*, pp. 170–283; Power (trans.), *Goodman*, pp. 221–310.

21 Rösener, *Peasants in the Middle Ages*, pp. 88–94.

22 Brereton and Ferrier (eds), *Ménagier*, pp. 116–24; Power (trans.), *Goodman*, pp. 195–204.

23 Brereton and Ferrier (eds), *Ménagier*, p. 136; Power (trans.), *Goodman*, p. 220.

24 Dyer, *Standards of Living*, p. 157; Rösener, *Peasants in the Middle Ages*, pp. 99–100.

25 I. Origo, *The Merchant of Prato. Daily Living in a Medieval Italian City* (Harmondsworth, 1963), pp. 172–6, 195.

26 C. Phythian-Adams, *Desolation of a City. Coventry and the Urban Crisis of the Late Middle Ages* (Cambridge, 1979), p. 239.

27 C. Klapisch-Zuber, 'Women servants in Florence during the fourteenth and fifteenth centuries', in B.A. Hanawalt (ed.), *Women and Work in Preindustrial Europe* (Bloomington, Indiana, 1986), p. 69; D. Romano, *Housecraft and Statecraft. Domestic Service in Renaissance Venice, 1400–1600* (Baltimore, 1996), p. 87; J. Heers, *Esclaves et domestiques au moyen âge dans le monde méditerranéen* (Paris, 1981), p. 147.

28 Brereton and Ferrier (eds), *Ménagier*, pp. 125–36; Power (trans.), *Goodman*, pp. 205–20.

29 P.J.P. Goldberg, 'Female labour, service and marriage in northern towns during the later Middle Ages', *Northern History* 22 (1986), p. 21.

30 J.C. Ward, 'Letter-writing by English noblewomen in the early fifteenth century', in J. Daybell (ed.), *Early Modern Women's Letter Writing, 1450–1700* (Basingstoke, 2001), pp. 35–6; P. Payne and C. Barron, 'The letters and life of Elizabeth Despenser, Lady Zouche (d. 1408)', *Nottingham Medieval Studies* 41 (1997), pp. 126–56.

31 E. Lamond, *Walter of Henley's Husbandry* (London, 1890), pp. 132–7, 140–1, 144–5.

32 *A Collection of Ordinances and Regulations for the Government of the Royal Household* (London, 1790), p. 37; Ward, *Women of the English Nobility and Gentry*, p. 217.

33 E.F. Jacob (ed.), *The Register of Henry Chichele, Archbishop of Canterbury, 1414–43*, 4 vols (Canterbury and York Society 42, 45–7, 1937–47), II (Canterbury and York Society 42), pp. 14–18.

34 L. Delisle, *Testament de Blanche de Navarre reine de France* (Paris, 1885), pp. 35–6.

5 Women and work in rural areas

It was taken for granted in many parts of medieval Europe, in both town and country, that women would be engaged in work which brought money into the household. Types of work varied according to opportunity and social and economic status. Women of all ages were employed in domestic service and laundry. Peasant women, living in villages or small towns,[1] worked on the land alongside their husbands or for an employer, and engaged in brewing, petty retailing, and carding and spinning for the textile industry. Much of the work done by women was connected with the household, and women used the skills learned during their upbringing and adapted and added to these to meet their adult needs. Household abilities enabled better-off peasants to produce for the market as well as for their own families.

Women's work was, however, subject to a range of gender and cultural restrictions, and this restricted the degree of agency they could exercise. Women's subordination applied to the realm of work as well as to other areas of their lives. Paid work had to be fitted around running the household and looking after the children. For this reason women cannot be said to have had a career structure and rarely had capital to invest in an occupation. They usually worked on a part-time or occasional basis and did not necessarily earn money throughout their lives; the wife of John Aldewyne, a butcher at Romford in Essex, brewed for the market while her husband was getting his business established and again when he retired.[2] The English Ordinance of 1363, laying down that men should follow one trade whereas women could follow several, recognised the casual nature of women's work. For most of their lives women were juggling with a large number of responsibilities and had to be adaptable. It was only as a widow, when she was regarded as a *femme sole*, that a woman was able to exercise a greater degree of agency, but her decision on whether to continue in her husband's occupation depended on what was permitted by local custom, on her age and the ages of her children, and on the chances of remarriage.

Political and demographic factors had a bearing on women's work. War, invasion and battles brought sudden change to many parts of medieval Europe, resulting in devastation and sometimes starvation. Demographic changes had a long-term effect. The rise in European population ended in the early fourteenth century, with severe famines in the decade 1310–1320. The impact of the Black Death was severe, with between one-third and one-half of the population dying in 1347–1350 and in subsequent plagues. Taking England as an example, historians are divided as to the effects on women. In his study of York and Yorkshire, Jeremy Goldberg argues for greater employment of women, enabling them to postpone marriage until their late twenties or not to marry at all. Other historians disagree, partly because the evidence is patchy, and it is likely that employment patterns varied regionally. York in the late fourteenth century was a large and growing city, but this was not the case everywhere. Moreover, in view of the numbers of single women in towns, many of them migrants, it is possible that they could not find marriage partners or were unable to raise a dowry.[3]

Although probably the majority of working women were married at some point in their lives, a number were on their own. Single adult women comprised a category unrecognised by the Church. They were more often found in the towns than the country, and most were poor and had low-status jobs.[4] There was always a danger that, living on their own and therefore not subject to male control, they would come under the suspicion of the authorities.

Domestic service

Although domestic service was carried out by children and teenagers, it was also an option for the older woman, making use of her domestic skills and experience. The servant was a female role acceptable to the authorities, since she came under the control of the master of the household; preachers such as Humbert de Romans and Jacques de Vitry addresses *ad status* sermons to servants, putting particular stress on sexual sins.[5] Looking at the poll tax evidence of 1377–1381 in England, it has been calculated that between 8 and 10 per cent of the population over the age of fourteen were in service in rural areas, with 15 per cent of rural households employing servants. The servants received a wage and board and lodging. Many were teenagers, working before they married, but some women worked for longer periods as servants, such as the widow Pernell Cooke of Greenwich, Kent, who went into service so as to have food and drink.[6]

Agricultural and general labourers

Farming was associated primarily with villages and small towns. Women might be engaged in helping their husbands with agricultural work, but they also worked outside the household in meeting obligations to the lord or were employed as wage labourers. Labour services decreased in the later Middle Ages, as lords adopted a policy of leasing their demesnes and servile obligations were relaxed, a process which took place earlier in France and west Germany than in England, and which operated in reverse in eastern

Europe where serfdom increased in the fifteenth century. The principal obligations were carried out by men, but there were occasions when female service was also required. At harvest time in particular, whether in the grain fields or the vineyards, it was expected that all able-bodied men and women would be available for work. Women were often paid wages rather than performing unpaid labour services. Around Seville in the late fifteenth century where cereals, olives and vines were cultivated, most peasant small-holdings were too small to support a family, and husband and wife took turns in being away from home to help with work elsewhere; women took their children with them when they were working as day labourers in the olive harvest.[7]

In England, the wife was generally responsible for the garden, dairy and poultry. How far she participated in the works demanded by the lord is uncertain, but English manorial court rolls and by-laws make it clear that the lord had priority in demanding workers for haymaking and harvest, and refusals to work were punished. At Littleport in Cambridgeshire in 1325, Mabel Beucosin was fined for leaving the village instead of working there as a wage labourer to reap the lord's and her neighbours' corn. The able-bodied were not allowed to glean, although the old and disabled were permitted to do so; it is probable that the farmer's consent had to be obtained.[8]

Women undertook a wide variety of agricultural work and, in addition to working at a number of jobs at haymaking and harvest, were found weeding, carrying corn, driving plough-oxen, spreading manure, thatching and breaking stones for roadmending. Women in Bohemia were responsible for beehives and making honey. Women in the Mediterranean region harvested olives and irrigated flax, while Castilian women took on harvest work. Women living on heathland in Suffolk, England, cut, dried and sold furze for fuel. Many women all over Europe worked with livestock. They were employed in sheep-shearing, and their responsibility for the dairy meant that they made butter and cheese.[9] The division of labour between men and women was not rigid, and women turned their hands to whatever needed doing and would earn them a little money.

Women were usually paid less than men. Pay reflected the local labour situation, the worker's skills and strength, and the urgency of the work as well as gender. The fall in population after the Black Death and the conse-quent shortage of labour benefited both men and women. Wages in the French grape harvest rose in the later fourteenth century, but fell after 1450 when the population was again rising; members of tenants' families were expected to work in the lord's vineyards, with women picking the grapes and men carrying away the baskets and being paid twice as much. Wages increased in England after the Black Death. According to the statute of Cambridge of 1388, women labourers and dairymaids were to receive 6 shillings a year, a figure comparable to the swineherd; the ploughman received 7 shillings and the carter and shepherd 10. However, Sandy Bardsley has shown that both before and after the Black Death the usual practice was to pay lower wages to women; thus in the East Riding of Yorkshire in 1363–1364 they received about 71 per cent of the man's wage. Quite apart from gender considerations, the woman's strength and skill were probably taken into account.[10]

Other labouring jobs were open to women. They carried out washing and cleaning. Washerwomen worked as servants within the household and also operated independently. According to the roll for levying the *taille* in Paris in 1313, there were ten laundresses in the city; probably there were more who were too poor to be taxed.[11] Women worked as labourers on building sites in Germany, Paris, Navarre and Seville, and in fourteenth-century Seville they were employed as masons and carpenters as well as labourers. Wages did not necessarily rise after the Black Death. The pay for women labourers at Toulouse was low over the period 1367–1443 and, as the work was seasonal, there was probably much hardship over the winter. Pay tended to be better when there was a great demand for workers; in the third quarter of the fifteenth century, pay for building labourers at Würzburg peaked at 9 pfennigs a day for women and 12.6 for men, and 1,472 women and 381 men were employed.[12]

Food processing and petty retailing

Food processing and retailing in villages and small towns enabled women to use household supplies for gain. The brewing of ale in England brings out the importance to women of food processing and also certain problems in interpreting their role. From the thirteenth century, manorial courts and the court leet, dealing with petty crime, prosecuted both women and men for offences against the assize of bread and ale, and the fines often amounted in practice to a licence to brew. Ale was drunk widely and therefore in demand. It was made from malted grain and lasted for only a short time, so frequent brewings were necessary. In many villages, brewing was largely in the hands of women. In her study of Brigstock in Northamptonshire before the Black Death, Judith Bennett distinguished between the 273 women who occasionally brewed for the market and the 38 who brewed regularly and controlled almost 60 per cent of the market. The larger group probably sold ale only when they had a surplus from their household requirements. The thirty-eight women came mainly from long-established families, were wives rather than widows or single women, and about one-third had husbands who were politically and economically influential in the community.[13]

Yet while the Brigstock alewives were predominant in the industry, elsewhere male brewers were more visible, accounting for 73 per cent of all brewing fines at Iver in Buckinghamshire and outnumbering female brewers at Alrewas in Staffordshire. Bennett has suggested that these differences can be related to the village economy; in Iver's pastoral economy, men had more time to brew than in the assarting and arable economy of Brigstock. It is also possible, however, that husbands were answering in the courts for their wives' activities or that, at Alrewas, they engaged in brewing on an occasional, part-time basis. In her study of Lincolnshire villages where pastoral farming was important, Louise Wilkinson argued that the male head of the household often answered for the brewing taking place there but that much of the work was done by women. At Havering in Essex and Ramsey in Huntingdonshire, women dominated brewing.[14]

The situation changed as brewing became more specialised after the Black Death. Many occasional brewers, especially unmarried women, ceased production. At Alrewas, the number of brewers fell substantially and there was greater specialisation. Women continued to brew, as did Rosa Kempe, wife of the smallholder William Heuster, who sold bread and was also a regular brewer.[15] However, the expansion of the market after the Black Death, due to higher standards of living and the growth of alehouses, made it increasingly difficult for women to compete. In addition, the development of guilds in the towns and the operation of regulations, as at Oxford, put the emphasis increasingly on male brewers. The introduction of hops, leading to the manufacture of a longer-lasting beer, affected brewing in south-east England in the fifteenth century, and this was very much a male trade, initially in the hands of immigrants from the Low Countries.[16] All these factors, taken together, diminished women's role in brewing by the end of the Middle Ages and cut off one of their means of obtaining supplementary income for their households.

Rural women engaged in marketing as a way to dispose of surplus products, but only the better-off peasants would have been able to use local markets regularly. At Sutton and Lutton in early fourteenth-century Lincolnshire women were selling ale and bread as well as other goods; a total of twenty-three female hucksters is recorded in the court rolls in 1306 and 1313, and thirty-three in 1314.[17] Women in rural areas also worked in the textile industry, although they were mainly to be found in the preliminary processes of shearing the sheep, washing the fleece, carding and combing the wool, and spinning the thread. These processes did not need expensive equipment (most women spun the thread on the distaff rather than the wheel) and could be done on an occasional basis.

Women living in villages and small towns found that most of their time was taken up with household tasks and child-care, and with looking after poultry, the dairy and the garden. Opportunities for paid work were few except at harvest time. Brewing, marketing and spinning gave them the option to make some extra money for the household, although brewing was increasingly a male industry by 1500.

Notes

1　Although small towns had craft occupations and often a market, many people gained their livelihood from farming.
2　M.K. McIntosh, *Autonomy and Community. The Royal Manor of Havering, 1200–1500* (Cambridge, 1986), p. 174.

3 P.J.P. Goldberg, *Women, Work and Life Cycle in a Medieval Economy: Women in York and Yorkshire c. 1300–1520* (Oxford, 1992), pp. 7, 202–43, 336; M.E. Mate, *Daughters, Wives and Widows after the Black Death. Women in Sussex, 1350–1535* (Woodbridge, 1998), pp. 38–40.

4 J.M. Bennett and A.M. Froide (eds), *Singlewomen in the European Past 1250–1800* (Philadelphia, 1999), pp. 16–17; C. Beattie, *Medieval Single Women. The Politics of Social Classification in Late Medieval England* (Oxford, 2007), pp. 2–12.

5 S. Farmer, '"It is not good that [wo]man should be alone." Elite responses to singlewomen in high medieval Paris', in Bennett and Froide (eds), *Singlewomen*, pp. 87–91.

6 M.K. McIntosh, *Working Women in English Society, 1300–1620* (Cambridge, 2005), pp. 46–8, 57.

7 M.B. Fernandez, 'Peasant and aristocratic women: their role in the rural economy of Seville at the end of the Middle Ages', in M. Stone and C. Benito-Vessels (eds), *Women at Work in Spain from the Middle Ages to Early Modern Times* (New York, 1998), pp. 13–20.

8 W.O. Ault, 'Open-field husbandry and the village community: a study of agrarian by-laws in medieval England', *Transactions of the American Philosophical Society*, new series, 55 part 7 (1965), pp. 12–15.

9 R.H. Hilton, *The Economic Development of Some Leicestershire Estates in the Fourteenth and Fifteenth Centuries* (Oxford, 1947), pp. 145–7; H. Dillard, *Daughters of the Reconquest. Women in Castilian Town Society, 1100–1300* (Cambridge, 1984), pp. 164–6; G. Bois, *The Crisis of Feudalism. Economy and Society in Eastern Normandy c. 1300–1500* (Cambridge, 1984), pp. 111–14; J. Klassen, 'Household composition in medieval Bohemia', *JMH* 16 (1990), p. 71; M. Bailey, *Medieval Suffolk. An Economic and Social History 1200–1500* (Woodbridge, 2007), p. 98.

10 E. Perroy, 'Wage labour in France in the later Middle Ages', *Economic History Review*, second series 8 (1955–6), pp. 234–6; A.R. Myers (ed.), *English Historical Documents 1327–1485* (London, 1969), p. 1004; P.J.P. Goldberg (ed. and trans.), *Women in England c. 1275–1525* (Manchester, 1995), pp. 176–9; S. Bardsley, 'Women's work reconsidered: gender and wage differentiation in late medieval England', *PandP* 165 (1999), pp. 3–29; J. Hatcher and S. Bardsley, 'Debate: Women's work reconsidered: gender and wage differentiation in late medieval England', *PandP* 173 (2001), pp. 191–202.

11 M.E. Wiesner, 'Having her own smoke. Employment and independence for singlewomen in Germany, 1400–1750', in Bennett and Froide (eds), *Singlewomen*, pp. 203–4; E.J. Hamilton, *Money, Prices and Wages in Valencia, Aragon and Navarre, 1351–1500* (Cambridge, Mass. 1936), p. 178; D. Herlihy, *Opera Muliebria. Women and Work in Medieval Europe* (New York, 1990), p. 146.

12 Hamilton, *Money, Prices and Wages*, pp. 177–8; Dillard, *Daughters of the Reconquest*, p. 161; Perroy, 'Wage labour in France', pp. 237–8; E. Uitz, *Women in the Medieval Town*, (trans. S. Marnie) (London, 1990), p. 64; S.E. Roff, '"Appropriate to her sex"? Women's participation on the construction site in medieval and early modern Europe', in T. Earenfight (ed.), *Women and Wealth in Late Medieval Europe* (Basingstoke and New York, 2010), pp. 108–34.

13 J.M. Bennett, *Women in the Medieval English Countryside. Gender and Household in Brigstock before the Plague* (Oxford, 1987), pp. 120–3.

14 Ibid., p. 125; H. Graham, '"A woman's work . . .": labour and gender in the late medieval countryside', in Goldberg (ed.), *Women in Medieval English Society*, pp. 137, 140, 142; L. Wilkinson, *Women in Thirteenth–Century Lincolnshire* (Woodbridge, 2007), pp. 132–6; McIntosh, *Working Women*, pp. 141, 153.

15 Graham, 'Woman's work', pp. 134–5, 137–9, 143.
16 J.M. Bennett, *Ale, Beer and Brewsters in England* (Oxford, 1996), pp. 6–12, 77–88, 111–15; P. Clark, *The English Alehouse: A Social History* (London, 1983), pp. 20, 29–31.
17 Wilkinson, *Women in Lincolnshire*, p. 137.

6   Townswomen and work

There are several parallels between rural women and the women of the larger towns as far as paid work is concerned. The same limitations apply – gender, subordination, household ties, lack of capital and the view that certain types of work were unfitting for a woman. Both urban and rural women worked alongside their husbands. There are similarities over the paid work undertaken as hucksters, brewers, spinners, washerwomen and labourers. However, some townswomen had the advantage of being recognised as *femmes soles* during their husbands' lifetime as well as when they were widows, thus being entitled to work as independent women. A few women became merchants and entrepreneurs, and many played an important part in the crafts; this was rarer in the Italian cities. Looking at the wide range of occupations in the large towns, women, particularly in northern Europe, had a greater degree of agency than in rural areas, although the openings for poor women remained limited.

Towns grew fast in the twelfth and thirteenth centuries; by 1347, the largest, such as Florence, had populations of over 100,000. After the Black Death and the consequent reduction of population, most towns gradually recovered in the fifteenth century. Towns were unhealthy places and recovery depended on immigration. Male migration is easier to trace than female, but women certainly moved to the towns as evidenced by the excess of women over men in both England and Germany. One-quarter of the households paying taxes had women heads at Trier in 1363 and at Basel in 1429, and nearly one-quarter at Frankfurt in 1495. Some of these households were headed by widows, but it is likely that a proportion were headed by single women. An analysis of nearly 300 households paying low tax at Trier shows widows heading 26 per cent, beguines 9 per cent, women designated by their occupations 21 per cent, and women identified only by their names 44 per cent.[1] It is probable that there were many single women in the last two categories. These women were mostly poor and had low status jobs. Greater awareness of the importance of demography and the use of a wider range of sources should eventually lead to better knowledge of migration patterns. In particular, the excavation of cemeteries and the study of skeletons should throw light on states of health and dietary patterns. Isotope and DNA analyses are promising tools being developed.[2]

Documentary research indicates that migration to the towns took place over comparatively short distances. For the period before the Black Death in England, toponymic surnames have been used to trace patterns of migration. Peter McClure has found that over half the migrants to Leicester, Nottingham, Norwich and York came from places within a twenty-mile radius of the towns. Using the same method for women migrating to Lincoln in the late thirteenth century, Louise Wilkinson found that out of seventy-three female migrants, forty-three came from places within a twenty-mile radius, twelve from more distant places in Lincolnshire and fourteen from other counties.[3] This method cannot be used after the Black Death when surnames became increasingly fixed.

Domestic service

As in rural areas, domestic service was carried out by children and teenagers many of whom probably migrated to the towns, and it was also an option for the older woman. Once the teenage servant had married, she might become a wet-nurse or governess. Some servants spent a long time in the same household; at Venice, Lena, the wet-nurse of Niccolo Barbarigo in 1440, was described as the companion to his widowed mother nearly thirty years later. Spanish women were found spending their lives in noble and urban elite households, acting as nurses, maids, bakers and cooks, and married and single women worked as servants in Germany and Paris; in Paris, domestic service was the largest women's occupation according to the roll of the *taille* for 1292, 197 servants being listed, as against 50 peddlers, which was the next largest category. Women sometimes returned to domestic service when they were widowed, but might have to leave their jobs if they were physically unable to carry out housework and child-care.[4]

In Florence, the increasing percentage of female servants in the fifteenth century as compared with men, and their rapid turnover, indicate that this was a better time for them than the periods before or after. Older women in particular appear to have benefited. Salaries were higher; women were able to earn 54 florins a year in the first half of the fifteenth century and 49 in the second, as against 14 florins in the second half of the fourteenth century, and 11 between 1500 and 1529. Women generally earned less than men, but on occasion received comparable wages, although problems arose in both Florence and Venice when wages were not paid regularly. Women did not fare as well in the early sixteenth century when larger numbers of male servants were employed.[5]

Food processing and petty retailing

Englishwomen in towns, as in the countryside, brewed ale before the Black Death, but the better-off women in the towns were better able to take advantage of the growing market for ale after 1350. However, the increase of regulation and the growing popularity of beer from *c.* 1450 eventually put an end to their activities. Women were also engaged in brewing in western and central Europe, as in Scotland, Denmark and Germany, although the evidence is less detailed than for England. Town councils supervised the industry and demanded fees from brewers, as at Muhlhausen in Thuringia. Hops were used earlier and more widely on the Continent than in England, and herb beer was also brewed. A contract survives between the authorities of Cologne and Fygen von Broikhusen and her husband by which Fygen was to teach two brewers of Cologne how to brew herb beer.[6]

As far as innkeeping was concerned, husbands and wives were found working together, but many women ran inns on their own. Some of these women were single or widows, but in a number of cases the wife ran the inn while her husband was in a different line of business. Innkeepers not only provided food, drink and lodging but were also involved in the trading transactions of their customers, arranging for storage and transport of goods, and giving credit. Purchases also took place at the inns. The town authorities considered that the inns reflected the town's reputation. After the Strasbourg fairs had been established in 1415, all the innkeepers, both men and women, and their servants were urged to treat visiting merchants honestly and to charge moderate prices.[7] Women innkeepers are found all over Europe. Daughters were trained in the business and at Ghent often married within the trade.[8] By the end of the Middle Ages, women were becoming restricted in certain regions. In Denmark, merchants increasingly took over beer production and sale in the fifteenth century and gained the right to sell imported beer through the municipal inn, and tavern owners were allowed to serve only Danish beer. As a result female innkeepers sank in status.[9]

Petty retailing was a popular way of earning extra money and hucksters are found all over later medieval Europe. Although men operated as small traders, women were particularly numerous in this line of business; for instance, at Coventry between 1377 and 1380, 45 per cent of those presented for forestalling and regrating (buying up goods before they arrived at the market, and holding them back until late in the day so as to push up prices) were women.[10] Trading was closely regulated, as seen in English court records with their fines for offences of selling at too high a price as well as of forestalling and regrating. Widows and single women operated on their own; wives worked in partnership with their husbands, or in some cases were independent *femmes soles* answerable for their own debts if their business ran into difficulties. One of the best known wives working on her own in England was Margery Kempe of Kings Lynn whose ventures into brewing and corn-milling both failed.[11]

Husbands and wives often divided their responsibilities, the wife sometimes taking over the retailing while her husband oversaw production. Thus, among German fishmongers, husbands caught the fish while their wives prepared and sold them. The wives of German bakers obtained the flour and other ingredients and did the baking. Butchers' wives in Shrewsbury were frequently summoned to court for leaving entrails and dung in the street; possibly they were responsible for preparing meat for sale.[12]

Most hucksters retailed food and drink, like the women of Exeter who sold ale, poultry, dairy products, salt, flour and oats. Some hucksters also dealt in clothing, as at Halesowen and Thornbury.[13] Women in Paris retailed foodstuffs, fuel and old clothes; according to the records of the *taille* of 1292, there were fifty female peddlars. Women poultry sellers were allowed to continue operating if they were widowed.[14] Hucksters were recorded in several German towns, such as Hamburg, Bonn and Frankfurt, and it appears that women were responsible for most of the retail distribution of food, drink and secondhand clothes. At Ofen, in eastern Europe, forty-five German and Hungarian women sold fruit, vegetables, poultry, cheese, game and herbs in the fifteenth century. Women in Nuremberg in the late fifteenth century were allowed to sell food and candles in the market, the authorities preferring this option for poor women rather than dispensing charity. Women worked as petty retailers in Denmark and also as the more important mercers who sold food and manufactured goods. They were included in the gild of merchants of Flensborg, founded in the early fifteenth century; according to the list of members of 1420–1531, thirty women on their own belonged to the guild, together with five who were married at the time of their entry. Becoming a mercer did not need capital and made use of household skills.[15]

Hucksters were also to be found in southern Europe. Among Venetian artisans, women engaged in food retailing, among other occupations. Women sold old clothes in Florence in the late thirteenth century, and according to the catasto of 1427, female heads of household sold dishes, fruit and vegetables, and food. Hucksters were also found at Bologna.[16] In the Iberian peninsula, women sold goods in both shops and the market, and these included textiles, bread, soap and garden produce. A survey for Seville of 1384 recorded female retailers, especially of food; barley, honey, milk, bread, fish, fruit and spices were listed.[17] Petty retailing provided women with the means of making money all over later medieval Europe. It was an occupation accepted by the authorities and continued into the early modern period.

Long-distance trade

In contrast to the many European women who made money as hucksters and retailers, few women were engaged in long-distance trade. Such trade required capital and expertise. Merchants also needed to be free to travel, especially before about 1300, and women with children were rarely able to do this. A few German women travelled as merchants to the Frankfurt fairs, and Scottish merchants in the fourteenth century were found travelling with their wives.[18] The women who worked as merchants usually came into trade as a result of their family connections; wives helped their husbands and widows carried on businesses, often until a son was old enough to take over. Wives took up mercantile responsibilities in Germany while their husbands were away from home; they made business decisions, dispatched merchandise and handled investments and loans, as did the wife of Hans Praun of Nuremberg in the 1470s. Some wives were responsible for keeping the business accounts; the wife of Matthias Runtinger (d. 1407) of Regensburg became responsible for book-keeping towards the end of her husband's life.[19]

Genoese women were both traders and investors in the late twelfth and early thirteenth centuries, investing in nearly 25 per cent of over 4,000 surviving *commenda* contracts for trading voyages between 1155 and 1216. In the early thirteenth century, a widow entrusted her trading partner with linen to be sold in Ceuta in north Africa, while another widow arranged with her partner for linen to be sold in Sicily. Genoese women never travelled as traders; the wife of Bonus Vasallus Crispini arranged with another merchant to deliver German cloth to her husband in Ceuta, and, in the event of his not being there, to sell the goods. Similar female activity is found in Venice, Marseilles and Montpellier in the thirteenth century.[20]

Over the later Middle Ages, however, women merchants were more usual in Europe north of the Alps. Widows of English merchants carried on their husbands' businesses. Marion Kent of York exported cloth and lead and imported a variety of goods in 1471–3, but withdrew from trade as her children grew up; most unusually, she was a member of the council of the York mercers' guild in 1474–5.[21] Women of the merchant class in Cologne in the fifteenth century engaged in trade. Fygen Lutzenkirchen continued with her husband's trading interests after his death in 1498, when she apparently handed over her silk workshop to her daughter. Other Cologne women traded as widows or helped their husbands during their lifetimes; they were active in a number of trades, such as metals, spices, flax and linen, woollen cloth and wine. Sometimes their trade was linked to other business interests, as when seamstresses traded in linen, presumably for making up and sale in their shops.[22] Women were found in the wine, woollen cloth and luxury trades in fourteenth-century Ghent, and occasionally as major moneylenders in Ghent and Bruges. Margaret van Ruuslede managed the family exchange in Bruges, Clare van der Ponten of Ghent dealt with wool sales when her husband was absent in 1384, while Celie Amelakens worked as a moneychanger and was one of only two women in Ghent to act as a tax-farmer in the fourteenth century.[23] Women drapers and merchants were found at Douai in the thirteenth and fourteenth centuries, and women drapers at Leiden in the fifteenth. At Montpellier, they were involved in the luxury trades and the grain and grape trade before the Black Death, and occasionally in moneylending.[24] These merchant women belonged to the elite and were exceptional in their activities. By the late fifteenth century, such activities were becoming even more unusual for women; at Douai, this came about as a result of legal, economic and political changes.[25]

The crafts

The craft workshop was essentially a family and household concern, under the control of the master craftsman, or sometimes his widow. Those working there comprised the family itself, servants and apprentices, together with journeymen and female employees who were paid a wage. It was taken for granted that the master's children had the right to be trained in his craft, as is made clear in the guild regulations of thirteenth-century Paris. The fullers, linen merchants, carvers of crucifixes, chandlers, makers of writing tablets and other trades all specifically referred to training the family's children.[26] As a result of the training of daughters and apprentices, and wives generally being allowed to help their husbands, women were found practising most medieval crafts. It was only rarely stated that a craft was unsuitable for them; the makers of Saracen tapestries at Paris, however, forbade women to work at the craft because the work was too hard for them, but allowed a widow who did not remarry to continue to run the workshop.[27] Many women on their own used the skills they had been taught to obtain work as employees, sometimes finding that the local economy provided opportunities for jobs, as with the women who sewed sails in the Arsenal at Venice.[28]

Household working arrangements were common among the crafts in later medieval Europe, and husband and wife often worked as a partnership, the input of both being vital to the success of the enterprise, with the wife taking over the running of the workshop in her husband's absence. Alternatively, husband and wife worked at different crafts, and their individual occupations might change during the course of their marriage. Where crafts were controlled by guilds, arrangements for women members varied; craftswomen might be admitted in their own right or wives might belong as a result of their husbands' membership.

Although artisan wives helped their husbands in all European towns, they were a less significant element in the workforce in Italy than in England, France, Germany, the Low Countries and Scandinavia. In both England and Germany, women worked in the food and drink trades, textiles and clothing, leather, metal and sometimes in building.[29] Women in Iberia also took up a variety of crafts – in addition to victualling and textiles, they were also found working in the leather and metal trades.[30] The Florentine *catasto* of 1427, however, indicates that the trades where women could work in Tuscany were restricted. Out of almost 7,000 heads of household, 315 women with occupations were listed, the majority having an assessment of less than 50 florins. This figure included women working in textiles (twenty-five weavers, ten spinners, three carders, two seamstresses and two hosemakers). Of the eighteen hucksters, fifteen had an assessment of over 100 florins, while the six laundresses, assessed at 8.5 florins, were at the bottom of the scale. Few women were in wealthy occupations. The three innkeepers had an average assessment of 266.67 florins, but there were only two wool merchants, assessed at 1,695.5 florins each.[31] No women appear to have worked as silkmakers, in contrast to the situation at Cologne. The picture of women in lowly occupations is mirrored at Bologna and Verona.[32] It is possible that women's opportunities were greater before the Black Death when women weavers were found taking apprentices, but even then they do not appear to have been as prominent in the workplace as women north of the Alps.[33]

The status of women in the workplace cannot be judged only on the basis of the number of crafts in which they were involved. The degree of control which they exercised over their work needs to be considered and for this their position in the guilds and their rights as widows have to be assessed. Widows' rights to take over the workshop on the death of their husbands varied, but widespread concern was expressed over untrained men coming into a craft and there may have been unexpressed anxiety for the future of the late master's children in the new household. Thirteenth-century evidence from Paris indicates that many widows had to give up their crafts if they remarried a man of a different trade; this applied, for instance, to the fullers and weavers, and the new husband of a cordwainer's widow had to purchase his mastership before she could carry on with the workshop.[34] The wives of Danish merchants helped their husbands but as widows generally lived off their property or went into retail trade. Craftsmen's widows were usually allowed to continue to work as long as they remained unmarried or remarried a man of the same craft.[35] In German towns, the widow could usually continue to trade, but might have to relinquish this if she remarried, and the situation was similar in England, although there were variations in practice from town to town. At York, widows carried on as weavers, dyers, pinmakers, founders, builders and chandlers, among other trades; the York butchers, however, decreed in 1498 that if a butcher's widow remarried a man of another trade, he was to reach agreement with the city and the guild before he could trade as a butcher himself. In London, widows of freemen were allowed to be freewomen, provided they did not remarry, and carry on their husbands' trades; they could take on and train apprentices, and have their own shops where they traded retail.[36] Matilda Penne, for instance, continued her husband's trade as a skinner after his death in 1379–80 for over twelve years. She was skilled in the specialist work of purchasing and preparing skins and making them up into fur linings. She trained her own apprentices and was bequeathed an apprentice by another skinner in 1386.[37]

Widows were more restricted in southern Europe. In Spain, they were allowed to continue to work if they had sons to succeed them. Artisan widows in fifteenth-century Valencia were permitted to carry on their husbands' trade if they had young sons; at Barcelona, according to an ordinance of 1402, a weaver's widow was forbidden to continue working unless she had a son aged twelve to succeed to his father's workshop.[38] A similar situation was found at Venice. Wives worked alongside their artisan husbands, who appointed them executors of their wills; however, it was rare for them to be in charge of workshops except for the period until their sons took over. At Genoa, Sofia, widow of Giovanni de Vilmercato, carried on her husband's weaving business and in her will of 1247 left her equipment to her apprentice, but workshops run by women were most unusual.[39] It was assumed that most widows of craftsmen would live on their dowries and on any bequest from their husbands. They were not expected to be in control.

Textiles

The term 'textiles' covers a vast array of crafts in the later Middle Ages. Not only does it include the making of woollen cloth, silk, linen and canvas and the multifarious processes involved, but also the making up of all types of clothing. Women's work ranged from the low-grade and poorly paid jobs such as washing fleeces and spinning to the more lucrative weaving and dyeing. Although the skills of textile manufacture were found all over Europe, the industry was concentrated in particular regions, such as Flanders, Florence and England for woollen cloth, and the north Italian towns, Paris and the Rhineland for silk; it was in these areas that women's opportunities for work were greatest. In contrast, in Denmark where the urban textile industry developed only in the later sixteenth century, women were unable to use their spinning and weaving skills to earn money.[40]

The majority of women worked in the less lucrative processes. As well as facing exploitation from employers, they came up against competition from charitable institutions, as when, in the fifteenth century, the hospital of the Innocents at Valencia purchased flax for the women inmates to spin into thread. Women in the Hôtel-Dieu at Chartres were also occupied in spinning.[41] Working women in the Spanish and Italian towns faced competition from slave labour. Although spinning did not pay well, it had the advantage of being a home-based occupation and could easily be combined with housework, child-care and gossiping with neighbours. It provided welcome supplementary earnings, but for women on their own it would have been difficult to earn much of a livelihood. Women were also engaged in combing and carding wool, preparatory to spinning, and in Valencia Moorish women took the silk off the cocoons. In some areas, men were also engaged in these processes, but spinning was almost always a female occupation in Europe north of the Alps. Male and female spinners were employed at Barcelona where detailed regulations in the fifteenth century covered the type and thickness of threads to be used for sails, and where both spinners and sellers were warned not to grease the thread to give it a better appearance.[42] Both men and women were engaged in carding and combing wool in thirteenth-century Genoa and then proceeding to the spinning and weaving.[43] In addition to home-working, some employers, like Jean Boine Broke of Douai, had workers on their own premises.[44]

Women also worked as weavers. In Barcelona, women linen weavers were allowed to qualify as masters and have their own workshop. Both men and women were engaged in weaving and dyeing in Valencia. Women were found as weavers and sometimes dyers in several parts of Italy, as well as in England, Flanders, France and Germany; an incomplete list of weavers from Strasbourg of 1434 named sixty-eight men and thirty-eight women, some of whom were described as widows or single women.[45] Numerous women worked as blue dyers in Ghent; the journeymen regarded them as a threat, but the guild responded that unrest would break out if they were not allowed to work.[46] In addition to the women involved in manufacture, seamstresses all over Europe produced various items of clothing and household furnishing, often specialising in particular items.

Women came into their own in the silk industry in the northern towns, in London, and especially in Paris and Cologne. The industry was largely in women's hands in London, although it never had its own guild. Silkwomen were found in London from the early fourteenth century, mainly making ribbons, laces and girdles, some of them running workshops, others employed as silk workers. They had a sense of common identity and combined to present petitions of grievance, as in their complaint to the mayor of London in 1368 against a Lombard merchant who, they alleged, was dominating the market in raw silk, and in their five petitions to parliament between 1463 and 1483 which led to acts of parliament prohibiting the import of ribbons and laces. The silkwomen bought raw silk and gold and silver thread from Italian merchants. They were allowed to take apprentices and attracted girls from as far away as Yorkshire. Several were married to mercers, and these marriages seem to have resulted in good business partnerships, as with Alice, married to Richard Claver (d. 1456), who worked during and after her marriage and whose will of 1489 mentions one apprentice and another three women who may well have been silk workers and former apprentices.[47]

In both thirteenth-century Paris and late medieval Cologne, luxury textile trades were dominated by women. According to the *Livre des Métiers*, Paris had several female guilds: the silk spinners using large spindles, silk spinners using small spindles, silk ribbon makers, silk weavers of kerchiefs (for covering the head), milliners, and the makers of Saracen alms purses. Mistresses were mentioned in a number of other luxury crafts, such as the embroiderers.[48] Such female guilds were exceptional in the later Middle Ages; apart from Paris and Cologne, they existed at Rouen for spinners, two types of linen merchants, ribbon makers and embroiderers.[49] Within the female guilds at Paris, there were detailed regulations on the number of apprentices and length of their training, and the employment of other workers. Thus, silk spinners using large spindles were restricted to three apprentices, as well as their and their husbands' legitimate children, and those using small spindles were limited to two.

Apprenticeship was supervised by the guild, which also checked out women workers from outside Paris. Length of apprenticeship varied within the guild. For spinners using large spindles, it was for seven years together with a payment of 1 *livre parisis*, or eight years without payment; the apprentice was to remain with her mistress until her term had been completed and mistresses were forbidden to exchange or sell their apprentices.[50] Work of high quality was insisted on; poor work was burnt by the guild of ribbon makers.[51] With the milliners, no mistress was allowed to take apprentices until she had been a mistress for twelve months.[52]

These women were highly skilled, but the regulations point to suspicions of malpractice. The weavers of silk kerchiefs were ordered to buy their silk only from the merchants and not from Jews or spinsters, and were forbidden to run up debts with the Jews, Lombards or anyone else.[53] The mercers complained that the spinsters sold the raw silk supplied to them to Jews and Lombards, or exchanged it for floss; they were using the silk as a pledge when they borrowed money. The silk spinners were summoned before the provost of Paris and told not to do this on pain of banishment.[54] It is not known whether this threat was sufficient to stop the practice.

Although some of the guilds had female officials, this was not invariably the case. Both the silk spinners using large spindles and those using small spindles had two male officials in charge of the guild. The ribbon makers were run by three masters and three mistresses, while the weavers of silk kerchiefs had three women in charge, and the Saracen purse makers had one male and one female official.[55] The existence of male officials is not altogether unexpected in view of contemporary ideas on women's weakness and the rarity of female office-holding.

The guild regulations do not throw light on all aspects of the crafts. The wages paid by mistresses to their workers are not known, nor is the number of workers employed. The ordinances of the embroiderers provide a long list of names, most of them female, as do those of the mistresses and women workers making Saracen-style alms purses, which name 124 women. The majority of women were working independently of the male members of their families. Some of these women were also named in the taxation lists of 1292 and 1313; in 1292, there were twenty silk-thread workers and fourteen silk workers, and in 1313 ten female silk spinners and seven silk-thread workers.[56] It is not clear how long the female guilds lasted; certainly they had disappeared by the fifteenth century.

Cologne was the only late medieval city where women had their own guilds. They worked in partnership with their husbands and also on their own. As in London and Paris, a distinction has to be drawn between the women directing operations and the workers. The products made by these women were renowned across Europe. The yarn makers were responsible for linen yarn, usually dyed blue. The guild was organised in the late fourteenth century, its charter being confirmed by the city council in 1397. The yarn maker was allowed to have three girls to help her, and once an apprentice had finished training and was admitted into the guild she was permitted to open a workshop. A mother who was a yarn maker was allowed to set up one daughter in an independent establishment and give her financial help, but not yarn. Much of the yarn was exported to Antwerp, a trade usually conducted by the yarn maker's husband. If she died, her husband was allowed to continue to run the workshop as long as he did not remarry a woman who was not a guild member. This provides an interesting reversal of the situation found with the widow in male crafts.

Gold beaters and gold spinners also received their guild charter in 1397. Gold spinning was women's work, and marriage to a husband who was a gold beater made for a good business partnership; the gold beater worked gold and silver into fine threads which the spinner then spun on their own or set round a textile thread. The spinner married to a beater was permitted to employ three girls, while the spinner on her own might employ four. Again, the work was for export, this time to northern Italy.

The numbers of yarn makers and gold spinners are not known, but the silk makers were numerous and some had considerable wealth. It has been calculated that between 1437 and 1504 116 silk makers running their own shops employed 765 apprentices, the majority employing between two and four. The most important was Tryngen Ime Hove, who trained thirty-nine apprentices between 1462 and 1501 and who probably bought about 5,000 pounds of raw silk a year in the first half of the 1490s. Silk makers mainly came of merchant families and were often married to merchants engaged in international trade, although they might also operate on their own. Silk grew in importance as an industry in the second half of the fifteenth century. The guild received its statutes in 1437 and it is significant that the silk maker was allowed to train four apprentices as well as her own daughters and could employ as many other workers as she wanted. Apprentices were attracted from Germany and the Low Countries, mainly from the Rhineland and Westphalia. The silk makers were primarily weavers, and spinners encountered problems even though they had their own guild from 1456; silk makers had to be reminded to pay wages in cash and not goods, but abuses remained within the outworking system.

The women's guilds at Cologne were unique for their time in western Europe. The guilds were run by men and women, the gold beaters and gold spinners electing two female and two male officials each year, as did the silk makers where Fygen Lutzenkirchen and her husband served alternately as officials for eighteen years; husband and wife were not allowed to hold office at the same time.[57]

Looking at the later Middle Ages as a whole, it is clear that women's opportunities to work varied from place to place, and that there were always certain restrictions, although these were greater in some parts of Europe than others. By 1500, however, there are signs that women's work was becoming more limited, except in huckstering, spinning, washing and low-grade employment. The growth of professional brewing limited domestic production. Regulations concerning the widows of craftsmen and traders became more stringent; whereas the widows of cordwainers, pursers and glovers in Copenhagen were allowed in 1460 to continue to run their husbands' workshops for as long as they liked, in 1514 they could do so for only one year.[58] Women weavers in England found that they were unable to continue in business.[59] Increasing restrictions cannot simply be explained by contemporary views on women, since the expectation that women should be passive and obedient applied throughout the Middle Ages. The answer lies rather in a range of economic, demographic and political factors, notably the effects of the drastic fall in population as a result of the Black Death and subsequent plagues, and the economic depressions of the late Middle Ages.

Although the immediate effect of the plague was to create a labour shortage, evidenced by the pressure for increased wages, the long-term fall in demand inevitably affected businesses despite the rise in the standard of living for many in society. Certainly the opportunities for women to take up employment grew in the second half of the fourteenth century. Where there was a high demand for the goods being produced, and where the legal and social situation allowed women to run workshops and conduct trade, women flourished both as craftswomen and merchants. Such was the situation at Cologne and in late medieval London. Yet not all women were able to benefit; women entrepreneurs were exceptional in the north Italian cities, and women in occupations such as spinning, wherever they lived in Europe, remained poor. Downturns in the economy, as in mid-fifteenth-century England, caused considerable hardship. By the later fifteenth century, population levels were beginning to rise and women found that employment opportunities became more limited. Even in domestic service, women found that many employers preferred to have male servants.[60]

Political factors also have to be taken into account. Changing fortunes in industry, as in Flanders in the fourteenth century, were due to both the economic and political situation and inevitably had an impact on work patterns. Revolt and war caused economic disruption, even if only temporarily, and affected businesses, often causing dislocation to trade. Women in war-torn areas probably found that little paid work was available and they had to take any occupation which offered remuneration. Occasionally, women benefited from the demand for military supplies, as when Lisbette Talboem sold cloth for captains' uniforms at Ghent in 1323, and the women of Görlitz supplied cloth, canvas and tools for the wars against the Hussites.[61]

Changes in the organisation of work in the late Middle Ages, notably the disappearance of the family unit of production, probably had an effect on women's role in the crafts and trade. Martha Howell has examined this question with reference to Leiden and Cologne. Although there are differences between the two cities, she found that women with high-status work benefited from the system of household production.[62] The growth of craft and trade guilds, dominated by masters, and exercising economic and political power, had a limiting effect on women's access to work. These guilds brought pressure to bear on the town authorities in their own protectionist interests. In Strasbourg in 1330, the weavers demanded that all women weavers should join the guild; many women could not afford the admission charges, and the council decreed that linen weavers need not join the guild, but those weaving woollen cloth had to be members. The guild pressed for further restrictions in the later fifteenth century, but the council continued to permit women to weave as long as they paid the guild charges.[63]

Similar pressure was brought to bear by guilds in other German towns. Women were allowed to weave only narrow cloth and veils at Hamburg in 1375. Although Cologne had its women's guilds, in other crafts in the fifteenth century only six out of forty-two can be described as guilds for men and women, and guild regulations often restricted women's role. Felt hat makers, for instance, forbade female workers in 1378, and this included wives, daughters and servants. Harness makers prohibited the use of female servants in 1494. Women were excluded from the guild-organised weavers and fullers in Leiden, and the wives of master fullers were forbidden to deal with their husbands' accounts on their own; women were allowed to operate as dyers, finishers and drapers.[64] Restrictions were found in guild regulations across Europe and limited women's work within the crafts.

These restrictions have to be set in the context of the protectionism of the guilds, the growing exclusiveness of masters, limitations on apprenticeship, and the expansion in the number of journeymen who might never be able to accumulate the resources to set up a shop of their own. If journeymen had to work as wage earners, their wives would be forced into lowly occupations, either because they had not had craft training or because there were no openings for them in masters' workshops. Moreover, as journeymen themselves became organised into guilds, they brought pressure to bear on female workers. Journeymen fullers at Leiden complained about masters' wives working in the craft and demanded that wives should no longer take down the cloth dried on tenter frames after fulling.[65]

During the later Middle Ages, women were engaged in a wide range of occupations and trades. Yet the variety of women's work, particularly in the crafts in Europe north of the Alps, should not obscure the fact that much of the work done by women was poorly paid and that women's guilds and wealthy female traders were the exception and not the rule. The assumption that the medieval urban family worked as a household unit generally applied in the crafts, but it fails to make allowance for women working independently and for the number of female wage earners working outside the home. The majority of women earned money on a part-time, casual basis, as spinners, washerwomen and hucksters, fitting their paid work in with their household tasks and child-care. Throughout the period, women found that there were limitations on what they could do: limitations of time, capital, social attitudes, legal restrictions and local regulation. Those women who ran workshops and were engaged in long-distance trade owed much to their fathers' and husbands' status and to circumstances; widowhood gave them a chance in certain parts of Europe to be in control of their affairs, at least in the short term. At the end of the Middle Ages, however, the openings for women to work in the crafts, in merchandise and in domestic service became increasingly restricted, and these developments continued into the early modern period.

Medical care and nursing

The impression that much work was casual and poorly paid is reinforced by women's experiences in medical care and nursing. The majority of women who engaged in nursing were poor; only few came from better-off families. Women worked occasionally as doctors, but they were few and far between. The growth of the universities meant that in the later Middle Ages the professions were almost completely closed to women. The Church and the law were staffed by men. Although many women had a deep spirituality and others an expert knowledge of the law, they were unable to use their personal qualities and expertise in a paid capacity. As with craftswomen and hucksters, they had to make use of their household skills and in looking after the sick performed a service to the community. The concept of women as carers for the body was taken for granted in the medieval world, and many women had their own recipes for petty ailments, but, although many women owned medical books, these were written in Latin and made use of medical terms which would have been incomprehensible to the untrained reader.[66]

References to women in the context of the universities are extremely rare and may be fiction rather than fact. Christine de Pizan has a story in the *Book of the City of Ladies* that when the fourteenth-century professor of canon law at Bologna, Giovanni d'Andrea, had to be absent, his daughter Novella gave lectures in his place, speaking behind a curtain so that her beauty should not distract the students. There is also an early fifteenth-century story of a woman who put on male clothing in order to attend the university of Cracow. She lived in a student hostel and proved a conscientious student, but her disguise was discovered after two years and she never gained a degree. According to the story, she became a nun and eventually an abbess.[67] The two stories suggest that except in a few rare cases university education was restricted to men, and the women who especially wished to study medicine had to do so by a different route.

Medical care

Medical employments for women had differing levels of acceptability in the later Middle Ages. Midwifery and nursing were regarded as suitable work, although individual women might find themselves prosecuted for misdemeanours and low standards. Medical practice for some women was acceptable, but here it was easy to transgress the norms established by male practitioners, especially when the medical faculty of a university was ready to prosecute, as at Paris. The medical profession in the later Middle Ages included various types of practitioner. Physicians were trained in the universities; surgeons were normally trained within the family or by apprenticeship, although in Italy surgery could also be studied at university; empirics specialised in particular areas of medicine and often in surgery. In addition, barbers carried out certain practices such as bleeding.[68] Because of their exclusion from the universities, women were likely to receive their training within their families and on the job. Stephanie, a doctor at Lyons in 1265, was the daughter of a doctor.[69]

Women practised all types of medicine and treated both men and women. However, their numbers were very small – although it is likely that many who practised locally and in a small way left no documentary record. The most famous woman doctor of the Middle Ages was Trotula of Salerno to whom many popular medical treatises on women's ailments were attributed and who was one of a number of female practitioners in Salerno in the eleventh and twelfth centuries.[70] Some women continued to practise at Salerno later in the Middle Ages, such as Trotta de Troya, who was given a licence to practise surgery in 1307, and was one of twenty-four women licensed to practise in the kingdom of Naples; thirteen were licensed to treat women but were not necessarily restricted to gynaecological matters.[71] Small numbers of women were found practising medicine of various kinds elsewhere in Italy, such as the four who matriculated in the guild of doctors, apothecaries and grocers at Florence between 1353 and 1408; it is significant that two of the four were daughters of doctors. No women seem to have entered the guild before or after, and it is possible that a shortage of doctors because of plague opened the profession to a few women. The hospital of Santa Maria Nuova at Florence had a female mistress and surgeons, but little is known about them.[72]

Numbers were small elsewhere in Europe. In France, 126 practitioners have been found, of whom 44 were midwives; this figure has to be set against 7,647 men. Eight women doctors, thirteen barbers and two midwives were recorded in the Paris rolls of the *taille* in 1292.[73] Only about a dozen female physicians, surgeons and midwives have been found in medieval England.[74] In contrast, fifteen women practitioners worked in Frankfurt-am-Main between 1387 and 1497. Women in German towns also worked as apothecaries, often being taught by fathers and husbands. A woman named Anna von Offenburg was a pharmacist at Basel in 1379 and again in 1431, and a female apothecary in Augsburg was ordered by the town government in 1445 to employ a trained male assistant.[75]

Some of the women working in medicine in Germany, Florence and Spain were Jewish, and in Spain Muslim medical practitioners were found occasionally. James II of Aragon (1291–1327) was anxious to employ university-trained physicians, often from Montpellier. In Spain, however, women practitioners did not face the pressure and criticism brought to bear in Paris by the university. James II intervened to protect several women surgeons in Barcelona. Women faced certain restrictions; a law of 1329 for Valencia allowed female doctors to care only for women and children and even then forbade them to give potions. This still permitted them to diagnose and recommend diet and external medication, such as ointments, and in fact women continued to treat men. Women also worked as apothecaries; Bernat de Calidis, an apothecary of Barcelona who was active in the 1330s, had two daughters married to Barcelona apothecaries, and pharmacists' widows continued to run their husbands' shops.[76]

Both male and female doctors were subject to criticism if they failed to effect a cure, but women were particularly liable to be prosecuted by the Church, town authorities or guilds. The actions were not necessarily successful. Marie de Gy, a physician of Dijon and the wife of a barber, was excommunicated when a man died at her house at the end of the fourteenth century, but she was still practising in Dijon as a widow in the early 1400s.[77] University-trained physicians were particularly anxious to control those whom they regarded as unqualified practitioners, and the faculty of medicine at the university of Paris made vigorous attempts to exercise control. In 1271, the faculty legislated against surgeons, apothecaries and herbalists who encroached on the role of the physician and prescribed medicines. By 1311, it claimed that their actions were based on a 200-year-old statute which would have predated the university's existence.[78] Several women were condemned in the early fourteenth century. Clarice of Rouen and her husband were excommunicated for illicitly practising the art of healing, and the surgeon Margaret de Ypra was forbidden to practice medicine in Paris and the suburbs in 1322 on pain of excommunication and a fine of 60 *livres parisis*.[79]

The most notorious case involving the university of Paris in 1322 concerned Jacoba (or Jacqueline) Felicie of Almania.[80] The faculty of medicine accused Jacoba of practising as a physician in and around Paris, examining urine, taking pulses, touching limbs and prescribing medicines, and of doing this without official approval. It alleged that she was totally ignorant of medicine. However, witnesses testified to her reputation and how she had cured men and women. Jeanne, wife of Denis Bilbaut, said that she had been cured of a fever by Jacoba after male treatment had failed, and Jeanne de Monciaco gave similar testimony for a kidney disease. Jean de St Omer testified that he had been cured by her when male physicians had failed and his wife supported his testimony. Other men who were cured included Odo de Cormessiaco, a friar at the Hôtel-Dieu; again, male treatment had been unsuccessful, whereas Jacoba had succeeded with her prescription of baths, massages and herbal applications. It was argued in her defence that the faculty's legislation was not valid and it was better for a woman physician to visit female patients; she was able to make a physical examination which was forbidden to a man and the patient would be more ready to talk about her illness to a woman than to a man. The woman physician was in a better position to effect a cure. The faculty was not impressed by these arguments and Jacoba was condemned.

Unlicensed practice continued, but during the fifteenth century women's medical activities were also attacked by the guilds, as was happening at the same time with the crafts. In certain towns, such as Montpellier, widows were allowed to practise provided that they did not remarry, but this was not the case everywhere. Jean Estevenet practised as a barber in Rheims for nearly twenty years before entering religion about 1450 at the age of seventy. He left his workshop to his wife, but the barbers' guild took action to prevent her from practising. Peretta Petone, a widow, was arrested in 1411 at the instigation of the Paris guild of surgeons, which claimed that she had not been approved to work as a surgeon. She claimed she had been trained in a provincial town by one of her relatives and had practised in Paris for eight years. Women were increasingly accused in the fifteenth century of practising witchcraft. In 1487, for instance, Jeanne Villain was accused of casting spells to cure wounds, and Henriette de Crans was burnt at Besançon in 1434 for sorcery after she was alleged to have cured the sick by spells and the invocation of the devil.[81] Women in medical practice found their position increasingly risky at the end of the Middle Ages.

Midwives and nurses

Midwives were responsible for gynaecological and obstetrical care. Their reputation varied widely and instances are found of prosecutions for malpractice, an extreme example being the case of Perrette de Rouen and Catherine la Petioune who obtained a stillborn baby for the benefit of a lord suffering from leprosy; it was believed that if the lord's face was anointed with the fat of the child it would be beneficial.[82] Midwives were present at childbirth at all levels of society. Asseline Alexandre was in attendance at the birth of the children of the duchess of Burgundy in 1371, 1377 and 1379, while Julienne worked in the lying-in room of the Hôtel-Dieu in Paris in 1378. Many midwives came of artisan or craftsman families. Asseline Alexandre was the wife of a Paris bourgeois and Catherine Lemesre the wife of a baker; Guillemette Vyard, wife of a shoemaker of Dijon, had to become a midwife in 1496 in order to survive because her husband had left two years before on a pilgrimage to Santiago de Compostela and never returned. Such women worked independently of their husbands, although it is likely that there was a greater degree of partnership when midwives were married to doctors, as at Mons and Ghent.[83]

Training was often informal; midwives learned from their own experience and that of other midwives. However, town authorities in France and Germany supervised midwives in the fourteenth and fifteenth centuries, and there is evidence of apprenticeships and examinations. Lille in the second half of the fifteenth century had an examination for midwives, consisting of an examination by a doctor and a report on their work during childbirth from the women they attended. Catherine Lemesre was admitted as a midwife in this way in 1461, and Agnes le Clerc in 1472. The references to sworn midwives in several French towns, such as Dijon, Rheims, Orleans and Paris, probably point to official approval, as does the employment of midwives by town governments in Germany and the Low Countries, as at Bruges from 1312 and Basel from 1455. In many towns, midwives were not allowed to leave without permission; a midwife named Gensane was forbidden to leave Apt in 1382 because several women were about to give birth.[84]

All women probably had to care for the sick at some point in their lives, and wives were expected to look after their families and servants. Nursing was regarded as women's work. It provided wives, widows and single women with employment, and it is likely that the twelve nurses listed in the rolls of the Paris *taille* of 1292 represented just the tip of the iceberg.[85] Nursing as an employment took several forms: wet-nurses fed and looked after babies and toddlers, women cared for the sick in hospitals, and women of higher status were appointed to supervise the care of elite babies and also of older girls, having the position of mistress rather than nurse.

The demand for wet-nurses provided good prospects of employment, and nurses in the first half of the fifteenth century could normally reckon on earning twice as much as a female servant.[86] Employment of a wet-nurse in the baby's own home enabled her to be carefully supervised; the household of Francesco, son of Lorenzo Priuli of Venice, consisted of himself and his wife, two children and four servants, two of whom were wet-nurses.[87] Yet for many working women the advantage of wet-nursing lay in its being carried on in the nurse's own home. She could therefore combine earning money with continuing to care for husband and family, as when the wife of a velvet-weaver in Valencia nursed the son of a local schoolmaster. This method of operation was found in many parts of Europe and at all social levels; in the early fifteenth century, the granddaughter of Katherine, Countess of Suffolk, was boarded with her wet-nurse in a nearby village.[88]

Wet-nurses and children's nurses also worked in municipal and institutional employment. By the fifteenth century, town authorities increasingly undertook the care of orphans and abandoned children. At Montpellier, the demand for nurses grew steadily from seven a year in the 1460s to twenty-six in the 1490s. Most of the women lived in Montpellier itself and the majority were married to craftsmen or agricultural workers. Most of the women were employed for short periods, but one woman spent nearly eleven years looking after three girls and a boy between 1479 and 1498. Wet-nurses were paid more than child-carers, and wages were higher in the first half of the fifteenth century than the second. Other southern towns also provided for wet-nursing, as at Tarascon and the Foundling Hospital at Florence.[89]

High expectations of nurses were expressed in treatises and hospital regulations. Whether they were servants or sisters who had taken religious vows, women tending the sick were expected to look after, wash and feed their patients gently and without complaint, even when they were exhausted.

Many hospitals were small and catered for the poor and for travellers as well as the sick; the hospital of St John the Baptist at Oxford had six sisters who were replaced by women servants in the 1380s. Problems of poverty and maladministration meant that the women's lives were often hard, and the sisters of the hospital of St Mary's Bishopsgate in London suffered from poor food and clothing in the fourteenth and fifteenth centuries.[90] Women were both more numerous and had more responsibility in the large hospitals of continental Europe, but the work was equally hard. At the Hôtel-Dieu in Paris, and elsewhere, there was a never-ending round of cleaning, bathing and feeding patients, and washing linen. Between 800 and 900 sheets had to be washed each week, and the great and little laundries were the centre of constant activity. For the majority of nurses, the work must have seemed unremitting and it is likely that many women took up the work not out of a sense of vocation but in order to secure a livelihood.

For the few women with posts of responsibility, there was the chance to exercise organisational skills. The prioress of the Hôtel-Dieu was the most important official in the hospital after the master. She administered the property attached to her office, had her own seal and presented her accounts in person to the chapter of Notre Dame cathedral. She was responsible for all the female staff, comprising forty sisters, thirty girls and novices, and the women servants, and she also supervised the sick rooms and the patients. Having entered the hospital as a novice and worked her way through all the departments, she knew the routine intimately. She was in charge of the linen on which she spent about half her revenues; over 1,500 sheets were in use, and each year she had to purchase more than 2,000 ells of new cloth.[91]

The prioress's duties were similar to those of women in other large hospitals. At the Holy Ghost hospital in Nuremberg, which was under the overall control of a master, three women, who were answerable to him, were responsible for the day-to-day running of the establishment. The custodian, helped by the mistress, was responsible for purchases of bedding, kitchen utensils and food; she was also responsible for any property of the patients, supervised the servants, and decided when patients should leave hospital. The mistress was primarily in charge of the kitchen and of the food which was served. A third woman was in charge of admissions, which could prove a difficult task; no patient with a contagious illness was to be admitted and all patients had to belong to or work for citizens' families. Women also held responsible positions at the Holy Ghost hospital in Munich where the mistress was in overall charge, with another woman responsible for the kitchen.[92]

Mistresses of royal and noble children had a very different life from the hospital nurse. It was usual throughout the later Middle Ages to appoint a woman, generally of a knightly or aristocratic family, to supervise royal children and those of the higher nobility. Lady Elizabeth Darcy, for instance, was in charge of the nursery under Edward IV and Henry VII, and she oversaw the servants attached to the nursery as well as the upbringing of the children. Boys over the age of seven were handed over to male tutors, but girls continued in the charge of a mistress until they grew up, and sometimes into the early years of their marriage.[93]

Helene Kottanner stands out among the mistresses of later medieval Europe, partly because of the events in which she was caught up in 1440 surrounding the birth and coronation of the Hungarian king, Ladislas the Posthumous, but also because she recorded her own version of these events in her memoirs. She was born into the lower nobility of Austria about 1400 and was married twice. In 1436, she is known to have been in Vienna at the court of Albert of Habsburg and his wife, Elizabeth of Luxemburg, possibly as governess to their daughter Elizabeth, born in the same year. Albert became Holy Roman Emperor and king of Hungary and Bohemia on the death of his father-in-law, Emperor Sigismund, the following year. His death in 1439 heralded a struggle for the succession between the Hungarian magnates who backed a Polish candidate and the queen who hoped to secure the kingdom for her unborn child. Throughout this period, Helene was in Hungary in charge of the baby Elizabeth and was apparently very much in the queen's confidence.

Helene's memoirs give a detailed account of the queen's actions. In particular, Elizabeth wished to get hold of the crown of St Stephen from the castle of Visegrad, and she asked Helene to do this. Helene realised the danger to herself and her children if something went wrong, but agreed to take on the task, provided that she was allowed a helper, and a Hungarian was engaged who was never named in the memoirs. The two journeyed to Visegrad on the pretext of fetching the queen's ladies-in-waiting. Helene was terrified on the night the theft took place and described her fears vividly; she prayed hard to the Virgin Mary to calm herself. The theft was successful and the crown was smuggled out of Visegrad concealed in a red velvet pillow. By the time Helene returned to the queen, the baby's birth was imminent, and Ladislas the Posthumous was born that night, with Helene present at the birth. Three months later, he was crowned at Székesfehérvár. Helene described how she cut up a vestment belonging to Emperor Sigismund and made the clothes for Ladislas to wear at the coronation; she looked after the child on the journey and held him during the coronation service. Shortly after the coronation, it was decided that the royal family should split up, with Helene accompanying the king, and her husband remaining with the queen. The memoirs break off shortly after Helene and Ladislas reached Austria.[94]

Few mistresses found that their employment involved them in such dramatic events, and it appears that Helene received little reward for her labours. The memoirs may have been written about 1450 to remind those in power of what they owed her.[95] Yet her care of the children and her close relationship with the queen were probably mirrored in the careers of many other mistresses.

Prostitutes

Prostitution was rarely a lucrative profession and it is probable that many young women were driven to it out of the need for money and food. It was very much an urban phenomenon and young women migrants or single women in the towns were vulnerable as a result of poverty, lack of training or a dowry and the absence of male kindred. Married women were also vulnerable if they had left or been deserted by their husbands. Prostitution epitomised the casual nature of women's work, the need to pick up whatever job was available at the time, and was often combined with other employment. In Exeter, for instance, prostitution was coupled with work as a servant, brewer, petty retailer or textile worker, and it has been calculated that about one-fifth of the fifty-five prostitutes recorded in the court rolls between 1373 and 1393 lacked relations in the town and were probably immigrants. A similar situation is found at York, and immigrants, both from outside London and from the Low Countries, are found in the stews (brothels) of Southwark.[96] Although some women took up prostitution on their own initiative, others were secured by pimps, procurers and procuresses, allegedly against their will, such as Isabel Lane, procured in London in 1439 for a group of Lombards and others. In some cases, mothers put their daughters into prostitution.[97]

Prostitutes were regarded as marginal women who needed to be kept under control. Although Louis IX of France attempted to expel public prostitutes in his ordinance of 1254, the decision two years later to ban them only from the centre of towns points to a realisation that prostitution could not be eradicated. Later legislation concentrated on controlling prostitutes. This attitude was similar to that of the Church. St Augustine considered that the existence of prostitutes was essential in human society in order to control lust, and this viewpoint was developed by later medieval thinkers, many of whom were more concerned to condemn homosexuality than prostitution.[98] Prostitutes were regarded as impure and were therefore expected to wear distinctive dress and not to frequent certain parts of the town. They had to be differentiated from respectable women. At the same time, it was considered that they had a social contribution to make in safeguarding marriage and providing sexual services for unmarried young men. It was widely thought that in this way homosexual and adulterous relationships were curbed.

Poverty, casual employment, immigration and rootlessness all had an impact on prostitution, and war and devastation also forced women to move. While women combined prostitution with domestic service, spinning and washing in Paris and German towns, prostitution probably appeared to many as the easiest way of earning money. The story of Marion du Pont, a prostitute of Paris, is typical. She was born at Corbie and after leaving the town worked as a servant and prostitute in Clermont, Beauvais and Senlis. She then moved to Paris, where she stole 15 *ecus* when she was visited in the Rue Glatigny in the Cité by a merchant who subsequently caught her trying to change the coins. She was put to death for theft.[99] In his study of Dijon and south-east France, Jacques Rossiaud found that many of the women came from humble families of the region and embarked on prostitution in their teens because they had been orphaned and lost touch with their families. About half had been forced into prostitution by their family or others. Jeanne was placed in service in a cookshop in Dijon by her father at around the age of fourteen because her mother had died and he had other children to bring up. She left the shop after she was raped one night and worked at weeding in the fields, as a building labourer and at casual prostitution. Unfortunately, her landlady learned about her prostitution and she was forced to leave.

There was also a large number of foreign prostitutes in the public brothels in Dijon and the Rhône valley, many of them from the Low Countries and northern France, hard hit by war in the fourteenth and fifteenth centuries.[100] Women from the Low Countries, France, Spain, Germany, Poland and Dalmatia were among the prostitutes in Florence in the fifteenth century, with Germany and the Low Countries making up 21.5 per cent between 1441 and about 1480; between 1486 and 1490, there were 115 Italians and 35 foreigners in the brothel quarter.[101]

Prostitutes found that, despite being on the margins, their services were always in demand, although the nature of the clientele varied somewhat from place to place. The clergy were the main clients in English cathedral cities and towns with large religious houses, and they formed a significant part of the clientele elsewhere; at Dijon, about one-fifth of the clients were members of the clergy. The demand for prostitutes was high in university towns. Prostitution was the largest form of employment for women, according to a household survey of Bologna of 1395, the prostitutes either living with their husbands or on their own. The brothel of La Pobla at Valencia was presumably popular with sailors as well as with notables and merchants; women were forbidden to be on board ship in 1473. At Florence, nearly three-quarters of the clients of the public brothel were non-Florentines and it was frequented mainly by artisans, labourers and small shopkeepers. At both Lyons and Dijon, the bath-house and brothel were frequented by men aged between about eighteen and forty, whether they were artisans, craftsmen or merchants. Married men were not supposed to be admitted, but there were ways of evading the regulations.[102] With the late age for men's marriage in southern Europe, the brothel provided a place for men to have sexual relations.

The regulation of prostitution varied between regions and over time. Non-institutional prostitution was to be found all over Europe throughout the later Middle Ages. Although subject to a measure of control from the Church and town authorities, the trade was in the hands of individual prostitutes or their procurers and took place in private brothels and other places such as lodging-houses, inns and taverns, as well as bath-houses. The latter were very near the margins of social acceptability, because although used for bathing, they were often notorious for prostitution, in spite of the attempts to separate bathing times for men and women; inventories of bath-houses included beds as well as baths.[103] In southern Europe and parts of Germany, mainly in the fourteenth and fifteenth centuries, the emphasis was put on institutional prostitution, regulated by the urban government.

Towns tried to control prostitutes and procurers who worked independently, but the regulations were usually ineffective. Some attempts were made to charge a licensing fee, and the fines on prostitutes in English urban court rolls may in fact constitute such a payment. Bruges operated an informal licensing system in the fourteenth century.[104] Dress regulations – such as the striped hood in London, and gloves and a bell on the head in Florence – were widespread in order to distinguish the prostitutes from 'respectable' women.[105] Attempts were also made to keep prostitutes out of particular areas, and certain streets became known as red light districts. In 1393, London prostitutes were forbidden to frequent all parts of the City and suburbs except the stews of Southwark and Cock Lane. In Paris, no particular part of the city was set aside for prostitution and the prostitutes were to be encountered on the banks of the Seine, in alleyways and the area surrounding the city, as well as in the Cité and other places.[106]

In southern Europe, freelance prostitution continued to flourish alongside public brothels. Regulations could not always be enforced, especially if a private establishment had powerful backers. Jeanne Saignant was in charge of the bath-house of St Philibert at Dijon for twenty years. She was married, and, more important, she had a protector who was in favour at the court of the duke of Burgundy. She was good company, and the attractions of her establishment included food as well as baths and prostitutes. She preferred married men as clients because they paid more. The city authorities finally took action against Jeanne in 1461 after she quarrelled with an influential woman client whose husband was secretary to the duke of Burgundy.[107]

Attempts were made to clamp down on illicit prostitution in Languedoc in the late fourteenth and fifteenth centuries. The prohibition of new brothels in Alès in 1454 and the letting of lodgings to concubines was greeted with an outcry and the decree was withdrawn. When prostitutes were driven out of their lodgings by the town authorities of Montélimar in 1423, they were given rooms in the inns. Their expulsion from the inns was proposed in 1438 at a time when there was a threat of plague; the innkeepers agreed, provided that the decree applied to taverns and bath-houses as well. The prostitutes returned to the inns once the plague was over and in 1447 the innkeepers had their right to receive private prostitutes confirmed by the dauphin, the future Louis XI.[108] This acceptance of independent prostitution in society was widespread.

Public brothels were established alongside private prostitution. The urban authorities in Languedoc issued general regulations in the thirteenth century banning prostitutes from certain areas of the town, excluding them from the streets of 'good men' at Arles and Avignon in the 1240s, and

Marseilles in the 1250s. Some towns regarded prostitutes as impure, and at Avignon they were forbidden to touch food in the market. Dress was regulated, as at Nîmes in 1353 where prostitutes' sleeves had to be of a distinctive material and colour.[109] It was only in the fourteenth century, however, that the authorities began to establish municipal brothels; one was set up by the consuls of Narbonne in 1335, one at Toulouse between 1363 and 1372, and one at Albi in 1393. Small towns also had their municipal brothel, as at Castres. This policy continued throughout the fifteenth century, when most towns in Languedoc had at least one brothel, and came to an end only in the sixteenth.[110]

Similar developments took place in Spain, Italy and Germany. The quarter of La Pobla in Valencia was walled off from the rest of the town in 1392, the wall being raised in 1444 so that it was difficult to climb. The quarter was regulated by both town and Crown, which set the prices of meals and rent of rooms. Before 1488, prostitutes were not forced to live in the quarter. At Florence, the Office of Onestà was set up in 1403 to watch over public morals and it proceeded to establish a public brothel and recruit and regulate prostitutes. Municipal brothels were founded in both large and small German towns in the fourteenth and fifteenth centuries, as at Frankfurt, Nuremberg, Augsburg, Ulm, Basel and Munich.[111] Such establishments were not set up in Paris or the Low Countries, nor by the major towns in England; the Southwark stews were patronised by Londoners but were on the land of the bishop of Winchester and outside the jurisdiction of the City. Apart from Southwark, England had licensed brothels only at Sandwich and Southampton.[112]

Historians have put forward a number of explanations as to why public brothels were established, and it is likely that demographic factors played a part. Many of the brothels were in southern Europe where early marriage was the norm for girls and late marriage the norm for men. A woman's honour required that she should be a virgin when she married and that she should have sexual relations only with her husband. Her honour was defended by her father, brothers and husband.[113] Unmarried men needed a sexual outlet, which was provided by the prostitutes or by homosexual activity. From the point of view of both the Church and state, prostitutes were preferable.

It is significant that Bernardino of Siena did not attack municipal brothels, either for the prostitutes themselves or those who frequented them; homosexuals, by contrast, were condemned. In his discussion of the Office of Onestà at Florence, Richard Trexler made a direct link with the demographic situation, seeing the Office as a means of fighting homosexuality and reversing the decline in the number of marriages and of births of legitimate children. The population of Florence had plummeted as a result of plague, from about 100,000 before the Black Death to about 26,000 in 1427. Whether the establishment of public brothels would encourage marriage is problematical, but clearly the town authorities were worried about the demographic situation and there were at this stage no moral objections to the brothels being set up. A double sexual standard operated in the later Middle Ages, and fornication by men was widely accepted. Rossiaud also emphasised the desire to encourage heterosexual relationships and coupled this with the dangers of violence by gangs of young men. Consorting with prostitutes helped to lessen young men's aggression and therefore defended the honour of 'honest' women.[114] Although contemporaries drew a clear distinction between 'honest' woman and harlot, the prostitute performed a social service in being available for sexual relations and could therefore be seen as part of the acceptable sexual order of society, whether she was protecting wives and daughters from male violence or deterring men from homosexual relationships.

Demographic considerations do not provide a complete explanation for the establishment of public brothels, which continued to be founded after the population of Europe had begun to rise again. The need to defend women's honour and to keep women under control, however, continued to hold true. It is likely that the overriding reason in the minds of the authorities was the desire to preserve public order, and in this context the situation in Castelnaudary is illuminating. In 1445, Charles VII allowed the opening of a public brothel.[115] According to the royal decree, the town wanted this because many young men and unmarried male servants lived in the town, and although there were prostitutes available, they did not have a house where they could live and work away from 'honest' people. Disturbances sometimes occurred. The king agreed to the building of such a house in the interests of law and order. The decree took it for granted that young unmarried men needed prostitutes, who should be separated from the 'respectable' people of the town. Living in their own house, the prostitutes could be more easily controlled than when they wandered all over the town. By setting up a public brothel, the needs of the inhabitants would be met and the town's reputation safeguarded. The authorities may also have seen the brothel as a profitable business enterprise. Many authorities would have agreed with those of Munich who in 1433 established a municipal brothel for the good of the city.[116]

All town governments wanted to maintain law and order, and the fear of disorder was very real in late medieval Europe. Brawls and violence were always liable to break out. Increased violence in La Pobla in Valencia helps to explain why all the prostitutes had to live there from 1488. It was usual practice for men to surrender their arms when they entered the brothel, as at Pamiers and in Venice. The restriction put on London prostitutes in 1393 was said to be due to the assaults and murders which had taken place when men met harlots, especially Flemings, at inns and places of ill-repute.[117] Admittedly, the authorities were biased against inns as well as against Flemish prostitutes, but it was only twelve years since parts of the City had been sacked during the Great Revolt.

Brothels varied considerably in size. The Château-Gaillard at Tarascon had a kitchen, common room and four bedrooms, together with a courtyard and garden, while the house at Dijon from 1447 had twenty bedrooms, each with a fireplace, and the house at Toulouse twenty-two bedrooms in addition to the common room and garden.[118] The rules laid down for individual houses provide an insight into the prostitute's life and into the control which was exercised over her. From the later fifteenth century, an increasing number of heads of brothels were men, with considerable powers over the running of the house. The rules of Castel Joyos at Pamiers of about 1500 laid down the payments made by the prostitute to the abbot, the name given to the manager of the brothel. If she ate at the abbot's table, she paid 4 *ardits* each for dinner and supper; if she did not, the abbot was ordered to sell her meat, bread and wine at the prices charged in the town. She paid the abbot 2 *ardits* a day for lodging. The abbot selected her customers, who made their payment to him for a night's stay.[119] The masters of German brothels provided two or three meals a day and were enjoined not to charge rent if the prostitute had no customers; the women paid the master a fixed sum for each customer. The master could not compel a woman to remain in the house, but could seize her property if she owed him money.[120] Fifteenth-century customs for the stews of Southwark appear to have tried to give the prostitute some independence of the stewholder. Her rent was fixed at 14 pence a week, and the stewholder was not to sell food, drink, candles or fuel, nor to lend the prostitute more that 6 shillings and 8 pence.[121] With the brothel on the Rialto in Venice, measures were taken to try to prevent the woman from running into debt at the inns and bath-houses; the owners were not to charge her more than 2 ducats a month for food, wine and rent, and were not to lend her money.[122] All the women were vulnerable if they ran into debt, especially if they were pregnant or were getting older or had few customers. Jeanne Saignant of Dijon kept her hold over her girls because they were indebted to her.[123]

Customs varied as to whether the prostitutes were free to leave the brothel. At Pamiers, they were expected to eat and sleep at the house. According to the regulations of the brothel opened on the Rialto at Venice in 1460, the prostitutes were allowed to leave the Rialto only on Saturday mornings, unless they had permission, and were to wear their distinctive clothes. German prostitutes were allowed to leave the brothel to go to church. The Southwark prostitute was allowed free access to her room and could not be forced to stay at the brothel against her will. It was usual across Europe for brothels to be closed on holy days, and often prostitutes had to leave during Holy Week (the week before Easter).[124]

As they grew older, a number of options were open to them. Some prostitutes married or went into domestic service. Some aspired to the position of abbess or female head of a brothel or manager of a bath-house, or entered the religious life in a house of repentant prostitutes. It is likely, however, that many ended their lives as vagabonds and beggars. Their situation became more restricted as the moral climate changed from the later fifteenth century. There was a widespread clampdown on prostitution which was increasingly denounced by churchmen. Towns in England tightened their regulations; Leicester expelled its prostitutes in 1467, and in 1482 York reissued its decree of 1301 forbidding prostitutes from staying in the city. Conditions for prostitutes likewise became more restricted.[125] These changes were to become more apparent during the sixteenth century.

Notes

1 P.J.P. Goldberg, *Women, Work and Life Cycle in a Medieval Economy: Women in York and Yorkshire c. 1300–1520* (Oxford, 1992), pp. 343, 372–3; M. Kowaleski, 'Singlewomen in medieval and early modern Europe: the demographic perspective', in J.M. Bennett and A.M. Froide (eds), *Singlewomen in the European Past 1250–1800* (Philadelphia, 1999), pp. 38–81; M.E. Wiesner, 'Having her own smoke. Employment and independence for singlewomen in Germany, 1400–1750', in ibid., pp. 192–3.

2 M. Kowaleski, 'Gendering demographic change in the Middle Ages', in J.M. Bennett and R.M. Karras (eds), *The Oxford Handbook of Women and Gender in Medieval Europe* (Oxford, 2013), pp. 181–96; I. Grainger, *The Black Death Cemetery, East Smithfield, London* (London, 2008), pp.1–3, 43–50.

3 P. McClure, 'Patterns of migration in the Middle Ages: the evidence of English place-name surnames', *Economic History Review*, second series 32 (1979), pp. 177–80; L. Wilkinson, *Women in Thirteenth-Century Lincolnshire* (Woodbridge, 2007), pp. 106–8.

4 Wiesner, 'Having her own smoke', pp. 199–200; D. Romano, *Housecraft and Statecraft. Domestic Service in Renaissance Venice, 1400–1600* (Baltimore, 1996), pp. 90–1, 165–6, 171, 179; *L'artisan dans la péninsule ibérique* (no editor; Nice, 1993), p. 104; D. Herlihy, *Opera Muliebria. Women and Work in Medieval Europe* (New York, 1990), p. 146.

5 C. Klapisch-Zuber, 'Women servants in Florence during the fourteenth and fifteenth centuries', in B.A. Hanawalt (ed.), *Women and Work in Preindustrial Europe* (Bloomington, Indiana, 1986), pp. 59–68.

6 E. Ewan, *Townlife in Fourteenth-Century Scotland* (Edinburgh, 1990), p. 32; G. Jacobsen, 'Women's work and women's role: ideology and reality in Danish urban society, 1300–1550', *Scandinavian Economic History Review* 31 (1983), pp. 17–18; R.W. Unger, 'Technical change in the brewing industry in Germany, the Low Countries and England in the late Middle Ages', *Journal of European Economic History* 21 (1992), pp. 281–9; M. Wiesner Wood, 'Paltry peddlers or essential merchants? Women in the distributive trades in early modern Nuremberg', *Sixteenth Century Journal* 12 (1981), p. 12; Uitz, *Women in the Medieval Town*, pp. 58–9; M.C. Howell, *Women, Production, and Patriarchy in Late Medieval Cities* (Chicago, 1986), pp. 135–6.

7 Uitz, *Women in the Medieval Town*, pp. 65–6; P. Dollinger (ed.), *Documents de l'histoire de l'Alsace* (Toulouse, 1972), pp. 135–8.

8 Herlihy, *Opera Muliebria*, pp. 145–6, 161, 176, 181; Wiesner Wood, 'Paltry peddlers', p. 12; Dillard, *Daughters of the Reconquest*, p. 163; D. Nicholas, *The Later Medieval City 1300–1500* (London, 1997), p. 265; H. Swanson, *Medieval Artisans. An Urban Class in Late Medieval England* (Oxford, 1989), pp. 19–23.

9 Jacobsen, 'Women's work and women's role', pp. 17–18.

10 R.H. Hilton, 'Women traders in medieval England', in R.H. Hilton, *Class Conflict and the Crisis of Feudalism* (London, 1985), p. 213.

11 S.B. Meech and H.E. Allen (eds), *The Book of Margery Kempe*, (*EETS* original series 212, 1940), pp. 9–11.

12 D. Nicholas, *The Domestic Life of a Medieval City: Women, Children and the Family in Fourteenth-Century Ghent* (Lincoln, Nebraska, 1985), p. 89; M.E. Wiesner, *Working Women in Renaissance Germany* (New Brunswick, New Jersey, 1986), pp. 116, 119; D. Hutton, 'Women in Fourteenth Century Shrewsbury', in L. Charles and L. Duffin (eds), *Women and Work in Pre-Industrial England* (London, 1985), p. 95.

13 M. Kowaleski, 'Women's work in a market town: Exeter in the late fourteenth century', in Hanawalt (ed.), *Women and Work in Preindustrial Europe*, pp. 147–51; R.H. Hilton, 'Lords, burgesses and hucksters', *PandP* 97 (1982), pp. 3–15, and reprinted in Hilton, *Class Conflict*, pp. 194–204; Hilton, 'Women traders', pp. 207–13.

14 Herlihy, *Opera Muliebria*, pp. 144–6; R. de Lespinasse and F. Bonnardot (eds), *Les métiers et corporations de la ville de Paris. treizième siècle. Le livre des métiers d'Etienne Boileau* (Paris, 1879), p. 148.

15 E. Ennen, *The Medieval Woman*, (trans.) E. Jephcott (Oxford, 1989), pp. 171, 202, 206; Wiesner Wood, 'Paltry peddlers', pp. 10–12; Uitz, *Women in the Medieval Town*, p. 46; G. Jacobsen, 'Women's work and women's role', pp. 7–11.

16 D. Romano, *Patricians and Popolani. The Social Foundations of the Venetian Renaissance State* (Baltimore, 1987), p. 61; Herlihy, *Opera Muliebria*, pp. 96, 154–9, 161.

17 Herlihy, *Opera Muliebria*, pp. 169–70; *L'artisan dans la péninsule ibérique*, pp. 104, 109–10.

18 Wiesner, *Working Women in Renaissance Germany*, p. 111; Ewan, *Townlife in Fourteenth-Century Scotland*, p. 81.

19 Uitz, *Women in the Medieval Town*, pp. 39–41; Wiesner, *Working Women in Renaissance Germany*, p. 111.

20 Uitz, *Women in the Medieval Town*, pp. 24, 37–8; M. Angelos, 'Women in Genoese *commenda* contracts, 1155–1216', *JMH* 20 (1994), pp. 299–312; S.A. Epstein, *Genoa and the Genoese, 958–1528* (Chapel Hill, North Carolina, 1996), pp. 101–2.

21 Goldberg, *Women, Work and Life Cycle*, p. 125; H. Swanson, *Building Craftsmen in Late Medieval York* (Borthwick Papers 63, York, 1983), p. 29; M. Sellers (ed.), *The York Mercers and Merchant Adventurers, 1356–1917* (Surtees Society 129, 1918), pp. 64, 67; W.R. Childs (ed.), *The Customs Accounts of Hull, 1453–90* (Yorkshire Archaeological Society Record Series 144, 1984), pp. 128, 142, 148, 154, 158–61, 167, 170–3.

22 M. Wensky, 'Women's guilds in Cologne in the later Middle Ages', *Journal of European Economic History* 11 (1982), p. 643; Howell, *Women, Production, and Patriarchy*, pp. 139–52.

23 Nicholas, *Domestic Life of a Medieval City*, pp. 81–2, 91–4; J.M. Murray, 'Family, marriage and moneychanging in medieval Bruges', *JMH* 14 (1988), pp. 115–25; J.M. Murray, *Bruges, Cradle of Capitalism, 1280–1390* (Cambridge, 2005), pp. 310–17.

24 Howell, *Women, Production, and Patriarchy*, pp. 70–4, 82, 164–7; K.L. Reyerson, 'Women in business in medieval Montpellier', in Hanawalt (ed.), *Women and Work in Preindustrial Europe*, pp. 122–33.

25 M.C. Howell, *The Marriage Exchange. Property, Social Place and Gender in the Cities of the Low Countries, 1300–1550* (Chicago, 1998), pp. 3–26.

26 Lespinasse and Bonnardot (eds), *Métiers et corporations*, pp. 107–11, 117–18, 127–9, 132–4, 140–4.

27 Ibid., pp. 102–6.

28 F.C. Lane, *Venice. A Maritime Republic* (Baltimore, 1973), p. 333.

29 The range of women's craft and trading activities is brought out in Swanson, *Medieval Artisans*, Wiesner, *Working Women in Renaissance Germany*, and Uitz, *Women in the Medieval Town*.

30 Dillard, *Daughters of the Reconquest*, pp. 158–9; *L'artisan dans la péninsule ibérique*, pp. 109–10, 114.

31 Herlihy, *Opera Muliebria*, pp. 158–60; only non-agricultural occupations were counted and of these, only the occupations which occurred at least twice in the survey.

32 Ibid., pp. 96, 157, 160–1.

33 J.C. Brown and J. Goodman, 'Women and industry in Florence', *Journal of Economic History* 40 (1980), p. 78.

34 Lespinasse and Bonnardot (eds), *Métiers et corporations*, pp. 107, 187; G-B. Depping (ed.), *Réglemens sur les arts et métiers de Paris, redigés au treizième siècle et connus sous le nom du livre des métiers d'Etienne Boileau* (Paris, 1837), p. 388.

35 Jacobsen, 'Women's work and women's role', pp. 6–16.

36 Ennen, *Medieval Woman*, pp. 201–2; Wiesner, *Working Women in Renaissance Germany*, pp. 113, 116, 133, 151; Swanson, *Medieval Artisans*, pp. 35, 42, 72, 74, 82, 100, 115–16; J.W. Percy (ed.), *York Memorandum Book BY* (Surtees Society 186, 1973), pp. 216–18; K.E. Lacey, 'Women and work in fourteenth and fifteenth century London', in Charles and Duffin (eds), *Women and Work in Pre-Industrial England*, p. 45; C.M. Barron and A.F. Sutton (eds), *Medieval London Widows 1300–1500* (London, 1994), pp. xxviii–ix.

37 E. Veale, 'Matilda Penne, skinner (d. 1392–3)', in Barron and Sutton (eds), *Medieval London Widows*, pp. 47–9.

38 J. Guiral-Hadziiossif, *Valence, port méditerranéen au quinzième siècle* (Paris, 1986), p. 465; C. Carrère, *Barcelone, centre économique à l'epoque des difficultés, 1380–1462*, 2 vols (Paris, 1967), I, p. 476.

39 Romano, *Patricians and Popolani*, pp. 56–7, 61; S.A. Epstein, *Wage Labor and Guilds in Medieval Europe* (Chapel Hill, North Carolina, 1991), pp. 94–5.

40 Jacobsen, 'Women's work and women's role', p. 4.

41 Hamilton, *Money, Prices and Wages*, p. 65; C. Billot, *Chartres à la fin du moyen âge* (Paris, 1987), p. 231.

42 Guiral-Hadziiossif, *Valence*, pp. 383–4; C. Carrère, *Barcelone, centre économique à l'époque des difficultés, 1380–1462* (Paris, 1967), pp. 198–9.

43 Epstein, *Genoa and the Genoese*, p. 100; Epstein, *Wage Labor and the Guilds*, p. 148.

44 *Cambridge Economic History of Europe*, 8 vols (Cambridge, 1941–89), II, M. Postan and E.E. Rich (eds), *Trade and Industry in the Middle Ages*, pp. 379, 381–2.

45 Carrère, *Barcelone*, p. 372; Guiral-Hadziiossif, *Valence*, pp. 383–4; H. Bresc, *Un monde méditerranéen. Economie et société en Sicile 1300–1450*, 2 vols (Rome, 1986), I, p. 210; Romano, *Patricians and Popolani*, p. 61; Wiesner, *Working Women in Renaissance Germany*, p. 172.

46 Nicholas, *Domestic Life of a Medieval City*, p. 101.

47 M.K. Dale, 'The London silkwomen of the fifteenth century', *Economic History Review* first series 4 (1932–4), pp. 324–35; K. Lacey, 'The production of "narrow ware" by silkwomen in fourteenth and fifteenth-century England', *Textile History* 18 (1987), pp. 187–204; A.F. Sutton, 'Alice Claver, silkwoman (d. 1489)', in Barron and Sutton (eds), *Medieval London Widows*, pp. 129–42.

48 Lespinasse and Bonnardot (eds), *Métiers et corporations*, pp. 68–72, 74–5, 83–4, 207–8; Depping (ed.), *Réglemens*, pp. 364–5, 379–86.

49 M. Kowaleski and J.M. Bennett, 'Crafts, gilds and women in the Middle Ages: 50 years after Marian K. Dale', *Signs* 14 (1988–9), p. 481.

50 Lespinasse and Bonnardot (eds), *Métiers et Corporations*, pp. 68–72. The ordinances of the silk spinners using small spindles are given in translation in E. Dixon, 'Craftswomen in the *Livre des Métiers*', *Economic Journal* 5 (1895), pp. 218–20.
51 Lespinasse and Bonnardot (eds), *Métiers et corporations*, pp. 74–5.
52 Ibid., pp. 207–8.
53 Ibid., pp. 83–4.
54 Depping (ed.), *Réglemens*, pp. 377–8.
55 Ibid., p. 386; Lespinasse and Bonnardot (eds), *Métiers et corporations*, pp. 68–72, 74–5, 84.
56 Depping (ed.), *Réglemens*, pp. 379–86; Herlihy, *Opera Muliebria*, p. 146; Kowaleski and Bennett, 'Crafts, gilds and women', pp. 481–3.
57 M. Wensky, *Die Stellung der Frau in der stadtkölnischen Wirtschaft in Spätmittelalter* (Cologne, 1980), pp. 61–186; Wensky, 'Women's guilds in Cologne', pp. 631–50; Howell, *Women, Production, and Patriarchy*, pp. 124–32.
58 Jacobsen, 'Women's work and women's role', p. 14.
59 For example, F.B. Bickley (ed.), *The Little Red Book of Bristol*, 2 vols (Bristol, 1900), II, pp. 127–8; an ordinance of 1461 laid down that female weaving was to be restricted to the weaver's wife.
60 C.M. Barron, 'The "Golden Age" of women in medieval London', in *Medieval Women in Southern England* (*Reading Medieval Studies* 15, 1989), pp. 35–58; J. Hatcher, 'The great slump of the mid-fifteenth century', in R. Britnell and J. Hatcher (eds), *Progress and Problems in Medieval England. Essays in honour of Edward Miller* (Cambridge, 1996), pp. 237–72; Klapisch-Zuber, 'Women servants', p. 66; P.J.P. Goldberg, 'Female labour, service and marriage in northern towns during the later Middle Ages', *Northern History* 22 (1986), pp. 35–6.
61 Nicholas, *Domestic Life of a Medieval City*, p. 95; Uitz, *Women in the Medieval Town*, p. 45.
62 M.C. Howell, 'Women, the family economy, and the structures of market production in cities of northern Europe during the late Middle Ages', in Hanawalt (ed.), *Women and Work in Preindustrial Europe*, pp. 198–222; Howell, *Women, Production, and Patriarchy*, pp. 9–46.
63 Wiesner, *Working Women in Renaissance Germany*, pp. 174–5.
64 Ibid., p. 176; Howell, *Women, Production, and Patriarchy*, pp. 70–4, 88–9, 91, 115, 134–7, 242 n. 41. The six 'mixed' guilds at Cologne comprised the bakers, brewers, linen weavers, silk embroiderers, needle makers and belt makers.
65 Howell, *Women, Production, and Patriarchy*, p. 91.
66 M.H. Green, *Women's Healthcare in the Medieval West* (Aldershot, 2000), pp. 1–76.
67 Christine de Pizan, *The Book of the City of Ladies*, (ed.) R. Brown-Grant (Harmondsworth, 1999), pp. 140–1. There is another story of a woman lecturing at Bologna in 1236; D. Herlihy, *Opera Muliebria. Women and Work in Medieval Europe* (New York, 1990), p. 116. M.H. Shank, 'A female university student in late medieval Krakow', *Signs* 12 (1987), pp. 373–80.
68 K. Park, *Doctors and Medicine in Early Renaisssance Florence* (Princeton, 1985), p. 8.
69 E. Wickersheimer, *Dictionnaire biographique des médecins en France au moyen âge*, 2 vols (Geneva, 1979), II, pp. 730, 732, 747.
70 M.H. Green (ed. and trans.), *The Trotula. A Medieval Compendium of Women's Medicine* (Philadelphia, 2001), p. 49; J.F. Benton, 'Trotula, women's problems, and the professionalisation of medicine in the Middle Ages', *Bulletin of the History of Medicine* 59 (1985), pp. 30–53.
71 Benton, 'Trotula', p. 50; M.H. Green, 'Women's medical practice and health care in medieval Europe', *Signs* 14 (1988–9), p. 442.

72 Park, *Doctors and Medicine*, pp. 71–2; J. Henderson, 'The hospitals of late medieval and Renaissance Florence: a preliminary survey', in L. Granshaw and R. Porter (eds), *The Hospital in History* (London, 1989), p. 82.

73 D. Jacquart, *Le milieu médical en France du douzième au quinzième siècle* (Geneva, 1981), pp. 47–8; Herlihy, *Opera Muliebria*, pp. 146–7.

74 Green, 'Women's medical practice', p. 440; C.H. Talbot and E.A. Hammond, *The Medical Practitioners in Medieval England* (London, 1965), pp. 10, 28, 100, 200, 209, 211.

75 Green, 'Women's medical practice', p. 444; L. Reutter de Rosemont, *Histoire de la pharmacie à travers les âges*, 2 vols (Paris, 1931), I, pp. 305–6.

76 M.R. McVaugh, *Medicine before the Plague. Practitioners and their Patients in the Crown of Aragon, 1285–1345* (Cambridge, 1993), pp. 51, 76–7, 104–7, 145.

77 Wickersheimer, *Dictionnaire biographique*, II, p. 538.

78 H. Denifle and A. Chatelain (eds), *Chartularium Universitatis Parisiensis*, 4 vols (Paris, 1889–97), I, pp. 488–90; P. Kibre, 'The faculty of medicine at Paris, charlatanism, and unlicensed medical practices in the later Middle Ages', in C.R. Burns (ed.), *Legacies in Law and Medicine* (New York, 1977), pp. 57–8.

79 Denifle and Chatelain (eds), *Chartularium Universitatis Parisiensis*, II, p. 267; Wickersheimer, *Dictionnaire biographique*, I, p. 100; II, p. 537.

80 Denifle and Chatelain (eds), *Chartularium Universitatis Parisiensis*, II, pp. 255–67; Wickersheimer, *Dictionnaire biographique*, I, p. 317; Kibre, 'The faculty of medicine at Paris', pp. 59–63; Jacquart, *Milieu médical*, p. 53. Parts of the case are translated in E. Amt (ed.), *Women's Lives in Medieval Europe. A Sourcebook* (New York and London, 1993), pp. 108–12.

81 Denifle and Chatelain (eds), *Chartularium Universitatis Parisiensis*, IV, pp. 198–9; Kibre, 'The faculty of medicine at Paris', pp. 63–9; Wickersheimer, *Dictionnaire biographique*, I, pp. 291, 397; II, pp. 506, 596; M.H. Green, *Making Women's Medicine Masculine. The Rise of Male Authority in Pre-modern Gynaecology* (Oxford, 2008), pp. 1–2.; Jacquart, *Milieu médical*, pp. 51–2.

82 Jacquart, *Milieu médical*, p. 50; D. Jacquart, *Supplément*, to Wickersheimer, *Dictionnaire biographique* (Geneva, 1979), p. 222.

83 Jacquart, *Supplément*, pp. 33, 54, 112, 195; E. Uitz, *Women in the Medieval Town* (trans. S. Marnie), (London, 1990), p. 68.

84 Jacquart, *Supplément*, pp. 12, 54, 81; Jacquart, *Milieu médical*, pp. 48–9; M.H. Green, 'Women's medical practice', p. 449; M.E. Wiesner, 'Early modern midwifery: a case study', in B. Hanawalt (ed.), *Women and Work in Preindustrial Europe* (Bloomington, Indiana, 1986), pp. 96–9.

85 Herlihy, *Opera Muliebria*, p. 147.

86 C. Klapisch-Zuber, 'Women servants in Florence in the fourteenth and fifteenth centuries', in Hanawalt (ed.), *Women and Work in Preindustrial Europe*, p. 65. See earlier, p. 61.

87 D. Romano, *Housecraft and Statecraft. Domestic Service in Renaissnce Venice, 1400–1600* (Baltimore, 1996), p. 87.

88 G. Navarro, 'L'artisanat de la soie à Valence à la fin du moyen âge' in *L'artisanat dans la péninsule ibérique*, p. 170; British Library, London, Egerton Roll 8776, m. 5.

89 L.L. Otis, 'Municipal wet-nurses in fifteenth-century Montpellier', in Hanawalt (ed.), *Women and Work in Preindustrial Europe*, pp. 83–93. See earlier, p. 25.

90 M. Carlin, 'Medieval English hospitals', in Granshaw and Porter (eds), *The Hospital in History*, pp. 32, 35; C. Rawcliffe, *Medicine and Society in Later Medieval England* (Stroud, 1995), p. 208; C. Rawcliffe, 'Hospital nurses and their work', in R. Britnell (ed.), *Daily Life in the Late Middle Ages* (Stroud, 1998), pp. 43–64; W. Page (ed.), *The Victoria History of London* (London, 1909), pp. 531–3.

91 E. Coyecque, *L'Hôtel-Dieu de Paris au moyen âge*, 2 vols (Paris, 1889–91), pp. 25–7, 31–7, 46–53, 79.
92 M.E. Wiesner, *Working Women in Renaissance Germany* (New Brunswick, New Jersey, 1986), pp. 38–42.
93 N. Orme, *From Childhood to Chivalry* (London, 1984), pp. 12–13, 17, 26–7.
94 M.B. Williamson (ed. and trans.), *The Memoirs of Helene Kottanner* (Woodbridge, 1998), pp. 1–6, 27–35, 40–5, 49–50, 52; E. Fugedi, *Kings, Bishops, Nobles and Burghers in Medieval Hungary* (ed. J. Bak), (London, 1986), Article I, pp. 175–80, 183, 186.
95 Williamson (ed. and trans.), *Memoirs of Helene Kottanner*, p. 6.
96 M. Kowaleski, 'Women's work in a market town: Exeter in the late fourteenth century', in Hanawalt (ed.), *Women and Work in Preindustrial Europe*, pp. 148, 154, 162; P.J.P. Goldberg, *Women, Work and Life Cycle in a Medieval Economy: Women in York and Yorkshire c. 1300–1520*, pp. 151–2, 155; M. Carlin, *Medieval Southwark* (London, 1996), p. 222.
97 Carlin, *Medieval Southwark*, p. 222; Goldberg, *Women, Work and Life Cycle*, p. 154; R.M. Karras, *Common Women. Prostitution and Sexuality in Medieval England* (Oxford, 1996), p. 48; H.T. Riley (ed.), *Memorials of London and London Life* (London, 1868), pp. 484–6.
98 L.L. Otis, *Prostitution in Medieval Society. The History of an Urban Institution in Languedoc* (Chicago, 1985), pp. 19–23; B. Geremek, *The Margins of Society in Late Medieval Paris*, (trans. J. Birrell) (Cambridge, 1987), pp. 211–14; J. Rossiaud, *Medieval Prostitution* (trans. L.G. Cochrane) (Oxford, 1988), pp. 72–85.
99 Geremek, *Margins of Society*, pp. 221, 225–8; M.E. Wiesner, 'Having her own smoke. Employment and independence for singlewomen in Germany, 1400–1750', in Bennett and Froide (eds), *Singlewomen*, p. 205.
100 Rossiaud, *Medieval Prostitution*, pp. 32–4, 179–81.
101 R.C. Trexler, 'La prostitution Florentine au quinzième siècle', *Annales ESC* 36 (1981), pp. 985–7, 1002.
102 Goldberg, *Women, Work and Life Cycle*, pp. 151–4; P.J.P. Goldberg, 'Pigs and prostitutes: streetwalking in comparative perspective', in K.J. Lewis, N.J. Menuge and K.M. Phillips (eds), *Young Medieval Women* (Stroud, 1999), pp. 175–6; Rossiaud, *Medieval Prostitution*, pp. 38–41; Herlihy, *Opera Muliebria*, pp. 157–8; J. Guiral-Hadziiossif, *Valence*, pp. 96–7; Trexler, 'La prostitution florentine', pp. 993–4.
103 Rossiaud, *Medieval Prostitution*, pp. 5–6.
104 Licensing is suggested at Exeter by the number of prostitutes and brothel-keepers appearing in the court rolls in the period 1373–93; Kowaleski, 'Women's work in a market town', p. 148. D. Nicholas, *Medieval Flanders* (London, 1992), p. 297.
105 Riley (ed.), *Memorials of London and London Life*, pp. 458–9; G. Brucker (ed.), *The Society of Renaisssance Florence. A Documentary Study* (New York, 1971), pp. 191–2.
106 Riley (ed.), *Memorials of London and London Life*, pp. 534–5; Geremek, *Margins of Society*, pp. 218–21.
107 Rossiaud, *Medieval Prostitution*, pp. 31, 35, 41, 45, 187, 191–3.
108 Ibid., pp. 60–1; Otis, *Prostitution in Medieval Society*, pp. 94–9.
109 Otis, *Prostitution in Medieval Society*, pp. 17–22, 77–81.
110 Ibid., pp. 29–35, 40–5.
111 Guiral-Hadziiossif, *Valence*, pp. 96–7; Trexler, 'La prostitution florentine', pp. 983–4, 996–1000, 1003–6; Wiesner, 'Having her own smoke', p. 205; Wiesner, *Working Women in Renaissance Germany*, p. 97; P. Schuster, *Das Frauenhaus. Stadtische Bordelle in Deutschland, 1350–1600* (Paderborn, 1992), pp. 77–85.

112 Karras, *Common Women*, pp. 35–43.
113 Goldberg, 'Pigs and prostitutes', pp. 180–3.
114 Rossiaud, *Medieval Prostitution*, pp. 11–14, 86–92, 96; Trexler, 'La prostitution florentine', pp. 983–4.
115 Otis, *Prostitution in Medieval Society*, p. 116; Rossiaud, *Medieval Prostitution*, pp. 193–5.
116 Schuster, *Das Frauenhaus*, pp. 40–1; the foundation was made for the *utilitas* of the city.
117 Otis, *Prostitution in Medieval Society*. pp. 83, 127–9; D. Chambers and B. Pullan (eds), *Venice. A Documentary History, 1450–1630* (Oxford, 1992), p. 121; Riley (ed.), *Memorials of London and London Life*, pp. 534–5.
118 Rossiaud, *Medieval Prostitution*, p. 5; Otis, *Prostitution in Medieval Society*, p. 53.
119 Otis, *Prostitution in Medieval Society*, pp. 54, 60, 82–5, 127–9; Rossiaud, *Medieval Prostitution*, pp. 199–200.
120 Wiesner, *Working Women in Renaissance Germany*, pp. 97–9.
121 Carlin, *Medieval Southwark*, pp. 213–17; R.M. Karras, 'The regulation of brothels in later medieval England', *Signs*, 14 (1988–9), pp. 411–21, 427–33; J.B. Post, 'A fifteenth-century customary of the Southwark stews', *Journal of the Society of Archivists*, 5 (1974–7), pp. 418–28.
122 Chambers and Pullan (eds), *Venice*, p. 122.
123 Rossiaud, *Medieval Prostitution*, p. 31.
124 This was the case at Perpignan: L.L. Otis, 'Prostitution and repentance in medieval Perpignan', in J. Kirshner and S.F. Wemple (eds), *Women of the Medieval World. Essays in honor of J.F. Mundy* (Oxford, 1985), p. 148.
125 Rossiaud, *Medieval Prostitution*, 19, 36–7; M. Bateson (ed.), *Records of the Borough of Leicester, 1103–1603*, 3 vols (Cambridge, 1899–1905), II, p. 291; L.C. Attreed (ed.), *The York House Books, 1461–90*, 2 vols (Stroud, 1991), I, p. 261; Wiesner, *Working Women in Renaissance Germany*, pp. 102–3.

7 Ethnic minorities
Jews, Muslims and slaves

For Christian women in later medieval Europe, gender and agency were set in the context of the law and teaching of the Church. This determined their subordination to men in a patriarchal society and their roles as daughter, wife, mother, widow and nun. The lives of the women who belonged to the ethnic minorities have to be seen in a different religious framework, such as Jewish or Muslim, although the concept of patriarchy applied to them all. The Jewish presence in Spain, southern France and Italy, like the Christian, can be traced back to Roman times. From there they moved north and were established in the Rhineland towns from the ninth century; they moved into the towns of northern France in the eleventh and twelfth centuries, and from there into England in the twelfth century. From the Rhineland they moved further into Germany as colonisation proceeded in the twelfth and thirteenth centuries. They were very much an urban phenomenon and are only rarely found in rural areas.

The Muslims of north Africa invaded Spain in the eighth century. Small Christian communities remained in the north, and it was from there that the Christian Reconquest moved south in the twelfth and thirteenth centuries and culminated in the capture of Granada in 1492. Large numbers of Muslims remained, mostly in the countryside in the later Middle Ages, especially in Valencia and Murcia, under the rule of the kings of Aragon and Castile.

Jews

Within the towns, Jews were regarded as a separate community. They were allowed their rights according to Jewish law, enforced by their own courts, provided that they met demands for taxes and dues from the local ruler. They were allowed to practise their religious faith which governed their way of life and morality, and had their own synagogues. According to the Fourth Lateran Council of 1215, their contact with Christians was limited to economic dealings; no Jews were to employ Christians and they were to build no new synagogues. For a long while, these recommendations were not observed in Spain, which had a prosperous and much larger Jewish population than in the north.[1]

The family was regarded as the key unit in Jewish society. All Jews were expected to marry. Marriage was regulated by Jewish law and the pro-creation of children was expected to take place within marriage. As in Christian society, marriages were usually arranged by parents; a dowry was paid by the bride's family and a gift was made to the bride by her husband; the latter was regarded as a protection for the wife in the event of divorce or widowhood. As a widow, she also kept her dowry and any inheritance. Boys and girls were married at the age of about eleven or twelve and the wed-ding was preceded by betrothal.[2] According to an Anglo-Jewish betrothal contract of 1271, Aaron, son of Rabbi Benjamin, was betrothed to Judith, daughter of Rabbi Hayim. Aaron was promised a dowry of 20 marks sterling and a religious book; the dowry was handed over and the money was to be lent at interest until Aaron was grown up. The wedding was planned for four years later, and Rabbi Benjamin was then to hand over to Aaron and Judith the 20 marks plus the interest, and provide them with suitable clothing; he also paid for the wedding feast out of the dowry's inter-est. Size of dowries varied according to the wealth of the family. In the small rural community of Santa Coloma de Queralt near Tarragona, Astrugona, wife of Boniuda Astruch, received a dowry of 6,000 *solidi* of Barcelona; she belonged to one of the wealthiest Jewish families and became a prominent businesswoman.[3]

As with Christian arranged marriages, affection is found between husband and wife. Husbands were punished for beating their wives and domestic violence constituted grounds for divorce. The husband was regarded as the owner of his wife's sexuality, but both husband and wife expected sexual satisfaction in marriage. Strict laws existed over sexual intercourse; it was not to take place during the wife's period and for seven days afterwards, and was resumed after she had taken the ritual bath on the eighth day. The wife's life was expected to centre on domestic activities and mother-hood, and many women also earned money for the household. Thus, early in the thirteenth century, Dolce, wife of Rabbi Eleazer ben Judah of Worms, was described by her husband as pious and good, caring for her husband, at least three daughters and her husband's students, and managing a large household; she was also a successful moneylender.[4]

With the birth of children, the mother was responsible for their care while they were infants, but the education of boys and girls diverged when they reached the age of about six. Boys then began their study of the Torah and learned Hebrew. This was not considered suitable for girls who were taught housekeeping, including the religious laws over food preparation and domestic rituals, and needlework. They would be expected to earn money when they married, so they received training in crafts or professions, and learned to read, write and do mathematics. Although women and girls attended the synagogue, they did not play a prominent role either there or in the government of the community. A few learned Hebrew, and women were sometimes in charge of women's prayers, as in thirteenth-century

Worms. In France, Germany and England, they were allowed to say grace at mealtimes and sat with their husbands and sons in the synagogue; this did not happen in Mediterranean Europe.[5]

Divorce was available to Jewish women. The husband was allowed to divorce his wife outright, whereas the wife could ask for a divorce on the grounds of domestic violence, infertility, desertion or serious incompatibility. In southern Europe, Jews were allowed to take two wives who had to be treated equally.[6]

Although family responsibilities were their primary duty, Jewish wives and widows earned money outside the household. As widows acted as the guardians of their children, earnings could be important to them. Jewish women, like Christian, were not confined to the house and were allowed to move freely about the town, although in Spain, probably because of Islamic influence, there was a tendency for them to remain at home. Many Jewish wives had the advantage of a certain amount of capital from the goods they brought to the marriage; widows had their dowry and the money assigned to them by their husbands at marriage. Having capital enabled them to exercise a considerable degree of agency. They undertook a wide variety of jobs, sometimes working alongside their husbands. Poor women often had to take low-grade jobs as petty traders, servants, nurses and wet-nurses.[7]

Better known are the women who worked as physicians and money-lenders. Jewish women worked in medicine in southern France, Germany, Italy and Spain. Many of the women working in Frankfurt were Jewish, as was Antonia di Maestro Daniele who entered the guild at Florence. Kings of Aragon protected Jewish women practitioners in their kingdoms. In southern France, Sarah de Saint-Gilles, a married Jew in Marseilles, taught medicine to an apprentice in 1326.[8]

Jewish women worked as merchants and moneylenders, either with their husbands or independently. Usury was forbidden by the Church and Jews were performing a financial service to their Christian neighbours. Yet their position was always precarious, partly because of outbreaks of anti-Semitism, and partly because their protection by the ruler made them vulnerable to royal demands for money. This is apparent in England where Henry III's demands for money in the 1240s and 1250s led to virtual ruin for the Jews. Licoricia of Winchester is first recorded as a widow and moneylender in 1234 and she built up her business in the 1240s to become the richest Jewish woman in England. She had a close relationship with Henry III and his court. The outbreak of the Barons' Wars in 1258 had a serious effect on her business, which retracted in the 1260s and 1270s; she was murdered in 1277.

The position of the Jews worsened in the later thirteenth century; Edward I's statute of 1275 forbade the charging of interest and compelled Jews to live in towns and wear a badge on their clothes. They continued to lend money and women played a prominent part. The royal scrutiny of 1276 found that at Exeter thirty-five out of 135 bonds had debts owed to two

Jewesses, Auntera and Tertia widow of Lumbard. The role of women money-lenders became more important in the 1280s, possibly because the Jews were expecting expulsion from the realm, which occurred in 1290; men departed in order to set up business elsewhere, expecting their wives and children to join them later. Clients came from all ranks of society, including knights, churchmen, craftsmen and men from the countryside.[9]

Jewish moneylending was also important on the continent. In Germany, women were responsible for one-third of the loans in forty-one towns between 1350 and 1400, with much of their business among poor borrowers. In certain places they also had a political role as tax collectors, and a few women, as at Regensburg, became citizens of their towns. In Picardy (in Northern France), major loans were made by Jewish men, but their wives specialised in making small loans, often to Christian women who probably needed the money for domestic purposes. In the south, at Perpignan, Jewish moneylending played an important part in the commercial growth of the town in the thirteenth century. Perpignan was situated at the crossroads between Spain and Southern France, and in the second half of the century it had a growing woollen industry and was hosting international fairs. Women's moneylending was less important than men's but widows particularly proved to be able businesswomen.[10]

In Spain some Jewish women were major entrepreneurs. Astrugona, wife of Boniuda Astruch of Santa Coloma de Queralt, worked independently in the 1290s and was engaged in the grain trade as well as in moneylending. She made her own partnership agreements, the most important of which was with a Jew of Montblanch, Iafuda Avenasagra. Astrugona and Iafuda made at least thirty-two joint loans. Her husband had his own business and there is no record of husband and wife working together.[11]

All Jews faced a precarious situation because of outbreaks of anti-Semitism, and violence and riots were triggered by local causes and by rulers' actions. The situation worsened in the late thirteenth and fourteenth centuries and particularly after the Black Death. Spain was relatively peaceful until the pogroms of 1391 after which Jews were expected to convert to Christianity or leave Spain; those who converted were known as *conversos*. There remained the problem that they were not regarded as genuine Christians; Jewish blood was regarded as impure and was not purified by baptism. Jewish expulsion came in 1492.[12] In France, prohibitions of usury and expulsions are found under Louis IX, with the final expulsion coming early in the fourteenth century. In Germany, Jews were expelled from many towns after the Black Death and moved into eastern Europe.

Muslims

Whereas Jews were found in many European towns in the thirteenth century, Muslims lived in Spain and Portugal, mostly in the countryside after the thirteenth-century Reconquest. From then until its capture in 1492, the only

Muslim kingdom was Granada. All Muslims, like the Jews, were under the ruler's protection. They were allowed to practise their religion and retained their customs, but their lives were increasingly restricted towards the end of the Middle Ages and persecution increased especially after the fall of Granada.

As elsewhere in Europe, Muslim women were primarily concerned with their households and children, but they were expected to live in seclusion and lacked the freedom of movement of Jewish and Christian women. Their marriages were arranged by male relatives and the code of honour dictated that they should be virgins when they married; Muslims were allowed to marry more than one wife. If the husband died, custody of the children was given to male kinsmen and the widow was expected to remarry. Changes as a result of the Reconquest would have been least noticed in Valencia, ruled by the king of Aragon, where it is estimated that in 1276 Muslims out-numbered Christian settlers by three to one; some communities continued to speak Arabic and had their own governors. At the same time there was an element of insecurity since Christian rulers feared attacks from Granada and local revolt.[13]

Women worked alongside their husbands or performed paid work, and this had to be fitted in with their household and child-care respon-sibilities. Occasionally, there is reference to a female Muslim medical prac-titioner; Alfonso IV of Aragon (1327–1336) was once treated before his accession by a woman Muslim surgeon. Muslim women, like Jews and Christians, worked as artisans in the smaller towns of Castile, such as Avila, but Muslims did not work in the larger centres. In Valencia, Moorish women took the silk off cocoons, and engaged in weaving and dyeing. They also worked on building sites although their wages were less than those earned by Christian women. Muslim women captured in war were enslaved.[14]

In many towns in Europe, Jews and Christians lived alongside each other; in Spanish towns, this applied to Muslims as well. Women had contacts as neighbours or on business and would meet as they went about daily tasks. Religious worship and prayer were confined to each ethnic group and sexual relations were discouraged or punished although they undoubtedly occurred; in Italian towns such as Padua, Venice and Milan, growing intolerance of the Jews and fears of pollution led to penalties for sexual relations between Jews and Christians becoming increasingly severe in the fifteenth century, but the enforcement of the law was uneven. Intermarriage was rare although some mixed marriages took place. Concubinage and prostitution was widespread in Muslim and Christian Spain, and Jewish prostitutes are also found.[15] Women were interdependent when it came to health and child-care, so Jewish families employed Christian servants and wet-nurses. Muslim women, many of them slaves, also worked as wet-nurses in Jewish and Christian families. A Jewish midwife in Marseilles attended Christian women in childbirth in the early fifteenth century. As has been seen,

Christian women went to Jewish moneylenders to obtain a loan. Jewish and Christian women shared their knowledge of cosmetics as well as health care.[16]

Slaves

The slave trade developed in the Eastern Mediterranean in the thirteenth century. Most slaves came from ethnic minorities as is seen in a notarial record of 1301 from Crete.[17] According to this, many slaves were purchased from the Turks and then sold to owners in Crete. Ethnic origins included the Tartars, Bulgars, Cumans and Turks. Manumission was possible but probably fairly rare. Slaves worked mainly in Mediterranean Europe, the men doing heavy work, and the women working in the household, often as wet-nurses, and vulnerable to being forced into sexual relations with the master. Female slaves were more numerous than male; in fifteenth-century Genoa, 1,610 women appear in notarial acts concerning slaves, as against 255 men.

They appeared in the Italian cities in increasing numbers after the Black Death. West African slaves were to be found in Portugal and Spain by the late fifteenth century; a negress from Guinea with her two-year-old daughter was sold to a lady of Barcelona in 1489.

Demand was high for girls and young women; in Sicily the highest prices of 60 or 62 florins were paid in the late fourteenth century for women in their mid-twenties. The control of foreign slaves, speaking their own language, posed problems for the housewife. Margherita Datini regarded them as untrustworthy, and they were generally viewed as quarrelsome, dangerous and promiscuous.[18]

Gender parallels exist between Christian, Jewish and Muslim women in the Middle Ages. All lived in a patriarchal society; women were regarded as subordinate to men and their responsibilities centred on marriage, household and children. All had only a limited degree of agency depending on their ethnicity, religion and marital and social status. The departure of most Muslims of wealth and standing to Granada or North Africa after the thirteenth-century Reconquest resulted in limited working opportunities for the remainder in low-grade occupations. Jewish women were able to enter certain professions and also urban crafts. Slaves had no option but to work for a master unless they were freed when they could look for work in the low-grade occupations. Whatever their status, all the ethnic minorities were vulnerable, whether from domestic violence, social or religious intolerance, or persecution. Periods of tolerance might suddenly end in violence, and, for the Jews, expulsion from many parts of Europe in the later Middle Ages.

Notes

1 M. Schaus (ed.), *Women and Gender in Medieval Europe. An Encyclopedia* (London, 2006), p. 426; J. Edwards, *The Jews in Christian Europe 1400–1700*

(London, 1988), pp. 11–12, 16, 24–38; J. Edwards (ed. and trans.), *The Jews in Western Europe 1400–1600* (Manchester, 1994), pp. 88–9, 91–2, 97–8.

2 J.R. Baskin, 'Jewish women in the Middle Ages', in J.R. Baskin (ed.), *Jewish Women in Historical Perspective* (2nd edn, Detroit, 1998), p. 110; R.L. Melammed, 'Sephardi women in the medieval and early modern periods', in ibid., pp. 134–5.

3 P. Skinner and E. Van Houts (trans.), *Medieval Writings on Secular Women* (London, 2011), pp. 71–4; Yom Tov Assis, *The Jews of Santa Coloma de Queralt* (Jerusalem, 1988), pp. 26–30.

4 Baskin, 'Jewish women in the Middle Ages', pp. 110–16; J.R. Baskin, 'Medieval Jewish models of marriage', in S. Roush and C.L. Baskins (eds), *The Medieval Marriage Scene: Prudence, Passion, Policy* (Tempe, Arizona, 2005), pp. 1–2, 16–18.

5 Baskin (ed.), *Jewish Women in Historical Perspective*, pp. 20–5; Baskin, 'Jewish women in the Middle Ages', p. 117; Melammed, 'Sephardi women', p. 131; J.R. Wegner, 'The image and status of women in classical Rabinic Judaism', in Baskin (ed.), *Jewish Women in Historical Perspective*, pp. 75–81; E. Baumgarten, *Mothers and Children. Jewish Family Life in Medieval Europe* (Princeton, 2004), pp. 14–16, 186–7.

6 Baskin, 'Medieval Jewish models of marriage', p. 4; Melammed, 'Sephardi women', p. 131.

7 Melammed, 'Sephardi women', p. 133; R.L. Winer, *Women, Wealth and Community in Perpignan, c. 1250–1300* (Aldershot, 2006), pp. 12–14, 45, 74–5.

8 K.P. Jankrift, 'Jews in medieval European medicine', in C. Cluse (ed.), *The Jews of Europe in the Middle Ages* (Turnhout, 2004), pp. 334–8; E. Wickersheimer, *Dictionnaire biographique des médecins en France au moyen âge*, 2 vols (Geneva, 1979), II, pp. 730, 732, 747; K. Park, *Doctors and Medicine in Early Renaissance Florence* (Princeton, 1985), p. 71.

9 P. Skinner (ed.), *The Jews in Medieval Britain. Historical, Literary and Archaeological Perspectives* (Woodbridge, 2003), pp. 41–63; S. Bartlet, P. Skinner (ed.), *Licoricia of Winchester* (London, 2009), pp. 21–109; H. Meyer, 'Gender, Jewish creditors and Christian debtors in thirteenth-century Exeter', in C. Beattie and K.A. Fenton (eds), *Intersections of Gender, Religion and Ethnicity in the Middle Ages* (Basingstoke, 2011), pp. 104–24.

10 M. Keil, 'Public roles of Jewish women in fourteenth and fifteenth-century Ashkenaz: business, community and ritual', in Cluse (ed.), *The Jews of Europe in the Middle Ages*, pp. 319–25; Winer, *Perpignan*, pp. 7–9, 13; W.C. Jordan, 'Jews on top: women and the availability of consumption loans in northern France in the mid-thirteenth century', *Journal of Jewish Studies* 29 (1978), pp. 39–56.

11 Yom Tov Assis, *The Jews of Santa Coloma de Queralt*, pp. 36–7, 48, 62, 101.

12 D. Nirenberg, *Communities of Violence. Persecution of Minorities in the Middle Ages* (Princeton, 1996), pp. 3–15; A. MacKay, 'The Hispanic-*converso* predicament', *TRHS*, 5th series, 35 (1985), pp. 159–79.

13 Nirenberg, *Communities of Violence*, pp. 23–5; M.D. Meyerson, *The Muslims of Valencia in the Age of Ferdinand and Isabel: Between Coexistence and Crusade* (Berkeley, 1991), pp. 248–51.

14 T.F. Ruiz, 'Women, work and daily life in late medieval Castile', in M. Stone and C. Benito-Vessels (eds), *Women at Work in Spain from the Middle Ages to Early Modern Times* (New York, 1998), pp. 111–12; J. Guiral-Haziiossif, *Valence, port méditerranéen au quinzième siècle* (Paris, 1986), pp. 383–4; H. Dillard, *Daughters of the Reconquest. Women in Castilian Town Society, 1100–1300* (Cambridge, 1984), p. 161.

15 T. Dean, *Crime and Justice in Late Medieval Italy* (Cambridge, 2007), pp. 146–50; Melammed, 'Sephardi women', pp. 131–2.

16 E. Baumgarten, *Mothers and Children*, pp. 7–8; R.L. Winer, 'Conscripting the breast: lactation, slavery and salvation in the realms of Aragon and the kingdom of Majorca, *c.* 1250–1300', *JMH* 34 (2008), pp. 64–84; V. Hoyle, 'The bonds that bind: moneylending between Anglo-Jewish and Christian women in plea rolls of the exchequer of the Jews, 1218–80', ibid., pp. 119–29; C. Caballero-Navas, 'The care of women's health and beauty: an experience shared by Jewish and Christian women', ibid., pp. 146–63; M.H. Green and D.L. Smail, 'The trial of Floreta d'Ays (1403): Jews and Christians and obstetrics in later medieval Marseilles', ibid., pp. 185–211.

17 Skinner and van Houts (trans.), *Medieval Writings on Secular Women*, pp. 63–70.

18 J. Heers, *Esclaves et domestiques au moyen âge dans le monde méditerranéen* (Paris, 1981), p. 145; C. Verlinden, 'L'esclavage en Sicile au bas moyen âge', *Bulletin de l'Institut belge de Rome* 35 (1963), pp. 19, 32, 62; C. Klapisch-Zuber, 'Women servants in Florence during the fourteenth and fifteenth centuries', in B. Hanawalt (ed.), *Women and Work in Preindustrial Europe* (Bloomington, Indiana, 1986), pp. 56–80; I. Origo, *The Merchant of Prato* (Harmondsworth, 1992), p. 197; S.A. Epstein, *Genoa and the Genoese, 958–1528* (Chapel Hill, North Carolina, 1996), pp. 266–70.

8 Women and power
Noblewomen and queens

Although women in town and country exercised influence informally within their families, their exercise of agency outside their households was rare. Women traders and craftswomen made their own decisions and managed their businesses, while many women probably exerted pressure on their husbands to achieve family goals. Public authority, however, was regarded as a male domain. Women were generally not regarded as fit to hold office or to play a leading part in politics or war. Their subordinate position was underlined in law, and in the belief that they were weak and irrational. Moreover, the growth of professional bureaucratic government during the later Middle Ages tended to diminish women's political opportunities, and to accentuate the distinction between the public and the private in a way that had not been the case earlier in the Middle Ages.

Only very infrequently did a woman hold office at village or town level. Although a number of women owed suit to manorial courts in England, they were hardly ever appointed to office; R.H. Hilton found women ale-tasters appointed on several occasions in fifteenth-century Halesowen, and sometimes a reeve's widow presented his account as part of the business of winding up his affairs.[1] Women were rarely office-holders in the guild or confraternity, or in town government. Margery Schireham held office in the customs system in Scotland, as did a few other women, but they may have owed their position to male kinsmen.[2] Midwives had an official position in several German towns, and instances have been found of women as supervisors of weights and measures, and in charge of gates and towers, tolls, and the sale of salt. In Bohemia, a woman might inherit the position of town judge, but it appears that the duties were carried out by a husband or male relative.[3] The few urban references to female office-holders, compared with the number of officials employed by the towns, underline the point that women were not considered suitable for office.

Joan of Arc appears to have been an outstanding exception to this lack of non-noble women in politics. She bridges the divide between religious and secular life. Her hearing of voices at Domrémy and her conviction that she was acting in obedience to God's will set her in the same tradition as the French women following a religious life who uttered prophecies. Her success in raising the siege of Orleans in 1429 and accompanying the king to Rheims for his coronation raised morale among Charles VII's forces, but the success was followed by military defeat and capture. She was handed over to the English and tried for witchcraft, and in 1431 was burnt to death at Rouen as a relapsed heretic. Charles VII made no effort to save her, and the orthodoxy of her faith was proclaimed only twenty-five years later.[4] From the point of view of the king's advisers, war was to be waged by men, not women, and it is noteworthy that when noblewomen were engaged in war preparations and sieges they did not wear armour or fight in battle. Women with a religious message might be revered, but they were always vulnerable to charges of sorcery.

It was noblewomen and queens who were to be found in the public domain, exercising authority outside their private family circle. The later medieval nobility comprised a very diverse social grouping, united by its lifestyle of lavish consumption, landholding and chivalric ethos, but differing widely in its degrees of wealth. Younger sons of the royal family and gentry families of modest estate were all regarded as noble, and their authority was exercised at local, regional and national levels. Women's participation in this authority stemmed from their family situation, and in the queen's case from her status and coronation. Whether they exercised power and jurisdiction depended in the first instance on law and custom, and also on family circumstances. Thus Margaret Paston was responsible for family estates and fortunes in Norfolk in the absence of her husband, and Margaret, Countess of Flanders, found herself heiress and ruler of the county as vassal of the king of France. Agency for these women implied an economic, social and jurisdictional relationship with men who were usually of lower status than themselves, and the ties were dependent on their own higher social position and wealth. Women needed to be able to exercise this power effectively, both through their households and in the courts, by coercion and by patronage. Long-term strategies underlying their actions were important; these can be difficult to trace, but usually centred on their families and children.[5]

Such political activity is found much more in certain parts of Europe than others. In areas such as England, France, the Low Countries, the kingdom of Sicily and the Latin Empire, where female inheritance was permitted in default of male heirs and where women received a landed dower, women as landowners often had a public role; women in northern Italy, on the other hand, rarely played a part in government.[6] This role was often more important during widowhood than during the marriage when it was assumed that the husband would carry out public obligations. As far as queens were concerned, custom again varied as to whether they could exercise authority during the incapacity or absence of their husbands, and during the minority of the heir. Some women found that they never had the chance to take on a public role; others preferred, or were compelled by their circumstances, to live a private life. A noblewoman whose sons were grown up at the time of her husband's death played a less significant political role than one entrusted with the guardianship of a minor heir.

In view of contemporary attitudes, it was to be expected that powerful noblewomen and queens were sometimes unpopular with their families and others. From the point of view of an adult son, it was galling to have a long-lived mother, and possibly other female relatives, holding a substantial portion of the estate in dower, and possibly also enjoying a large inheritance into the bargain. The wealth and political activities of the son could be hampered as a result and some sons went so far as to take their mothers to court to try to regain some of their lands.[7] Remarriage led to tension and sometimes conflict. Margaret Beaufort appears to have thought out her second and third marriages carefully, and it was probably an advantage that she had only one child, Henry Tudor. Fighting erupted in Flanders and Hainault in the 1240s and 1250s between the sons of Margaret, Countess of Flanders, by her first and second marriages, and Louis IX's arbitration of 1246 did not secure peace.[8] The remarriage of queens was particularly likely to cause political repercussions, as when the widow of John of England, Isabella of Angoulême, married Hugh de la Marche in 1220, allying herself with the son of the man to whom she had formerly been betrothed. Isabella claimed that Hugh would be a powerful ally for Henry III against France, but this proved not to be the case. The remarriage of Henry V's widow, Katherine of France, to Owen Tudor was a clear *mésalliance*, leading to acts of parliament in 1428 and 1430 forbidding marriage to a dowager queen without royal permission.[9]

Tensions within the family often had wider ramifications. Queens have suffered more than most women from the denigration of contemporaries and posterity. This was sometimes due to political failure, but frequently to misogynist attitudes and the need to blame someone other than the king. When the unpopular queen is examined in context, she is often found to have been in the grip of events beyond her control, and cannot fairly be blamed for the failure of her policies. Queens enjoyed success as well as failure, as did their husbands and sons. Recent writing has shown how a queen's reputation also depends on the writings of later commentators, influenced more by their own age than by contemporary evidence. This appears to have been the case with Isabeau of Bavaria, wife of Charles VI of France, who was extravagant but did not deserve the sexual accusations levied against her.[10] Modern historians base their high opinion of Blanche of Castile, mother of Louis IX, on her contribution to the rise in power of the Capetian monarchy, setting on one side the invective which contemporaries uttered against her. In discussing both queens and noblewomen, historians' attitudes as well as evidence have to be carefully assessed.

Politics and marriage

Politics were an integral element in the lives of noblewomen and queens from their earliest years and played a prominent part in their marriage. As with other groups in European society, marriages were arranged and were usually seen as the means of sealing an alliance or securing an inheritance. It was very rare for a noblewoman to live in the world unmarried. Noble girls were generally married young, especially if they were heiresses, and political considerations often appear to have been uppermost in the choice of husband, with the women themselves having little say. When building up his support in Naples in 1436, Alfonso V of Aragon promised Raimondo Orsini, Count of Nola, the hand of Leonor of Urgel; Leonor resisted and had to be forced aboard the galley at Barcelona which was to take her to Naples. The marriage of Boniface of Montferrat in 1204 to Margaret of Hungary, the widow of the Byzantine emperor, Isaac II Angelos, was probably connected with his landed ambitions in Thessalonika and Greece.[11] Marriage strategies were essential to the build-up of family power and were therefore planned carefully. Edward III of England appears to have been particularly lucky, securing for his second son Lionel of Clarence the heiress to the earldom of Ulster, for John of Gaunt, his third son, the heiress of the duchy of Lancaster, and for his youngest son Thomas of Woodstock the heiress to half the earldom of Hereford, Essex and Northampton. John of Gaunt (by his second marriage) and Edmund of Langley married the daughters and heiresses of Pedro the Cruel of Castile, while Lionel by his short-lived second marriage forged an alliance with the Visconti of Milan.

Similar political considerations operated with the marriage of a queen, although here the choice was often conducted on the international plane and, once married, she was more likely to be isolated from kin and country-men. It was rare for a king to make a sudden, unexpected marriage, as Edward IV of England made with Elizabeth Woodville. Far more usual were the marriages to seal peace treaties, such as the marriage of Isabella, daughter of James I of Aragon, to the future Philip III of France, confirming the treaty of Corbeil between the two kingdoms in 1258. Edward II's marriage to Isabella, daughter of Philip IV, was aimed at securing peace through a political alliance. Marriages were often designed to secure lands – the four marriages of the Emperor Charles IV all increased his territory and influence.

When women were heiresses to a kingdom there was intense competition over their marriages, often combined with conflict over the succession. On the death of Louis the Great in 1382, it took some years for his elder daughter Mary and her husband Sigismund of Luxemburg to establish themselves in power in Hungary. The younger daughter, Jadwiga, elected by the Poles as their ruler in 1384 at the age of eleven, was persuaded to break her engagement to William of Habsburg, and married to Jagiello of Lithuania. Possible candidates for queenship were useful pawns in the diplomatic game. John of Gaunt took his two unmarried daughters on his expedition to Castile in 1385–9; his alliance with Portugal was sealed by the marriage of his daughter Philippa to John of Aviz, while his renunciation of his claim to the Castilian throne was marked by the marriage of his daughter Catherine, granddaughter of Pedro the Cruel, to the eldest son of John I of Castile. Catherine described herself in a letter of 1412 as 'undoubted queen of Castile and Leon'.[12]

Women of the nobility and those destined to become queens were expected to adapt to life in their new homes. Their youth may have made adaptation easier, although views on this differed. Eleanor of Castile was unwilling in 1282 to send her eldest daughter to Aragon to marry the heir to the throne for another eighteen months or two years and was backed up by her mother-in-law, Eleanor of Provence; her daughter was thirteen at the time and therefore marriageable, but her mother and grandmother probably felt that she needed to be more mature before she was sent to a foreign court. On the other hand, Queen Constance of Aragon was eager to receive her.[13] Royal brides could certainly feel isolated when they were allowed to keep only a few of the servants they knew and when they found that their bridegroom already had a mistress at court. Mothers-in-law also posed problems, Blanche of Castile showing jealousy of Louis IX's feeling for Margaret of Provence, so that they had to snatch secret meetings.[14] Language or dialect could also be a barrier and any queen coming to a new country encountered new customs. In some cases, there was an element of culture shock, even though the influence of French court culture was widespread. Although the Iberian and French royal families mostly married within their own geographical areas, the majority of English queens originated from the Continent, coming from various parts of France, the Low Countries, Castile and Bohemia. Many of the later medieval Scandinavian queens originated from the Baltic region, but Waldemar II of Denmark married Dagmar of Bohemia and subsequently Berengaria of Portugal, while Eric of Pomerania married Philippa, daughter of Henry IV of England.

Some contact was maintained with natal families. Meetings were rare, although the four daughters of Raymond Berengar of Provence and their mother met in 1254 at the court of Louis IX; the meeting reunited Margaret, married to Louis IX, Eleanor, wife of Henry III, Sancia, married to Richard of Cornwall, and Beatrice, the wife of Charles of Anjou.[15] Usually, contact was maintained by letter. Blanche of Castile heard the news of the Castilian victory at Las Navas de Tolosa in 1212 in a letter from her sister Berenguela. Philippa of Lancaster corresponded from Portugal with Thomas Arundel, Archbishop of Canterbury, and Bishop Despenser of Norwich, sending gifts as well as letters. She asked Richard II to provide a benefice for her chancellor who wanted to retire to England, and corresponded with her brother Henry IV in connection with the marriage of the earl of Arundel and Beatrice, bastard daughter of John of Aviz.[16] The correspondence points to a continuing interest in English affairs.

Once married, queens and women of the higher nobility had their own households and landed resources; less important noblewomen ran their households in conjunction with their husbands. It was in the household context that these women, like others in society, could exercise their influence informally and in ways which were acceptable in the medieval world. The expression of piety was regarded as the mark of the good wife, provided that it did not take on greater importance than her relations with her husband. Pious activities, such as attendance at Mass, almsgiving or making a religious foundation, were widely recorded. The woman was the head of a predominantly male household among whose members she dispensed patronage, providing offices, clerical benefices and presents in return for good service. She sometimes used her position to advance her own family and people from her natal region, as when Eleanor of Provence secured advantageous marriages in England for men and women from Savoy.[17] Through their officials, the noblewoman and the queen administered lands and exercised jurisdiction. Intercession with their husbands on behalf of members of the family and household, tenants or subjects was regarded as both important and acceptable. The queen's duty was to foster peace. The variety of everyday business undertaken by a queen is exemplified in the letters of Margaret of Anjou, wife of Henry VI of England. They throw light on the running of her estates and her relations with tenants, and at the same time show her enjoyment of hunting as a recreation. She was concerned to promote the fortunes of her officials, whether by marriage, gifts or Church preferment, and she was anxious to provide for former servants who were ill or had fallen on hard times. The letters show Margaret's awareness of her rights and a determination to further the fortunes of those connected to her.[18]

The lady's lifestyle had a direct bearing on the reputation of her family. Hospitality and feasting increased the family's contacts with kin, royalty, nobility and local lay and religious figures, and thus had a direct bearing on the influence which a family could wield. Livery served a similar purpose, visibly binding the household officials and other retainers into a unity. In 1313, Mahaut, Countess of Artois and Burgundy, purchased crimson cloth for her knights, crimson medley for her clerks, striped and marbled cloth for her squires and striped cloth for the servants, the robes displaying membership of the household and differentiation within its hierarchy.[19] On ceremonial and chivalric occasions, the woman was expected to play her part, whether as hostess or guest, at jousts and tournaments, banquets and balls. Her bearing and her activity within the household gave her status and influence.

Noblewomen and family

Although wives exercised authority informally through their households, husbands controlled their wives' estates, and during marriage many wives largely disappear from the historical record. During the thirteenth century, they acted alongside their husbands, especially where dowry, dower and inheritance were concerned, but it is probable that their involvement in family property matters did not go beyond this.[20] The knight of La Tour-Landry recommended that wives should counsel their husbands secretly, a process which leaves little record and indicates that their public role after marriage was expected to be discreet.[21] In the early years of the marriage what was crucial was the birth of the heir, or preferably the birth of several sons, in order to secure the future of the lineage. Both husband and wife were concerned that the family should continue to flourish, and although the wife was subsumed into her marital family, concern for her natal family was also expressed. When Anne de Laval married Jean de Montfort in 1405, shortly after the death of her only brother, it was arranged that Jean should not only succeed her father but also take his name. In other cases where the wife was heir to her father, the first son succeeded his father and the second his mother, sometimes taking the mother's family name.[22] The birth of children therefore benefited both the marital and the natal family.

Noblewomen's seals reinforced this double identity, particularly in cases where the woman was an heiress. The iconography of the seal, whether it was active or passive, military or religious, displayed the woman's sense of identity. In France and Britain, where the use of seals in society increased greatly in the thirteenth century, most noblewomen used their own name and their husband's title, while the heiress used her name and patronymic together with her father's arms. The 1220 seal of Garsande, Countess of Provence and Forcalquier, delineated one title on each side of the seal; on the side inscribed countess of Forcalquier, she was portrayed fully armed, as if to emphasise her hereditary lordship in the county. Devorguilla de Balliol stood on her seal portrayed as a widow, holding in her right hand her husband's Balliol shield and in her left her father's shield with the lion of Galloway; the shields of the earldom of Chester and of her maternal grandfather, David of Scotland, were a reminder of family ancestry.[23] Such claims from the past might have an important bearing on the family's future, and men and women made use of them to further the fortunes of their children and therefore of the lineage.

Family strategies were intertwined with politics, but political activity by the wife depended on her husband's wishes and career. Even though the wife often took over responsibilities for land and family when her husband was absent or incapacitated, it cannot be taken for granted that he would permit her to take control. Yet in an age when warfare was frequent and husbands were summoned to serve the ruler in counsel as well as war, women were often found running estates, holding castles and raising ransoms. Marie, daughter of Jean, Duke of Berry, and married in 1400 to the heir of the duke of Bourbon, found herself in charge of the duchy for twelve years after her husband was captured at the battle of Agincourt in 1415. Although she took over affairs straightaway, it was only two years later that her husband formally authorised her to act during his absence and while their son was under age. Marie found herself embroiled in Burgundian-Armagnac feuds, and after her father's death in 1416 fought to secure her own inheritance in Auvergne. She never succeeded in obtaining her husband's release because he accepted the treaty of Troyes in 1420 and subsequently recognised

Henry VI as king of France. She retired from power in 1427, once her husband had formally transferred authority to their son. Two years before, Charles VII had ceded Auvergne to the Bourbons.[24] Marie was involved in a complex and tense political situation. She was concerned for both the Bourbon and the Berry inheritance, and aimed to safeguard a strong power-base for her son.

Other husbands trusted their wives to act in the best interests of the family. Elizabeth Berkeley, wife of Richard Beauchamp, Earl of Warwick, managed her own inheritance during her marriage, and in the absence of her husband in France took action to secure possession of Berkeley Castle, despite the fact that an earlier entail precluded her succession to her father.[25] The four Valois dukes of Burgundy all involved their wives in the government of their estates to a greater or lesser degree. Margaret, daughter and heiress of Louis de Male, Count of Flanders, and wife of Philip the Bold, often acted on her husband's behalf in the county in the 1370s and 1380s, and she took charge of Flanders in 1404–5 after her husband's death. Margaret of Bavaria, wife of John the Fearless, ruled Flanders on and off between 1405 and 1409; she was virtually in charge of the duchy and county of Burgundy between 1409 and 1419 while her husband was immersed in French politics, and held the duchy together after John's murder at Montereau. Isabella of Portugal carried out various government commissions for her husband, Philip the Good, and Margaret of York, wife of Charles the Bold, was involved in diplomacy and raised money and soldiers for the duke's wars. In the months after his death in 1477, she supported and advised the inexperienced Duchess Mary at a time when her whole inheritance was threatened with disintegration.[26]

Wives of the lesser nobility and gentry similarly took on their husbands' responsibilities. While her husband John I was in London, Margaret Paston looked after the family's interests in Norfolk, defended their property and supervised the estates. She received detailed instructions from her husband, as in 1465 when he complained that money had not been sent to him in London, advised her as to how his household and livelihood were to be well governed, and specified various payments to churches for work done. He regarded his son John II as lazy, but Margaret had interceded for him.[27] Margaret's letters show that she was capable of acting on her own initiative and was fully aware of the political situation in the county.

Even if the wife played an important role during her husband's lifetime, she enjoyed greater independence as a widow, and it was at this time that exercise of agency was likely to be at its greatest. The legal independence conferred by widowhood in feudal society enabled the widow to run her estates, and her power might be considerably increased through guardianship of her children and their lands, although this was rare in Germany and not permitted in Normandy. The degree of her influence varied according to the extent of her estates, her family circumstances and her personality. Margaret Paston continued to be involved in family and local affairs after her husband's death. The childless widow, Marie de St Pol, Countess of Pembroke, ran her estates in England and Wales and also made periodic visits to her lands in France, even during the Hundred Years War.[28] Widows exercised jurisdiction on their estates and met the obligations which were due to their lord or to the Crown. They also held office. Ela, Countess of Salisbury, acted as sheriff of Wiltshire in 1227–8 and between 1231 and 1237, but the king stressed that she held the office by royal grant and not by hereditary right; Isabella of Ghistelles wrote to the count of Flanders to inform him that she was unable to perform her late husband's service of chamberlain at Pentecost, 1317.[29] Many noble widows found that they were faced with litigation but showed little inclination to give up their claims or estates. Matilda, Countess of Norfolk, told Henry III that she had handed over the lordship of Chepstow to her son, but in fact was still holding it at her death in 1248.[30]

Widows of the higher nobility especially were a power to be reckoned with. Alda Ferrández, daughter of the last Almohad ruler of Valencia, married into a powerful Aragonese family, and as a widow continued to hold much of the family's lands. She was involved in the Union revolt of the nobles in the 1280s, and subscribed to the oath as 'the noble lady Alda Ferrández, daughter of the former noble king of Valencia'.[31] Women's political allegiances were carefully watched; in 1417, the widow of Amanieu de Madailhan, Jeanne d'Armagnac, was described to Henry V as being of great power with his enemies.[32] Widowed queens might be equally dangerous. Jeanne of Evreux, widow of Charles IV of France, and Blanche of Navarre, widow of Philip VI, supported the rebellion in 1364 of Charles of Navarre, while Barbara of Cilly, widow of the Emperor Sigismund, was suspected of supporting the claims of the Jagiello kings of Poland to the Bohemian throne.[33]

Such reports show that sometimes women took their own political line, and this independence often came about as a result of war. Although women normally performed their feudal obligations by deputy, on one occasion they found themselves present in a parliament. The circumstances were exceptional. In 1259, the Byzantines were victorious over the Latins at the battle of Pelagonia; William de Villehardouin, prince of Achaia, was taken prisoner and ordered to surrender three of his strongholds. Two years later, a parliament was held at Nikli, attended mainly by the wives and widows of the Latin lords who had been killed in battle or taken prisoner. A long debate ensued over the surrender of the castles. The chronicles report only the men's speeches (at least four men were present), but the decision to accept the Byzantine terms, and to send the daughters of the marshal and constable to Constantinople as hostages, was taken by the parliament as a whole. The argument was accepted that if William died in prison, his family would suffer; if freed, he would have a chance to retake the castles.[34] The women presumably considered that they were acting in the present and future interests of their families and of the continuation of the Latin presence in Greece.

Although noblewomen might make their own decisions at a time of rebellion and war, there is no doubt that they were vulnerable if the situation turned against them. The most graphic accounts of vulnerability are those by the women themselves. English widows, for instance, found themselves bereft of resources at times of rebellion if their lands and goods were confiscated by the Crown. Elizabeth de Burgh's account of her treatment by Edward II after her husband died as a rebel in 1322 shows how she feared for the life of her children and was forced to give up the part of her inheritance wanted by the king and her brother-in-law, Hugh le Despenser the Younger. She did not feel wholly secure until Edward III became king five years later.[35]

The autobiography of Leonor López de Córdoba tells of how she was caught up in the struggle between Pedro the Cruel and Henry of Trastamare. She was married as a child to a rich noble related to Pedro's family. When Henry came to power, her father was beheaded in Seville because of his support for Pedro; and his whole family was imprisoned for nine years. Plague swept through the prison, and only Leonor and her husband survived. Released on Henry's death, her husband found that he could not recover his property, and Leonor was taken in by her aunt. After seven years, her husband reappeared and he and Leonor lived in poverty. When plague came to Córdoba, Leonor left for Aguilar with her aunt, but her son and adopted son both died. Later in her life, Leonor enjoyed high favour with Queen Catherine of Lancaster, then regent of Castile, but around 1412 she fell from grace and it was after this that she wrote her autobiography.[36] Like other members of society, noblewomen found that their fortunes were not necessarily secure.

Noblewomen and rule

Certain countesses found that their responsibilities went further than the administration of their estates and guardianship of their children, and that their title conferred many of the functions of ruler. This was particularly true of France and the Low Countries where counties owed allegiance to the king of France or the Holy Roman Emperor but where intervention by the overlord was generally infrequent. On the death of the Latin Emperor Baldwin IX of Flanders, his heirs were his daughters Jeanne and Margaret, who ruled the county through their husbands and on their own for much of the thirteenth century; in the last part of her life, Margaret co-ruled with her son. The county of Champagne was in the hands of a widowed regent between 1201 and 1222. Theobald III of Champagne died shortly before setting out on the fourth crusade, and Theobald IV was born posthumously; his mother, Blanche of Navarre, exercised power throughout his minority.[37]

Mahaut, Countess of Artois and Burgundy, is one of the best recorded widows of the later Middle Ages. She was an heiress in her own right, succeeding her father, Robert II, in the county of Artois in 1302. Her husband was Otto IV, Count of Burgundy, who was killed in the Flemish wars the following year, leaving her with a son and two daughters. From then until her death in 1329 she ruled the county of Artois and acted on behalf of her son, a minor, in the county of Burgundy. Like other widows, she was keen to maintain her rights in the interests of her family. With the death of her son in 1317, the county of Burgundy passed to her daughter Jeanne, married to Philip V of France.[38]

Artois was involved in the opposition to the Crown and the rise of the provincial leagues after the death of Philip the Fair in 1314, and grievances were directed against Mahaut as well as against the Crown; demands were made that Mahaut should respect ancient custom. Trouble continued after Louis X's grant of liberties to the county in 1315, and Mahaut had to face a rival claim to the county from her nephew Robert, and a charge of causing Louis X's death by sorcery. Although she was exonerated and Robert's claim was dismissed, the litigation again points to the vulnerability of a widow in politics. It was not until 1319 that Mahaut could make a triumphant return to her castle of Hesdin. It was doubtless an advantage to her that she was related to the royal family by descent, but the scandal concerning her daughters, who married sons of Philip the Fair, was directly linked to the charge of sorcery, as Mahaut was said to have concocted a potion to reconcile Philip V and Jeanne, and to have engineered the death of Louis X.[39] Philip the Fair arrested all three of his daughters-in-law in 1314, accusing Mahaut's daughter Blanche of adultery and Jeanne of concealing what had been going on. Jeanne proved her innocence, but Blanche was condemned to imprisonment and ended her life as a nun.

Mahaut ruled her county through her officials, and the accounts of her *baillis* were checked three times a year. She enforced law and order; she confiscated the lands in Artois of the lord of Oisy when he invaded the estates of the beguinage of Cantimpré and the abbey of Verger, which were both under Mahaut's protection. She issued charters to the towns of Artois, as when she protected the cloth industry of St Omer against competition from rural areas. She also exercised power through dispensing patronage and favours, and the complexity of her noble and political connections can be traced in her household accounts. Through these networks, Mahaut could intercede, mediate and recommend candidates for offices and reward. She herself had plenty of openings for office on her estates and in her household and administration and, like other noblewomen, also exercised ecclesiastical patronage.[40]

The noblewomen who ruled their lordships in the later Middle Ages were relatively few in number. Far more numerous were the widows with their dower estates and the wives exercising political influence informally through their husbands and households. They became involved in political activity because their circumstances compelled them to do so and were vigorous in their defence of rights, land and family. Some of them ran their estates much more successfully than others. What is clear at all levels of the nobility is that family and political concerns were inextricably linked, and women were often acting on behalf of their children and thinking of the future well-being of the family. The importance of the family unit is brought out in Christine de Pizan's discussion of the wise princess. The princess built up her reputation for piety, good conduct, loyalty and obedience to her husband. She watched over the upbringing and education of her children and ensured that they were often with her. At the same time, she took steps to promote peace between the prince and his barons, and kept a watchful eye on the revenues of her household.[41] Christine urged that she should have the training to be able to do this and, in view of the expectation in various parts of Europe that wives and widows should be able to take over from their husbands, she was being sensible and realistic in her views.

The ceremonial roles of the queen

In many respects, there were parallels between the life of the noblewoman and that of the queen, especially as far as the higher nobility was concerned. Both exercised influence through their households, administered land and revenues, and enjoyed a noble lifestyle. Yet the queen had responsibilities towards all the subjects of the kingdom, especially the duty of providing an heir to the throne, and her coronation set her apart from the nobility. In certain European kingdoms, she came to exercise considerable authority, even becoming regent or ruler.

The queen was not crowned in all European kingdoms; amongst Castilian rulers, both anointing and coronation were an exception to the norm.[42] Where the rites are known, there were significant differences between the queen's coronation and the king's. The coronation gave the queen a national identity, emphasised the importance of her marriage and fertility, and at the same time made clear her inferiority to the king. All these points were made at the coronation of French queens, as in that of Jeanne de Bourbon, wife of Charles V.[43] The *Coronation Book* of Charles V contains illustrations of Jeanne's coronation, which followed her husband's in Rheims cathedral on 19 May 1364. The king remained seated on his throne during his wife's coronation. From the twelfth century, queens were anointed as well as crowned. However, whereas the king was anointed with holy chrism, said to have been sent from heaven for the baptism of Clovis, the queen was anointed with consecrated oil and only on the head and breast; the sacerdotal element in the coronation was thus reserved for the king. The anointing assured the queen's spiritual renewal and fertility; the ceremony reinforced her marriage vows. The birth of a legitimate heir was crucial for the future of the kingdom and was especially important for Jeanne de Bourbon, as she and Charles V had no living child after eighteen years of marriage; two girls and a boy had died, but four children were born to them in the next few years. The queen did not take a coronation oath, but her regalia symbolised her undertakings on behalf of the kingdom: the ring, symbolising the Holy

Trinity, underlined her orthodoxy and her duty to fight heresy, and the rod her charitable duties to the poor. The prayers requesting that she should be granted the virtues of the women of the Old Testament can be interpreted as prayers for fidelity, courage and fertility. The subservience of the queen to the king was symbolised by her smaller throne placed on the north side of the choir and her smaller sceptre, and she was not acclaimed when she was crowned.[44] However, like the king, she received communion in both kinds in the course of the Coronation Mass.

The emphasis on fertility and the concern for a legitimate heir are understandable in view of the crises likely to occur in the event of a disputed succession. Even in the Holy Roman Empire where the emperor was elected, there was a tendency with both the Luxemburgs and the Habsburgs to try to ensure a son's succession. With women who failed to become pregnant for several years, like Henry VI's queen, Margaret of Anjou, there must have been both relief and rejoicing when their son Edward was born eight years after their wedding. Similar anxieties were aroused if the king died young or shortly after his marriage; the widow's pregnancy led to hopes of a son, but the birth of a daughter could provoke a succession crisis, as happened after the death of Louis X of France. An even greater crisis erupted if the king was unable or unwilling to consummate the marriage. Ingeborg of Denmark, second wife of Philip Augustus of France, was repudiated immediately after her coronation in 1193 and divorced soon afterwards. Ingeborg always maintained that the marriage had been consummated, but even when Philip Augustus took her back in 1213, her rights as queen were not fully restored.[45] Ingeborg's repudiation was not a unique case. A marriage was arranged between Pedro the Cruel of Castile and Blanche of Bourbon, but before her arrival he fell in love with Maria de Padilla. The marriage took place in 1353, but Blanche was quickly repudiated and imprisoned. Eight years later, she was executed.[46]

During her husband's lifetime, the queen's principal duty, besides the birth of children, was participating in the ceremonial life of the court and advertising the power and prestige of the royal family at court and on progresses through the kingdom. The queen, as royal wife and mother, had a definite part to play and was expected to be both pious and just, interceding with her husband when asked to do so. She might be expected to be present when portentous matters of policy were discussed, as when Jeanne de Bourbon sat on the king's right hand at the meeting of the *parlement* of Paris in 1369 when it was decided to renew the war with England. The queen entertained foreign rulers who visited the court; Jeanne had two meetings with the Emperor Charles IV when he was in Paris in 1377–8.[47] Queens enjoyed the recreation and ritual of tournaments. Charles of Anjou, his queen and her ladies presided over the joust when their son, Charles of Salerno, was knighted. At the splendid tournament at St-Denis in May 1389, Isabeau of Bavaria and her ladies, richly dressed, presided over the lists and enjoyed the feasting and dancing in the evenings. It was the ladies who conducted the knights into the lists and distributed the prizes at the end of the day.[48]

On progresses, the queen was greeted with pageants and spectacles which had a definite political message. Isabeau of Bavaria made a ceremonial journey in August 1389 from the abbey of St-Denis to Notre Dame cathedral in Paris for her coronation. She was greeted at the first gate by angels and an image of the Virgin Mary with the Child Jesus, and at the second by a scene of Paradise from which two cherubim descended and placed a gold and jewelled crown on her head. At Le Châtelet, a figure of St Anne had been placed on the seat of justice, flanked by a white hart and a lion; an eagle, symbolising a bird of prey, flew out but was seized by twelve maidens armed with swords.[49] The message of heavenly favour and the importance of upholding justice was clear.

Visits by king, queen or prince to towns within the kingdom were the occasion for carefully planned symbolic ritual. When Margaret of Anjou visited Coventry in 1456, it was the importance of her motherhood which was underlined. It was customary to give the queen a present, but half of the gift was kept in reserve for when the prince visited the town. Five pageants were prepared for her progress through the city, with speeches directly relevant to her and her son. Thus, at the first station, under a representation of the tree of Jesse, the prophets Isaiah and Jeremiah likened her to the root of Jesse and asserted that, just as mankind rejoiced at the birth of Jesus, England would rejoice over her son and his knightly courage. At the second station, Edward the Confessor and St John the Evangelist prayed for the well-being of the royal family and praised Margaret for her virtue. Margaret and Edward were praised by the Cardinal Virtues at the third station, Margaret for her motherhood and Edward as the prince who would bring peace to the kingdom. The Nine Worthies appeared at the fourth station and offered their service and loyalty to the queen, and at the last station St Margaret of Antioch appeared slaying the dragon and offering her prayers on behalf of her namesake.[50] The virtues of loyalty and service, and the queen's supreme duty of providing an heir, were visibly displayed.

Political activity, regency and rule

The amount of power which a queen might exercise during her husband's lifetime was limited. She did not have a formal role on the king's council and had to exert her influence in informal ways, through intercession and through her household. Contemporaries looked to her religious and charitable role, and Elizabeth of York's piety helped to enhance the reputation of Henry VII.[51] The queen could make her wishes known to officials and others, but could not necessarily enforce them. For instance, Kunigunde, the Hungarian queen of Ottokar II of Bohemia (1253–78), had strong views on promoting the fortunes of Slavs in the Church. She wrote to Agnes, Abbess of Trebnitz and daughter of Henry II of Silesia and Anna of Bohemia, criticising her for her support of German rather than Polish or Bohemian friars; Kunigunde considered that it was Agnes's duty to assist the Slavs.[52]

It was only when the king was unable to act, whether through absence or defeat, that queens sometimes played a more active political role by right of her status as royal wife or mother. In this role she had to show political expertise to ensure the success of royal policies, a character-trait which women were not expected to have. Margaret of Provence accompanied her husband Louis IX on his crusade, and was left at Damietta when Louis led the crusaders towards Cairo. She gave birth to her son John Tristan three days after hearing that Louis had been taken prisoner. She suffered from nightmares that the Saracens were entering her chamber and found an old knight to stay by her and keep her safe. Despite her fears, she realised that Damietta was an important bargaining-counter for the king's release and persuaded the merchants of Pisa and Genoa not to abandon the town. When Damietta had to be surrendered to the Muslims, she sailed to Acre to await Louis.[53]

In Aragon, seven queens acted as their husbands' political partners. The office of lieutenant to govern a particular part of the kingdom was used in the thirteenth century; the first appointment of a queen came in 1310. Often the queen acted for a short period, but Maria of Castile, wife of Alfonso V the Magnanimous (1416–58), acted as lieutenant-general of Catalonia between 1420 and 1423, and 1432 and 1453 while her husband conquered and then ruled the kingdom of Naples. This involved her in peace-keeping, justice and administration, and she kept in close touch with Alfonso who sent her detailed instructions. Theresa Earenfight sums her up as prudent, fair and effective.[54]

The acceptability of the queen taking action in an emergency is also seen in the time of Isabeau of Bavaria whose husband, Charles VI, suffered from periodic bouts of insanity from 1392 until his death thirty years later. After his first attack of madness, Charles made her the guardian of the dauphin until he came of age at thirteen, and a member of the regency council. She played an important role in mediating between the dukes of Burgundy and Orleans, and in the early fifteenth century her authority was increased. In 1403, she became the head of the regency council which was to rule the country while the king was incapacitated. She was unable to control the kingdom during the civil war after the murder of the duke of Orleans in 1407, and by the time of the treaty of Troyes in 1420 was very much in the hands of the Burgundians.[55] It would have taken an exceptionally strong ruler to dominate the noble factions of the time.

There is no doubt that motherhood increased a queen's power, but practice varied in European kingdoms as to whether a queen was allowed to become the regent during her son's minority. In France, from the late twelfth century, the king's mother was entrusted with the role of regent, although she did not necessarily act on her own. When Philip Augustus left for the third crusade in 1190, the regency was entrusted to his mother, Adela of

Champagne, and her brother the archbishop of Rheims, together with a regency council. Blanche of Castile was the most famous regent of medieval France, designated by her husband Louis VIII in 1226 to govern the kingdom during the minority of Louis IX, although there is little indication that she had been politically active under her husband. Blanche had to defeat noble rebellion and foreign invasion. Through her diplomacy she safeguarded the Crown's gains in the south. She proved vigorous and able in her consolidation of the kingdom and was not deterred by opposition from pursuing policies which she considered to be in the Crown's interests. According to Joinville, Louis attached much importance to his mother's advice, and the fact that he recalled her as regent during his time on crusade testifies to the success of her earlier rule.[56] His piety owed much to his mother's teaching. Later kings designated their queens as regents, although not all were called on to act. At the outbreak of the Hundred Years War, Philip VI appointed his wife as head of the government of the realm, should the necessity arise. In 1374, Charles V specified that Jeanne of Bourbon was to be their children's guardian, assisted by the dukes of Burgundy and Bourbon, and she was forbidden to remarry until her eldest son came of age. Louis XI entrusted power to his elder daughter Anne de Beaujeu during the minority of Charles VIII.[57]

This reliance on women in France was in marked contrast to practice in England. Although the queen might be appointed regent during the king's temporary absence, as was Eleanor of Provence in 1253–4, it was more usual to appoint regency councils when the heir was a minor, as happened for Henry III, Richard II and Henry VI. Margaret of Anjou claimed the regency during her husband's madness in 1453–4, and the birth of Prince Edward in October 1453 and his creation as prince of Wales strengthened her position. However, it was Richard, Duke of York, who was created Protector and Defender of the realm in March 1454.[58] Events of the later 1450s and 1460s show Margaret exercising power without a formal title; her efforts to secure her husband's restoration ended in defeat and exile in 1471.

Several queen-mothers acted as regents in the Iberian kingdoms, but were expected to work with male members of the royal family. Henry III of Castile (d. 1406) was succeeded by his two-year-old son John II, entailing a thirteen-year minority. The regency was shared by his uncle, Ferdinand of Antequera (d. 1416) and his mother, Catherine of Lancaster, who divided their responsibilities, with Catherine taking the north and Ferdinand the south. On Ferdinand's death, Catherine remained sole regent until her death in 1418. The queen-mother was designated regent for Alfonso V of Portugal (1438–81) and, because of fears of interference from her brothers, it was proposed that she should share the regency with the king's uncle. However, she found her position untenable and fled to Castile.[59]

Other female relatives might play a part in regency government and in Castile as well as Aragon women played prominent political roles. Berenguela of Castile, the sister of Blanche of Castile, was married to Alfonso IX of Leon, but because of their close relationship the marriage was dissolved in 1204. On the death of her father, Alfonso VIII of Castile, his son Henry succeeded to the throne at the age of eleven, with his sister Berenguela as guardian. Henry died three years later, in 1217, and at that point Berenguela was recognised as ruler of Castile. She abdicated in favour of her son Ferdinand III, but she remained in power, arranging for his marriage to Beatrice, daughter of Philip of Swabia, and dominating affairs. On the death of Alfonso IX of Leon, it looked as if conflict would break out over the succession, but this was averted by Berenguela and Alfonso's first wife Teresa of Portugal. Ferdinand III succeeded and Leon and Castile were united. Berenguela derived her power from her family (as a child she was recognised as heir to Castile) and from her position as wife in Leon and as mother; her power was also based on her estates and on her adept use of patronage. She succeeded in never being seen as a threat, despite her gender.[60] Although individual regents might encounter problems, the idea of a woman in power in Spain was accepted, and this also applied to a woman ruling in her own right.

In eastern and northern Europe, there is a great contrast between the problems women faced in Hungary and their acceptance in Scandinavia. The queen's role as regent was problematical in any kingdom having to deal with disputed succession, civil war and strong factions among the nobility. Moreover, it was most unusual for women in Hungary to have the right of inheritance. Louis the Great persuaded the Hungarian nobility to accept his daughter Mary as his successor so that Mary, who was married to Sigismund of Luxemburg, was elected and crowned 'king', although in her charters she was described as 'queen by grace of God'. Her mother Elizabeth Kotromanic was made regent on Louis's death in 1382. Elizabeth came from the Balkans where women were found playing important political roles, and she had support from certain Hungarian magnates, but in view of the extent of faction was unable to avoid conflict. The throne was disputed by Charles of Durazzo, who was crowned but subsequently murdered by the queen's men; Elizabeth and Mary were imprisoned and Elizabeth put to death. Sigismund and Mary eventually established their position. Likewise there were serious problems of faction when Elizabeth of Luxemburg tried to secure the succession of Ladislas the Posthumous.[61] In such a situation, the success of a woman regent was most unlikely – only a strong king could dominate the factions.

The regency of queens in Scandinavia again stemmed from the political circumstances of the time, but they did not encounter the traumatic fortunes women met with in Hungary. Although queen-mothers were found acting as regent for young sons in the mid-thirteenth and early fourteenth centuries, it was the successful rule of Margaret I which set the pattern for later regencies. Margaret was the daughter of Waldemar Atterdag of Denmark and was born in 1353. She married Haakon VI of Norway when she was ten years old, and her son Olaf was born in 1371. The Danes chose Olaf as their king in 1375 on Waldemar's death, preferring him to Albert of Mecklenburg, king of Sweden, who was Olaf's cousin and the son of Margaret's elder sister. Margaret became regent of Denmark and also of Norway where Olaf succeeded his father in 1380. She made peace with the Hanseatic League and restored to Denmark the royal castles in Scania which had been handed over to the League at the time of the Peace of Stralsund of 1370. She regained Schleswig and Holstein, and defeated and captured Albert of Mecklenburg in 1389. Olaf had died two years before; Margaret was named guardian of Denmark and Norway, but did not rule on her own. She chose her great-nephew, Eric of Pomerania, as elected king of Denmark, Norway and Sweden, and he was crowned at Kalmar in 1397 in the presence of nobles of all three kingdoms. Margaret continued to be a strong force in government until her death in 1412, and did not allow Eric a free hand.

It is noteworthy that she never ruled in her own right. She recognised the necessity of a male ruler and the importance of working with the Scandinavian nobility, but saw her position in terms of daughter, wife and mother. Any regency in Denmark and Sweden was regarded as temporary, and the same was true of Norway in 1387. After 1397, Margaret's aim was to strengthen the Union of Kalmar. She wanted to develop the personal power of the ruler, while at the same time establishing good relations with the nobility. This policy comes out clearly in her instructions to Eric on his first visit to Norway in 1405.[62] Her success paved the way for other women within the Scandinavian ruling families in the fifteenth century. Margaret chose and trained Eric's wife, Philippa of Lancaster, and Philippa served as regent during Eric's absence of 1423–5, taking action over the Hanse and safeguarding the Union of Kalmar. Dorothea of Brandenburg, the wife of Christian I of Denmark, was involved in foreign diplomacy, military activity and coping with her husband's debts.[63]

Where women were allowed to be regents and guardians, their power emanated from their role as mothers. They had the opportunity to exercise political power within the family context, and some were able over a period of time to develop sustained policies for their kingdoms. Only a few were strong and ruthless enough to be able to defeat serious magnate opposition, and in this situation they needed to be sure that their regency was firmly grounded in their husband's designation or in acceptance by their marital family. The number of women regents is relatively small, but even fewer women had the chance of exercising power in their own right. Some women, like Margaret of Denmark and Berenguela of Castile, deliberately set their faces against this option. Others knew that certain kingdoms deliberately excluded women rulers and were not prepared to reverse the exclusion in an emergency, as Louis the Great of Hungary did with his two daughters. No woman would be considered as Holy Roman Emperor; such an exalted position was suitable only for a man.

The situation in France changed in the course of the fourteenth century. The need to consider the claims of a queen never arose before the early fourteenth century because all Capetian rulers invariably had a son and heir. Louis X's death without a son in 1316 gave rise to a novel situation. His posthumous son died soon after birth, and his daughter Joan might be considered of dubious legitimacy because of the scandal involving her mother, Blanche of Artois, who had been condemned for adultery.[64] The throne was seized by her uncle Philip V, and on his death without a son in 1322 his brother Charles IV seized power. The dynasty came to an end with Charles's death in 1328. The lawyers then decided that no claimant who traced his claim through a woman could be considered as a possible successor and this left the way open for the heir whose claim was transmitted by male ancestors, Philip VI of Valois. The subsequent declaration of Salic law forbidding female rights of inheritance to the Crown meant that women could never rule as queens in their own right, although their role as regents continued.

Elsewhere, female claims were more acceptable. In England, there was no female ruler between the twelfth and sixteenth centuries, but rights were transmitted through women. The Yorkists traced their claim through the daughter of Edward III's second son, Lionel of Clarence, who married into the Mortimer family; her granddaughter was the mother of Richard, Duke of York, and the grandmother of Edward IV. The kingdom of Naples under the Angevins accepted the rule of women regents and queens, although Joanna I's succession in 1343 was disputed by the Angevins of Hungary and by Charles of Durazzo (d. 1348). Neither she nor Joanna II (1414–35) can be regarded as successful queens and both were childless. Their failures were not simply due to gender. Tensions were already apparent in the kingdom in the reign of Robert the Wise (d. 1343) and the monarchy increasingly lost control over its territories and its nobility because of faction and conflict.[65]

There was always a danger that weak male and female rulers would be manipulated by favourites or relatives, and women were vulnerable sexually as well as politically. On the death of James II, the last Lusignan king of Cyprus, in 1473, his wife Caterina Corner inherited the crown and ruled until 1489. Their son had died at the age of one. Although Cyprus technically continued to be an independent kingdom, it was in reality ruled by Venice and the Corner family who built up their interests and fortunes in the island over the fifteenth century. In 1489, Caterina was recalled to Venice and resettled at Asolo.[66]

In Spain, female rights of inheritance were accepted more easily in theory than in practice. The proclamation by Peter IV of Aragon in 1347 of his daughter Constance as his heir was underpinned by the opinion of canon and civil lawyers who could see no reason against this. However, opponents pointed to the French model and to the exclusion of women from the succession by the wills of earlier Aragonese kings. The Union of Aragon ensured Constance's rejection as heir. From this time, women were excluded, although claims through women were accepted – Ferdinand of Antequera

(1412–16) was the son of John I of Castile and of Leonor, daughter of Peter IV.[67]

During the fifteenth century, the only woman to succeed as ruler of Castile was Isabella, sister of Henry IV (d. 1474).[68] She was recognised as heir to the throne by her brother in 1468, in preference to the king's daughter Juana who was suspected of being illegitimate, and she agreed to abide by Henry's choice of husband. In fact, she made her own choice when she married Ferdinand of Aragon in 1469. Henry IV retaliated by proclaiming his daughter as his heir and on his death Isabella had to fight for her right to rule. She was established as undisputed queen in 1479. Her rule is often seen as a partnership with her husband, but it is evident that she had her own initiatives and policies. Her marriage to Ferdinand established a personal union between Aragon and Castile, with each partner dominant in the kingdom each had inherited. Isabella had the right to have the final say in decisions in Castile, while acting as her husband's consort in Aragon. Contemporaries commented on Isabella's qualities: her consciousness of her royal rights, her energy and capacity for hard work, and her love of justice, which was possibly greater than her husband's. Isabella was also concerned for moral reform and was guided by Francisco Jimenez de Cisneros, her choice as archbishop of Toledo. The policy of crusade against Granada and the line taken towards Muslims and Jews had deep roots in late medieval Castilian history. As a result of their joint rule, Isabella and Ferdinand reversed the failures of their immediate predecessors, strengthened the monarchy, and set their two kingdoms on the path which Spain was to pursue in the sixteenth century. In politics, Isabella broke the accepted mould for a medieval queen, but in one respect she and Ferdinand failed, in that their son did not grow up to succeed them.

The opportunities for noblewomen and queens to play a public and political role varied widely. Law and tradition played a major part in determining the roles which these women undertook. In some respects, the opportunities open to noblewomen and queens became more restricted in the later Middle Ages, although in Germany and northern Italy the opportunities were already limited in the early thirteenth century. Even in the regions where women were allowed to take on a political role, family circumstances might well preclude this. Many powerful widows lived in retirement. Agnes of Habsburg, widowed in 1301 on the death of Andrew III of Hungary, left Hungary and settled by the monastery of Königsfelden, founded by herself and her mother. She adopted a religious way of life, but also exercised considerable influence over the Habsburg family and local politics.[69] She typifies a very large number of high-born women who found that they could exercise power most effectively by bringing persuasion to bear on their male kinsmen.

It was taken for granted that the noblewoman or queen would enjoy a lavish lifestyle and conform to contemporary expectations of splendour and display. Her power depended at least partly on her ability to impress, and she advertised her status through costly possessions and residences as well as by means of gifts to the Church and commemoration of members of her family. She had her own cultural interests, which her wealth and taste allowed her to follow up through her employment of writers, artists and craftsmen. These aspects of the noble life will be addressed in the next chapter in the context of laywomen's patronage of the arts.

Notes

1 R.H. Hilton, *The English Peasantry in the Later Middle Ages* (Oxford, 1975), p. 105; J.M. Bennett, *Women in the Medieval English Countryside. Gender and Household in Brigstock before the Plague* (Oxford, 1987), pp. 22–6; Public Record Office (London), SC6/844/8,9.
2 E. Ewan, *Townlife in Fourteenth-Century Scotland* (Edinburgh, 1990), p. 128.
3 E. Uitz, *Women in the Medieval Town*, (trans.) S. Marnie (London, 1990), pp. 98–9; J. Klassen, 'Household composition in medieval Bohemia', *JMH* 16 (1990), pp. 71–2.
4 M. Warner, *Joan of Arc, the Image of Female Heroism* (London, 1981). See later, pp. 201, 211, 226–7 for other examples of prophecy.
5 The importance of 'power as process' is emphasised by P. Stafford, 'Emma: the powers of the queen in the eleventh century', in A.J. Duggan (ed.), *Queens and Queenship in Medieval Europe* (Woodbridge, 1997), pp. 10–11.
6 See earlier, pp. 36–9, 62–4 for discussions of inheritance and dower. Elisabetta, widow of Carlo Malatesta, had a share in the government of Rimini after his death in 1429; P.J. Jones, *The Malatesta of Rimini and the Papal State. A Political History* (Cambridge, 1974), pp. 168, 173.
7 E.g. in England: R.E. Archer, 'Rich old ladies: the problem of late medieval dowagers', in A. Pollard (ed.), *Property and Politics: Essays in Later Medieval English History* (Gloucester, 1984), pp. 15–35; M. Altschul, *A Baronial Family in Medieval England: the Clares, 1217–1314* (Baltimore, 1965), p. 100.
8 M.K. Jones and M.G. Underwood, *The King's Mother. Lady Margaret Beaufort, Countess of Richmond and Derby* (Cambridge, 1992), pp. 40–1, 58–60; D. Nicholas, *Medieval Flanders* (New York, 1992), pp. 156–7.
9 F.M. Powicke, *King Henry III and the Lord Edward. The Community of the Realm in the Thirteenth Century*, 2 vols (Oxford, 1947), I, pp. 171–2, 176, 188–9; W.W. Shirley (ed.), *Royal and Other Historical Letters Illustrative of the Reign of Henry III*, 2 vols (Rolls Series, London, 1862–6), I, pp. 114–15; H.G. Richardson, 'The marriage and coronation of Isabella of Angoulême', *EHR* 61 (1946), p. 297; B. Wolffe, *Henry VI* (London, 1981), p. 45.
10 R. Gibbons, 'Isabeau of Bavaria, queen of France (1385–1422): the creation of a historical villainess', *TRHS* sixth series 6 (1996), pp. 54–70, 73.
11 J.M. Klassen (ed.), *The Letters of the Rožmberk Sisters: Noblewomen in Fifteenth-Century Bohemia* (Woodbridge, 2001), p. 17; A. Ryder, *Alfonso the Magnanimous King of Aragon, Naples and Sicily, 1396–1458* (Oxford, 1990), p. 218; P. Lock, *The Franks in the Aegean* (London, 1995), pp. 37, 58–9.
12 M.A.E. Wood, *Letters of Royal and Illustrious Ladies of Great Britain from the Commencement of the Twelfth Century to the Close of the Reign of Queen Mary*, 3 vols (London, 1846), I, p. 86.
13 J.C. Parsons, 'Mothers, daughters, marriage, power: some Plantagenet evidence, 1150–1500', in J.C. Parsons (ed.), *Medieval Queenship* (Stroud, 1994), p. 63; M. Prestwich, *Edward I* (London, 1988), pp. 315, 321, 325–6. The marriage did not in fact take place.

14 N. de Wailly (ed.), *Jean Sire de Joinville, Histoire de St Louis, Credo et Lettre à Louis X* (Paris, 1874), pp. 330–3; G. Sivéry, *Blanche de Castille* (Paris, 1990), pp. 203–7.

15 M.W. Labarge, *Women in Medieval Life. A Small Sound of the Trumpet* (London, 1986), pp. 56–7.

16 Sivéry, *Blanche de Castille*, pp. 40–1; M.D. Legge (ed.), *Anglo-Norman Letters and Petitions from All Souls MS 182* (Oxford, 1941), pp. 73–4, 353–4, 360–2, 372–3; Wood, *Letters of Royal and Illustrious Ladies*, pp. 80–1; F.C. Hingeston (ed.), *Royal and Historical Letters during the Reign of Henry IV*, 2 vols (Rolls Series, London, 1860), II, pp. 83, 87, 92, 96, 99.

17 M. Howell, *Eleanor of Provence. Queenship in Thirteenth-Century England* (Oxford, 1998), pp. 50–4.

18 C. Monro (ed.), *Letters of Queen Margaret of Anjou and Bishop Beckington and Others, Written in the Reigns of Henry V and Henry VI* (Camden Society old series 86, 1863), pp. 89–99, 100–1, 106–9, 117–18, 122–3, 126–8, 134–41, 156–65.

19 M. Vale, *The Princely Court. Medieval Courts and Culture in North-West Europe 1270–1380* (Oxford, 2001), pp. 125–6.

20 R. Hajdu, 'The position of noblewomen in the *pays des coutumes*, 1100–1300', *JFH* 5 (1980), p. 127.

21 William Caxton, *The Book of the Knight of the Tower*, (ed.) M.Y. Offord (EETS supplementary series 2, 1971), pp. 35–8.

22 P. Contamine, *La noblesse au royaume de France de Philippe le Bel à Louis XII. Essai de synthèse* (Paris, 1997), pp. 217–18.

23 B. Bedos-Rezak, 'Women, seals and power in medieval France, 1150–1350', in B. Bedos-Rezak, *Form and Order in Medieval France. Studies in Social and Quantitative Sigillography* (Aldershot, 1993), pp. 65–6, 68, 71–2; B. Bedos-Rezak, 'Sceaux seigneuriaux et structures sociales en Dauphiné de 1170 à 1349', in ibid., pp. 38–9; C.H. Hunter Blair, 'Armorials on English seals from the twelfth to the sixteenth centuries', *Archaeologia* second series 39 (1943), p. 21.

24 A. Leguai, *Les Ducs de Bourbon pendant la crise monarchique du quinzième siècle* (Paris, 1962), pp. 35–9, 84, 87–104, 130, 191–4, 199–201.

25 C.D. Ross, 'The household accounts of Elizabeth Berkeley, Countess of Warwick, 1420–1', *Transactions of the Bristol and Gloucestershire Archaeological Society* 70 (1951), pp. 81–105.

26 R. Vaughan, *Philip the Bold. The Formation of the Burgundian State* (London, 1962), pp. 38, 114, 151–2; R. Vaughan, *John the Fearless. The Growth of Burgundian Power* (London, 1966), pp. 15–16, 173–92; R. Vaughan, *Valois Burgundy* (London, 1975), pp. 76, 82; C. Weightman, *Margaret of York Duchess of Burgundy 1446–1503* (Stroud, 1989), pp. 63, 76, 102–22.

27 N. Davis (ed.), *Paston Letters and Papers of the Fifteenth Century*, 2 vols (Oxford, 1971, 1976), I, pp. 126–31.

28 *Calendar of Patent Rolls, 1340–3* (London, 1900), pp. 77, 126; ibid., *1350–4* (London, 1907), pp. 362–3, 506; ibid., *1354–8* (London, 1910), pp. 48, 51, 170, 203, 409, 422, 460.

29 F.W. Maitland (ed.), *Bracton's Note Book*, 3 vols (London, 1887), III, pp. 248–9; Vale, *The Princely Court*, p. 29.

30 J.G. Edwards (ed.), *Calendar of Ancient Correspondence concerning Wales* (Board of Celtic Studies, University of Wales History and Law Series 2, Cardiff, 1935), p. 29.

31 R.I. Burns, 'Daughter of Abú Zayd, last Almohad ruler of Valencia: the family and Christian seignory of Alda Ferrándis 1236–1300', *Viator* 24 (1993), pp. 143–87.

32 R. Boutruche, *La crise d'une société. Seigneurs et paysans du Bordelais pendant la guerre de cent ans* (Paris, 1947), p. 240.

33 G. Fourquin, *Les campagnes de la région Parisienne à la fin du moyen âge, du milieu du treizième siècle au début du seizième siècle* (Paris, 1964), p. 254; J.M. Bak, 'Queens as scapegoats in medieval Hungary', in Duggan (ed.), *Queens and Queenship*, p. 231.

34 J. Longnon (ed.), *Livre de la conqueste de la princée de l'Amorée* (Paris, 1911), pp. 120–3; J. Schmitt (ed.), *The Chronicle of Morea* (Groningen, 1967), pp. 290–9; K.M. Setton (ed.), *A History of the Crusades*, 6 vols (Madison, Wisconsin, 1955–89), II, R.L. Wolff and H.W. Hazard (eds), *The Later Crusades, 1189–1311*, pp. 246–8; Lock, *The Franks in the Aegean*, p. 305.

35 British Library, London, Harley MS 1240, fos 86v–87r; translated in J.C. Ward (ed. and trans.), *Women of the English Nobility and Gentry 1066–1500* (Manchester, 1995), pp. 116–19.

36 A.K. Kaminsky and E.D. Johnson, 'To restore honor and fortune: "The autobiography of Leonor López de Córdoba"', in D.C. Stanton (ed.), *The Female Autograph. Theory and Practice of Autobiography from the Tenth to the Twentieth Century* (Chicago, 1987), pp. 70–80; E.A. Petroff (ed.), *Medieval Women's Visionary Literature* (Oxford, 1986), pp. 302–3, 329–34.

37 Nicholas, *Medieval Flanders*, pp. 151–61, 176–81; T. Evergates, *Feudal Society in the Bailliage of Troyes under the Counts of Champagne, 1152–1284* (Baltimore, 1975), p. 3.

38 J-M. Richard, *Mahaut Comtesse d'Artois et de Bourgogne* (Paris, 1887), pp. 3–5, 15.

39 Ibid., pp. 16–42.

40 Ibid., pp. 42–7, 60–8, 414–16; G. Espinas and H. Pirenne (eds), *Recueil de documents rélatifs à l'histoire de l'industrie drapière en Flandre*, 7 vols (Brussels, 1906–66), I, pp. 61–2, 79–82, 125–6.

41 Christine de Pisan, *The Treasure of the City of Ladies or The Book of the Three Virtues*, (ed.) S. Lawson (Harmondsworth, 1985), pp. 35–79.

42 T.F. Ruiz, *The City and the Realm: Burgos and Castile 1080–1492* (Aldershot, 1992), article 13, pp. 109–10.

43 M.C. Facinger, 'A study of medieval queenship: Capetian France, 987–1237', *Studies in Medieval and Renaissance History* 5 (1968), pp. 17–20; C.R. Sherman, 'The queen in Charles V's *Coronation Book*: Jeanne de Bourbon and the *Ordo ad reginam benedicendam*', *Viator* 8 (1977), pp. 255–98; A.D. Hedeman, 'Copies in context: the coronation of Charles V in his *Grandes Chroniques de France*', in J.M. Bak (ed.), *Coronations. Medieval and Early Modern Monarchic Ritual* (Berkeley, California, 1990), pp. 73–80.

44 Women were often associated with the north side of the church; R. Gilchrist, *Gender and Material Culture. The Archaeology of Religious Women* (London, 1994), pp. 133–5.

45 G. Conklin, 'Ingeborg of Denmark queen of France, 1193–1223', in Duggan (ed.), *Queens and Queenship*, pp. 39–52.

46 J. O'Callaghan, *A History of Medieval Spain* (Ithaca, New York, 1975), pp. 420, 423.

47 Sherman, 'The queen in Charles V's *Coronation Book*', pp. 288–9.

48 J. Dunbabin, *Charles I of Anjou. Power, Kingship and State-Making in Thirteenth-Century Europe* (Harlow, 1998), p. 200; M. Thibault, *Isabeau de Bavière reine de France. La jeunesse 1370–1405* (Paris, 1903), pp. 118–28, 433–6.

49 Thibault, *Isabeau*, pp. 130–63, 437–43; L.M. Bryant, 'The medieval entry ceremony at Paris', in Bak (ed.), *Coronations*, pp. 88–118.

50 M.D. Harris (ed.), *The Coventry Leet Book*, 2 vols (EETS original series 134–5, 138, 146, 1907–13), I, pp. 285–92. The Cardinal Virtues comprised righteousness, temperance, strength and prudence. The Nine Worthies of chivalry were Hector

of Troy, Alexander the Great, Joshua, David, Judas Maccabeus, Julius Caesar, Arthur, Charlemagne and Godfrey of Bouillon.

51 A. Crawford, 'The piety of late medieval English queens', in C.M. Barron and C. Harper-Bill (eds), *The Church in Pre-Reformation Society. Essays in honour of F.R.H. Du Boulay* (Woodbridge, 1985), pp. 51–3.

52 J. Freed, *The Friars and German Society in the Thirteenth Century* (Cambridge, Massachusetts, 1977), pp. 75, 164.

53 De Wailly (ed.), *Joinville, Histoire de St Louis*, pp. 216–19.

54 T. Earenfight, 'Absent kings: queens as political partners in the medieval crown of Aragon', in T. Earenfight, *Queenship and Political Power in Medieval and Early Modern Spain* (Aldershot, 2005), pp. 34–5, 40–6; T. Earenfight, *The King's Other Body. Maria of Castile and the Crown of Aragon* (Philadelphia, 2010), pp. 1–9, 42–66, 71–130.

55 Gibbons, 'Isabeau of Bavaria', p. 34.

56 De Wailly (ed.), *Joinville, Histoire de St Louis*, pp. 40–5, 62–3.

57 A. Poulet, 'Capetian women and the regency: the genesis of a vocation', in Parsons (ed.), *Medieval Queenship*, pp. 108–15; H. Lightman, 'Political power and the queen of France: Pierre Dupuy's treatise on regency governments', *Canadian Journal of History* 21 (1986), pp. 299–312; Sivéry, *Blanche de Castille*, pp. 87–90, 124–69; Sherman, 'The queen in Charles V's *Coronation Book*', p. 288.

58 Howell, *Eleanor of Provence*, pp. 111–27; R.A. Griffiths, *The Reign of Henry VI. The Exercise of Royal Authority, 1422–61* (London, 1981), pp. 722–3.

59 O'Callaghan, *A History of Medieval Spain*, pp. 541, 546, 550–1, 566, 605, 607; Wood, *Letters of Royal and Illustrious Ladies*, I, pp. 85–8.

60 M. Shadis, 'Berenguela of Castile's political motherhood: the management of sexuality, marriage and succession', in J.C. Parsons and B. Wheeler (eds), *Medieval Mothering* (New York, 1996), pp. 335–58; M. Shadis, *Berenguela of Castile (1180–1246) and Political Women in the High Middle Ages* (Basingstoke and New York, 2009); J. Bianchini, *The Queen's Hand. Power and Authority in the Reign of Berenguela of Castile* (Philadelphia, 2012).

61 J.M. Bak, 'Roles and functions of queens in Arpádan and Angevin Hungary (1000–1386 A.D.)', in Parsons (ed.), *Medieval Queenship*, pp. 16, 20–1; J.M. Bak, 'Queens as scapegoats in medieval Hungary', in Duggan (ed.), *Queens and Queenship*, pp. 229–31; see earlier, p. 107.

62 I. Shovgaard-Petersen, 'Queenship in medieval Denmark', in Parsons (ed.), *Medieval Queenship*, pp. 33–9; S. Imsen, 'Late medieval Scandinavian queenship', in Duggan (ed.), *Queens and Queenship*, pp. 58–61.

63 Imsen, 'Late medieval Scandinavian queenship', pp. 55–6, 62–3; Shovgaard-Petersen, 'Queenship in medieval Denmark', p. 39.

64 The increased sanctification of monarchy in the thirteenth century precluded any successor who was illegitimate; C.T. Wood, 'Queens, queans and kingship: an inquiry into theories of royal legitimacy in late medieval England and France', in W.C. Jordan, B. McNab and T.F. Ruiz (eds), *Order and Innovation in the Middle Ages. Essays in honor of Joseph F. Strayer* (Princeton, 1976), pp. 385–7, 390–400.

65 Sancia of Majorca was regent for a short time after the death of her husband, Robert the Wise; Robert designated her in his will. R.G. Musto, 'Queen Sancia of Naples (1286–1345) and the Spiritual Franciscans', in J. Kirshner and S.F. Wemple (eds), *Women of the Medieval World. Essays in honor of John H. Mundy* (Oxford, 1985), pp. 187–90; Ryder, *Alfonso the Magnanimous*, pp. 16–17, 23–33, 77–8, 316.

66 B. Arbel, 'The reign of Caterina Corner (1473–89) as a family affair', in B. Arbel, *Cyprus, the Franks and Venice, Thirteenth to Sixteenth Centuries* (Aldershot, 2000), pp. 67–87.

67 O'Callaghan, *A History of Medieval Spain*, pp. 416, 432, 539, 543–4.
68 P.K. Liss, *Isabel the Queen. Life and Times* (Oxford, 1992); R. Menéndez Pidal, 'The significance of the reign of Isabella the Catholic, according to her contemporaries', in R. Highfield (ed.), *Spain in the Fifteenth Century 1369–1516* (London, 1972), pp. 385, 390–9, 401.
69 V. Honemann, 'A medieval queen and her stepdaughter: Agnes and Elizabeth of Hungary', in Duggan (ed.), *Queens and Queenship*, pp. 109–19.

9 Laywomen and the arts

Throughout the later Middle Ages, women are found among the patrons and practitioners of the arts. Their interests ranged over building, painting and sculpture, music, and books and literature. Yet the degree of their involvement can be difficult to establish. Although household accounts and contracts throw considerable light on particular works, their sporadic survival means that the details of many commissions are now unknown. Wills give information about women's books and precious objects, but by no means provide a full inventory and rarely say how and when the items were obtained. Occasionally, the portrait of a woman donor throws light on her role as patron. Moreover, by their very nature, many works of art have not survived. Fabrics, tapestries and wooden objects are perishable, plate was liable to be melted down, either in an emergency or to be refashioned according to later taste, and buildings were demolished or altered so as to conform to current styles and needs. Religious and literary works may survive only in later copies. Wars and religious and political upheavals in the modern period have contributed to further destruction. In assessing women's role in the arts, the historian can present only a partial picture. What is clear is that medieval women derived both interest and enjoyment from the arts.

Women patrons were mostly members of the elite, namely wealthy and patrician townswomen, and members of gentry, noble and royal families. Yet less powerful women also played a part in patronage, through combining with others of their parish, confraternity or guild; many churches of the later Middle Ages were built and furnished as a result of the co-operative efforts of both men and women. Men were in a much better legal and economic position to become patrons, however. Wives were restricted during marriage in that their resources were managed by their husbands. Patronage by married couples took place, but the degree of input by the wife is rarely known; it is usually not clear whether a husband's patronage was supported by his wife. The widow was in a much better position to exercise patronage through use of her dowry or inheritance. Yet her wishes might be circumscribed if her resources were too meagre to do more than support herself and her family, or if her family – or in northern Italy her *mundualdus* (legal guardian) – prevented her from executing her plans.

The reasons why a woman exercised patronage have to be set in the context of her life and aspirations. From her own point of view, whether as a wife or more likely a widow, she had to consider her needs during her lifetime and her salvation after her death. She had her own tastes and preferences. The lifestyle of the elite, with its emphasis on splendour and display, and its demands for fine clothes, costly fabrics and tapestries, gold and silver plate, and elaborate ceremonial in daily life, religious worship and recreation, entailed patronage of skilled artists and craftsmen. Yet to see all this as only meeting the woman's individual needs is to take too narrow a view. She had her allotted place in society and was expected to fulfil it by displaying her social status and meeting its obligations. Inevitably, this involved patronage of those who could supply her demands. She had her own prestige and that of her peers in society to consider.

Much of her patronage was linked not just with her equals but with her family. During her lifetime, she might well be concerned with furthering the projects of father or husband and maintaining establishments associated with her natal or marital family over several generations. These projects included work on houses and castles, and religious and charitable foundations. Gifts to such foundations were likely to be most lavish when the woman had no children to succeed her. The most usual artistic project associated with the family, however, was the provision of tombs, whether for herself or for members of her family, and this was coupled with the ritual of burial and the provision of requiem masses for the soul of the deceased. The commissioning of the tomb provided suitable commemoration of the dead and also advertised the importance of the family; it safeguarded the reputation of the family for the future. For the majority of the elite, such commemoration was important in the context of the locality or region, but had a much wider significance with members of the higher nobility and royalty.

Fashion was an important element in patronage; it applied to all the arts and is particularly noticeable in tombs. Catherine King has shown how fashions varied among the Italian cities, with fine tombs being usual for lawyers in Bologna and Padua, and effigies of the dead being provided in Naples, as in other parts of the feudal world. Such portrayals were rarer in the republics of Venice and Florence.[1] Contemporary religious ideas also had an influence on fashion, and contempt of the body led to the depiction of decay on fifteenth-century English tombs.[2] The importance attached to the prayers of the poor was reflected in the carving of mourners on the sides of some late medieval tombs. Devotion to the saints was mirrored in tomb sculpture, as in the commissions of Mahaut of Artois.

Tapestries, plate and religious objects were purchased from master craftsmen, and purchasers had the power of choice over what they wanted, as was also the case with their purchase of books. Only the wealthiest women had craftsmen working within their households. Elizabeth de Burgh had goldsmiths in her household in the 1330s, making altar vessels, images, jewellery and plate, and from time to time she employed illuminators as well.[3] For major projects, it was usual to commission a mason, carpenter, painter, metalworker or other craftsman, and specify the project in detail. This gave the lady and her officials the opportunity to have a say in what she wanted and the chance of legal remedy if the terms of the commission were not met. It is only rarely that the lady's own views were documented, even though they may well have been important. The description in the will of 1439 of Isabella Despenser, Countess of Warwick, concerning the form her effigy was to take indicates that at least some women knew exactly what they wanted. She was to be depicted naked, with her hair cast back, and St Mary Magdalen placing her hands across her breast. On either side of her head were to be carved the figures of St John the Evangelist and St Anthony, and her coat of arms impaled with her husband's and supported by two griffins was to be placed at her feet. Poor men and women holding their rosaries were to be sculpted around the tomb.[4] Here, noble rank, contempt for the body, religious devotion and the hope of salvation were presented in combination.

The richness of the buildings and furnishings of the later medieval Church is well known and it was provided by the gifts and legacies of men and women, both religious and lay. Women played an important part in making and enhancing religious establishments, whether these were monasteries, cathedrals, parish churches or their own chapels. Such patronage is found among women of differing degrees of wealth and applies to building, painting, carving, metalwork and books. The range of involvement is particularly obvious in the case of building. At the bottom end of the scale, parishioners combined their resources in order to produce a church suited to their aspirations. Margery Koo in the mid-fifteenth century gave 6 shillings and 8 pence towards the elaborate Perpendicular porch of the parish church of Woolpit in Suffolk. Marion Fenkele, who wanted to be buried near the window which her husband had newly glazed in Stowmarket parish church, left £2 for the repair of the aisle of St Mary there, and 4 shillings towards the painting of St Christopher in the chapel at Gipping.[5] The painting has disappeared, but the porch at Woolpit remains as a splendid example of fifteenth-century work.

These examples of small-scale patronage can be contrasted with the work of Mahaut, Countess of Artois, whose wealth, family feeling and piety made her a lavish donor. She made gifts to religious houses and hospitals in Paris, such as 100 *livres parisis* to the Hôtel-Dieu in 1320 for repairs after a fire. She had a special devotion to St James and was present when the foundation stone was laid for the church and hospital of Saint-Jacques to which she later gave stained glass windows. Her main building projects were in her own county. As well as work on her residences, to be considered below, she rebuilt the convent of Poor Clares at St Omer in 1322 which had been founded by her father and herself. She was also responsible for building the Dominican nunnery of La Thieulloye at Arras, the hospital at Hesdin which opened to the sick in 1323, and the Carthusian monastery at Gosnay. Although relatively little of her work survives, her household accounts and contracts throw considerable light on the form and furnishings of the buildings. The 1324 account for installing the nuns at La Thieulloye and furnishing the convent amounted to just over 1,000 *livres parisis*.[6] Marion Fenkele, Margery Koo and Countess Mahaut represent the extremes of this type of patronage. Yet all three have elements in common: concern for both community and family as well as the wishes of the individual woman to carry out good works in the hope of gaining salvation.

Much of Mahaut's religious building took place in the 1320s, although donations and provision for the dead span her lifetime. Whether the spurt in building activity was galvanised by the death of her son and heir Robert in 1317 and the knowledge that her inheritance would pass to her daughter Jeanne, or by her victory over Robert of Artois is not known. However, childlessness is known to have acted as a spur for charity and patronage with certain medieval men and women. This was the case with Sibilia Cetto of Padua, who used her wealth to build the church and convent of St Francis and next to it a large hospital. Sibilia came of a mercantile and propertied family, and was married twice to doctors of law. She inherited her father's property, and her wealth and legal expertise were both important to her plans. Although her second husband, Baldo Bonafari, whom she married in 1393 when she was in her forties, acted as her agent, evidence during his exile from Padua between 1406 and 1413 and after his death in 1418 indicates that Sibilia was capable of carrying out her plans herself. As she had no child by either of her marriages, she could devote her wealth to the hospital, and Baldo was apparently happy to go along with this. The hospital's foundation stone was laid in 1414 and the contracts point to concern both for privacy and for high-quality materials and decoration in the quarters for men and women. Baldo completed the contracts for building the church, but the work was carried out after his death. Hospital, monastery and church were united by a portico along the facade. Baldo and Sibilia were buried in the church, Sibilia dressed in the habit of a Franciscan nun as she had requested.[7]

Many women contributed furnishings to churches, whether these were altar vessels, books or images. The amount expended on these gifts varied enormously according to the resources and social status of the donor, but a common factor exists in the desire of many women to perform this type of good work. The idea of community contribution comes out especially with those women who could afford only a small gift, as seen above with Margery Koo and Marion Fenkele. As well as groups of parishioners, a guild might decide to pay for a particular work. In the early sixteenth century, a sisterhood at Perugia commissioned an altarpiece of the Nativity for their chapel in the church of St Anthony; the group assisted women who wished to marry and also gave help at childbirth, so the Nativity was a fitting subject. On the predella of the altarpiece was the figure of the Virgin Mary sheltering the women of the sisterhood under her cloak, and flanked by saints, including St Anne.[8] Such group commissions can be paralleled by paintings commissioned by nuns, as at the convent of Poor Clares of Santa Maria di Monteluce at Perugia where there was considerable building work on the church and convent buildings in the mid-fifteenth century, and decoration of the external church, used by the public, with works of art.[9]

Gifts of paintings and other items by individual women are found across Europe. In 1392, the widow Domina Tema, who had married into the Sismundi family of Pisa, included among her religious bequests the sum of 40 florins for a fine panel painting of St Basil and other saints, to be placed above St Basil's altar in the church of St Cecilia. Matilda, Countess of Nevers (d. 1257), gave stained glass to the cathedral at Bourges. Philippa, Countess of March (d. 1381), left most of her chapel furnishings to the abbey of Bisham, founded by her father who was buried there. These comprised vestments, service books, chalices, cruets, silver chandeliers, paintings and embroideries, together with a gold tablet which she had purchased and two silver basins with the arms of Mortimer and Montagu, her marital and natal families. All these were to serve the altar of St Anne in front of which she was to be buried. Mahaut, Countess of Artois, bought alabaster images from Jean Pépin de Huy of Paris for herself and for religious houses. She also purchased ivory objects from Jean le Scelleur; in 1325, an ivory statue of the Virgin Mary under a canopy cost 19 *livres* and a cedar cross with Christ's figure in ivory 8 *livres*.[10]

Many of these gifts would have had no identifying mark and it would probably soon be forgotten who had given them. Some donors, however, wanted to be remembered, presumably in the hope that prayers would continue to be said for themselves and their families. The arms on the basins given by Countess Philippa and the depiction of the sisters sheltering under the Virgin's cloak show that these patrons wanted their donations to be remembered. Pictures of donors are to be found on paintings and stained glass. John and Catherine Goldale were painted along with the four Fathers of the Church on the pulpit at Burnham Norton in Norfolk, with an inscription asking for prayers. Eleanor Despenser was possibly represented as the small naked figure in the east window at Tewkesbury abbey; she probably made a major contribution to the rebuilding of the east end of the church in the 1320s and 1330s. The portrait of Altabella Avogaro as an old woman at prayer appears on the 1484 altarpiece in her funerary chapel at the church of San Fermo Maggiore in Verona.[11]

While many women could afford to contribute to the fabric and ornaments of a church, only the wealthy were able to afford a tomb within the building. It was with the tomb that the elements of individual, family and fashion coalesced. The tomb was the way to bring out the social position and importance of both family and individual and to secure remembrance for the future, in some cases down to the present day. By providing the tomb, and sometimes its setting of a family chapel, the woman was able to patronise high-class and up-to-date craftsmanship while she carried out her obligations to her family. In a few cases, a new foundation was made to serve as the family mausoleum. In 1323, Elizabeth Richenza, the Polish widow of Wenceslas II of Bohemia, founded a Cistercian nunnery in Old Brno, intending the church to be the burial place of herself and her family; she was buried there in 1335.[12] Some widows carried out their husbands' plans for commemoration, as when Andreuccia Acciaiuoli rebuilt the old choir of the church of Santa Maria Novella at Florence to serve as the family chapel in the 1380s according to the plan of her husband, Mainardo Cavalcanti, but she seems to have made the decision that the stained glass windows should depict the lives of Christ and St John the Baptist, and she added her own and her father's patron saints, St Andrew and St James the Great, to the altarpiece. She took care that the tomb's inscription should praise her husband's service to Queen Joanna of Naples.[13]

Mahaut, Countess of Artois, was fully alive to her responsibilities to her family and took steps to ensure commemoration. She sent friars to find her father's body after the battle of Courtrai and had it taken in a magnificent cortège across Artois before its burial in December 1304 at the abbey of Maubuisson; this Cistercian nunnery, founded by Blanche of Castile, was often used as the burial place of members of the royal family and their kindred. Several years later, Mahaut had a tomb made for her father's second wife, Agnes of Bourbon. In 1310, her husband's body was moved to the abbey of Charlieu where he was reburied next to his parents. Her son Robert was buried in the church of the Cordeliers in Paris, and Mahaut herself at Maubuisson near her father, although her heart was placed next to her son in Paris.

Mahaut commissioned the tombs of her husband Otto and her son Robert from the Paris craftsman, Jean Pépin de Huy. The contract of 1312 for Otto's tomb specified a marble chest with an alabaster effigy of Otto, depicted as an armed knight with sword and shield. A lion was to lie under his feet and two angels were to be placed on either side of the pillow under his head, with 140 *livres parisis* to be paid for the effigy. The tomb chest was to be arcaded, with figures in the arcades; no detail is given, but they may have represented poor mourners or possibly ancestral figures. Other craftsmen were employed to depict the arms on the shield and to paint and gild the tomb which was then to be sent to the abbey of Charlieu. In the case of Robert, Jean Pépin de Huy contracted to make the tomb for 440 *livres parisis*.[14]

The provision of tombs had an influence on the transmission of artistic styles. After Isabella of Portugal married Philip the Good, Duke of Burgundy, in 1430, she kept in touch with her natal family, although she never revisited her homeland. She sent Flemish works of art to decorate the family funerary chapel in the abbey of Batalha. She also contributed financially to the tomb of her nephew James in the church of San Miniato near Florence, although she had no say in the design. For her marital family, Isabella acted on her husband's behalf to commission a tomb for Louis de Male, his wife and his daughter Margaret of Flanders in the church of St Peter at Lille. Margaret of Flanders was her husband's grandmother and it was through her that the county of Flanders had come into the possession of the dukes of Burgundy. Isabella negotiated the contract for the tomb with Jacques de Gérynes, coppersmith of Brussels. Louis de Male was to be depicted in armour, with his wife and daughter on each side. Around the tomb there was to be a latten arcade with figures of Louis's descendants, identified by their heraldic shields and names. The total cost of the tomb came to 2,000 gold crowns.[15]

Although women had fewer resources and opportunities than men to exercise religious patronage, their role was by no means negligible. The same can be said of their secular patronage, which reflected their social expectations and lifestyle. They desired up-to-date residences and splendid furnishings. Although ancestral connections sometimes had a bearing on secular patronage, the wife, or more probably the widow, was principally concerned with her immediate needs and those of her family. Self-advertisement was, if anything, more important than with religious patronage.

Mahaut, Countess of Artois, carried out building work on many of her residences and in some cases, as at Hesdin and at the family residence in Paris, continued work begun by her father. She rebuilt the castle of Bapaume almost entirely, and all her castles underwent alteration and regular repair. The castle of Conflans was also enlarged and possibly nearly completely rebuilt. Contracts with painters indicate that the interiors of her residences were highly decorated. The agreement with the Paris painter, Peter of Brussels, for decorating a gallery at Conflans provided for the painting of two episodes from the life of her father, one a knightly scene with members of the court throwing two barrels of wine into a fountain (the story behind this is unknown) and the other a scene of galleys and armed ships at sea, probably referring to his expedition to Sicily. An inscription was to be placed above the painting, and the agreed cost came to 48 *livres parisis*.[16] When work such as this is set alongside Mahaut's patronage of cloth merchants and mercers, embroiderers, tapestry makers, jewellers and metal workers of all kinds, it is clear how culturally influential she was. She was by no means unique in her activity, however. Bonne de Bourbon, wife of Amadeus VI of Savoy, was largely responsible for building the house at Ripaille which has been described as the first house in Savoy to be built for comfort rather than defence. In England, Elizabeth de Burgh refurbished and added to her castles at Clare in Suffolk and at Usk, and her house at Great Bardfield in Essex, and decided towards the end of her life to build herself a house in London.[17]

Two aspects of secular patronage need to be looked at particularly, namely painting and books. Patronage of painters by noblewomen and queens was found throughout the later Middle Ages as part of the desire to live in a splendid and colourful setting, and it was also essential on ceremonial occasions. In the fifteenth century, however, certain Renaissance women patronised individual artists with the aim of building up a collection of their works. Wives and widows took their place alongside male members of their families in commissioning works of art. Alternatively, they were concerned to develop the style of local artists along lines which they preferred. Bianca Maria Visconti, wife of Francesco Sforza of Milan, sent Zanetto Bugatto to the studio of Rogier van der Weyden in 1463 so that he might benefit from Rogier's teaching. Her letter reflects the high opinion she had of Rogier's work.[18]

The best known woman patron of art is Isabella d'Este, wife of Gian Francesco II Gonzaga of Mantua, who began to plan her collection for the room known as the Grotta in her palace at Mantua in 1496.[19] She wrote to the leading painters of the day, specifying what she wanted, and the letters testify to her demands as patron, as well as to the reluctance of certain painters to do her bidding. She was not lavish in payment. Mantegna, the court painter at Mantua, provided her with two allegorical paintings, but she had difficulty in securing a work from his brother-in-law, Giovanni Bellini of Venice. In the spring of 1501, Bellini was fully occupied with his work on the Doge's palace and he disliked the allegorical subject suggested by Isabella, especially if it was to hang beside Mantegna's paintings. About eighteen months later, Isabella decided to have a picture of the Nativity, with St John the Baptist, instead; Bellini painted a picture of the Virgin and Child and St John the Baptist. Isabella received the painting in 1504 and paid Bellini's minimum price of 50 ducats, but she continued to badger him for an allegorical picture. Bellini pointed out that he disliked a detailed specification, preferring to give his imagination a free rein.

Isabella was successful in obtaining a painting of the Battle of Love and Chastity from Perugino, although it was nearly three years before the work was delivered. She was advised by scholars as to the pagan myths, and the contract laid down in great detail what the painting should contain. Attention was focused on the battle between Pallas Athene and Diana, representing chastity, against Venus and Cupid, the former supported by nymphs, and the latter with a following of fauns, satyrs and cupids. Even the background was not left to the imagination of the painter; the olive tree and the myrtle were to be included as emblems of Pallas and Venus, and the battle was to be watched by Jupiter, Mercury and others standing on the bank of a river or by the sea. One hundred gold florins were to be paid for the work. Difficulties arose over Perugino not following the instructions to the letter and over the size of the figures, since Isabella wanted the paintings in the Grotta to match. She grew impatient and her letter acknowledging receipt of the picture was not enthusiastic; the picture was well drawn and coloured but not well finished, and she would have preferred it to have been painted in oils.

Leonardo da Vinci had made a charcoal drawing of Isabella when he visited Mantua in 1500, and in the years that followed she was anxious to secure a work from him. She asked for a religious subject but did not attempt to tie him down to detail. However, the painting she hoped for never appeared. She failed to obtain a painting from Giorgione, and hoped that Raphael would paint a life-size portrait of her son Federico. The letters from her and her agents show how persistent and nagging a patron could be and how finicky as to the contents of a painting. The desire to put pressure on the painter to get the work done quickly is apparent. On the other hand, if artists had plenty of work they could afford to be choosy over commissions. Bellini, it appears, wanted to keep in favour with Isabella, while at the same time stalling over carrying out her wishes.[20]

Such patronage as Isabella's was possible only for wealthy and powerful women. Many of the elite, however, appreciated art through manuscript illumination, and an increasing number came to own books in the fourteenth and fifteenth centuries. Bell argues that whereas twelve European women are known to have owned a single book each in the thirteenth century, forty-one did so in the fourteenth and seventy-six in the fifteenth century. During the fifteenth century, twenty-nine women owned between two and ten books, thirteen between eleven and fifty, and thirteen between fifty-one and two hundred. Gabrielle de la Tour, Countess of Montpensier, had 200 volumes in her possession when she died in 1474.[21] These must be regarded as minimum figures; there are few inventories of books, and wills and household accounts do not provide the total number of works in a lady's library. Moreover, research continues to uncover new evidence of book ownership.

During the fourteenth and fifteenth centuries, growing numbers of elite women were able to read. Literacy indicates growing trust and use of the written word, and this is also seen in women's readiness to express themselves more freely in letters than they had done earlier. Letters became a normal vehicle for conducting business, keeping up with friends and family and conveying news.[22] Furthermore, the book became an integral part of their lifestyle. According to the Sachsenspiegel, compiled about 1215, it was acceptable for women to own devotional books, and women of the later Middle Ages came to possess psalters and Books of Hours in increasing numbers, while at the same time enjoying histories and romances for recreation. Books read aloud became the focus for a social gathering, while mothers found books invaluable not only for teaching their daughters to read but also for inculcating religious and moral values and preparing the girl for adult life. Books became affordable to a wider circle in the fifteenth century as manuscript books became less expensive and printed works began to appear.[23] Many works, however, remained luxury items, to be displayed rather than handled. The whole book with its illuminations and binding was an object of beauty and value.

The books which women owned covered a variety of subjects, but devotional works appear to have been especially important. Books of Hours were designed to meet the needs of an individual man or woman; the person commissioning the work could make a choice of the prayers or saints' lives to be included, and also the subject matter of the illustrations. The Book of Hours replaced the psalter as the private devotional work in the fourteenth and fifteenth centuries. It comprised the Little Office of the Virgin Mary, a collection of eight services to be said at set times by day or night. The services had the same names as the Office used by the clergy and by monks and nuns, but were shorter; they included psalms, readings and hymns. The Book of Hours also usually included a calendar of saints' days and festivals, the Office of the Dead, the seven penitential psalms and individual prayers. Much of the material was in Latin, but there are instances of the whole book being written in the vernacular.[24] Some of the Books of Hours were works of art in their own right, such as the Hours of Jeanne d'Evreux, wife of Charles IV of France, with its illustrations by the Paris artist, Jean Pucelle. Many books depicted the owner at prayer, as in the late fifteenth-century Hours of Joanna of Castile who is shown kneeling in front of a picture of the Virgin and Child with her patron saint, St John the Evangelist, beside her. Some patrons were shown receiving communion; a Book of Hours by the Master of the Munich Golden Legend of about 1435 thus depicted an anonymous female patron, probably with her husband and sons in the margin, and her pet ermine at the bottom of the page.[25]

Devotional works, and also histories and romances, were appreciated on several levels. As well as objects of beauty and value, text and paintings gave the reader information, entertainment and the opportunity to meditate and pray. Some of the illustrations probably provoked wonder and laughter. Women enjoyed their books and did not regard them simply as objects to be collected and admired. Evidence survives to show that they made use of them. Mahaut Countess of Artois ordered a desk for reading; Isabeau of Bavaria appointed Catherine de Villiers to take charge of her books and a trunk was purchased so that she could take them on her journeys. On the death of Jean, Duke of Berry, in 1416, his daughter Marie, Duchess of Bourbon, asked for forty titles from his collection.[26]

Mahaut of Artois likewise took books with her on her travels. She used religious works in the education of her children, spending 70 *sous* on a psalter for her daughter Blanche, then aged about seven. Mahaut's tastes ranged widely. In 1305, she had the *Croniques des Rois de France* copied and illuminated, and also possessed an abridged version. She enjoyed romances, making purchases of several at Arras in 1308 and 1310, including the *Histoire de Troyes*, *Perceval* and *Tristan*. She had her own copy of *The Travels of Marco Polo*. Her tastes changed after her son's death and she restricted herself to religious works on which she spent a considerable amount; a two-volume Bible, bound in red leather and purchased in 1325, cost 15 *livres*. She also possessed volumes of *Lives of the Saints* and *Lives of the Church Fathers*, three Books of Hours, the Miracles of the Virgin Mary, and a French translation of *The Consolation of Philosophy* by Boethius.[27]

The Valois dukes of Burgundy were famous for their libraries, and Margaret of York, third wife of Charles the Bold, continued the Burgundian tradition of patronage and collection. Some twenty-six works can be associated with her, several of them copied from books in the ducal library and all of them in French. Two were historical works, *Les Chroniques de Flandre* and Jean Mansel's *La Fleur des Hystoires*. The rest were religious and devotional works and included sermons by Jean Gerson and others, Books of Hours, works by the Fathers of the Church, and devotional and moral volumes. She also owned *The Consolation of Philosophy* by Boethius. Some of the works were translated for her from Latin. Her lives of the saints included the *Life of St Colette* who had received support from an earlier duchess. These books were finely written and illuminated. Nicholas Finet's devotional work, *Benoit Seront les Misericordieux* (Blessed are the merciful), was written at the Carthusian monastery at Herines and illustrated by Jean Dreux, whose two miniatures depicted Margaret performing the works of mercy and kneeling at prayer in a Brussels landscape.[28] Margaret's books were very much in the medieval tradition, just as Isabella d'Este's patronage has to be considered in the context of the Italian Renaissance.

Although the wills of Englishwomen often concentrated on the bequest of religious books, they enjoyed secular works as well. Alice Chaucer, Duchess of Suffolk, is known to have owned religious service books and didactic works, but she also possessed a French romance and Christine de Pizan's *Book of the City of Ladies*. She may have been jointly responsible with her husband in commissioning a copy of Lydgate's *Siege of Thebes*. About a century earlier, Isabella of France, the widow of Edward II, owned *chansons de geste*, a romance of the Trojan war, and three Arthurian romances. It was not only the higher nobility and royalty who owned romances. Anne Paston, for example, had a copy of Lydgate's *Siege of Thebes*. Similar patterns of book ownership are found among nuns as among laywomen. Eleanor de Bohun, Duchess of Gloucester, divided her books among her son and three daughters, the youngest of whom was a Minoress.[29]

Book ownership points to women's importance in the transmission of authors and works. This applied especially to queens and members of the nobility who brought books to their new home on marriage. The Book of Hours of Marie de St Pol, Countess of Pembroke, may well have been brought from Paris when she came to England as a bride. Beatrice of Naples, wife of Matthias Corvinus of Hungary, was criticised for her patronage of foreign painters and writers. Isabella of Portugal derived her interest in books from her natal family as well as from her husband, and was responsible for cultural transmission between Burgundy and Portugal. She sent Christine de Pizan's *Treasure of the City of Ladies* or *The Book of the Three Virtues* to her niece, the queen of Portugal, where it was translated into Portuguese, and she arranged for the Portuguese translation of *The Imitation of Christ* by Thomas à Kempis. *The Triumph of Ladies* by Juan Rodriguez de la Camera was translated from Portuguese into French. Cultural transmission also took place when a library was broken up. In addition to the books of the duke of Berry which passed to Marie, Duchess of Bourbon, the *Très Riches Heures* was inherited by his daughter Bonne, Countess of Savoy, and the *Belles Heures* was purchased by Yolande of Aragon, Countess of Anjou and Queen of Sicily, for 300 *livres*.[30]

For women of royal, noble and gentry families, book ownership was often combined with the patronage of authors, translators and painters. Women's influence was all the greater because of the emphasis on the use of the vernacular in their books. Women rarely understood much Latin. Books commissioned included Books of Hours, such as the *Savoy Hours* made for Blanche of Burgundy, Countess of Savoy, in the second quarter of the fourteenth century, and originally containing over 200 illustrations. Matthew Paris wrote his *Life of St Edmund of Abingdon* for Isabella de Warenne, Countess of Arundel. Froissart enjoyed the patronage of several women, including Philippa of Hainault, wife of Edward III, Isabella Countess of Coucy, Blanche of Lancaster, and Jeanne of Brabant and her husband. Lydgate was patronised by a number of prominent fifteenth-century noble-women, including Alice Chaucer, Duchess of Suffolk, Anne, Countess Stafford, Anne Mortimer, Isabella Despenser, Countess of Warwick, and Margaret Talbot, Countess of Shrewsbury.[31]

The advent of printing, heralding a revolution in book production and ownership, also had its need of patrons. Margaret of York was William Caxton's first patron. After serving as the governor of the Merchant Adventurers at Bruges from 1461, he had moved into Margaret's service by 1471. He completed his translation of *The Recuyell of the Historyes of Troye* under her patronage and the work was printed in Bruges in 1475, to be followed by a French edition. His second English book printed in Bruges, *The Playe and Game of Chess*, was dedicated to her brother George, Duke of Clarence, and was followed shortly by his departure for London where he established his printing-press at Westminster with the help of several court patrons, including Lady Margaret Beaufort, the mother of Henry VII. Isabella d'Este also patronised printing, commissioning works by Petrarch, Dante and Virgil from Aldus Manutius of Venice.[32]

Patronage of the arts was essential, and the majority of those supported were men. Women, however, also worked as artists and writers. Relatively few of these women are known, although it is likely that many wives and daughters practised anonymously in family workshops. Enough names survive to show that women were skilled scribes, illuminators and embroi-derers, while others ran workshops which were involved in building and furnishing religious and lay establishments. A few women were employed in noble and royal households as singers, dancers and instrumentalists. Women scribes have been found at Nuremberg, while female illuminators worked in Paris, Cologne, Lille and Bruges. Certain women were described as illuminators in the rolls of the *taille* for Paris in the late thirteenth and early fourteenth centuries, and in the case of widows were presumably running their own workshops. Perronnelle d'Auteuil and her husband Ernoul de Nuce were both described as illuminators in the 1290s; Ernoul died in 1299, and Perronnelle continued to be listed as an illuminator and to pay tax. She must have taken over from her husband as head of the workshop.

The importance of the book trade in Paris provided good work opportunities for scribes, artists and their families in the fourteenth and fifteenth centuries. Jean le Noir and his daughter Bourgot worked for Yolande of Flanders, Countess of Bar, for Charles V in Paris, and subsequently for the duke of Berry in Bourges. At a time when guilds were becoming more restrictive, the artists' guild at Bruges continued to admit women, eighteen women being full members in 1461–2; whereas women comprised 12 per cent of the membership in 1254, the figure had risen to 25 per cent in the 1480s. Women illuminators were also found in London; Matilda Myms bequeathed her materials and tools for making pictures to her apprentice William.[33]

The demand for elaborate clothes and costly vestments meant that skilled embroiderers were in demand. Many women undoubtedly had this skill, whether they were working in their own households or for pay, but most is heard of male workshops. In Paris around 1300, women were prominent in the silk crafts as well as in embroidery, and eight embroiderers were listed in the roll of the *taille* for 1292. Mabel of Bury St Edmunds carried out major commissions for Henry III, making a chasuble and offertory veil in 1239, and four years later a red samite banner embroidered in gold with the images of the Virgin Mary and St John. Women were not found working in the skilled building trades, but as widows continued to be responsible for workshops. Catherine Lyghtefote supplied building materials for the royal palace at Sheen in the 1380s and subsequently married the mason Henry Yevele.[34]

Women writers were relatively few in number, whether they worked in religious establishments or in the lay world. Women's mystical writing was regarded as acceptable, although carefully vetted by churchmen, and the circulation of manuscripts for some mystics was very small. Women troubadours were found in southern France around 1200. In the north, the outstanding woman writer was Christine de Pizan. It is likely that there were more women poets and writers than are now known, but their work was concealed by anonymity; there is no way in which women's authorship can be deduced from subject matter, style or the handwriting of the scribe. Moreover a work known to have been by a woman might lose its authorship in later copies. In the thirteenth century a woman wrote a *Response* to Richard de Fournival's *Bestiaire d'amour*. Richard was a well-known scholar and Churchman; the woman wrote anonymously. It is significant that out of seventeen surviving manuscripts of the *Bestiaire* only four have the *Response*. Several copies of Christine de Pizan's *Faits d'Armes et de Chevalerie* have no reference to her authorship.[35]

This anonymity and suppression of authorship was probably due partly to misogyny. Women as weak and irrational beings were not expected to be writers, although mystical writing which did not make use of reason was acceptable under supervision. Yet the explanation also lies with education, as typified by the *Bestiaire d'amour* and *Response*. Richard relied on ancient texts for his authorities, mainly making use of Aristotle. The female author of the *Response* was by no means overawed by this, relying instead on divine authority in arguing for the nobility and dignity of women. In view of their lack of advanced education, women writers were dependent on their senses, imagination, religious knowledge and experience. Their works inevitably lacked the authority of male authors.

Certain women succeeded in emerging as authors. A group of trobairitz, or women troubadours, was present in Occitan society in the second half of the twelfth and first half of the thirteenth century. Their number is uncertain because some women wrote anonymously, and it is not possible to make a clear differentiation between poems written by men and women. Women composed only a tiny proportion of troubadour poetry, about forty poems out of 2,500. Several of the trobairitz were of noble birth or familiar with noble society, such as Comtessa de Dia, Comtessa de Proensa, Maria de Ventadorn, and Castelloza from the Auvergne. Little is known about their lives. They wrote *cansos* and debate poems, and also composed music; the music survives for Comtessa de Dia's 'A chantar', a lament for a man whom she has loved but who has cheated her. Out of twelve *cansos* in all, Comtessa de Dia wrote four and Castelloza four. The twenty-four debate poems are mainly dialogues between a troubadour and a woman, although occasionally between two women; many debated courtly love, and the trobairitz could express herself as a woman from whom the lover was seeking favours, or could impersonate a man. The poems, taken as a whole, shed light on women's desires and aspirations, and are a remarkable achievement at the turn of the twelfth and thirteenth centuries.[36]

As a woman making her living by authorship, Christine de Pizan was exceptional in the late medieval world. At the same time she was typical of the women who, finding themselves widowed with a family to support, turned their skills into the means of making a living. Christine was born in Venice about 1364, but spent nearly all her life in France. Her father was appointed court astrologer to Charles V, and at the age of fifteen Christine married the court notary, Etienne de Castel. His death after a happy marriage lasting ten years left her on her own in a difficult financial situation, with three children and her mother and niece to support. She made use of her court contacts to get her children established; her son joined the household of the earl of Salisbury in England and her daughter entered the Dominican nunnery at Poissy. Christine had been educated by her father and continued to educate herself during her widowhood. She possibly began earning her living as a copyist and may eventually have had her own workshop. She was becoming known as a poet by the end of the 1390s, and from about 1402 embarked on her serious prose works. In old age she retired to a nunnery, possibly to Poissy, and continued to write. Her work on Joan of Arc was written in 1429, the year that Joan raised the siege of Orleans. Christine probably died soon after.[37]

In receiving the patronage of Louis, Duke of Orleans, and his wife, Philip the Bold and John the Fearless, Dukes of Burgundy, Jean, Duke of Berry, and Charles VI and Isabeau of Bavaria, Christine had to be ready to tackle a wide variety of subjects. These were mostly secular, although underlain by a strong sense of religion and morality, and several express Christine's firmly held views. Christine's lyric poetry was in the courtly love tradition which was popular in court circles. In *Le Livre du Dit de Poissy*, she described a visit to the convent in the spring of 1400. The nunnery was described in an idealised way, and her depiction of the group riding there through the forest is typical of this genre of poem. So was the court of love which she and her companions held on their return ride.[38]

In contrast to her poetry, she wrote prose works on war and history and these bring out her concerns over the factional nature of French politics and her desire for peace. Her biography of Charles V was commissioned by his brother, Philip the Bold, and Christine made use of chronicles as well as her memories of the court. She deliberately brought out Charles's virtues, and the biography was very much a eulogy of the king. The work was possibly intended as a model for the dauphin, Louis, Duke of Guienne (d. 1415). Christine had a strong interest in education, writing advice for her son as well as discussing the education of a knight in the *Epistre d'Othea*, and developing her ideas further in the *Livre du Corps de Policie* of 1407 and the *Livre de la Paix* of 1412–13, which were written for the dauphin. Both these works were in the medieval didactic tradition of treatises for the instruction of princes. In the *Livre de la Paix*, she discussed the virtues that the ruler should cultivate, such as truth and justice, and strength and mercy, and made use of a wide range of biblical, classical and later medieval sources.[39]

It is possible that her *Faits d'Armes et de Chevalerie* was commissioned by John the Fearless who had gained control of the dauphin in 1409. In this work, Christine made use of the treatise by the Roman author Vegetius, as well as more recent sources. Although she made use of Roman examples, her work was relevant to the contemporary French situation of war and instability. She discussed the concepts of the just war and the laws of war, including the treatment of prisoners and of the civilian population. Her discussion of military leadership and discipline, and of open warfare and sieges, was immediately applicable to her own time. Christine's anxiety over the state of France lasted throughout the later part of her life.[40] She always hoped for the establishment of peace, at one point urging Isabeau of Bavaria to use all her efforts to avoid civil war.[41] Yet she realised that war was inevitable, and her writing on warfare showed a realism well removed from the idealism of some of her poetry.

Christine was realistic in her views on human nature, but at the same time her strong moral sense made her unwilling to tolerate what she regarded as false assumptions and hypocrisy. She had no patience with contemporary expressions of misogyny, and her forthright views on women's ability and wisdom led to considerable debate in her own time and since. Christine was a principal protagonist in the Querelle de la Rose of 1398–1402, attacking the popular poem, *Roman de la Rose*, for its misogyny. This poem about a lover seeking the rose was written by Guillaume de Lorris about 1225, and expanded about fifty years later by Jean de Meun, who intensified the misogynist elements in the poem. Christine objected to the poem's attitude to women, seeing no point in Jean de Meun's remarks about their vicious and evil behaviour. Although she was supported by Jean Gerson, chancellor of the university of Paris, many influential figures sided against her, criticising not only her opinions but her presumption in putting them forward. Gontier Col attacked her for daring to criticise a man as learned and famous as Jean de Meun, and insulted her by inferring that women were over-emotional.[42] Such men possibly saw Christine as a threat and were not to be convinced by her views.

Christine's views on women were given in most detail in *The Book of the City of Ladies* and *The Treasure of the City of Ladies or The Book of the Three Virtues*, written in 1404–5.[43] The second work was written for the dauphin's wife, Margaret de Nevers, daughter of John the Fearless. *The Book of the City of Ladies* opens with Christine pondering disconsolately in her study on the misogyny which she found in the authorities. She is visited by three women, representing Reason, Justice and Rectitude, who gently rebuke her for her depression and tell her that she is to build a city for virtuous and praiseworthy women. The book then describes the building of the city in a series of conversations between Christine and the three ladies. In Parts I and II, the foundations of the city are dug, houses built and inhabitants brought in; particular women are described, mainly taken from pagan mythology and history, but also from the Old Testament and from more recent times; Christine made use of Boccaccio's work *De Claris Mulieribus (On Famous Women)*, although he mainly described classical women. Part III sees the high towers completed, and these lofty parts of the city are inhabited by the women saints, ruled over by the Virgin Mary. Christine emphasises the great contribution which women have made to the world, and Reason stresses that God has given women not only the ability to take in all sorts of knowledge but to discover new forms of knowledge for the benefit of the world.

In *The Treasure of the City of Ladies*, Christine turns her attention to women of her own time. Most of the work discusses the princess and the women of the court; this would be particularly relevant to Margaret de Nevers, and Christine had had most opportunity to observe women in this group. Her advice to the princess can be paralleled by what was going on in contemporary royal and noble households. It was rooted in religion and morality, and Christine was aware of the temptations which confronted the princess. Her watchwords for the princess are peace and prudence.

Unusually, Christine included all ranks of women in her book, although the lower social groups were discussed more cursorily than the princess. She included gentlewomen, nuns, wives of merchants and artisans, servants, prostitutes, labourers' wives and the poor. She obviously disliked extravagant display among these groups, criticising costly clothing and excess splendour in the chambers of merchants' wives after the birth of a child. Yet much of her advice was sensible, although her knowledge of the poorer groups was limited. She wrote chapters on how the old should behave towards the young and vice versa, recommending older people who were critical of the young to remember their own youth; correction when needed should be gently administered, and the old should not spend their time complaining about the young. The wife of the artisan should treat her husband kindly so that he did not spend his time in the tavern, help him to oversee his workers, and advise him not to allow too much credit. Christine abhorred prostitution and urged prostitutes to renounce their way of life. Idealising comes in with her remarks on the wives of labourers and poor women, as she urged them to patience in this world in the hope of winning a heavenly crown. Such an attitude was found widely in noble circles.

Christine considered that women were capable, rational and intelligent, and that they had been slandered by classical and medieval authorities. She realised that women varied, that not all were virtuous enough to be admitted to the city of ladies, but her positive view of women was unusual in her time. Christine's defence of women's abilities has led to her being applauded as a modern voice. Yet in many respects she accepted the status quo. She accepted the hierarchical ordering of society, arguing that every woman should keep to her own position in life. In her address to all women at the end of *The Book of the City of Ladies*, she emphasised that it was not the best thing in the world to be free. Women should make the most of their marriages, rejoicing if they had loving, good and wise husbands; if their husbands were a mixture of good and bad, they should thank God that they were no worse, while wives with cruel husbands should try to make them more reasonable. All women should cultivate virtue and confound men's criticisms. In her acceptance of the existing social order, Christine was no feminist.

Christine was influential beyond the borders of France in the fifteenth century and some of her work continued to be read after 1500. The *Faits d'Armes et de Chevalerie* survives in several copies, some of which were well used; a copy was given by John Talbot, Earl of Shrewsbury, to Margaret of Anjou in 1455, and the work was translated into English and printed by Caxton. There are over twenty manuscripts of the *Treasure of the City of Ladies or The Book of the Three Virtues*. Anne de Beaujeu made use of it in writing her book of advice for her daughter. Copies of *The Book of the City of Ladies* were owned by Isabeau of Bavaria, the duke and duchess of Berry and their daughter Marie, Duchess of Bourbon, and Margaret of Bavaria, the wife of John the Fearless, and in England by Alice Chaucer, Duchess of Suffolk. Some of Christine's works belonged to members of the ruling house of Savoy, with at least three owned by Yolande, the daughter of Charles VII of France and wife of Amadeus IX. Nevertheless, some of Christine's works did not enjoy wide popularity; the *Livre de la Paix* survives in only two copies.[44] The feminist movement and the growing interest in women's history and literature in the later twentieth century, however, has triggered a new interest in Christine.

By the fifteenth century in northern Italy, certain women were receiving a humanist education and were attempting to participate in humanist circles. These women belonged mainly to families of the ruling courts or the professional elite and received their education in the classics from humanist tutors or from their fathers and brothers. Isabella and Beatrice d'Este were given a typical medieval education in religion and social skills, such as music and dancing, but they also studied Cicero and Virgil and Greek and Roman history with Battista Guarino. Cecilia Gonzaga of Mantua and her brothers were taught by Vittorino da Feltre. Fathers encouraged their daughters to become learned, as in the case of Laura Cereta of Brescia. Some of these women won fame for their classical learning and rhetoric. Cassandra Fedele of Verona was praised in the late fifteenth century for her oration at the university of Padua on behalf of a kinsman, and Nicolosa Castellani Sanuti of Bologna used her learning to challenge the 1453 sumptuary decree of Cardinal Bessarion, making her case on behalf of the women of Bologna. Yet there was widespread feeling among both men and women that such learning was unfeminine. Isotta Nogarola, along with her brother and sister, was accused by an anonymous writer of Verona of promiscuity and incest since, he alleged, a learned woman is never chaste. Some women married and abandoned their learning, as did Ginevra, another of Isotta's sisters; some resumed their humanist interests as widows, like Laura Cereta, although she encountered misogyny and hostility; some, like Cecilia Gonzaga, entered the religious life. Isotta Nogarola continued to live in the world but pursued a solitary life in retirement and abandoned humanism in favour of religious studies. Once learned girls had grown up, there was no way in which they would be accepted into male humanist circles. They were expected to conform to the social norms laid down for women. In this way they did not pose a threat to male scholars.[45]

Although the number of known women artists and writers is relatively few, most elite women enjoyed the arts in a variety of forms. Works of art, whether tapestries, precious metalwork or illuminated books, constituted an essential part of their lifestyle and were highly prized. Craftsmen and women displayed their skills in the production of such objects. In her patronage of the arts, the noblewoman pursued a family and an individual agenda. The commissioning of buildings and works of art redounded to the prestige of the family, while books served a more individual need. Tombs met the aspirations of both family and individual, as the reputation of both was upheld by the splendour of the monument, and personal commemoration was combined with the reputation of the family to whom the deceased belonged. Moreover, patronage had a wider cultural importance in spreading knowledge of styles, artists and authors more widely, and in making works increasingly accessible through translation and the use of the vernacular. Royal and noble patrons, and the work of women illuminators and of writers such as Christine de Pizan, show that women were undoubtedly significant in the world of culture.

Notes

1 C.E. King, *Renaissance Women Patrons. Wives and Widows in Italy c. 1300–1550* (Manchester, 1998), p. 3.
2 For example, the tomb of Alice Chaucer, Duchess of Suffolk, in the parish church of Ewelme, Oxfordshire.
3 Public Record Office, London, E101/91/27, m. 4; E101/91/30; E101/92/2, m. 1, 2, 14; E101/92/9, m. 10.
4 F.J. Furnivall (ed.), *The Fifty Earliest English Wills* (EETS original series 78, 1882), pp. 116–17.
5 P. Northeast (ed.), *Wills of the Archdeaconry of Sudbury 1439–74, Part 1 1439–61* (Suffolk Records Society 44, 2001), pp. 130, 230.
6 J-M. Richard, *Mahaut Comtesse d'Artois et de Bourgogne* (Paris, 1887), pp. 86–9, 256, 263–5, 399–409.
7 King, *Renaissance Women Patrons*, pp. 63–72.
8 Ibid., pp. 200–6.
9 J.M. Wood, *Women, Art and Spirituality. The Poor Clares of Early Modern Italy* (Cambridge, 1996), pp. 102–11.
10 S.K. Cohn, Jr., *The Cult of Remembrance and the Black Death* (Baltimore, 1992), pp. 81–4; M.H. Caviness, 'Anchoress, abbess and queen: donors and patrons or intercessors and matrons?', in J.H. McCash (ed.), *The Cultural Patronage of Medieval Women* (Athens, Georgia, 1996), p. 138; J. Nichols, *A Collection of All the Wills of the Kings and Queens of England* (London, 1780), p. 99; Richard, *Mahaut Comtesse d'Artois*, pp. 317–18, 321.
11 King, *Renaissance Women Patrons*, pp. 154–6.
12 P. Crossley, 'The architecture of queenship: royal saints, female dynasties and the spread of Gothic architecture in central Europe', in A.J. Duggan (ed.), *Queens and Queenship in Medieval Europe* (Woodbridge, 1997), pp. 284–7.
13 King, *Renaissance Women Patrons*, pp. 100–3.
14 Richard, *Mahaut Comtesse d'Artois*, pp. 84–5, 88, 312–17, 378–9, 392–3.
15 C.C. Willard, 'The patronage of Isabel of Portugal', in McCash (ed.), *Cultural Patronage*, pp. 312–14; A.M. Morganstern, *Gothic Tombs of Kinship in France, the Low Countries and England* (Philadelphia, 2000), pp. 140–8.
16 Richard, *Mahaut Comtesse d'Artois*, pp. 256–7, 262, 268–97, 323–58.
17 E.L. Cox, *The Green Count of Savoy. Amadeus VI and Transalpine Savoy in the Fourteenth Century* (Princeton, 1967), pp. 287–9; J.C. Ward, 'Elizabeth de Burgh, Lady of Clare (d. 1360)', in C.M. Barron and A.F. Sutton (eds), *Medieval London Widows 1300–1500* (London, 1994), pp. 32, 37–40; J.C. Ward, 'Elizabeth de Burgh and Great Bardfield in the fourteenth century', in K. Neale (ed.), *Essex Heritage* (Oxford, 1992), pp. 53–5.
18 D.S. Chambers, *Patrons and Artists in the Italian Renaissance* (London, 1970), pp. 151–2.
19 Ibid., pp. 124–50.
20 K. Clark, *Leonardo da Vinci* (Harmondsworth, 1959), p. 100. Isabella's life and activities are discussed by Julia Cartwright, *Isabella d'Este, Marchioness of Mantua, 1474–1539. A Study of the Renaissance*, 2 vols (London, 1903).

21 S.G. Bell, 'Medieval women book owners: arbiters of lay piety and ambassadors of culture', in M. Erler and M. Kowaleski (eds), *Women and Power in the Middle Ages* (Athens, Georgia, 1988), p. 151.

22 K. Cherewatuk and U. Wiethaus (eds), *Dear Sister. Medieval Women and the Epistolary Genre* (Philadelphia, 1993), pp. 3–6, 8–15; J.C. Ward, 'Letter-writing by English noblewomen in the early fifteenth century', in J. Daybell (ed.), *Early Modern Women's Letter Writing, 1450–1700* (Basingstoke, 2001), pp. 29–41.

23 Bell, 'Medieval women book owners', pp. 152, 154, 156–7, 162–5.

24 J. Backhouse, *Books of Hours* (London, 1985), pp. 3–4; J. Bossy, 'Prayers', *TRHS* sixth series 1 (1991), pp. 139–40.

25 Caviness, 'Anchoress, abbess and queen', p. 141; Backhouse, *Books of Hours*, pp. 5, 9, 65, 70.

26 Bell, 'Medieval women book owners', pp. 155, 157–8; R. Gibbons, 'The piety of Isabeau of Bavaria, queen of France, 1385–1422', in D.E.S. Dunn (ed.), *Courts, Counties and the Capital in the Later Middle Ages* (Stroud, 1996), pp. 215–16.

27 Richard, *Mahaut Comtesse d'Artois*, pp. 99–106; Bell, 'Medieval women book owners', pp. 154, 157; M. Vale, *The Princely Court. Medieval Courts and Culture in North-West Europe 1270–1380* (Oxford, 2001), pp. 212, 279.

28 M.J. Hughes, 'Margaret of York, duchess of Burgundy. Diplomat, patroness, bibliophile and benefactress', *The Private Library* third series 7 (1984), pp. 12–15; M.J. Hughes, 'The library of Margaret of York, duchess of Burgundy', ibid., pp. 53–78; C. Weightman, *Margaret of York Duchess of Burgundy 1446–1503* (Stroud, 1989), pp. 203–8.

29 C.M. Meale, '". . . alle the bokes that I have of latyn, englysch and frensch": laywomen and their books in late medieval England', in C.M. Meale (ed.), *Women and Literature in Britain 1150–1500* (Cambridge, 1993), pp. 134–5, 139, 141; F. Riddy, '"Women talking about the things of God": a late medieval sub-culture', in Meale (ed.), *Women and Literature*, pp. 107–11; Nichols, *Collection of All the Wills*, pp. 180–3.

30 H. Jenkinson, 'Mary de Sancto Paulo, foundress of Pembroke College, Cambridge', *Archaeologia* 66 (1915), pp. 420, 426, 432–3; J.M. Bak, 'Queens as scapegoats in medieval Hungary', in Duggan (ed.), *Queens and Queenship*, pp. 231–2; Willard, 'The patronage of Isabel of Portugal', pp. 308–12; Bell, 'Medieval women book owners', p. 155.

31 M.M. Manion, 'Women, art and devotion: three French fourteenth-century royal prayer books', in M.M. Manion and B.J. Muir (eds), *The Art of the Book. Its Place in Medieval Worship* (Exeter, 1998), pp. 21–3; K.K. Jambeck, 'Patterns of women's literary patronage: England, 1200–c. 1475', in McCash (ed.), *Cultural Patronage*, p. 242; P.E. Bennett, 'Female readers in Froissart: implied, fictive and other', in L. Smith and J.H.M. Taylor (eds), *Women, the Book and the Worldly* (Woodbridge, 1995), p. 13; Meale, 'Laywomen and their books', pp. 137–8; J. Boffey, 'Lydgate's lyrics and women readers', in Smith and Taylor (eds), *Women, the Book and the Worldly*, pp. 139–49.

32 Weightman, *Margaret of York*, pp. 209–12; J. Summit, 'William Caxton, Margaret Beaufort and the romance of female patronage', in Smith and Taylor (eds), *Women, the Book and the Worldly*, pp. 151–65; Bell, 'Medieval women book owners', p. 158; J.H. McCash, 'The cultural patronage of medieval women: an overview', in McCash (ed.), *Cultural Patronage*, p. 33.

33 E. Uitz, *Women in the Medieval Town*, (trans.) S. Marnie (London, 1990), pp. 98–100; M.W. Labarge, *Women in Medieval Life. A Small Sound of the Trumpet* (London, 1986), pp. 224–7, 230–3; R.R. Sharpe (ed.), *Calendar of Wills proved and enrolled in the Court of Husting, London, A.D. 1258–A.D.1688*, 2 vols (London, 1889–90), p. 576.

34 D. Herlihy, *Opera Muliebria. Women and Work in Medieval Europe* (New York, 1990), pp. 147–8; Labarge, *Women in Medieval Life*, pp. 228–9; J. Alexander and P. Binski (eds), *Age of Chivalry. Art in Plantagenet England 1200–1400* (London, 1987), p. 45; see earlier, pp. 96–8.

35 J. Boffey, 'Women authors and women's literacy in fourteenth- and fifteenth-century England', in Meale (ed.), *Women and Literature*, pp. 166–71; J. Beer, 'Woman, authority and the book in the Middle Ages', in Smith and Taylor (eds), *Women, the Book and the Worldly*, pp. 61–9; C.C. Willard, 'Pilfering Vegetius? Christine de Pizan's *Faits d'Armes et de Chevalerie*', in ibid., p. 37.

36 L.M. Paterson, *The World of the Troubadours. Medieval Occitan Society, c. 1100–c. 1300* (Cambridge, 1993), pp. 256–65; C. Neuls-Bates (ed.), *Women in Music. An Anthology of Source Readings from the Middle Ages to the Present* (New York, 1982), pp. 21–7; T. Sankovitch, 'The trobairitz', in S. Gaunt and S. Kay (eds), *The Troubadours. An Introduction* (Cambridge, 1999), pp. 113–26; W.D. Paden (ed.), *The Voice of the Trobairitz. Perspectives on the Women Troubadours* (Philadelphia, 1989), pp. 13–14, 227–37. Comtessa de Proensa has been identified with Garsende de Forcalquier, Countess of Provence.

37 Christine's life and work are discussed in C.C. Willard, *Christine de Pizan. Her Life and Works* (New York, 1984). A selection of Christine's works in translation can be found in C.C. Willard (ed.), *The Writings of Christine de Pizan* (New York, 1994).

38 Christine de Pisan, *Oeuvres Poétiques*, (ed.) M. Roy, 2 vols (Paris, 1891), II, pp. 159–222.

39 J. Chance (ed.), *Christine de Pizan's Letter of Othea to Hector* (Woodbridge, 1997); C.C. Willard (ed.), *The 'Livre de la Paix' of Christine de Pisan* (The Hague, 1958).

40 Willard, 'Pilfering Vegetius?', pp. 31–7.

41 M.D. Legge (ed.), *Anglo-Norman Letters and Petitions from All Souls MS 182* (Oxford, 1941), pp. 144–9.

42 A. Blamires (ed.), *Woman Defamed and Woman Defended* (Oxford, 1992), pp. 148–66, 286–9.

43 The second work is available in a recent critical edition; C.C. Willard (ed.), *Le Livre des Trois Vertus* (Paris, 1989). Both works are available in translation; Christine de Pizan, *The Book of the City of Ladies*, (trans.) E.J. Richards (New York, 1983); Christine de Pizan, *The Book of the City of Ladies*, (trans.) R. Brown-Grant (Harmondsworth, 1999); Christine de Pisan, *The Treasure of the City of Ladies or the Book of the Three Virtues*, (trans.) S. Lawson (Harmondsworth, 1985).

44 Willard, 'Pilfering Vegetius?', pp. 31, 37; Labarge, *Women in Medieval Life*, p. 237; McCash, 'Cultural patronage', p. 31; Willard (ed.), *Le Livre des Trois Vertus*, p. xviii; Willard (ed.), *The 'Livre de la Paix' of Christine de Pisan*, p. 46; G. Mombello, 'Christine de Pizan and the house of Savoy', in E.J. Richards (ed.), *Reinterpreting Christine de Pizan* (Athens, Georgia, 1992), pp. 187–204.

45 Julia Cartwright, *Beatrice d'Este Duchess of Milan, 1475–97. A Study of the Renaissance* (London, 1903), pp. 36–9; M.L. King, 'The religious retreat of Isotta Nogarola (1418–66): sexism and its consequences in the fifteenth century', *Signs* 3 (1977–8), pp. 807–22; M.L. King, 'Book-lined cells: women and humanism in the early Italian Renaissance', in P.H. Labalme (ed.), *Beyond their Sex. Learned Women of the European Past* (New York, 1980), pp. 66–90; L. Panizza and S. Wood (eds), *A History of Women's Writing in Italy* (Cambridge, 2000), pp. 25–9.

10 Religious life
Nuns and nunneries

The twelfth and thirteenth centuries saw a substantial increase in the opportunities for women to live a religious life. The life of the nun had long been the main option for unmarried girls and women as well as for widows, but women of the later Middle Ages could also join communities of beguines, tertiaries or penitents, or live a religious life in the world. Many women opted for the life of a nun, and popular preachers and reformers found that they had to cater for women as well as men, as women flocked to them in considerable numbers. Norbert of Xanten, Robert of Arbrissel and Gilbert of Sempringham in the twelfth century, and St Francis and St Dominic in the thirteenth, were faced with enthusiastic women followers for whom they had to establish communities; gifts of property and money from male and female patrons enabled them to build up foundations. At the same time, women joined houses of the long-established Benedictine order or became canonesses, following the Rule of St Augustine, and Cistercian customs were adopted among groups of women. A few women became sisters in the military orders or joined the Carthusians where they lived a communal life, unlike the solitary life of the monks. The prohibition of new monastic orders at the Fourth Lateran Council of 1215 presented difficulties for women like St Clare and St Birgitta who wished to have their own Rules of life, and the Benedictine and Augustinian Rules provided the basis for most nunneries in the later Middle Ages.[1] Throughout the later Middle Ages, the religious life for women posed problems of control for the Church, which felt that it was dangerous to have groups of women who were not subject to male guidance and control.

Women joined the Franciscan and Dominican friars early on. Dominic's original foundation for women at Prouille in 1206 constituted part of his campaign against the Cathar heresy. The convent housed women who had been handed over by their parents to the heretics to be educated, but who had subsequently been converted to the religious life of the Roman Church. The account of the foundation referred to their parents' poverty and presumably this was one of the reasons why they could not return home and marry. The original foundation housed twelve nuns, who lived an austere and enclosed life of prayer and poverty, their days being divided between the

Office or *Opus Dei* (services in the convent church), private prayer and meditation, and manual work such as spinning.[2] Dominic envisaged them as a model for the locality through their way of life, and he and other early friars saw them as playing a constructive role in the Dominican mission through their prayers; in writing to Diana d'Andolò, patroness and nun at the house of St Agnes at Bologna, Jordan of Saxony asked for her prayers.[3]

The life and subsequent canonisation of St Clare of Assisi have made the early Franciscan nuns better known than the Dominican nuns. Clare was born into a wealthy family of Assisi around 1194. After discussions with St Francis she left home against her parents' wishes at about the age of eighteen and made her profession to Francis; her hair was cut and she dressed in poor clothing. To start with, she lived in Benedictine communities, but she wanted a Franciscan lifestyle and she, her sister and other recruits were housed at the church of San Damiano, which Francis had restored.[4] Her way of life was probably similar to that of the women's communities described by Jacques de Vitry in 1216 in the region round Perugia. These women renounced possessions and lived by the work of their hands.[5] Clare and her nuns, who became known as Poor Clares, lived a life of poverty, but were apparently not enclosed in the early years.

Clare regarded the life of individual and corporate poverty as essential for the imitation of Christ. Yet although this was regarded as acceptable to start with for the friars, it raised concern for the nuns, since the Church did not regard it as suitable for them to live and work in the world. It is significant that the degree of contact between Francis and the nuns gradually decreased; it has to be remembered that women were regarded as sexual temptresses and as liable to succumb to temptation. Moreover, the friars were increasingly reluctant to have their time taken up with providing spiritual and temporal services for women's houses. On the issues of poverty and enclosure, Clare was adamant that poverty was essential to her vision, and spent much of her life endeavouring to secure this. Shortly before his death in 1216, Clare obtained from Pope Innocent III the Privilege of Poverty which was granted to all the Poor Clares, present and future, and which saw them as living in poverty in imitation of Christ – it laid down that no one could force them to accept possessions. Yet only two years after Innocent's death, Cardinal Ugolino, later to become Pope Gregory IX, imposed on the Poor Clares an enclosed, largely Benedictine rule and set aside the issue of poverty. As pope, Gregory reissued the Privilege of Poverty in 1228 but in a watered-down form, not applicable to nunneries in the future. At the same time, he envisaged all houses of Poor Clares, apart from San Damiano, as accepting gifts of money and land. Although Innocent IV approved Clare's own Rule, incorporating poverty, just before she died in 1253, most Poor Clares came to follow Urban IV's Rule promulgated ten years later which confirmed Gregory IX's position; only Clare's own house and the foundation of Agnes of Prague were exempted from the provision for the holding of property.[6]

The mendicants had a strong influence on women's religious life in the later Middle Ages, not only among their nuns but also among women living in informal communities and pursuing a lay life in the world. The nuns' houses grew in size and their orders spread over Europe, but with a greater density in some regions than others. A ceiling of 160 nuns was imposed on Prouille in 1283, and six daughter-houses were founded in southern France and Spain in the late thirteenth and early fourteenth centuries. Dominic established a convent at Madrid and was responsible for bringing to fruition Innocent III's plan to unite the nuns of Rome in the house of San Sisto. By the early fourteenth century, there were about 150 Dominican nunneries in Europe, nine in France, seventy-four in Germany, forty-two in Italy, eight in Spain, six in Bohemia, three in Hungary and three in Poland. The only English house was at Dartford, founded in the mid-1340s during the reign of Edward III.[7] The expansion of the Poor Clares began early. Clare's sister Agnes was sent to the convent of Monticelli near Florence in 1219 where, although homesick for San Damiano, she was cheered by the fervour of the nuns. She subsequently went to Verona, Padua, Venice and Mantua. By 1228, there were twenty-three houses of Poor Clares in Italy. The first house outside Italy was established at Rheims in 1220, while in Spain the earliest convent was probably founded at Pamplona in 1230. The order was popular in Germany, where twenty-five houses were set up, and in France, where one of the best known houses was at Longchamp, founded in 1255 by Isabella, sister of Louis IX. Only four houses were established in England, where the nuns were known as Minoresses. In eastern Europe, Agnes of Prague, daughter of Ottokar I of Bohemia, was influential in her own house at Prague and among members of her family; her sister founded the house at Breslau in 1257. There were also houses of Poor Clares in the Crusader States and Cyprus.[8]

Regional patterns emerge from these foundations, notably the small number of houses in England and in parts of eastern Europe where only a limited number of patrons appear to have been interested in mendicant foundations for nuns, where there was less urbanisation, and where there do not seem to have been large numbers of women wishing to adopt this form of the religious life. Varied trends are also apparent within nations. In Germany, Cistercian nunneries were concentrated particularly in the dioceses of Cologne, Liège and Mainz, whereas mendicant nuns were found far more in the dioceses of Strasbourg and Constance. J.B. Freed attributes this to the earlier urbanisation of the northern area where the Cistercians were especially active in the early thirteenth century, and the later arrival of the friars in Germany. Once they arrived, the response in the towns was swift: by 1237, there were five Dominican nunneries in Strasbourg, and this had increased to seven, together with one house of Poor Clares, by the 1280s.[9]

A smaller group of nunneries belonging to the later Middle Ages was those for reformed prostitutes and these can be associated with widespread preaching on penance, often by the friars. Such communities were often dedicated to St Mary Magdalen. They were found from the early thirteenth century and by 1300 most major towns had such a house, which has been described as complementing the town brothel. The houses were not always enclosed and the sisters did not necessarily stay for life. At Perpignan, the sisters went out in pairs to beg for alms and were often given grain and olive oil. According to the statutes of 1339 of the sisters of St Catherine of Montpellier, entrants had to bring their bed, clothes and the sum of 100 *sous*, and could leave to marry within the first year, although they would not receive a dowry; they were expelled if they refused to be imprisoned for offences.[10]

The increase in the number of nunneries added to the opportunities for women to follow an institutional religious life. In addition to mendicant convents, houses belonging to the older orders continued to be founded into the fourteenth century, although the number diminished markedly after the Black Death. Santuccia Carabotti founded a strict Benedictine nunnery near Gubbio in the thirteenth century and later reformed twenty-four other houses.[11] There were always more male houses. Even when the number of nunneries was at its peak, there was by no means an even spread of houses throughout Europe, and it was only in the larger towns that women had much choice as to which house to enter. In Lorraine, Toul had eight male houses and none for women, Nancy had two for men and two mendicant houses for women, and Metz a total of twenty-seven monasteries, of which nine were for nuns, and these included Benedictine, Premonstratensian, Augustinian, Dominican and Franciscan foundations.[12] Yet in the course of the later Middle Ages, there were considerable similarities between the orders in their enclosed way of life, and mendicant and Benedictine nuns would find many points in common.

Nuns and the male orders

The nunneries' dependence on men for spiritual and temporal services posed major problems. Women were not admitted into the orders of the Church and always needed men as chaplains, confessors and priests to celebrate Mass. Although nuns who held office in the convent were allowed to break the rule of enclosure, they were dependent on male labourers and bailiffs on their estates, and some orders required a man to run the convent's affairs. Monks and friars were reluctant to devote time to directing women, considering that other aspects of their work were more important, and there was always the underlying fear of sexual scandal. Men also saw women's houses as a financial drain.

The problem had arisen in the twelfth century with large numbers of women wanting to follow the religious life. Norbert of Xanten, Robert of Arbrissel and Gilbert of Sempringham saw the answer to women's religious needs in the establishment of double monasteries, but differed in the role they gave to women. Robert of Arbrissel at Fontevrault put the abbess in overall charge of the house, and the same policy was adopted in Fontevrault's dependencies; throughout the later Middle Ages, the role of abbesses and prioresses continued to be important. Gilbert of Sempringham established both a prior and prioress in his double houses, with final authority resting with the prior. Norbert of Xanten accommodated his male and female followers in the double house at Premontré and founded other houses in France and Germany. Yet after his death in 1134, the leaders of the order were hostile to the idea of the double monastery, and as early as 1141 a statute was passed for its suppression. This proved unenforceable, as did the decision in 1198 not to admit sisters in the future. However, the decree of 1270 proved more effective; it again forbade the admission of sisters and expelled all the women in the order to other houses. Some Premonstratensian nunneries continued to exist, but the attitude of the male members of the order was clear.[13]

The popularity of the Cistercians meant that women as well as men were attracted to the order, but the Cistercians showed their hostility towards women from early on. There was nothing to stop nunneries from imitating Cistercian customs, but most convents appear to have been received into the order only in the thirteenth century, in some cases well after their foundation. From 1213, when it was decreed that all Cistercian nuns were to be enclosed, the statutes of the general chapter referred to female as well as male houses. It is possible that this change came about as a result of pressure from patrons and from women who wanted to observe the Cistercian rule, and also from the Premonstratensian edict of 1198; this last argument was put forward by Jacques de Vitry.

A particularly influential patron may well have been Alfonso VIII of Castile who wanted to ensure that the nunnery he founded in 1187, Las Huelgas de Burgos, was accepted as a Cistercian house. The abbess here was especially powerful and is reputed to have heard nuns' confessions and to have preached sermons. Las Huelgas was envisaged as head of all Cistercian nunneries in Castile, and Alfonso petitioned the general chapter in 1187 for the chapter of abbesses to be held there. This may have come as a shock to the general chapter, which commented that although it would be pleased to see such a meeting it could not compel abbesses to attend.

After 1213, the Cistercians remained anxious to limit the number of women's houses, and in 1220 and 1228 attempted to put an end to the incorporation of nunneries, although without complete success. This was probably due to pressure from prominent churchmen and nobles. In 1230, the abbey of Vezella in Lombardy became a member of the order at the request of the pope, and six years later the abbey of Biaches-lès-Peronne joined at the request of Louis IX and Blanche of Castile. The acceptance of Marham in Norfolk, founded in 1249, as a Cistercian abbey may well have been helped by its foundress Isabella being the daughter of William de

Warenne and Matilda Marshal, and the widow of Hugh d'Aubigny, Earl of Arundel, all members of the higher nobility.[14]

The friars also came under pressure to meet the needs of religious women and were similarly reluctant to minister to them. The rapid expansion of women's houses exacerbated the problem. Although Dominic regarded women's communities as important as powerhouses of prayer, his followers were unwilling to tie up their manpower in female houses; Dominic's plan to have six friars at the nunnery of San Sisto in Rome was unrealistic in the context of the order's expansion. By the 1260s, although friars had duties of correction and visitation, they did not have to be resident, and nuns' chaplains did not necessarily have to be friars.[15]

There was no getting away from a male presence in the nunnery and the best that could be achieved was a compromise which was acceptable to both sides. Quite apart from the fact that men were indispensable for the spiritual life and regarded as essential for worldly business, the emphasis on the enclosed life for the nun meant that her contacts with the world were inevitably limited. The stress on formal institutions and enclosure was obvious from the early twelfth century with the work of Robert of Arbrissel and Norbert of Xanten. Suspicion of informal groups was widespread, as will be seen in the next chapter. Regulations on enclosure were tightened in the thirteenth century, and St Clare's experience exemplified the difficulties facing women who wanted to live the apostolic life in imitation of Christ. Pope Boniface VIII's decretal, *Periculoso*, of 1298 insisted that all nuns should be subject to lifelong enclosure within their communities; they were forbidden to leave their houses and to receive unauthorised visitors, and heads of houses were to conduct their business by proxy. The main concern was to protect the nuns' chastity and to distance them from any sexual temptations.[16]

Although measures were taken to enforce the decree, it was never completely effective. In his injunctions to the Benedictine nunnery of Barking, Essex, in 1279, Archbishop John Pecham had already underlined the importance of enclosure, but at the same time realised that there were occasions, such as the imminent death of a parent, when the nun should be allowed to leave the community.[17] Heads of houses and their officials were unable to do all their business by proxy, and the information available on nuns' lives makes it clear that by no means all were subject to perpetual enclosure.

The life of a nun

The lives of nuns across Christendom displayed both uniformity and variety. They showed uniformity because, in spite of the numerous orders for women, the emphasis on enclosure and a life devoted to the *Opus Dei*, private prayer and work were to be found in virtually every nunnery in Europe. Although customs varied, the basic structure of the nun's life remained remarkably uniform. Variety was to be seen in the size of houses, their relative wealth or poverty, the types of women recruited, the standards maintained, and the relationships with rulers, churchmen and the local community.

Women were attracted to the religious life in large numbers, especially in the twelfth and thirteenth centuries. This is apparent in the need to set limits as to the numbers a house could support. The house of Santa Maria di Monticelli at Florence was limited to thirty-three nuns by Gregory IX in 1235; Gregory set the same limit at Santa Maria di Monteluce at Perugia, but the nuns numbered fifty-seven when the church was consecrated in 1253.[18] Numbers fluctuated over time, partly because of economic problems and poverty and partly because of social factors and changing ideas about the religious life. The Black Death had the same impact on the nunneries as on the population at large, and some houses disappeared as a result. Agnes de Bowes was said to be the sole survivor of Wolthorpe priory, Northamptonshire, after the Black Death, and the house was merged with St Michael's, Stamford, in 1354.[19] War exacerbated economic difficulties in some parts of Europe. The problem of poverty was addressed in *Periculoso* where it was laid down that nunneries with limited resources were not to accept further novices. The Benedictine priory of Saint-Zacharie near Marseilles, dependent on the abbey of Saint-Victor of Marseilles, suffered increasing poverty in the fourteenth century, partly as a result of Saint-Victor exploiting its property in the abbey's interests. The abbey progressively limited the number of nuns from ninety-eight in 1322 to thirty in 1376, twenty-four in 1402 and five in 1461.[20]

In Florence and Venice, on the other hand, the early age of marriage for girls and the late age for men, together with the rising cost of dowries, led to expansion in the number and size of nunneries. The five houses at Florence in the mid-thirteenth century grew to twenty-four in 1336, and a further increase took place in the fifteenth and early sixteenth centuries. Nunneries came to be concentrated within the city, and the average number of religious and lay women within a convent grew from 20 in 1428 to 97.8 in 1515. The Benedictine house of Le Murate, founded by a recluse of poor family in 1390, grew rapidly in the mid-fifteenth century and attracted nuns of higher social status; the number of inmates was fixed at 150 in 1461 by Pope Pius II, but it is likely that the nuns numbered 200 in the early sixteenth century.[21]

Entry to a nunnery usually required the payment of a dowry and the provision of clothing and equipment. Poor women were more likely to be numbered among the lay sisters, who did much of the manual work, than among the nuns. At the same time, simply to describe nuns as noble is to make use of a very broad term which can give the misleading impression that nuns came only from the wealthiest families. The pattern of recruitment varied at different places and was partly dependent on the house's reputation. Some nunneries certainly drew women of high birth. The house of Poor Clares at Pavia, founded in 1379, admitted only noble ladies over the age of forty.

Amesbury in Wiltshire, belonging to the order of Fontevrault and numbering 117 nuns around 1300, attracted Eleanor of Provence, widow of Henry III, her granddaughter Mary, and Eleanor of Brittany (d. 1342), who subsequently became abbess of Fontevrault. Other convents, however, attracted gentry, yeomanry and townspeople. In her study of nunneries in the diocese of Norwich, Marilyn Oliva found that a considerable number of nuns came from the middling social ranks of East Anglia and few from the higher nobility. Many houses recruited from their surrounding parishes and were often both small and poor. In the Rhineland and south-west Germany, Cistercian and mendicant nuns in the thirteenth century were drawn from noble, ministerial and knightly families, and from urban patricians and burghers, a similar pattern to that in France. Florentine nuns mostly originated from middling families and there was no insistence that they should be members of the wealthiest social groups; lay sisters came from the lower urban classes and often from the country.[22] It can be said that nuns usually came from the better-off groups of society, but they did not necessarily belong to the nobility.

It is rare for the sources to give information as to why women became nuns, unless they are describing the life of a saint. Religious vocation, lack of a dowry, revolt against marriage, family pressures and widowhood all had a part to play. Certain religious writings, such as the *Letter on Virginity*, played on the desire not to marry and the sufferings in marriage itself.[23] The Church always regarded the life of the virgin as the ideal. Some women appear to have been forced by their families to enter a convent and possibly also compelled to leave. Margaret de Prestwich claimed that she was forced to make her profession; she fled and married, and was pronounced free of the nunnery in 1383. Hawise de Basevil allegedly left the convent at Rusper in Sussex to claim a family inheritance. Beatrice, daughter of Hugh, Count of Burgundy, alleged that her parents compelled her to enter the Benedictine house of Baume-les-Dames and that she stayed there for several years for fear of her brother, Count Otto, before finally appealing to the pope.[24]

Families evolved their own strategies as to which of their children should enter the religious life. Although a dowry was needed, it tended to be smaller than the dowry paid for marriage. For example, a dowry of 100 florins was usual in fifteenth-century Florence, while John Fox bequeathed £10 for his daughter to become a nun at Marham in Norfolk. Such a dowry was easier for a Florentine or Venetian father to raise than one for marriage and he could be sure that his daughter would lead a life acceptable to the elite. Wills often throw light on parental policies. The will of Gauffrid de Tarare of the Lyonnais, dating from the first half of the fourteenth century, reveals that he had two daughters who were nuns, and he wanted three others to take up the religious life, although he gave them the option to choose.[25]

Certainly there were nuns who had a strong religious vocation. Clare of Montefalco became the abbess of an Augustinian house in 1291 and was renowned for her asceticism and ecstasies, as well as for her devotion to the

Passion of Christ. Caterina Vigri (d. 1463) was lady-in-waiting to Margaret d'Este but in the late 1420s became a Poor Clare at the house of Corpus Domini in Ferrara, later transferring to Corpus Domini at Bologna as head of the house; she used her mystical visions in her writings and paintings. Matilda of Lancaster, Countess of Ulster, entered religious life as a widow, although she asserted that she had always wanted to be a nun.[26] The convent of Corpus Domini at Venice in the early fifteenth century, as described by Sister Bartolomea Riccoboni, gives a picture of a group of women dedicated to the religious life, whether they had entered as girls or widows. Her accounts of individual nuns in the necrology stress their religious fervour and their devotion to Christ and the Eucharist. Thus Caterina Costantini was very humble and much given to prayer and weeping, Marina Ogniben entered the convent with her sister without family permission and had a vision of Christ when she received Communion, and Chiara Buonio performed the humblest chores with great joy.[27]

The age for entering a convent varied. In Florence a girl often entered religion at the age of nine and took her vows at thirteen. In England, the girl frequently entered in her mid-teens.[28] The practice of entering the convent young probably helped integration into the religious life and enabled the girl's education to be geared towards her life as a nun. Entry as a virgin, to become the bride of Christ at profession, was regarded as the ideal, but many women entered as widows. At profession, the novice made her vows of poverty, chastity and obedience, which bound her to the religious life until her death. The Rule of St Benedict provided for a communal life and this set the basic framework for the nuns. The Augustinian Rule was less precise, but the timetable for the canonesses was similar to that of the nuns. The performance of the Office in church took place at intervals throughout each day, with matins, or the night office, taking place an hour or so after midnight, and lauds at daybreak, followed at intervals by prime, terce, sext, none, vespers and compline. There was at least one daily Mass, usually after terce. The meeting of the chapter took place after prime, and the main meal was eaten in the middle of the day. In the intervals between the services, the nuns worked or meditated privately. The basic *Opus Dei* was added to in the course of the later Middle Ages, with extra Masses on feast days, frequent communion in some houses, and the preaching of sermons. Dominican nuns had a special devotion to the Virgin Mary, and sang the Little Office of the Virgin every day, together with other acts of worship in her honour. Their affective devotion to her and to Christ and his Passion is also apparent in their prayers and reading.[29] The performance of the *Opus Dei* was carefully checked at visitations. Archbishop Eudes Rigaud of Rouen was frequently critical of the nuns' chant. After visiting the Benedictine priory of Villarceaux in 1249, he pointed out that all services should be celebrated regularly and at the proper times, and that all nuns should attend punctually unless they were ill or excused by the prioress.[30]

All the services were in Latin and it is unlikely that all the nuns fully understood the chants. Many later medieval nuns were probably able to read in the vernacular as a result of education before their entry or because they were taught in the nunnery itself, and some were able to write as well. It is less clear how many understood Latin. A few convents were exceptional in their learning, such as Unterlinden in Colmar, where many nuns had a good knowledge of Latin and whose sister-book was the only one among the German Dominicans to be written in Latin. Most nuns probably learned enough Latin to understand the psalter, which constituted a major part of the *Opus Dei*, as well as the Pater Noster, Ave Maria and other prayers. The readings at mealtimes in the refectory were often in Latin, and it is known that this posed problems to German Dominican nuns and to Poor Clares; in the fifteenth century, the Dominicans substituted readings in the vernacular. The vernacular was used for the Rule, for sermons and presumably for the nuns' private prayers, and this was probably also the case in England.[31]

The importance of books to the later medieval nun has to be assessed from scattered evidence. It was Benedictine custom to issue a book to each nun at the beginning of Lent; this is known to have taken place at Barking abbey in Essex, which owned works in English and French.[32] Certain German Dominican nunneries had large collections of books; 370 works were listed in a fifteenth-century catalogue for St Catherine's house at Nuremberg. The dispersal of monastic libraries in England after the Dissolution makes it impossible to know the full extent of convent book ownership, but it is possible to gain certain pointers. In the diocese of Norwich, in addition to service books, several houses had bibles and devotional texts in the vernacular. Flixton had part of the Old Testament in French, and Thetford the New Testament in English; Bruisyard and Campsey Ashe possessed saints' lives, the Golden Legend and a Life of Christ in French and English. Individual nuns also had their own books, the majority in English or French.[33]

The ability to read constituted a bridge between the *Opus Dei* and work. Some nuns were authors, with many, especially in Germany and Italy, recording mystical experiences. The sister-books were written in the first half of the fourteenth century and contained biographies of nuns, concentrating on their virtues and religious practices. They were used to instruct nuns in the religious life. Two very different authors show the range of writing with which some nuns were engaged. Teresa de Cartagena came of a prominent *converso* family of fifteenth-century Burgos. Her grandfather was a Jewish rabbi and scholar who, together with his children, was converted to Christianity in 1390 and who subsequently became prominent in the royal court of Castile, being appointed bishop of Cartagena in 1402 and bishop of Burgos ten years later. Teresa was born around 1415–20, was well educated and, according to her own account, attended the university of Salamanca, probably studying in a convent there. At some subsequent time she became deaf and entered a silent world. She became a nun, possibly a Poor Clare at Burgos, and lived the rest of her life very much in isolation.

Her work, *Grove of the Infirm*, written in Spanish, explored the nature and purpose of suffering. She urged sufferers to use their sickness to seek spiritual joy and to grow in virtue, pointing out that the sick could not enjoy the blessings of the world and it was useless to hanker for worldly things. Rather, the sufferer had to cultivate patience and persevere in doing good works for love of God. Her second work, *Wonder at the Works of God*, was written because of the incredulity with which *Grove of the Infirm* was received. Teresa did not write to justify herself but to emphasise the goodness and mercy of God. She commented on her weak womanly understanding but stressed that she was directed by the grace of God. She wanted to show the greatness of God's blessings to all.[34]

Bartolomea Riccoboni produced a historical narrative work. Little is known about her apart from her entry into the newly founded convent of Corpus Domini at Venice in 1394 at the age of twenty-five. She wrote her chronicle and necrology in the Venetian dialect. The necrology described nuns who had died, praising their spiritual achievements, while the chronicle brings out her love for the community and its high standards. At the same time, the work shows an awareness of the world beyond the convent walls, as in her account of the banishment from Venice of Giovanni Dominici, who had taken the house under his protection, and of the Great Schism, seen very much from the point of view of the Venetian pope, Gregory XII. Like Teresa, Bartolomea presented herself as weak and inadequate but felt strongly that the urge to write came as a result of divine inspiration. She wanted to inform the nuns who came after her.[35]

More nuns were engaged in copying books than in authorship, but there is only partial evidence for this activity since it is rare to be able to attribute a book to a particular copyist. There was some copying of books in German nunneries in the thirteenth century, and the fifteenth-century nuns of the reformed house at Langendorf prepared parchment and transcribed and bound books as well as doing spinning and weaving. The Poor Clares wrote and illuminated manuscripts, and Caterina Vigri was renowned as a mystic, writer, copyist, painter and musician; her breviary which was completed around 1452 used pictures as well as words as the focus for devotion.[36]

Nuns also engaged in sewing and embroidery, although again the evidence is sparse. In view of women's skills in needlework, it is likely that many nuns pursued this type of work. Some German houses were active in this area; wall hangings were made for the church at Quedlinburg in the late twelfth or early thirteenth century, and also in the fourteenth century at the Cistercian house at Wienhausen, one of them with the story of Tristan and Isolde. A set of vestments is known to have been made at Göss in the late thirteenth century. Le Murate at Florence was famous for its gold and silver embroidery which was done in Lent and helped to keep the house solvent. Savonarola was critical of this activity and also ordered the nuns to stop making their little books; the nuns are known to have copied and illuminated manuscripts.[37]

Although nuns employed male labourers, servants and lay sisters, some nuns are known to have carried out manual work. Much depended on the status and relative prosperity of the house. Cistercian nuns performed labouring jobs, like the nuns of La Ramée who were occupied with agricultural work. On the whole, however, nuns doing manual labour were in a minority, and a fifteenth-century nun at Ankerwick in Buckinghamshire complained that the nuns had had to prepare their food for several months since there were no servants in the brewhouse, bakehouse or kitchen.[38]

The Rule of St Benedict provided for a moderate diet, with two cooked dishes being served and possibly a third dish of fruit or vegetables. One pound of bread a day was allowed for each monk. Meat was not to be served, except to the sick. The abbot was given discretion to increase the amount of food when greater labour was to be performed. As far as later medieval nunneries were concerned, there was great variety in diet, depending on the religious life and economic circumstances of the house. Sometimes poverty meant that the diet was sparse. Moreover, in the stricter orders, fasting was regarded as a form of renunciation and penance, and some nuns deliberately starved themselves as part of their religious discipline. This was the case with St Clare, as with the early Dominican nuns at Unterlinden in Colmar and elsewhere.[39] On the other hand, dietary rules might be considerably relaxed when particular feast days came to be celebrated with pittances or extra dishes of food.

All nuns followed the general pattern of worship, prayer and work, but those who held office had particular responsibilities to the community. The number of officials varied according to the size and wealth of the house, but the hierarchy mirrored that found in lay society, with the abbess or prioress as the head, then the officials such as the sacrist and the cellarer, and then the nuns, lay sisters and servants. The obedientiaries, as the officials are often called, had specific areas of responsibility, although their titles and areas of work varied from house to house. Some convents had a treasurer to deal with finances, others gave this responsibility to the abbess, prioress or cellarer. The cellarer was usually responsible for the house's property, the sacrist for the church, the precentrix for music and chant, the chamberer for clothing, the hosteller for guests and the almoner for charity.[40] Houses with a male prior, like Saint-Zacharie near Marseilles, had their property and finances dealt with by him. Many women appointed to office, however, found that they had considerable power and had to take difficult decisions; they needed intelligence, ability and integrity, and had to be able to work with their fellow nuns as well as with people outside the convent, usually men. The need for experience is brought out by the fifteenth-century Office of the Cellaress at Barking abbey. She had to collect the rents from the abbey's manors, ensure that the abbey had sufficient stocks of grain, livestock and fish, arrange for pittances on anniversaries, pay various wages, and ensure that the buildings she was responsible for at the abbey and on the manors were kept in good repair.[41]

The choice of abbess and prioress was of even greater importance, as she had to provide spiritual and material leadership, and the nuns owed obedience to her. Visitations suggest that poor leadership led to problems at a number of nunneries. The abbess or prioress was responsible for the economic well-being of the house, working with her officials and coming into contact with lay and ecclesiastical authorities. Evidence from English nunneries indicates that serious problems arose when accounts were not properly kept and the house fell into debt. She was responsible for discipline and had to provide spiritual guidance for the nuns; it was recorded of Isabetta Tommasini, prioress of Corpus Domini at Venice, that she was very learned in the Scriptures and sounded like a doctor of theology when she preached in chapter. The abbess was also responsible for any daughter-houses or cells of the convent. The election of abbess or prioress was regularised by the Fourth Lateran Council. She was normally chosen by her nuns and confirmed by the diocesan bishop, head of the order, or sometimes by the king. It has often been assumed that she was elected from the elite, but recent work on the diocese of Norwich has shown that office-holding reflected the social composition of the individual house and that ability and experience counted for more than birth.[42]

The later Middle Ages have been regarded by historians as a time of relaxed standards in the religious life. Certainly the enthusiasm and growth of the twelfth and thirteenth centuries were not maintained in the fourteenth and fifteenth, but movements for reform and visitation articles show a desire to maintain high standards. Visitation documents have to be treated with caution as they do not provide a full picture of life at the house, and the visitor had particular questions in mind to which he required answers. His brief was to find and correct faults. Three areas in particular caused concern: the communal life, private property and the issue of chastity. All these matters provoked a variety of responses and have to be set in the context not only of the religious life but of changes in secular living standards as well.

The greater emphasis on privacy in elite life in the world was reflected in the breakdown, to varying degrees, of communal life in nunneries. For the Benedictine convents of the Holy Roman Empire, eastern France and the Low Countries which evolved into houses of secular canonesses, the *Opus Dei* was virtually the only communal element in their lives. These canonesses came from noble and knightly families, held their own prebends, took their meals in their own houses, owned private property and made visits to their families. Some followed a religious pattern of life, but it was clearly different from that intended originally for the enclosed nun.[43] This development can be compared with the evolution of the Benedictine house of La Celle les Brignoles, a priory attached to the abbey of St Victor of Marseilles. This house had more than 100 nuns at its thirteenth-century peak, in spite of being limited to fifty in 1227 and to forty in 1362. Girls normally entered at about the age of twelve, although there were some adult and widowed entrants. The house had a common refectory but not a dorter.

From around 1300, the nuns lived in little houses in the park with their own outhouses and chicken runs, although they came together in church and in the refectory on feast days. They were allowed to make family visits and to go out on business. References in nuns' wills to furs and jewels point to the existence of private property.[44]

The breakdown of communal life was widespread in other parts of Europe and although visitors might regard it as deplorable, there was little they could do to enforce a reversal of the trend. Florence witnessed an emphasis on individual life in convents, and visitation reports from English houses complained about the growth of privacy. At Godstow, Oxfordshire, in 1432, the refectory was ordered to be repaired and at least twelve nuns were to eat there every day.[45] The often close link between the nun and her family helps to explain how nuns came to hold private property, in spite of their vow of poverty. In some cases, they were given property to support them during their life as a nun, in others they received an inheritance or bequest. Some nunneries were given a papal dispensation to hold private property, as the nuns of Salzinnes were permitted by Innocent IV in 1245.[46]

Visitors paid most attention to sexual scandals. With the emphasis put on virginity and enclosure, the issue of chastity was bound to be of major concern. From the modern point of view, it is important to try to understand the circumstances of a particular nunnery and its local society. The Dominican nuns of Zamora can be taken as a case in point. The house was founded in 1259 and twenty years later, when it was subject to episcopal visitation, there appears to have been a complete breakdown of monastic life and obedience. The Rule was not observed, nor was the *Opus Dei* celebrated at the proper times. Nuns and friars engaged in sexual activity, taking each other as lovers. The convent had fractured into two parties, one faction threatening the prioress and depriving her of her office. On the face of things, here was a scandalous situation. However, the scandal concealed ecclesiastical conflict between the bishop of Zamora and the Dominicans which had been going on for several years and explains the two factions, that of the prioress, supporting the bishop and unable to control the convent, and that of the nuns, supporting the friars. By 1281, the convent had split, with a substantial group settling at Benevente, and the prioress submitted her case to Rome. It was several more years before the conflict was resolved. The situation also has to be considered in the context of Spanish politics and the Spanish Church. Celibacy of the clergy had not been achieved in thirteenth-century Spain, and both Ferdinand III and Alfonso X of Castile allowed clergy to bequeath property to their children; attempts by the papal legate to enforce celibacy were unpopular among the Castilian bishops.[47] The whole situation was more complex than it appears at first.

The prevalence of sexual offences in Normandy has been analysed by Penelope Johnson with reference to the visitations by Eudes Rigaud, Archbishop of Rouen, of seventeen women's houses in the mid-thirteenth century.[48] Of these houses, eight came up with sexual offences, with twenty-six nuns out of a total of 587 breaking the vow of chastity. The majority of men involved were churchmen connected with the nunnery. The three houses where the greatest number of incidents were recorded all had further serious problems. The report on Villarceaux in 1249 found that over half the nuns had broken their vow and therefore Eudes insisted on the proper performance of the *Opus Dei*, a communal refectory and dorter, no excess in dress and no departure from the house without permission; no guest was to be allowed to sleep within the enclosure. At the same time it was clear that the priory could not support the number of nuns, and Eudes wanted the accounts to be properly kept by the prioress and audited. He finished by saying that his recommendations were to be read in chapter once a month and that he would be harsher the next time if they failed to do this. The other two priories of Saint-Saëns and Saint-Aubin likewise faced additional problems linked with poverty.

This evidence from Normandy indicates that it was only a small minority of nuns who were involved in sexual relationships. Such scandals were made much of in the visitations, although the effect on the nun herself went unrecorded. One can only wonder about the feelings of women like Beatrice de Hawkesworth who ran away from Esholt priory in Yorkshire in 1303 to have her baby at home and was subsequently readmitted, or Isabella Gervays of Winchester who connived in her own abduction and returned to the nunnery pregnant.[49] Research indicates that problems within the nunnery itself were conducive to relaxed discipline. The majority of nuns were living a less communal life than earlier on, but this was due as much to social changes as to monastic abuses. They continued to worship and work within the enclosure and to live a religious life, although without the degree of enthusiasm and fervour which characterised many nuns of the thirteenth century.

Late medieval reform

Certain reforms were afoot in the late Middle Ages. A particularly influential foundation was established at Vadstena by St Birgitta of Sweden, famed also for her sanctity and her writings. The house was situated on land given by King Magnus in 1346 and built by her son. Birgitta herself never saw the convent as she left Sweden in 1349 and died at Rome in 1373, but she drew up its Rule and made strenuous efforts to get it accepted. Vadstena was a double house, with sixty enclosed nuns and twenty-five monks who shared the abbey church and lived a life of poverty. The nuns had a special devotion to the Virgin Mary, as well as to the Passion and Death of Christ, while the monks were expected to carry out a preaching ministry. Birgitta stressed the importance of books and study; nuns were engaged in copying, and the library contained about 1,500 books by the early modern period. The abbess controlled the temporal affairs of the house, but the monks were in spiritual charge. Birgitta claimed that the Rule was communicated to her by Christ, but both Clement VI and Urban V turned it down, Urban in 1370 sanctioning the Augustinian Rule for two separate houses at Vadstena. It was only in 1378 that Bridget's Rule was accepted by Urban VI. The order was patronised by the Danish royal family in the late fourteenth and fifteenth centuries. Queen Margaret was brought up by Birgitta's eldest daughter and brought pressure to bear to secure Birgitta's canonisation in 1391. She and her successors were generous patrons, and both Margaret and Philippa of Lancaster became lay sisters at Vadstena. Houses belonging to the order were established in Italy, Germany and Poland as well as in Scandinavia. In England one house at Syon in Middlesex was founded by Henry V.[50]

The emphasis on poverty was at the root of the Franciscan reform of St Colette of Corbie (d. 1447), the daughter of a carpenter, who became a beguine, Poor Clare and then a recluse in her search for the religious life. In 1406, she had visions of St Francis urging her to reform his order, and received permission from Pope Benedict XIII to found a house of Poor Clares where poverty would be upheld. She achieved this at Besançon in 1408 and carried on with her reform, establishing new houses and reforming old ones, notably in France, Flanders and Savoy.[51] Reform was also carried out by individuals, making use of existing Rules and aiming to reinvigorate monastic life. The combination of religious reformer and patron led to the foundation of a number of new houses of female mendicants in northern Italy. The house of Corpus Domini at Venice was founded by the Benedictine nun Lucia Tiepolo, who felt called upon to found a new Benedictine house on the edge of the city. As a result of the patronage of Isabetta and Andreola Tommasini, and the intervention of the Dominican, Giovanni Dominici, the house became Dominican and was consecrated in 1394. The house of Corpus Domini at Ferrara was established about 1406 as a community of laywomen by Bernardina Sedazzari, a merchant's daughter. Bernardina had been a Benedictine nun both as a girl and as a widow. Her plan to set up an Augustinian enclosed house ran into difficulties, but in 1452 the house had its position confirmed as part of the order of St Clare. It was here that Caterina Vigri spent much of her life as a nun, and the house became a focus for reform in the late fifteenth century.[52]

The reform of existing houses often entailed drastic change in the way of life. Reform usually came from outside and was sometimes impossible to achieve because of internal opposition, political factors and vested interests. The papal legate in Germany, Cardinal Nicholas of Cusa, attempted to enforce strict enclosure and a ban on private property in the mid-fifteenth century. The nuns at Sonnenburg agreed to reform, but then changed their minds and turned for support to Sigismund, Duke of Austria; as a result, the new abbess installed by Nicholas made no headway. Some reform was achieved by Johann Rode (d. 1439) in the Rhineland, and he was also associated with the reform in north Germany which emanated from the abbey of Bursfeld. Among the nunneries reformed was Langendorf in Saxony where rules were drawn up for the elaborate performance of the *Opus Dei* and for daily life. The duties of officials were specified, and no one was to be elected abbess under the age of twenty-nine, an indication of the importance attached to mature leadership. Johann Busch was also engaged in the reform of nunneries, although not always with success. In one case, it was the town authorities who called for reform. The leading citizens of Ulm marched on the house of Poor Clares at Söflingen, taking with them a new abbess and a number of reformed nuns. The existing abbess refused to be deposed but in the end had to accept certain reforms.[53] The reforms indicate that some houses achieved high standards in the fourteenth and fifteenth centuries, and certain reformers and nuns were anxious to return to the original spirit of their monastic Rules. The whole movement of monastic reform was to face much greater upheaval in the sixteenth century.

Nuns and lay society

The emphasis on enclosure did not mean that nuns were completely cut off from the world outside the convent. Even the most rigorous houses had their contacts with nuns' families and local authorities, as did houses with a more relaxed lifestyle. All convents had their concerns with property and revenues, they had to maintain relationships with patrons and lay and ecclesiastical powers, and were expected to offer hospitality, charity, education and spiritual services to individuals and communities.

Most people knew nunneries and their officials as landowners, farmers, rent collectors and holders of courts. As such, nuns faced the same problems as lay landowners in the later Middle Ages, with labour difficulties, falling incomes and sometimes devastation by war. The Carthusian, Margaret of Oingt, commented in one of her letters on the late wheat harvest and storm damage in the convent's vineyards. In the pillaging in France in 1358, the nuns of Poissy, Longchamp and Maubuisson all had to take refuge in Paris.[54] Nunneries were on the whole poorer than male houses, and the large number of poorly endowed nunneries often had a hard time, with debt being the result of contemporary economic and political circumstances, and not only due to poor management. Businesslike leadership was a real asset but could not always be secured. The priory of La Celle les Brignoles was fortunate to have efficient women of affairs and coped better than others with the crisis of the late Middle Ages. Even when money was tight, it was possible to remain clear of debt, as several houses in East Anglia found. The question of cash flow has been identified as the root problem with the three houses of the order of Fontevrault in England, but they weathered the agrarian crisis of the fourteenth century by adapting to change; in the early 1300s, Nuneaton leased out its mills, churches and the marketplace in Nuneaton, but continued to exploit most of its estates directly. Berenice Kerr points out that although much of the administration was carried out by lay brothers and laymen, it was the prioresses who appointed the officials and were ultimately responsible.[55] At the other end of the scale, there were houses suffering extremes of poverty and debt which were tempted into short-term and ineffective remedies. In his report on the Norman priory of Villarceaux, Eudes Rigaud warned nuns not to recruit any more until their number had fallen.[56] There were too many nuns for the priory's resources and although novices' dowries were a welcome source of cash, the nun would probably have to be maintained in the house for twenty or thirty years.

Like their lay counterparts, nuns had to be ready to defend their property and privileges and this inevitably brought them into contact, and sometimes conflict, with the lay world. One instance shows the lengths to which nuns might go. The wealthy abbey of Notre-Dame-aux-Nonnains at Troyes had a close connection with Pope Urban IV who was a native of the town and had been baptised in the church. He gave his family house to the nunnery, together with papal bulls granting them a forty-day indulgence and protection of their property. He then decided to build a church of canons dedicated to St Urban on the site of his parents' house, and although the nuns handed the property back, they were hostile to the papal plans. After Urban's death, they twice broke down the doors of the new church, and two years later the abbess, nuns and armed men prevented Giles, Archbishop of Tyre, from entering the church. They were found guilty and excommunicated. It was only in 1283 that they paid compensation to the canons and the excommunication was lifted.[57] Few defences of rights were so drastic, but the episode shows that nuns were quite capable of standing up for themselves.

Nuns offered hospitality and charity to the lay world. Of these, least is known about charity, as much of it was probably given in kind. Hospitality could be subject to abuse, involving houses in excessive expenditure, especially if wealthy guests made long stays in the nunnery or the house was expected to look after political detainees, as when Roger Mortimer's daughters were sent to nunneries after he escaped from the Tower of London in 1324.[58] The granting of corrodies, where payment was made for future maintenance, was also an economic drain on nunneries. It was common for noble girls all over Europe to be educated in convents, sometimes remaining there to become nuns. This was widespread in the Poor Clare houses of southern France as well as in England, Italy and elsewhere.[59]

Apart from material considerations, the nuns offered the elite of lay society an important spiritual dimension. Guests and pupils might be from nuns' families or be numbered among the house's patrons, or belong to the wider network of the gentry and urban elite. Many of these people wanted the spiritual and not just the material benefit that came from contact with the nuns. The desire for confraternity with a monastic house was widespread. At the male Cistercian house of Berdoues in Gascony, women were promised burial in the abbey church by 1237, and as members of the abbey's confraternity, had the right to be buried in the Cistercian habit.[60] Papal indulgences were sought for permission to enter enclosed orders. In 1290, Blanche of Navarre, wife of Edmund, Earl of Lancaster, was permitted to visit the monastery of Provins with twelve matrons, and any house of the Poor Clares in France and England with eight, although she was not allowed to eat or spend the night with the nuns. Marie de St Pol had her own apartment built in the Minoresses' abbey of Denny in Cambridgeshire, overlooking the nuns' church.[61] Widows who boarded at a convent, in return for payment, had the advantage of security and could at the same time participate in the religious life, whether they were at Le Murate at Florence or Carrow outside Norwich, which had at least 250 boarders between the late fourteenth and mid-fifteenth century, most of whom were female.[62]

Some nunneries catered for pilgrims, as at the house of St Clare in Assisi. Clare was canonised in 1255, two years after her death, and the convent moved from San Damiano into Assisi where the new buildings were designed to provide a shrine for her body.[63] Many nunneries catered for the local community through their churches. Some owned the patronage of parish churches, giving them the right to appoint the parish priest. Some nuns' churches served the parish as well as the nuns, and certain nunneries allowed lay people to be buried in their cemeteries. The nuns' principal religious duty was, however, to offer prayer and intercession for those who requested it. Here they were at a great disadvantage compared with the monks. Over the later Middle Ages, the offering of the Mass on behalf of the living and the dead became increasingly popular. The nuns had to employ priests to meet this demand, whereas in male houses the Masses were celebrated at no extra cost to the monastery by monks who were increasingly in priestly orders. With patrons who asked for Masses over a long period or in perpetuity, the cost to the nuns was likely to outstrip the endowment. The prayers of the nuns continued to be requested and valued through the later Middle Ages. The sisters of San Piero Martire at Florence declared in 1478 that they had always been exempt from taxation because of their strict life and constant prayers for the town; they claimed that such prayers, coming from people of great religion, were worth more to Florence than 2,000 horses. Abbess Scolastica Rondinelli (d. 1475) of Le Murate emphasised the continuous twenty-four-hour cycle of prayer when she was writing to people outside the convent.[64]

More unusual was the role of nun as spiritual counsellor outside the convent. Isabetta Tommasini, of Corpus Domini at Venice, was described in the house's necrology as the source of good advice; many men and women, religious and lay, came to her for counsel and she was able to help them. Spiritual advice was also dispensed in writing. Margaret of Oingt (d. 1310) was a nun, and later prioress, at the charterhouse of Poleteins. She was a visionary and mystic, writing in Latin and Provençal. She was hesitant in speaking of her experiences, and in her letters attributed them to a third person, or spoke reluctantly of what she herself had witnessed. In one letter, after an anonymous brother had asked for advice on the penance he should perform, she made use of her visions of Christ's birth and death for the salvation of mankind. Another letter describes a vision, said to have been experienced by another, for the consolation of the recipient.[65]

Nuns had an integral role to play in the medieval world. The life of the convent met a demand from both women and their families. Nuns and nunneries were never as numerous as monks and monastic houses; many of the nunneries were poor, and the degree of male control intensified over the later Middle Ages. Yet nunneries offered certain women more than the religious life. Abbesses and prioresses were in a position of power both inside and outside the convent, and the well-being of the house and of local communities depended largely on their leadership and that of their officials. Nunneries were by no means cut off from the world, as contacts were maintained with nuns' families, with patrons, guests and boarders, with peasants and labourers on their lands, and with townsmen who supplied their needs. In view of the amount of contact with the world, relaxations of the Rule were bound to occur over a period of time. Yet the late Middle Ages saw a measure of reform, and although very strict houses were in a minority, it is likely that many nuns continued to live a disciplined and fulfilled religious life.

Notes

1 M. Parisse, *Les nonnes au moyen âge* (Le Puy, 1983), pp. 66–80.

2 V.J. Koudelka and R.J. Loenertz (eds), *Monumenta Diplomatica Sancti Dominici* (Monumenta Ordinis Fratrum Praedicatorum Historica 25, Rome, 1966), p. 181; R.B. Brooke, *The Coming of the Friars* (London, 1975), pp. 167–8, 184; M-H. Vicaire, 'L'action de Saint Dominique sur la vie regulière des femmes en Languedoc', in *La femme dans la vie religieuse du Languedoc* (Cahiers de Fanjeaux 23, Toulouse, 1988), pp. 217–40.

3 A. Walz (ed.), *Beati Jordani de Saxonia Epistulae* (Monumenta Ordinis Fratrum Praedicatorum Historica 23, Rome, 1951), pp. 4–60; Brooke, *Coming of the Friars*, pp. 187–8. Carmelite nuns are not found before the mid-fifteenth century, and only became of importance in early modern and modern times; K.J. Egan, 'The spirituality of the Carmelites', in J. Raitt (ed.), *Christian Spirituality. High Middle Ages and Reformation* (London, 1987), p. 56.

4 Thomas of Celano, *Legenda Sanctae Clarae Virginis*, (ed.) F. Pennacchi (Assisi, 1910), pp. 4–16; P. Ranft, 'Clare of Assisi and the thirteenth-century Church', *JMH* 17 (1991), pp. 123–5.

5 R.B.C. Huygens (ed.), *Lettres de Jacques de Vitry* (Leiden, 1960), pp. 75–6.

6 E. Amt (ed.), *Women's Lives in Medieval Europe. A Sourcebook* (New York and London, 1993), pp. 235–45, gives Clare's Rule in translation; E.A. Petroff, *Medieval Women's Visionary Literature* (New York, 1986), pp. 242–5, gives the Testament of St Clare in translation; Ranft, 'Clare of Assisi', pp. 125–32; C. Gennaro, 'Clare, Agnes and their earliest followers: from the poor ladies of San Damiano to the Poor Clares', in D. Bornstein and R. Rusconi (eds), *Women and Religion in Medieval and Renaissance Italy* (Chicago, 1996), pp. 43–51; J.R.H. Moorman, *A History of the Franciscan Order from its Origins to the Year 1517* (Oxford, 1968), pp. 38–9, 205–13. Most Poor Clares followed Urban IV's Rule, but Longchamp in France, the English houses, and the Colonna house in Rome followed the Isabella Rule, devised by the sister of Louis IX; there are minor differences between the two Rules.

7 Vicaire, 'L'action de Saint Dominique', pp. 218, 224–5; Brooke, *Coming of the Friars*, pp. 185–6; B.M. Bolton, 'Daughters of Rome: all one in Christ Jesus', in

W.J. Sheils and D. Wood (eds), *Women in the Church* (Studies in Church History 27, Oxford, 1990), pp. 107–15, and reprinted in B. Bolton, *Innocent III: Studies on Papal Authority and Pastoral Care* (Aldershot, 1995), pp. 101–15; M. de Fontette, 'Les dominicaines en France au treizième siècle', in M. Parisse (ed.), *Les religieuses en France au treizième siècle* (Nancy, 1985), p. 97; Paul Lee, *Nunneries, Learning and Spirituality in Late Medieval English Society. The Dominican Priory of Dartford* (Woodbridge, 2001), pp. 14–16.

8 H. Grundmann, *Religiöse Bewegungen im Mittelalter* (Berlin, 1935), pp. 312–14; Petroff, *Medieval Women's Visionary Literature*, pp. 245–6; Gennaro, 'Clare, Agnes and their earliest followers', pp. 42, 48; J.M. Wood, *Women, Art and Spirituality. The Poor Clares of Early Modern Italy* (Cambridge, 1996), p. 66; Moorman, *History of the Franciscan Order*, pp. 39, 209–11; A.F.C. Bourdillon, *The Order of Minoresses in England* (Manchester, 1926), pp. 11–23; J.B. Freed, *The Friars and German Society in the Thirteenth Century* (Cambridge, Massachusetts, 1977), pp. 58–9; G. Brunel-Lobrichon, 'Diffusion et spiritualité des premières clarisses méridionales', in *La Femme dans la Vie Religieuse du Languedoc*, pp. 261–80.

9 Freed, *Friars and German Society*, pp. 49–50, 142–3, 156.

10 Parisse, *Nonnes au moyen âge*, pp. 82–3; L.L. Otis, 'Prostitution and repentance in late medieval Perpignan', in J. Kirshner and S.F. Wemple (eds), *Women of the Medieval World. Essays in Honor of John H. Mundy* (Oxford, 1985), pp. 140, 149–60; L.L. Otis, *Prostitution in Medieval Society. The History of an Urban Institution in Languedoc* (Chicago, 1985), pp. 72–5; K.L. Jansen, 'Mary Magdalen and the mendicants: the preaching of penance in the late Middle Ages', *JMH* 21 (1995), p. 21.

11 C.W. Bynum, 'Religious women in the later Middle Ages', in Raitt (ed.), *Christian Spirituality*, p. 122.

12 M. Parisse, *La Lorraine monastique* (Nancy, 1981), pp. 135–6, 139.

13 P. Ranft, *Women and the Religious Life in Premodern Europe* (Basingstoke, 1996), pp. 46–54; S. Roisin, L'efflorescence cistercienne et le courant féminin de piété au treizième siècle', *Revue d'Histoire Ecclesiastique* 39 (1943), p. 350; J.A. Gribbin, *The Premonstratensian Order in Late Medieval England* (Woodbridge, 2001), pp. 7–8; B.M. Kerr, *Religious Life for Women c. 1100–c. 1350. Fontevraud in England* (Oxford, 1999), pp. 178–9, 239.

14 Roisin, 'L'efflorescence cistercienne', pp. 344–53; S. Thompson, *Women Religious. The Founding of English Nunneries after the Norman Conquest* (Oxford, 1991), p. 96; S. Thompson, 'The problem of the Cistercian nuns in the twelfth and early thirteenth centuries', in D. Baker (ed.), *Medieval Women* (Studies in Church History Subsidia 1, Oxford, 1978), pp. 227–52; Ranft, *Women and Religious Life*, pp. 54–7; M. Shadis, 'Piety, politics and power: the patronage of Leonor of England and her daughters Berenguela of Leon and Blanche of Castile', in J.H. McCash (ed.), *The Cultural Patronage of Medieval Women* (Athens, Georgia, 1996), pp. 204–7.

15 De Fontette, 'Les dominicaines en France', pp. 100–6; Moorman, *History of the Franciscan Order*, pp. 213–15.

16 J.A. Brundage and E.M. Makowski, 'Enclosure of nuns: the decretal *Periculoso* and its commentators', *JMH* 20 (1994), pp. 143–55.

17 C.T. Martin (ed.), *Registrum Epistolarum Johannis Peckham, Archiepiscopi Cantuariensis*, 3 vols (Rolls Series, London, 1882–6), I, pp. 81–6; J.C. Ward (ed. and trans.), *Women of the English Nobility and Gentry 1066–1500* (Manchester, 1995), pp. 209–13.

18 Wood, *Women, Art and Spirituality*, pp. 67, 99.

19 D. Logan, *Runaway Religious in England, c. 1240–1540* (Cambridge, 1996), p. 259.

20 Brundage and Makowski, 'Enclosure of nuns', p. 145; P. Leclerq, 'Le prieurie de Saint-Zacharie en 1403 d'après le Livre de Raison de son prieur', *JMH* 1 (1975), pp. 382–99.
21 R. Trexler, 'Le célibat à la fin du Moyen Age: les religieuses de Florence', *Annales ESC* 27 (1972), pp. 1330–7, 1345–6; K.J.P. Lowe, 'Female strategies for success in a male-ordered world: the Benedictine convent of Le Murate in Florence in the fifteenth and early sixteenth centuries', in Sheils and Wood (eds), *Women in the Church*, pp. 209–12.
22 Moorman, *History of the Franciscan Order*, p. 413; Kerr, *Religious Life for Women*, pp. 109–10, 116, 237; M. Oliva, *The Convent and the Community in Late Medieval England. Female Monasteries in the Diocese of Norwich, 1350–1540* (Woodbridge, 1998), pp. 52–61; J.B. Freed, 'Urban development and the *cura monialium* in thirteenth-century Germany', *Viator* 3 (1972), pp. 317–20; Parisse, *Les nonnes au moyen âge*, pp. 131–3; Trexler, 'Le célibat à la fin du Moyen Age', pp. 1338–40.
23 B. Millett and J. Wogan-Browne (eds), *Medieval English Prose for Women. Selections from the Katherine Group and Ancrene Wisse* (Oxford, 1990), pp. xiv–xx, 2–43.
24 Logan, *Runaway Religious*, pp. 83–9, 256, 259; Parisse, *Les nonnes au moyen âge*, pp. 245–6.
25 Trexler, 'Le célibat à la fin du Moyen Age', p. 1340; Oliva, *Convent and Community*, p. 50; M-T. Lorcin, 'Retraite des veuves et filles au couvent. Quelques aspects de la condition féminine à la fin du Moyen Age', *Annales de Démographie Historique* (1975), pp. 198–9.
26 D.H. Farmer, *The Oxford Dictionary of Saints* (Oxford, 1997), p. 104; Wood, *Women, Art and Spirituality*, pp. 123–40; *Calendar of Entries in the Papal Registers relating to Great Britain and Ireland: Papal Letters, 1342–62* (London, 1897), p. 112; *Petitions to the Pope, 1342–1419* (London, 1897), pp. 22–3.
27 Sister Bartolomea Riccoboni, *Life and Death in a Venetian Convent: the Chronicle and Necrology of Corpus Domini, 1395–1436*, (ed. and trans.) D. Bornstein (Chicago, 2000), pp. 64–7.
28 Trexler, 'Le célibat à la fin du Moyen Age', pp. 1342–3; Oliva, *Convent and Community*, pp. 45–6.
29 P.D. Johnson, *Equal in Monastic Profession. Religious Women in Medieval France* (Chicago, 1991), p. 134; Lee, *Nunneries, Learning and Spirituality*, pp. 141, 151–2.
30 J.F. O'Sullivan (ed.) and S.M. Brown (trans.), *The Register of Eudes of Rouen* (New York, 1964), pp. 49, 129, 285, 477.
31 M-L. Ehrenschwendtner, '*Puellae litteratae*: the use of the vernacular in the Dominican convents of southern Germany', in D. Watt (ed.), *Medieval Women in their Communities* (Cardiff, 1997), pp. 52–3; Kerr, *Religious Life for Women*, pp. 127–8; Lee, *Nunneries, Learning and Spirituality*, pp. 150–1.
32 Kerr, *Religious Life for Women*, p. 125; A.I. Doyle, 'Books connected with the Vere family and Barking abbey', *Transactions of the Essex Archaeological Society* new series 25 part 2 (1958), pp. 239–43.
33 Lee, *Nunneries, Learning and Spirituality*, p. 154; Oliva, *Convent and Community*, pp. 64–72.
34 D. Seidenspinner-Núñez (ed.), *The Writings of Teresa de Cartagena* (Woodbridge, 1998), pp. 4–16, 44–7, 86–8, 102–3, 109; A. Minnis and R. Voaden (eds), *Medieval Holy Women in the Christian Tradition c. 1100–c. 1500* (Turnhout, 2010), pp. 105–10.
35 Riccoboni, *Life and Death in a Venetian Convent*, pp. 5, 10, 25, 41–63.
36 L. Eckenstein, *Woman under Monasticism. Chapters on Saintlore and Convent Life between A.D. 500 and A.D. 1500* (Cambridge, 1896), pp. 237–8, 416; Wood, *Women, Art and Spirituality*, pp. 128–34.

37 Eckenstein, *Woman under Monasticism*, pp. 233–6; Lowe, 'Female strategies for success', pp. 216–17.

38 Roisin, 'L'efflorescence cistercienne', pp. 365–6; A. Hamilton Thompson (ed.), *Visitations of Religious Houses in the Diocese of Lincoln*, 3 vols (Canterbury and York Society 17, 24, 33, 1915–27), II, p. 4.

39 P. Dollinger (ed.), *Documents de l'histoire de l'Alsace* (Toulouse, 1972), pp. 118–21.

40 Oliva, *Convent and Community*, pp. 83–102.

41 British Library, London, Cotton MS Julius D viii, fos 40r–47v; translated extracts can be found in Ward (ed. and trans.), *Women of the English Nobility and Gentry*, pp. 213–16.

42 Thompson (ed.), *Visitations*, I, pp. 44–5; II, pp. 2–4; Riccoboni, *Life and Death in a Venetian Convent*, p. 100; Johnson, *Equal in Monastic Profession*, pp. 169–72, 195; Oliva, *Convent and Community*, pp. 91–3, 105–10; M. Oliva, 'Aristocracy or meritocracy? Office-holding patterns in late medieval English nunneries', in Sheils and Wood (eds), *Women in the Church*, pp. 197–208.

43 M. Parisse and P. Heili (eds), *Les chapitres de dames nobles entre France et Empire* (Paris, 1998), pp. 15, 21–69; Parisse, *Les nonnes au moyen âge*, pp. 206–14.

44 P. L'Hermite-Leclerq, 'Le monastère de La Celle les Brignoles (Var) au treizième siècle', in Parisse (ed.), *Les religieuses en France*, pp. 75–88.

45 R.C. Trexler, *Synodal Law in Florence and Fiesole, 1306–1518* (Rome, 1971), pp. 98–9; Thompson (ed.), *Visitations*, I, pp. 66–8.

46 Johnson, *Equal in Monastic Profession*, pp. 107–12.

47 P. Linehan, *The Ladies of Zamora* (Manchester, 1997), pp. 4–5, 42–58, 146–7, 161–74.

48 Johnson, *Equal in Monastic Profession*, pp. 112–30; O'Sullivan (ed.) and Brown (trans.), *Register of Eudes of Rouen*, pp. 48–50, 129, 199, 225–6, 285, 306, 319, 353, 364, 369–70, 383–4, 411, 430–1, 470–1, 477–8, 513, 559, 569, 687. Parts of the 1249 visitation of Villarceaux priory, the 1253 visitation of Saint-Saëns, and the 1260 visitation of Saint-Aubin are included in Amt (ed.), *Women's Lives in Medieval Europe*, pp. 248–51.

49 Logan, *Runaway Religious*, pp. 84, 259, 262.

50 J.B. Holloway (ed.), *St Bride and her Book* (Woodbridge, 1992), pp. 7–11, 16–17; B. Morris, *St Birgitta of Sweden* (Woodbridge, 1999), pp. 160–72; S. Imsen, 'Late medieval Scandinavian queenship', in A.J. Duggan (ed.), *Queens and Queenship in Medieval Europe* (Woodbridge, 1997), pp. 61–2.

51 Farmer, *Oxford Dictionary of Saints*, p. 108; Moorman, *History of the Franciscan Order*, pp. 414–15.

52 Riccoboni, *Life and Death in a Venetian Convent*, pp. 4–5, 26–34; M.M. McLaughlin, 'Creating and recreating communities of women: the case of Corpus Domini, Ferrara, 1406–52', *Signs* 14 (1988–9), pp. 293–310.

53 S. Hilpisch, *History of Benedictine Nuns*, (trans.) M.J. Muggli and (ed.) L.J. Doyle (Collegeville, Minnesota, 1958), pp. 51–7; Eckenstein, *Woman under Monasticism*, pp. 414–23; F. Rapp, 'La réforme des maisons de dames nobles dans le diocèse de Strasbourg à la fin du Moyen Age', in Parisse and Heili (eds), *Les chapitres de dames nobles*, pp. 71–86.

54 R. Blumenfeld-Kosinski (ed.), *The Writings of Margaret of Oingt, Medieval Prioress and Mystic* (Woodbridge, 1997), p. 65; G. Fourquin, *Les campagnes de la région parisienne à la fin du moyen âge, du milieu du treizième siècle au début du seizième siècle* (Paris, 1964), p. 230.

55 L'Hermite-Leclerq, 'Le monastère de La Celle les Brignoles', p. 87; Oliva, *Convent and Community*, pp. 90–9; Kerr, *Religious Life for Women*, pp. 129–236.

56 O'Sullivan (ed.) and Brown (trans.), *Register of Eudes of Rouen*, p. 50.

57 Johnson, *Equal in Monastic Profession*, pp. 86–8.

58 *Calendar of Close Rolls, 1323–7* (London, 1898), pp. 88–9.
59 Brunel-Lobrichon, 'Diffusion et spiritualité des premières clarisses méridionales', p. 268.
60 C.H. Berman, 'Women as donors and patrons to southern French monasteries in the twelfth and thirteenth centuries', in C.H. Berman, C.W. Connell and J.R. Rothschild (eds), *The Worlds of Medieval Women. Creativity, Influence and Imagination* (Morgantown, Virginia, 1985), pp. 56–7.
61 *Papal Letters, 1198–1304* (London, 1894), pp. 522, 526; P.M. Christie and J.G. Coad, 'Excavations at Denny abbey', *Archaeological Journal* 137 (1980), pp. 141, 152–4.
62 Lowe, 'Female strategies for success', p. 219; Oliva, *Convent and Community*, pp. 117–18.
63 Wood, *Women, Art and Spirituality*, pp. 43–51.
64 Trexler, 'Le célibat à la fin du Moyen Age', p. 1329; Lowe, 'Female strategies for success', p. 219.
65 Riccoboni, *Life and Death in a Venetian Convent*, p. 100; Blumenfeld-Kosinski (ed.), *The Writings of Margaret of Oingt*, pp. 62–3, 65–6.

11 Religious life

Beguines, penitents and recluses

Until the twelfth century, women who wished to follow the religious life had to become nuns, an option which only a minority could take up. The popular preachers of the twelfth century, such as Norbert of Xanten and Robert of Arbrissel, gathered followings of women from a wide range of backgrounds and established them in monastic foundations. By the later twelfth century, other forms of religious life were emerging, with growing numbers of lay-women becoming beguines and penitents and living their lives in a non-institutional setting. These groups posed new problems for the Church in that they did not take formal vows or follow a monastic rule. They lived among a group of women or at home and, over time, pressure was brought to bear on them to live an institutional life. Recluses, however, were recognised by the Church, which regarded their solitary life as valid and covered by ecclesiastical rituals and customs.

These forms of religious life were widespread and many women experimented with them before finding the way of life best suited to their religious needs. Ivetta of Huy fulfilled her duties as wife and mother before turning to the care of lepers, establishing a hospital and community, and eventually becoming a recluse. Juliana Falconieri (d. 1341) became a tertiary, belonging to a third order of friars, in her own home before joining a group of women and drawing up a Rule for female Servite tertiaries.[1] Penitents, beguines and recluses all exercised influence on the rest of society in the later Middle Ages, and included saints and mystics among their numbers.

These new movements attracted both men and women, but there always seem to have been many more beguines than beghards, the male adherents, in the Low Countries, northern France and the Rhineland, while the penitential movement in Mediterranean regions drew large numbers of women. The movements attracted girls, married couples and widows, and extended over much of Europe, the *beatas* of Spain and the *bizzoche* of Italy being very similar to the beguines in northern Europe. It was unusual, however, to find beguines in England.[2] The movements grew out of the ferment of popular religious developments of the twelfth century, with the theme of poverty and the desire to live a life of renunciation of worldly goods providing a common factor between the followers of the preachers, the mendicant movement and the beguines.[3] There was, however, a marked difference from the women who became nuns, in that the beguines did not look to a particular figure as inspiration or founder, and although close relationships developed with monastic houses and the friars, there was no sense of setting up a new order.

Becoming a beguine or penitent rather than a nun was a matter of deliberate choice for many women, and although some families sought to dissuade them, parental pressure was a less significant factor than for nuns. Although the movements provided religious opportunities for women from lower social groups, many beguines came from a similar background to the nuns and could have become nuns had they so wished. It was only in the later fourteenth and fifteenth centuries that the majority of beguines came from middling and lower social groups.[4] It is probable that in some areas where there were large numbers of women wanting to follow a religious life, there were not enough nunneries to meet the demand. Flemish nunneries, for instance, were few in number and catered mainly for the nobility. According to Jacques de Vitry, there were not enough Cistercian houses for the many women who wanted to live a life of poverty and austerity; the Cistercians instead supported the beguines and provided them with spiritual services, receiving in return an insight into the women's mystical devotion to Christ and the Eucharist.[5]

Although rural groups of women are recorded, the majority of beguines and penitents are associated with the towns, and it is likely that social and economic as well as religious factors influenced the growth of the movements. This was the period when towns were growing rapidly all over Europe, and the greatest concentrations of towns were to be found in the same areas as those where beguines and penitents were flourishing. The towns relied on immigration of both men and women, who often arrived in adolescence or early adulthood. Unmarried women and widows probably settled together in households in order to gain security and mutual support, and such groups might be following a lay or religious life. It is likely that many towns had a surplus of women, making it difficult to marry; in addition, some women may have been too poor to accumulate a dowry. In a patriarchal world, life as a beguine or penitent meant freedom from male control.

Cultural factors may also have been present. The town with its commercial economy and emphasis on manufacture, sale and profit, as well as the possession of material goods, may well have sparked a reaction in some people, a desire to renounce wealth and live in imitation of Christ. The element of renunciation was uppermost in the religious life of beguines, just as it was in the life of certain nuns such as St Clare. Such renunciation could spark conflict within families. Ivetta of Huy as a widow distributed large sums to the poor, leading her father to remove her children, thinking that she was giving away their inheritance; her children were returned to her when she agreed to safeguard their property.[6]

The early beguines were concentrated in the diocese of Liège, with women such as Ivetta of Huy, Juliana of Cornillon, and Mary of Oignies, who is well known as a result of the *Life* written by Jacques de Vitry. He was concerned to justify the orthodoxy and way of life of the beguines, at a time when the Cathar and Waldensian heresies were causing the Church serious concern; he was urged to write the *Life* by Bishop Fulk of Toulouse who had been exiled from his diocese because of Cathar heresy. Mary was born in 1177 into a well-off family of Nivelles, and married at the age of fourteen. She showed religious traits as a child and lived a pious life as a married woman. Eventually she persuaded her husband that they should live in chastity and give away their goods to the poor; they spent the next fifteen years caring for lepers at Willambroux. Mary's ascetic piety became widely known, and to get away from the crowds her husband agreed that she could become a lay sister and recluse in a hermitage dependent on the Augustinian priory at Oignies-sur-Sambre. It was here that Jacques de Vitry met her in 1211, two years before her death, and became her confessor.[7]

Many of the features of Mary's life were typical of the *mulieres sanctae* (holy women) of the region: her renunciation of wealth and marital relations, her asceticism and care for the sick and outcasts of society, her contemplative life as a recluse and her devotion to the Eucharist. Jacques de Vitry interpreted her renunciation of the world as the means by which she deepened her religious life. She was a visionary and prophetess and foresaw the Albigensian crusade, although she was unable to carry out her desire to go to Languedoc and be martyred for her faith. She also performed miracles of healing. There is no doubt that Jacques de Vitry was impressed by her and accepted her guidance. She was his inspiration as a preacher and had an influence on his career. He also had a high opinion of her fellow beguines, as he had of the similar women he met near Perugia in 1216 when he was on his way to Rome to become bishop of Acre. His intention was to gain papal approval for the religious women of the diocese of Liège, France and Germany. Unfortunately, he arrived after the death of Innocent III who had brought the Humiliati, Franciscans and Dominicans into the Church, and after the Fourth Lateran Council had prohibited the formation of new religious orders. Honorius III gave oral approval for the women to live a communal life and Gregory IX put the women under papal protection in 1233. Yet problems remained because of the informal nature of the beguines.[8]

Many of the same characteristics, bound up with the desire to follow Christ, were found with the groups in Italy. The Humiliati came under suspicion of heresy in the late twelfth century, but were incorporated into the Church by Innocent III in 1201 as three orders, the first and second comprising monks and nuns, and the third order for laymen and laywomen who lived in their own homes, following a life of prayer and fasting, work and service to the poor. The Franciscan Order of Penitents for lay people adopted a similar way of life by 1221, and wives could join the groups with their husbands' consent. Apart from regular meetings of the group, the individual member was expected to recite the seven canonical hours or, if illiterate, the Pater Noster and Ave Maria; confession and communion took place three times a year.[9] Many groups of penitents in the towns developed spontaneously, as with the three women of Padua who established themselves as a small community of penitents under the supervision of a parish priest in 1213; the group developed into the convent of St Cecilia by 1225.[10] Such communities burgeoned, but at the same time the Church wanted to harness and control these and other spontaneous groups.

Looking at the areas where the beguines flourished in the thirteenth and early fourteenth centuries, women on their own and in small informal groups were found alongside an increasing number of larger foundations. The beguines were numerous in the Rhineland. In Strasbourg in the late thirteenth and early fourteenth centuries, they were concentrated in particular parts of the city, notably near mendicant convents. There were also many beguines in the villages round the city. An analysis of the beguines whose place of residence is known has found that about one-third came from citizen families, one-third from artisans and one-third from outside the city. Most of the beguines lived in communities and tended to congregate with women from similar backgrounds. In central Strasbourg, the women were mainly artisan, whereas near the Dominican convent three houses of wealthy beguines were established before 1276. There was a considerable concentration near the Franciscan house in the west of the city, where most of the beguines were from artisan families or were immigrants. Some small convents were founded before the clampdown on beguines in Strasbourg in 1318.[11]

Cologne is thought to have had 169 beguine houses. According to the St Albans chronicler Matthew Paris, there were 2,000 beguines in the city in 1243, and he regarded these women as very much a German phenomenon. This figure may not be an exaggeration, since there were 1,170 beguines in the city in the mid-fourteenth century. They were first recorded in the city in the 1220s, and property deeds reveal a considerable amount of beguine activity in the second half of the thirteenth and early fourteenth centuries. Houses came to be established, with fifty-four known to have been founded by 1300. As at Strasbourg, many beguines lived near the Dominican and Franciscan convents.[12] Other German cities also had substantial numbers of beguines – Frankfurt is said to have had fifty-seven houses, Basel twenty and Nuremberg twenty-two. Mainz had twenty-eight houses but they were very small, and there were only around sixty beguines there in the fourteenth century.[13]

Although there were strong similarities between the beguines of the Rhineland towns and those of the Low Countries, the presence in the latter of powerful patrons helps to explain the foundation of substantial beguinages. From the 1230s, groups of beguines began to acquire property and establish small convents and court beguinages. They worked in hospitals near the convent or in other works of charity. The movement was again primarily urban, although some rural groups have been found in northern France. Of the patrons, the most important were Jeanne and Margaret, successive countesses of Flanders, who through their influence and grants were able to establish beguinages in many of the major towns. Convents were mostly small and rarely had their own chapel; the beguines used the parish church and were directed by the parish priest. The court beguinages contained a number of individual houses and convents grouped round the chapel, communal buildings and hospital, and some were recognised as parishes in their own right. The largest was probably the house of St Elizabeth at Ghent, set up in the 1230s and early 1240s, and possibly having 400 inmates at the end of the Middle Ages. The beguines of Bruges were organised into a parish in 1245, and in the same year the house of Cantimpré at Mons was established. Countess Margaret was responsible for founding the important beguinage of St Elizabeth at Lille, and both Jeanne and Margaret patronised the house of Champfleury at Douai. Local patrons were also found, but the patronage of the two countesses was outstanding.[14]

It is difficult to calculate the number of beguines at any one time. Douai is known to have had fifteen beguinages, of which the house of Champfleury housed at least 100 beguines by 1273; the beguinage of Wetz, usually described as a hospital, had over eighteen inmates, while the house of Pilates was founded for ten poor beguines. There is no means of counting the number of beguines living in small groups or on their own. There were substantial numbers in other parts of the Low Countries and northern France; in the county of Artois, Arras had nine houses with between twelve and seventy-two women each, while St Omer in 1322 had 395 beguines in the great convent and twenty smaller ones.[15]

Beguinages were also to be found in other French towns, such as Besançon and Rheims; the house at Rheims, founded in 1249, is known to have had noble inmates. In Paris, the beguinage founded by Louis IX was modelled on Ghent and was placed under Dominican supervision.[16] In Provence, the beguines were associated with Douceline de Digne, who founded the beguinage of Roubaud around 1240. Her brother was a Franciscan and the house was intended to combine the worship of God and the care of the sick. Most of the beguines came from urban families, and although many lived an austere life, this was not true of all.[17]

The lack of vows and of a formal rule make it difficult to elucidate the daily life of the beguine, but the Ghent memorandum of 1328, produced for the visitation of the house of St Elizabeth, throws light on beguine practices and enables a comparison to be made with the life of the nun. New entrants underwent a year's probation, after which profession was informal since no vows were taken. The beguine was always free to leave the house but while she was an inmate she was not allowed to be absent without the mistress's agreement, or to go out on her own. She was expected to be obedient to the grand mistress, who was chosen by the beguines themselves or by the founder. The grand mistress enjoyed a position of authority but, because of the more fluid nature of the beguinage, did not have as much power as a Benedictine abbess. She was expected to rule the house with the advice of senior beguines and sometimes also the town authorities. The beguine wore a grey habit, and many lived an austere life, sleeping on straw mats, not making use of linen sheets, and fasting on bread and water. Emphasis was placed on living the life of the poor. After getting up at dawn, the day was divided between prayer and work. The beguines heard Mass and then spent the day working in silence and continuing to pray. They returned to church for Vespers, further prayer and meditation. Sundays and holy days were spent at Mass and in prayer and contemplation, and hearing sermons.[18] The beguines were especially devoted to the Passion of Christ and the Eucharist. Juliana of Cornillon initiated the feast of Corpus Christi in the Roman Church; the feast was established at Liège in 1246 and was promulgated by Pope Urban IV eighteen years later. Mary of Oignies is said to have eaten only the Host at the end of her life. The thirteenth-century visionary, Elizabeth of Spalbeek, received the stigmata and was regarded by Philip, abbot of Clairvaux, as a female St Francis. He emphasised women's missionary role in spreading the Gospel through use of their bodies, arguing that because of their concern with the physical side of nature they were in a special position to imitate Christ.[19]

Manual work was essential for the poor beguines so that they could make their contribution to the support of the house; the Ghent memorandum singled out sewing and laundry work. Nursing the sick was the most common occupation and many beguinages were associated with hospitals. Some of the beguines at St Elizabeth's were responsible for the upbringing of girls, sent to the house by their wealthy parents, and beguine schools were also found elsewhere. Some houses brewed beer for sale, and many were engaged in processes connected with the woollen and linen cloth industries. However, industrial problems and guild restrictions limited the work which the beguines could do. The use of the spinning wheel was prohibited in three of the houses founded in Strasbourg after 1318, and there was friction between the guild of silk spinners of Cologne and the beguines in the fifteenth century.[20]

The beguines and penitents exercised a religious and caring influence on the society around them. From the point of view of the women themselves, both movements provided ways for townswomen in particular to follow the religious life, either on their own or in groups, without having to make the lifelong commitment which they would have had to do if they became nuns. The way of life could be lived in the context of home and family, and of urban work patterns; the housekeeper-companion of the young wife of the Ménagier of Paris was a beguine. Although many of the women, especially early on, came from well-off families, this form of life was open to poorer women who used their working and caring skills to earn a livelihood within the group. Women attracted by the ideal of poverty and renunciation made use of the skills learned during their upbringing as part of their religious life. Although beguines and penitents are found before the advent of the friars, they came to be strongly influenced by the mendicants as spiritual guides.

At the same time, the ascetic way of life led certain beguines and penitents into spiritual ecstasy and mysticism, and some were eventually canonised. Some of these women had a considerable impact on patterns of devotion and on local society and politics, although sometimes their influence spread further afield. The hope of Jacques de Vitry and Fulk of Toulouse that Mary of Oignies would become a model of orthodoxy for women did not in fact materialise; Fulk was unable to return to his diocese until 1229 and died two years later, and no version of the *Life* of Mary of Oignies in Occitan is known.[21] Other women were more influential, even if it was only in their own locality. The mystic Mechtild of Magdeburg lived most of her adult life as a beguine in the city and became known as a strong critic of the local clergy; it was their hostility which led her to become a nun at Helfta in her old age. The blind and disabled Margaret of Città di Castello (d. 1320) became a penitent attached to the Dominicans when she was fourteen years old, and lived a life of asceticism and charity. She came to be regarded in her lifetime as the protector of the town, praying to God on its behalf and acting as intercessor in local quarrels. Margaret of Cortona (d. 1297) became a Franciscan penitent after the death of her lover, and lived a life of harsh austerity while caring for the sick. After her death, she continued to be regarded as the protector of Cortona and a new church was built round her tomb decorated with frescoes of her life. Her reputation grew in Cortona and beyond.[22]

Notwithstanding the reputation and influence of beguines and penitents, they posed a problem to the Church and to lay authorities as well. Here were women who, even if they had a connection with a house of monks or friars, were not bound to lifelong enclosure and therefore were seen as out of control. Such a situation where women lived and moved freely was regarded as dangerous to the social order. A parallel situation had arisen with the Poor Clares and enclosure had soon been imposed as a solution. By the mid-thirteenth century, it was clear that the beguines were not a temporary phenomenon; they were acquiring property and establishing convents. Towns were volatile places, subject to faction and disorder, and no authority wanted to have a group which it could not govern. Patrons such as Jeanne and Margaret, Countesses of Flanders, wanted to foster the beguine movement but within a controlled environment. The beguinage at Lille was established to stop the beguines from wandering round the town, and its rules were drawn up by Count Guy de Dampierre, son of Countess Margaret, in the late thirteenth century and subsequently by Philip the Bold, Duke of Burgundy, in 1401.[23] Urban patrons probably had similar considerations in mind, thinking in terms of spiritual benefits and also the need to control a potential problem. In Cologne, several mid-thirteenth-century patrons belonged to the urban elite which dominated the town government; Richmudis Wipperfurth was daughter of the burgomaster Ludwig of the Muhlengasse and in 1267 founded a beguinage for fifty women near the Dominican convent.[24]

The Church's attitude towards the beguines moved from approbation to hostility over the thirteenth and early fourteenth centuries. Although the beguines were under papal protection from 1233, hostility continued among local clergy, as with Bruno, Bishop of Olmütz, who recommended to the pope in 1273 that the beguines should be married or become members of an approved order. The Council of Lyons the following year was concerned with the number of unauthorised groups and reiterated the pronouncement of 1215 forbidding the establishment of any new order.[25]

The anxieties expressed in 1274 were not confined to the Church's lack of control over religious women. Heresy was still regarded as a real danger in the later thirteenth century. *The Mirror of Simple Souls*, written by the beguine Margaret Porete, was condemned as spreading the heresy of the Free Spirit and its author was burnt at the stake in Paris in 1310. Margaret contended that, as the soul progressed from the valley of humility to the mountain of contemplation, it was liberated and so completely absorbed into God that all ethical obligations disappeared. There are serious doubts as to whether the book was heretical, but the fact remains that the heresy of the Free Spirit was regarded by the Church as a threat.[26]

Moreover, certain women penitents in southern France and Italy were strongly influenced by the Spiritual Franciscans who were condemned by Pope John XXII. Their influence is apparent in the life of Delphine de Puimichel (d. 1360). She and her husband, Elzéar de Sabran, came of prominent Provençal families. Elzéar belonged to the nobility of Angevin Naples, and the couple were well known at the court of Naples, which became a refuge for the Spiritual Franciscans. Widowed after a chaste marriage in 1323, Delphine decided to get rid of all her property and ten years later took a vow of poverty and formed a small community with her followers, aiming to live as a group of equals. She is known to have begged for alms on the streets of Naples. This emphasis on poverty and equality was likely to have been the result of Spiritual Franciscan influence; Delphine had come under Franciscan influence since she was a child, and her friend, Queen Sancia of Naples, is known to have protected her brother, Philip of Majorca, who was a Spiritual Franciscan. Delphine ended her life as a recluse in Provence.[27]

The Council of Vienne of 1311–12 specifically focused on the beguines, their lack of Rule, and their heresy on the Trinity and the nature of God. The two decrees can be compared with Boniface VIII's decretal, *Periculoso*, issued at the end of the thirteenth century, which insisted on enclosure for nuns. The first decree, *Cum de quibusdam mulieribus* (Concerning certain women), denied the beguines the right to call themselves religious because they did not promise obedience, renounce private property nor follow an approved Rule, even though they wore the habit and had connections with religious houses. Their way of life was absolutely forbidden for the future. The last sentence of the decree, however, contains a contradiction, as Pope

Clement V ended by saying that there was no intention to stop devout women from living as inspired by God, provided that they lived a life of penance, humility and chastity in their communities. The second decree, *Ad nostrum*, condemned the heresy of the Free Spirit. Both decrees were published in 1317 after revisions by John XXII.[28]

What happened to the beguines after the Council of Vienne mirrors the contradictions in the decree. The action taken, usually after a delay, varied according to the attitude of local ecclesiastical authorities and rulers, but the general trend was towards institutionalisation. The archbishop of Cologne had shown his hostility towards beghards and beguines in 1307, and in 1318 he decreed that beguines were to be integrated into approved orders. This move took place over the fourteenth century, but as late as 1421 the archbishop was ordered by Pope Martin V to suppress small unregulated convents. In contrast, at Würzburg, the beguines continued to flourish throughout the fourteenth century and later, and were accepted by the local clergy.[29]

Patrons appear to have accepted the move to greater regulation. It is interesting to find that the peak in numbers of new convents comes both before and after the Council of Vienne. Some foundation dates are uncertain, but between 1280 and 1320 seventy-nine beguine convents were founded, compared with eighteen in the 1260s and 1270s and thirty-four between 1320 and 1350. The fifteen houses founded between 1350 and 1400 shows that the time of expansion for the beguines was over.[30] The clampdown of 1317 was followed by the foundation of numerous convents for beguines in Strasbourg, and altogether there may have been eighty-five houses in the city. Foundations were made by the inhabitants of Strasbourg: twenty-three by patricians, twenty-six by less wealthy citizens and at least twenty-three by craftsmen. The founders included twenty-seven women, fifteen of whom were from the artisan group. Founders often reserved places in the houses for kinsmen and friends, and in some houses a prebendal system was in operation. In contrast, all the beguinages in Basel were closed down after investigation in 1409 and 1411.[31]

In the Low Countries, the backing of powerful patrons, both ecclesiastical and lay, ensured the survival of the beguinages. The bishops conducted an inquiry into beguinages in the 1320s. The bishop of Tournai found that beguines were pursuing a praiseworthy life. Beguines in Flanders were supported by Count Robert and those in court beguinages were fully cleared in 1328. The tone of the Ghent memorandum underlines the spiritual value of the community and emphasises that it was well ordered, and this was corroborated in the visitation. Founders' descendants had no wish to see these communities disbanded, but nearly ninety communities had closed by 1400, partly for demographic reasons and also because of changing views on the religious life.[32]

One solution after 1317 was for the beguines and penitents to become members of the third orders of the friars (or tertiaries) which developed in the late thirteenth century and were designed to cater for the religious needs of lay people whether they were single, married or widowed. By the fourteenth century, some members of the third orders were living in communities and taking monastic vows, while at the same time continuing with their occupations. By the fifteenth century, some of the communities were enclosed.[33] The Rules of the third orders provided a solution for the beguines which was satisfactory to the Church and had been under consideration even before the Council of Vienne. In 1303, the Franciscan chapter of Upper Germany insisted that any beguinage which it was to supervise should follow the Rule of the third order or hand over all its property rights to the friars. The Franciscans would then supply confessors and carry out a yearly visitation of the house. Similar moves are found at Strasbourg after 1318 when the Rules of the third orders were widely adopted, and this process continued through the fourteenth century. At Tournai, Augustinian communities as well as those of the Franciscan third order grew in the fourteenth century.[34]

The heyday of the beguines was in the thirteenth and early fourteenth centuries, before the Council of Vienne. Beguinages continued to exist well into the modern period but were no longer significant pioneers in the religious life for laywomen. Yet groups emerging in the late Middle Ages show that the desire to combine the religious life with life in the world remained, and this was particularly apparent with the Brethren of the Common Life. The first group of Sisters of the Common Life was established by Gerard Groote at Deventer in the 1370s. The Brothers and Sisters held property in common and followed a life of poverty, chastity and obedience without taking formal vows. The Sisters combined prayer with working for their living and practised charity. They were allowed to leave the community but, if they did so, had no right to return. By the mid-fifteenth century, there were about 100 houses, mainly in Holland and West Germany, and the women's houses outnumbered the men's. There are obvious parallels between the Sisters and the beguines, and it is significant that most of the Sisters came to follow the third rule of St Francis in the second half of the fifteenth century.[35]

Several of the best known Italian penitents of the thirteenth century were members of the third order, such as Angela of Foligno and Margaret of Cortona; the hospital which Margaret founded was run by a community of tertiaries. The most famous medieval tertiary was undoubtedly St Catherine of Siena. Some women progressed from being tertiaries to becoming nuns, such as Clare of Montefalco whose community in 1290 decided to change from being one of Franciscan tertiaries to a house of Augustinian nuns. The life of the tertiary, combining renunciation and prayer with service to the community, continued to be attractive throughout the late Middle Ages in many parts of Europe.

The life of St Francesca of Rome (1384–1440) sums up the ideals of this form of life. Francesca belonged by birth and marriage to the Roman nobility. At the age of thirteen she married Lorenzo Ponziani and lived in his family home with his brother and sister-in-law, Vannozza, to whom Francesca grew very close. The two women lived virtually a double life. On the one hand, Francesca had all the usual duties of wife and mother, responsible for household and children at a time of war and unrest (Rome was captured by Ladislas of Naples in 1408). At the same time, the two women attended Mass, heard sermons, begged for alms and devoted themselves to the poor and ill, notably in the Hospital of Santo Spirito. Francesca's husband knew of her activities and was willing for her to live a religious life within the bonds of marriage; Francesca promised to live with him until he died.

A group of mainly noble women formed round Francesca, continuing to live at home and becoming known as the Oblates of Mary. Some years later they obtained their own house where they lived as a group and were called the Oblates of Tor de'Specchi. Francesca became the head of the community after Lorenzo's death in 1436. These women were not enclosed, took no vows and wore lay dress. Their life was divided between prayer and meditation, reading and charity. They were very popular in the city and came to be accepted by the Church hierarchy. Canonisation proceedings opened soon after Francesca's death, although she did not become a saint officially until 1608.[36] This group of women was by no means unique in the fifteenth century. Women still wanted to experience religious life in the context of the world, both in Italy and in other parts of Europe.

In contrast, for some women the religious life was achieved by becoming a recluse or anchoress.[37] This was acceptable to patriarchal culture and was sanctioned by the Church. Within their cells anchoresses were not subject to male control, and this way of life was increasingly popular in the thirteenth and fourteenth centuries. Within their cells, they prayed for the local community, dispensing spiritual counsel in person and through their writings. The story of Verdiana of Castelfiorentino (d. 1241) can be regarded as typical. She was born into a poor Tuscan family and, after going on pilgrimage to Santiago de Compostela and Rome, decided to become a recluse. Emerging unharmed after frequent attacks by snakes, she gained a reputation for sanctity as well as asceticism. She died after thirty-four years in her cell, and her tomb became a place of local pilgrimage, her help being especially invoked against snake bites.[38]

The initiative to become an anchoress came from the woman herself, who might be either a nun or a lay person, single or widowed, and the Church had procedures for trying to ensure that the desire was genuine. When Beatrice Franke, a Benedictine nun, wished to become an anchoress at the parish church of Winterton, the bishop of Lincoln asked John Horton, abbot of Thornton, to examine her before granting a licence. The parishioners of Winterton were in agreement, and it was also important to ensure that the anchoress had adequate financial support. Beatrice was enclosed in 1435 in a cell on the north side of Winterton church.[39] The rite of enclosure included part of the Mass for the dead, in that the anchoress was henceforth regarded as dead to the world, and she took a vow to remain enclosed for the rest of her life. After entering her cell, the door was locked and sealed. The cell had a window into the church so that she could participate in the celebration of Mass and adore the Host, which was placed in the pyx hanging above the altar. Through an outside window the anchoress could talk to callers, although Aelred of Rievaulx, writing for his sister in the twelfth century, urged her to beware of idle gossip. Some anchoresses had a maidservant as their contact with the outside world. The author of the *Ancrene Riwle*, written about 1230 for three noble ladies on the Anglo-Welsh border, allowed the anchoress to keep a cat.[40] Cells were simple, with one or two rooms and possibly a small yard or garden, so the anchoress had as much space as would be found in the houses of the poor.

Not all anchoresses kept their vow of lifelong enclosure. Colette of Corbie lived as an anchoress for four years before she felt called to reform the Franciscans.[41] All lived a simple life devoted to prayer and meditation, but religious practices and austerity varied. The author of the *Ancrene Riwle* prescribed a vegetarian diet and warned against excessive fasting; the three recluses might entertain women and children but not men unless they had the permission of their spiritual director. They were forbidden to engage in business. Their clothing was to be plain and warm, with no jewellery. Idleness was to be avoided, and they were urged to work on plain needlework. The religious life laid down by the author of the *Ancrene Riwle* focused on the control of the senses and on penance. The anchoresses were given a daily structure of prayer and the writer stressed the need to control one's inner feelings which cause temptation and sin. The heart could be open to the way of love at the centre of the Christian life only if it was purged by confession and penance. A parallel can be drawn with the manuals for confessors being produced at about the same time in the wake of the decrees of the Fourth Lateran Council on yearly confession and communion. There is little sign of the devotion centred on the Mass, as found with Mary of Oignies and other beguines. According to the *Ancrene Riwle*, the anchoresses were allowed to receive communion fifteen times a year, but there is no discussion of the importance of the Eucharist in their devotional lives.[42]

Fourteenth-century English treatises laid far more emphasis on contemplation. Richard Rolle's *The Form of Living* was written for Margaret Kirkby, a nun of Hampole who was enclosed in 1348. The renunciation of the world and the temptations which were likely to be encountered in the solitary life occupied the first half of the work, but in contrast to the *Ancrene Riwle*, the second half concentrated on the contemplation of Christ's love which Rolle saw as the way to grow in the spiritual life. Some anchoresses, notably Julian of Norwich, experienced mystical visions. Little is known of Julian's life, apart from the fact that she received a series of visions in 1373 at the age of thirty while she was seriously ill. At some subsequent time she became an anchoress at St Julian's church in Norwich and it was here that she was visited by Margery Kempe about 1413.[43]

The anchoress was enclosed but through her window remained in contact with the world. The danger, as Aelred of Rievaulx realised, was that this would become a place for gossip, and the author of the *Ancrene Riwle* recommended that the anchoress should be selective in whom she saw. Yet the anchoress was often sought out for spiritual advice, and bequests to recluses in English wills indicate that the women were highly valued. Margery Kempe consulted Julian of Norwich about her heavenly revelations, feeling anxious that she might have been deceived. She considered that Julian was an expert in these matters and would give her good advice. Julian told her to carry out God's commands and pointed out that the gifts of tears and devotion came from heaven. Margery was urged to persevere and not to fear worldly slander.[44]

The role of Julian of Norwich can be compared with that of Lame Margaret of Magdeburg, who lived in the first half of the thirteenth century. Margaret was enclosed at about the age of twelve next to St Alban's church and then, because of criticism from the clergy, was moved by her confessor to a cell next to the Dominican convent. Margaret's visions centred on the Virgin Mary and later on Jesus Christ, and these experiences gave her authority as a counsellor. According to the Life written by her confessor, she summoned sinners to her and discussed religious and moral matters with her fellow citizens.[45] Being enclosed did not mean that the anchoress was ignorant of what was going on in the world around her. Through her prayers for the community as well as her advice, she might wield considerable influence.

Jeanne-Marie de Maillé (1331–1414), who came of a noble family of the Loire region, also had close links with the world. After the death of her husband in 1362, she lived the life of a penitent, caring for the sick and distributing her fortune to the poor and to churches. She had been under a strong Franciscan influence since childhood, and in 1386 she was enclosed at the Franciscan convent at Tours and became known as a visionary and prophetess. She was supported by Marie of Brittany, wife of Louis I of Anjou, who asked her to be godmother to one of her sons, and Jeanne-Marie is said to have performed a cure on Yolande of Aragon. Her prayers were asked for the kingdom of Cyprus, and Charlotte de Bourbon, wife of King James II of Lusignan, asked her in 1409 for an effective ointment that she made herself. Few recluses operated on an international stage, but Jeanne-Marie had close ties with a number of noble networks.[46]

Laywomen wishing to lead a religious life had a number of options in the later Middle Ages. They could live as penitents and beguines, on their own, in groups or in their own homes. Most combined a life of prayer with work and charity. Although the Church accepted the recluse as following a valid way of life, many in the hierarchy were critical of women living informally, without taking vows and following a Rule. Yet these women often found spiritual protection and guidance from established monastic houses and especially from the friars. It was under the auspices of the friars that the third orders developed which catered for large numbers of women. Although numbers decreased in the fifteenth century, laywomen following a religious life remained important in many parts of Europe into the early modern period. Some of these women influenced both their directors and the world around them through their way of life and their devotions. The later Middle Ages saw an increasing number of female saints and mystics who were to be found among the beguines, penitents, tertiaries and recluses, as well as among nuns. The significance of these influential women will be discussed in the next chapter.

Notes

1 A.B. Mulder-Bakker, 'Ivetta of Huy: *mater et magistra*', in A.B. Mulder-Bakker (ed.), *Sanctity and Motherhood. Essays on Holy Mothers in the Middle Ages* (New York, 1995), pp. 225–58; P. Ranft, *Women and the Religious Life in Premodern Europe* (Basingstoke, 1996), p. 84.

2 N.P. Tanner, *The Church in Late Medieval Norwich 1370–1532* (Toronto, 1984), pp. 64–6, has found slight evidence of communities resembling beguinages in the town.

3 C. Neel, 'The origins of the beguines', *Signs* 14 (1988–9), pp. 321–41; B. Bolton, '*Mulieres sanctae*', in D. Baker (ed.), *Sanctity and Secularity: The Church and the World* (Studies in Church History 10, Oxford, 1973), pp. 77–95.

4 W. Simons, *Cities of Ladies. Beguine Communities in the Medieval Low Countries, 1200–1565* (Philadelphia, 2001), p. 90.

5 S. Roisin, 'L'efflorescence cistercienne et le courant féminin de piété au treizième siècle', *Revue d'Histoire Ecclesiastique* 39 (1943), pp. 360–5, 370, 372–3; P. Galloway, 'Beguine communities in northern France, 1200–1500', in D. Watt (ed.), *Medieval Women in their Communities* (Cardiff, 1997), p. 95.

6 Mulder-Bakker, 'Ivetta of Huy', p. 236.

7 *Acta Sanctorum*, June, vol. V (Paris and Rome, 1867), pp. 542–88; B. Bolton, '*Vitae Matrum*: a further aspect of the *Frauenfrage*', in D. Baker (ed.), *Medieval Women* (Studies in Church History Subsidia 1, Oxford, 1978), pp. 253–73; Bolton, '*Mulieres Sanctae*', pp. 77–95; Simons, *Cities of Ladies*, pp. 39–47; A. Vauchez, *Saints, prophètes et visionnaires. Le pouvoir surnaturel au moyen âge* (Paris, 1999), pp. 175–88.

8 R.B.C. Huygens (ed.), *Lettres de Jacques de Vitry* (Leiden, 1960), pp. 75–6; E.W. McDonnell, *The Beguines and Beghards in Medieval Culture* (New Brunswick, New Jersey, 1954), pp. 156–7.

9 Ranft, *Women and the Religious Life*, pp. 64, 81–2; A. Vauchez, *Les laïcs au moyen âge. Pratiques et expériences religieuses* (Paris, 1987), pp. 106–7.

10 A. Rigon, 'A community of female penitents in thirteenth-century Padua', in D. Bornstein and R. Rusconi (eds), *Women and Religion in Medieval and Renaissance Italy* (Chicago, 1996), pp. 28–38.

11 D. Phillips, *Beguines in Medieval Strasburg. A Study of the Social Aspect of Beguine Life* (Stanford, California, 1941), pp. 19, 26–7, 31, 45–9, 69–70, 87–90, 119–20, 138, 145; J-C. Schmitt, *Mort d'une hérésie. L'Eglise et les clercs face aux béguines et aux béghards du Rhin supérieur du quatorzième au quinzième siècle* (Paris, 1978), pp. 40–1, 143–4.

12 H.R. Luard (ed.), *Matthaei Parisiensis Monachi Sancti Albani Chronica Majora*, 7 vols (Rolls Series, London, 1872–83), IV, p. 278; Phillips, *Beguines in Medieval Strasburg*, p. 145; Schmitt, *Mort d'une hérésie*, pp. 39–40; R.W. Southern,

Western Society and the Church in the Middle Ages (Harmondsworth, 1970), pp. 323–5, 327–8.

13 Phillips, *Beguines in Medieval Strasburg*, p. 145; Schmitt, *Mort d'une hérésie*, pp. 40, 144.

14 Simons, *Cities of Ladies*, pp. 36, 48–51; M. Lauwers and W. Simons, *Béguins et béguines à Tournai au bas moyen âge* (Tournai, 1988), pp. 12–17; B. Delmaire, 'Les béguines dans le nord de la France au premier siècle de leur histoire, vers 1230–vers 1350', in M. Parisse (ed.), *Les religieuses en France au treizième siècle* (Nancy, 1985), pp. 129–30; McDonnell, *Beguines and Beghards*, pp. 205–12; D. Nicholas, *Medieval Flanders* (London, 1992), pp. 141–2; Galloway, 'Beguine communities', pp. 98–100.

15 Galloway, 'Beguine communities', p. 98; Delmaire, 'Les béguines dans le nord de la France', p. 131; Simons, *Cities of Ladies*, pp. 56–9.

16 McDonnell, *Beguines and Beghards*, pp. 99, 224–5.

17 L.M. Paterson, *The World of the Troubadours. Medieval Occitan Society, c. 1100–c. 1300* (Cambridge, 1993), pp. 246–8.

18 McDonnell, *Beguines and Beghards*, pp. 138–40, 544–5; Jean Béthune (ed.), *Cartulaire du béguinage de Sainte-Elisabeth à Gand* (Bruges, 1883), pp. 73–6; E. Amt (ed.), *Women's Lives in Medieval Europe. A Sourcebook* (New York and London, 1993), pp. 263–7.

19 M. Rubin, *Corpus Christi. The Eucharist in Late Medieval Culture* (Cambridge, 1991), pp. 169–85; W. Simons and J.E. Ziegler, 'Phenomenal religion in the thirteenth century and its image: Elizabeth of Spalbeek and the Passion cult', in W.J. Sheils and D. Wood (eds), *Women in the Church* (Studies in Church History 27, Oxford, 1990), pp. 117–26.

20 McDonnell, *Beguines and Beghards*, pp. 271–4, 544; Phillips, *Beguines in Medieval Strasburg*, pp. 158–9, 208.

21 Vauchez, *Saints, prophètes et visionnaires*, p. 187.

22 'Beatae Margaritae Virginis de Civitate Castelli', *Analecta Bollandiana* 19 (1900), pp. 21–36; *Acta Sanctorum*, February, Volume III (Paris and Rome, 1865), pp. 302–63; F. Beer, *Women and Mystical Experience in the Middle Ages* (Woodbridge, 1992), p. 79; Bornstein and Rusconi (eds), *Women and Religion in Medieval and Renaissance Italy*, p. 2; D.H. Farmer, *The Oxford Dictionary of Saints* (Oxford, 1997), p. 328. The cult of Margaret of Cortona is discussed in J. Cannon and A. Vauchez, *Margherita of Cortona and the Lorenzetti. Sienese Art and the Cult of a Holy Woman in Medieval Tuscany* (Philadelphia, 1999).

23 Galloway, 'Beguine communities', pp. 102–3.

24 J.B. Freed, *The Friars and German Society in the Thirteenth Century* (Cambridge, Massachusetts, 1977), p. 49.

25 Southern, *Western Society and the Church*, p. 329.

26 M.G. Sargent, 'The annihilation of Marguerite Porete', *Viator* 28 (1997), pp. 253–79; A.M. Haas, 'Schools of late medieval mysticism', in J. Raitt (ed.), *Christian Spirituality. High Middle Ages and Reformation* (London, 1987), pp. 142–3; M. Lambert, *Medieval Heresy. Popular Movements from Bogomil to Hus* (London, 1977), pp. 176–9.

27 Vauchez, *Les laïcs au moyen âge*, pp. 83–92, 111, 211–24; R.G. Musto, 'Queen Sancia of Naples (1286–1345) and the Spiritual Franciscans', in J. Kirshner and S.F. Wemple (eds), *Women of the Medieval World. Essays in honor of John H. Mundy* (Oxford, 1985), pp. 179–83, 190–214.

28 Southern, *Western Society and the Church*, p. 330; McDonnell, *Beguines and Beghards*, pp. 523–9; Lambert, *Medieval Heresy*, p. 178.

29 J.K. Deane, '*Geistliche schwestern*: the pastoral care of lay religious women in medieval Würzburg', in F.J. Griffiths and J. Hotchin (eds), *Partners in Spirit. Women, Men and Religious Life in Germany, 1100–1500* (Turnhout, 2014), pp. 237–70.

30 Lambert, *Medieval Heresy*, p. 176; Southern, *Western Society and the Church*, pp. 324–5, 330–1.

31 Phillips, *Beguines in Medieval Strasburg*, pp. 145–53, 161–75; Schmitt, *Mort d'une hérésie*, pp. 40, 85–90, 143–4.

32 Béthune (ed.), *Cartulaire du béguinage de Sainte-Elisabeth à Gand*, pp. 76–8; Simons, *Cities of Ladies*, pp. 133–6; Lauwers and Simons, *Béguins et béguines à Tournai*, pp. 34–6; Galloway, 'Beguine communities', p. 100.

33 B. Hamilton, *Religion in the Medieval West* (London, 1986), pp. 77–8.

34 Phillips, *Beguines in Medieval Strasburg*, pp. 179, 182–3; Lauwers and Simons, *Béguins et béguines à Tournai*, p. 21.

35 O. Grundler, '*Devotio moderna*', in Raitt (ed.), *Christian Spirituality*, pp. 176–9; Ranft, *Women and the Religious Life*, pp. 85–6.

36 *Acta Sanctorum*, March, vol. II (Paris and Rome, 1865), pp. *89–*219; A. Esposito, 'St Francesca and the female religious communities of fifteenth-century Rome', in Bornstein and Rusconi (eds), *Women and Religion in Medieval and Renaissance Italy*, pp. 197–218; Farmer, *Oxford Dictionary of Saints*, p. 191; Ranft, *Women and the Religious Life*, pp. 98–101.

37 Few women became hermits; there were obvious dangers to women from living in the wilds.

38 A. Vauchez, *La sainteté en occident aux derniers siècles du moyen âge* (Rome, 1981), pp. 229–30; L.H. McAvoy (ed.), *Anchoritic Traditions of Medieval Europe* (Woodbridge, 2010), pp. 2–12; L.H. McAvoy, *Medieval Anchoritisms. Gender, Space and the Solitary Life* (Woodbridge, 2011), pp. 1–9.

39 A. Hamilton Thompson (ed.), *Visitations of Religious Houses in the Diocese of Lincoln*, 3 vols (Canterbury and York Society 17, 24, 33, 1915–27), I, pp. 113–15.

40 Beer, *Women and Mystical Experience*, p. 121; Simons, *Cities of Ladies*, p. 74; B. Millett and J. Wogan-Browne (eds), *Medieval English Prose for Women. Selections from the Katherine Group and Ancrene Wisse* (Oxford, 1990), pp. xi–xii, xxix–xxxiv; Ranft, *Women and the Religious Life*, p. 44; M.B. Salm (trans.), *The Ancrene Riwle* (Exeter, 1990), p. 185.

41 Ranft, *Women and the Religious Life*, p. 87.

42 Salm (trans.), *The Ancrene Riwle*, pp. xix–xx, 7–20, 182–8.

43 Beer, *Women and Mystical Experience*, pp. 122–9; A. Louth, *The Wilderness of God* (London, 1991), pp. 63–4.

44 Salm (trans.), *The Ancrene Riwle*, p. 28; A.K. Warren, *Anchorites and their Patrons in Medieval England* (Berkeley, California, 1985), pp. 283–4; S.B. Meech and H.E. Allen (eds), *The Book of Margery Kempe* (EETS original series 212, 1940), pp. 42–3.

45 A.B. Mulder-Bakker, 'Lame Margaret of Magdeburg: the social function of a medieval recluse', *JMH* 22 (1996), pp. 155–69.

46 Vauchez, *Les laïcs au moyen âge*, pp. 225–36.

12 Mystics and saints

Women saints and mystics proliferated in the thirteenth and fourteenth centuries. Although they were to be found particularly in the Low Countries, parts of Germany and the towns of northern and central Italy, they were by no means confined to these areas. One of the best-known visionaries of the fourteenth century was Birgitta of Sweden. Margaret of Oingt was a French Carthusian nun, while Margery Kempe came from Kings Lynn in Norfolk. There was a tendency for more of the northern mystics to be nuns and the southern to be tertiaries, but this can be taken only as a broad generalisation. The convent of Helfta in Saxony became the centre of the cult of the Sacred Heart in the thirteenth century, and there was a high level of mysticism among German Dominican nuns, but Dorothea of Montau lived as a lay-woman for most of her life, becoming a recluse only shortly before her death. The best known of the Italian women visionaries were members of the mendicant third orders, such as Margaret of Cortona, Angela of Foligno and Catherine of Siena, but mystics were also to be found among Italian nuns, such as Caterina Vigri who was a nun at the Observant convents at Ferrara and Bologna. Many of these women were influential in their own communities and localities, while some achieved an international reputation.

The background and experience of these women were extremely varied. On the whole, they did not come from the lower orders of society. Some became nuns at an early age and their whole experience was bounded by convent life. Of the mystics at Helfta, Mechtild of Hackeborn entered the nunnery at the age of seven and Gertrude the Great at the age of five. Extreme piety often developed during childhood, but for Gertrude this grew fully only when she began to have visions from the age of twenty-five. Margaret von Ebner was a Dominican nun for over thirty years before she started to have mystical experiences. Catherine of Siena, on the other hand, began to have visions as a child and was sure of her way of life as a tertiary and a mystic by the time she was in her teens. For women such as Catherine, virginity and the religious life went together, but virginity was not a prerequisite for many women saints in the later Middle Ages. Birgitta of Sweden was assured by both God and the Virgin Mary that the states of virgin, wife and mother were all regarded as virtuous.[1]

Some women changed their way of life as they grew older. Mechtild of Magdeburg moved to Helfta in 1270, at about the age of sixty, having spent most of her life as a beguine in Magdeburg. Other women had to fulfil the obligations of marriage and motherhood before they could fully embark on their lives in religion. Although Margery Kempe experienced visions of Christ early in her married life, it was not until after about twenty years of marriage and the births of fourteen children that her husband agreed that they should live a life of chastity; from that point her life as a visionary intensified. Angela of Foligno rejoiced when the deaths of mother, husband and children left her free to pursue the religious life. The attempt to combine piety with worldly demands posed difficulties. Dorothea of Montau, who was a peasant's daughter, was beaten by her artisan husband when she failed to carry out her household tasks of shopping and cooking. Some women practised chastity within marriage. Birgitta of Sweden was the mother of eight children, but she and her husband had periods of sexual abstinence. Birgitta was extremely pious from childhood, but her piety deepened during her widowhood.[2]

Few women mystics received much education, which was only to be expected in the medieval world. Clare of Montefalco saw mysticism as far more beneficial to the soul than academic knowledge.[3] Helfta was, however, exceptional. The nunnery was founded in 1229 and was strongly influenced by Cistercian and Dominican spirituality. Gertrude of Hackeborn, elected abbess in 1251, insisted on a high level of learning. Nuns were taught the *trivium* of grammar, rhetoric and logic, and some studied the subjects of the *quadrivium*, arithmetic, astronomy, geometry and music. According to her account, Gertrude the Great thoroughly enjoyed her studies, especially classical literature, but from the age of twenty-five devoted herself completely to mysticism and religious writing.[4]

Women's mystical experience was rooted in their sexuality and emotions. Contemporary views on the nature of women emphasised their emotions and lack of reason, and in their religious lives they used this emotional side to great effect, taking what were generally regarded as their weaknesses in order to exercise influence and power. With the priesthood limited to men, the clerical route to holiness was closed to women and they were unable to pursue an active preaching ministry in the world. The emotive and affective piety of the age led both men and women to similar religious devotions, but mysticism was more central in female than in male experience, and female mystics based their claims to authority on their visions of the supernatural.[5] They were especially devoted to the Passion and Death of Christ, to the Eucharist and to the Virgin Mary. Women made full use of their bodies and senses to bring themselves into contact with God and on the whole developed asceticism to a more marked degree than was found among male mystics.

Recent work on saints and mystics has been concerned to set them in the context of their place and time, and to look at changes in the expressions of sanctity. The study of saints' lives has involved much more questioning of the relationship of the male author and the saint herself, and the extent to which he exercised control and edited the information he was given in order to ensure that his work would be acceptable to the Church. Masculine and feminine views of gender clashed and in many cases the former prevailed with the women appearing less assertive than they really were. Clare of Assisi saw herself as God's mother, sister and bride, and as a follower of St Francis living in imitation of Christ. Male hagiographers, on the other hand, stressed the concept of the saint as the bride of Christ, living in imitation of the Virgin Mary.[6]

Poverty and renunciation

Women mystics saw their way to the imitation of Christ through renunciation of what would have been their normal life in the world: renunciation of family ties, wealth, a comfortable lifestyle, beauty, food and drink. The obedience which in the world they would have owed to father and husband was given to God. It was easier for men to renounce wealth since they had it in their possession; women's inheritances and dowries were held by fathers and husbands unless they were widows. Widows were found giving away their possessions and sometimes those of their families to the poor, as in the case of Clare Gambacorta of Pisa.[7] It was easier for religious women to give up their beauty, food and drink, because all three were an integral part of their upbringing; in preparation for marriage, girls were expected to make themselves attractive with fine clothes, hairstyles and make-up, and to learn to provide a variety of fine foods for the household. Catherine of Siena was urged as a teenager to make herself attractive to men.[8] The adoption of a life of poverty meant renouncing all the things with which the girl or woman was familiar.

Many women went to extremes in their austerities and asceticism. Their practices of self-mutilation and rejection of food have been investigated in depth by Caroline Walker Bynum, who sees fasting as the means to keep the body under control and to overcome the sins of both lust and gluttony. The ultimate aim of these women was to follow Christ and to identify with the suffering of the human Jesus, especially in his Passion and Crucifixion. This desire brings out the direct connection between asceticism and mysticism.[9] Bodily discipline took a variety of forms. Birgitta of Sweden as a widow tied knotted ropes round her waist and round each leg and knee next to the skin, and also wore a hair shirt. Beatrice of Ornacieux is said to have carried burning coals but not to have felt the burns, to have flagellated herself until the blood ran and in imitation of Christ's death to have driven blunt nails through her hands, although this drew water rather than blood and the wounds soon healed. When she could do nothing else, she walked barefoot through snow and ice.[10] Such examples could be multiplied and show that for many religious women holiness involved physical suffering.

Fasting constituted an identification with the life of the poor but was taken much further, going well beyond the fasts laid down by the Church. Confessors and spiritual directors urged women to eat. Mary of Oignies was reputed only to have partaken of the Eucharist in the time before she died. According to Thomas of Celano, St Francis forbade Clare of Assisi from taking no food at all on Mondays, Wednesdays and Fridays in Advent and Lent, and insisted that she should have a small amount of bread each day. Clare expected her nuns to fast, but not to the same extent. Catherine of Siena's inability to eat worried her confessors as well as herself. Her decision to adopt a diet of bread, raw vegetables and water appears to have been part of her conflict with her family when she rejected marriage and was determined to take up her religious vocation. She subsequently gave up bread and lived on water and herbs, which she either vomited or spat out. She gave up water for a month in January 1380 and died in the following April. She was a woman who seems literally to have been unable to eat from her early twenties.[11]

Such a situation may be linked with anorexia, as has been suggested by Rudolph M. Bell. Catherine exhibited symptoms of the anorexic in her loss of appetite, eating followed by vomiting, sleeplessness and bursts of hyperactivity. She herself referred to her inability to eat as an infirmity; in one of her visions, Christ commanded her to eat at the family table and this she was unable to do. Other women may have been suffering from depression and hysteria. The terrors experienced by Beatrice of Ornacieux verge on the hysterical, as at the Christmas Mass when after many doubts she received communion, only to find it turn to flesh and blood in her mouth;[12] according to the doctrine of transubstantiation, the consecrated host was the body of Christ. Ecstasy and even frenzy at the Eucharist were widespread and may be connected with the extreme asceticism to which these women subjected themselves. Rudolph Bell also sees their behaviour as a response to patriarchal social structures. Catherine rebelled against her family as a teenager and her adult life is interpreted as shaped by her experiences as a child and her relationship with her parents. Older women's anorexic behaviour is construed by Bell as rebellion against early marriages and the subservient role of wives and mothers.[13] The element of rebellion may have been present in some cases, but the asceticism cannot be explained by secular reasons alone. The desire to participate in the suffering of Christ was uppermost in the minds of many religious women, and contemporary society saw poverty and asceticism as marks of sanctity. The writers of saints' lives, such as Jacques de Vitry, emphasised the austerities as indicating that the woman was on the road to becoming a saint.

It is likely that it was not always realised what damage extreme fasting does to the body, but some medieval women along with their spiritual directors were not convinced that their fasting was in accordance with God's will. Catherine of Siena referred to her inability to eat as an infirmity. Angela of Foligno found that the Eucharist was a substitute for food, but in time she centred her attention on achieving humility rather than concentrating on fasting and abstinence. She wanted to identify with the human Jesus, and in one of her visions He assured her that her whole life, including eating, drinking and sleeping, was pleasing to Him; God always blessed what she ate and drank. She made use of food imagery, as when the devil taunted her as to whether she was worthy to wash lettuce, and she replied that she was worthy only to gather manure.[14]

Suffering was viewed as an integral part of the imitation of Christ. Just as Christ had suffered during his Passion and Crucifixion, so anyone following him had to accept pain. The women's austerities have to be interpreted as control rather than hatred of the body. The body was certainly regarded as of far less importance than the soul but, although it was held in contempt, it was created by God, and a rejection of God's physical creation was tantamount to heresy. Women kept their bodies and impulses under control through their rejection of food and drink and their acceptance of suffering. Suffering was in any case regarded as the normal fate of women from earliest times, when Eve was told by God that she would give birth to children in sorrow.[15] The acceptance and even the welcoming of suffering were widespread among religious women. The necrology of the convent of Corpus Domini at Venice contains many accounts of long illnesses and patience during sickness, as with Margarita Piacentini who was ill for fifteen months before her death, Caterina Rosso who was ill for six years, and Giovanna da Loreto who suffered from dropsy. Julian of Norwich asked God for the gift of illness and it was when she was thought to be terminally ill that she was given her *Revelations*. For those women, like Elizabeth of Spalbeek, who received the stigmata, the marks of Christ's wounds on the hands, feet and side, the link between suffering and the imitation of Jesus reached a climax.[16]

Suffering was seen as an element in penitential discipline, and penance for sins committed was regarded as the essential preliminary and accompaniment to the holy life. The writings of the mystics portrayed penance as an inherent part of religious development. The importance of penance was emphasised by the Church at the Fourth Lateran Council which laid down that all lay Christians were to receive communion at Easter after they had made their confession to a priest. Religious women's penitential practices and devotion to the Eucharist went well beyond this precept. The 'journey' of Angela of Foligno was described as a series of twenty-six steps whereby she was first purged by suffering, tears, repentance and confession before she received her visions of Christ which centred on the Passion and Crucifixion. The first six steps put her in a state of self-knowledge. After her first visions, she went through a period when she felt that God had abandoned her, but in her final vision she perceived the complete goodness of God. *The Book of Margery Kempe* described three years of temptations when Margery was acutely aware of her unworthiness and repented with sorrow and weeping. Temptations were often depicted in concrete terms as visitations by demons. Julian of Norwich was visited by devils on her sickbed and came to believe that the struggle against sin was the human equivalent of Christ's Passion.[17] Although not all women experienced tears and visions, the feelings of unworthiness and contrition and the need for repentance were found among religious women across Europe. Only by overcoming sin could spiritual growth take place.

Affective devotion

The life of suffering fused with the life of devotion which was centred on the human Christ and on the Eucharist. Meditations focused on the birth and death of Jesus, the women seeing themselves as present at the Nativity and Crucifixion and helping to care for and play with the infant Christ. Many women also had a deep devotion to the Virgin Mary, but often saw her primarily in the context of their devotion to Christ. Birgitta of Sweden had a vision of the birth of Jesus when she visited Bethlehem, and described the scene in the stable as the baby was born and Mary worshipped him before she fed him and wrapped him in swaddling clothes. Joseph came in and helped her to put the child in the manger. Margery Kempe had visions of Mary swaddling the Christ child and of Christ's Presentation in the Temple. Some religious women, like Gertrude the Great, saw themselves as breast-feeding Jesus. When the Virgin Mary appeared to Agnes of Montepulciano, she allowed Agnes to hold the child, but Agnes was then unwilling to give him back. Works of art and religious objects fostered devotion. Margaret von Ebner was given a carved doll depicting the child Jesus in 1344, probably by her confessor, and by means of the doll was able to meditate on Christ and deepen her spiritual understanding. For her, the doll became a real baby who needed to be fed, kissed and played with, and who demanded to be picked up at night when Margaret wanted to sleep. The child also talked to Margaret, and in this way she learned about his life and suffering and about the nature of his love for humanity.[18]

Devotion to the Passion and Crucifixion was widespread in later medieval Europe and by no means confined to those following a religious way of life.[19] It was fostered by paintings and carvings. Angela of Foligno commented that when she saw paintings of the Cross or the Passion, Christ's suffering was brought home to her, although eventually she avoided paintings as being too far removed from reality. Several of the *Revelations* of Julian of Norwich centred on the sufferings of Christ which are described in graphic detail, appropriate to the affective and emotive piety of the age, such as the wounds Jesus received from the crown of thorns and the dying body on the Cross, pale and turning blue. Julian developed these themes to bring out the goodness and love of God towards humanity, but her starting point was the crucifix facing her in what was thought to be her final illness.[20]

The intensity of this form of devotion is exemplified by Clare of Montefalco (d. 1308). When her nuns opened her heart after her death, they found what they thought to be the emblems of the Passion, and in her gall bladder three stones symbolising the Trinity. Such a claim aroused scepticism among the authorities, but the vicar of the bishop of Spoleto was convinced that it was genuine and his report led to canonisation proceedings. Clare had identified herself during her lifetime with the sufferings and death of Christ and for her, as for many others, austerity of life was combined with her spiritual experience. Her devotion can be compared with Vanna of Orvieto who re-enacted the Passion on Good Friday.[21]

Devotion to the Eucharist was closely bound up with devotion to Christ's Passion. It was also inextricably linked with the women's fasting, heavenly food being regarded as of far greater importance than earthly fare. According to the doctrine of transubstantiation, the priest at Mass consecrated the bread and wine, as Jesus had done at the Last Supper, and they were transformed into the body and blood of Christ. From the thirteenth century, the usual practice was for the laity to take communion in one kind, receiving only the bread, known as the host, but this signified a partaking of Christ and therefore devotion to the Eucharist was intimately bound up with the concept of the imitation of Christ.

The desire to receive the Eucharist frequently was accepted only reluctantly by the Church, and the right to take communion more often than once a year had to be sanctioned by the woman's confessor or spiritual director. Although Dorothea of Montau was allowed daily confession and communion as an anchoress, this was not permitted earlier in her life.[22] Some women were reluctant to make their communion because of feelings of unworthiness. Beatrice of Ornacieux felt unable to take communion one Christmas, although she had three times made a great effort to confess all her sins. When she plucked up courage to receive the host, she felt that she tasted flesh and blood. Margaret of Cortona on one occasion took the host like a patient swallowing medicine because of her feelings of unworthiness.[23] Many religious women experienced visions in the context of the Eucharist. The Christmas communion of Beatrice of Ornacieux sparked off a period of intense contemplation over the three days of the festival, during which she did not eat or sleep. Beatrice of Nazareth once saw a vision of Jesus standing on the altar, and Angela of Foligno saw Christ as a boy of about twelve years old, very handsome and with an air of authority. On one occasion, when Vanna of Orvieto was ill and unable to attend church, a heavenly light is said to have shone over her and a white host appeared and entered her mouth.[24]

Mystics saw Christ in various guises and described their relationship with him in a number of ways. Their close bond with Jesus gave them authority and enabled them to bypass to some extent the structures of the Church. For them absolution from sin was bestowed direct from heaven; Angela of Foligno described how she received Christ's forgiveness at the intercession of the Virgin Mary. Some mystics saw themselves as assisting in the celebration of the Eucharist, as John the Baptist allowed Ivetta of Huy in one of her visions. They did not restrict themselves to a single form of relationship. Angela of Foligno was addressed by Christ as daughter and bride when he told her that he loved her more than any woman in the valley of Spoleto. Julian of Norwich saw Christ as mother, brother and saviour.[25] The language in which religious women expressed their love for Christ derived from their sexuality, gender and experience, and it was primarily to the human and suffering Christ that they were relating. Although similar language and images are found among medieval male mystics, for women the gender relationship was central.

The image of Christ as bridegroom was one frequently recorded among religious women. This image brought out not only love of Christ but also the need for obedience to his commands. Some women experienced a mystic marriage with Christ, as did Catherine of Siena about 1366, and Margery Kempe in the church of the Apostles at Rome in 1414; God told Margery that he would show her his secrets, and that she would live with him for ever. The relationship might be expressed in sensual and erotic terms, the Song of Songs providing an influential source. Angela of Foligno described how on one Holy Saturday she lay in the tomb with the dead Christ, kissing his chest and mouth, and they held each other tightly. The beguine Hadewijch, writing in the first half of the thirteenth century, described union with Christ in physical terms, with the mystic being taken into the body of Christ; this occurred in visions or at the time of the Eucharist. For her, love was to be achieved only by suffering and was never a state of peace.[26]

Birgitta of Sweden described union with Christ in more prosaic terms.[27] Christ announced that he had chosen Birgitta to be his bride for such pleasure as was right to have with a chaste soul. To prepare herself for her husband, the bride had to cleanse herself from sin and to be aware of all the blessings he had conferred on her in her creation; he had given her body and soul, endowed her with health and material possessions, and redeemed her through his death. The bride was expected to do her husband's will, to love him above all things and to desire nothing else. If Birgitta carried this out, her reward in heaven would be great. Yet although Christ loved her, he would be merciful only if she did his will. It was right for the bride to tire herself in service to her husband so that she could then rest with him. These ideas were largely adapted from those concerning medieval marriage in the world.

Some medieval mystics saw themselves in a maternal role, caring for the infant Jesus. Christ was also seen as mother, emphasising his nurturing role.[28] The feminine aspect of God was discussed by churchmen down to the fourth century and is found again with St Anselm and St Bernard in the eleventh and twelfth centuries. The theme comprised a major element in the *Revelations* of Julian of Norwich. Julian saw God as epitomising the human relationships of father, mother and lord. She saw Christ as saviour and mother in the sense that all beings were born of him; Mary as his mother was mother to all who were redeemed by him. She also visualised God as creator being united to humanity as the husband is to his beloved wife and sweetheart, and saw Christ as brother in that he had shared mankind's experience in his life and death on earth. Christ was both creator and sustainer; people owed their existence to Christ, and this for Julian was the essence of motherhood, the mother's love and tenderness being found in Christ. The pain of childbirth was paralleled by the pain of the Crucifixion; while the human mother breastfed her child, Jesus fed people with his own blood, as shed on the Cross.[29] For Julian, a mother always loved her child and was wise, kind and good. Her disciplining of her child was comparable to the way Jesus cared for his people. By using the maternal images, Julian was able to build up her picture of a caring saviour.

Groups of mystics were found living in communities, especially in Germany. Sisterbooks were compiled in a number of Dominican nunneries, as at Colmar, Töss and Engelthal, giving biographies of pious nuns and an account of their visions. The nuns lived a harsh life, and in addition to their devotion to the Eucharist, their visions concentrated on the childhood and death of Jesus and on union with him as bridegroom. Margaret von Ebner was only one among many Dominican visionaries.[30] The best known group of mystics were nuns at the abbey of Helfta in and soon after the time of the Abbess Gertrude of Hackeborn (1251–91). The community was joined by the beguine Mechtild of Magdeburg in 1270, and her arrival may have encouraged the development of mysticism at Helfta, notably in the abbess's younger sister, Mechtild of Hackeborn, and later in Gertrude the Great, both of whom had been brought up in the nunnery from the time they were children. Mechtild of Magdeburg recorded her visionary experiences before coming to Helfta in *The Flowing Light of the Divinity*; only the last of the seven books was written at Helfta. The work was written in Low German and survives in High German and Latin translations. Mechtild was influenced by vernacular love poetry and she used erotic language in her love poems to God, seeing the soul as his bride and God as lover and husband as well as king and judge. Divine love of the soul was at the centre of her visions. In 1291 Mechtild of Hackeborn dictated the *Book of Gostlye Grace* to two nuns who recorded it in Latin. Gertrude started to write the *Herald of God's Loving Kindness* in Latin in 1289 and it came to include an account of her life, prayers and visions. All three women had a strong devotion to the Eucharist and regarded Christ's suffering as central to the religious life. All emphasised the importance of obedience to God's commands.

The two younger mystics showed greater confidence in their writings; Mechtild of Magdeburg was the only one to speak of her weakness as a woman, possibly due to the criticism she had encountered during her life as a beguine. Mechtild of Hackeborn and Gertrude the Great are particularly associated with the development of the cult of the Sacred Heart of Jesus. His heart was seen as a refuge and dwelling place, as when Christ, speaking to Mechtild of Hackeborn, likened his heart to a kitchen, the space in the house which was open to all. Mystic union was seen in the terms of the

Sacred Heart, the soul being taken into Christ through his wounded side and joined to his heart. Both visionaries used erotic language and their own female experience; the cleansing flow of blood from the Sacred Heart has parallels with menstruation.[31]

The visions of later medieval mystics concentrated particularly on the humanity and suffering of Christ; life in the world was seen in terms of austerity, struggle and penitence. This meant that other aspects of the divine were neglected. In writing of the fourteenth century, Richard Kieckhefer perceived a lack of balance, a failure to see the implications of the Resurrection of Christ as well as of his Passion and Death.[32] The concentration on the human Christ meant that less attention was paid to God the Father and the Holy Spirit, and the Virgin Mary's role often came over as teacher and intercessor rather than as a major figure in her own right; she was probably of greater importance in male visions. Julian of Norwich described her as the mother of Christ and therefore of humanity, but did not develop the theme. In women's visions, Mary appeared as facilitator. In Mechtild of Magdeburg's vision of the Mass of John the Baptist, she was guided through the service by the Virgin Mary and at the end suckled the lamb, the symbol of Christ. Mary also appeared as interpreter to many of the religious women, as she did to Birgitta of Sweden, many of whose prophecies came from the Virgin Mary.[33]

Influence and power

Austerity and intense meditation comprised only one side of the lives of many of these religious women. Active service in the world, often taking the form of charity to the poor and sick, and to outcasts, combined love of God with love of one's neighbour. Such service could be exercised from home or from a community, and enabled the woman to identify herself with the most helpless of society and to see Christ in the midst of their sufferings. Some women took their involvement to extraordinary lengths. Angela of Foligno described how she washed the hands and feet of a leper and then drank the washing water; lepers were regarded as untouchables in medieval society. A scab off one of the leper's sores stuck in her throat and it tasted as sweet as the host at the Eucharist. Catherine of Siena described how she drank the pus from a woman's cancerous sore.[34]

Care of the sick and the distribution of food were two of the works of mercy which Christians were expected to carry out and which women, with their responsibility for the household, were especially well fitted to do. Although religious women fasted, they showed no reluctance in distributing food to the needy, and this applied at all social levels. Zita of Lucca (d. 1272) worked as a servant of the Fatinelli family and gave away food. Elizabeth of Hungary (d. 1231), wife of the Landgrave of Thuringia, distributed food from her table. According to legend, when her husband accused her of giving away food, the bread in her basket turned to roses.

Religious women were also associated with food miracles, as when Catherine of Siena after her death is said to have cooked the family dinner for a woman who had gone to church.[35] Numerous other feeding miracles were associated with Catherine, bringing out the contrast between her asceticism and her generosity to others.

Many religious women worked in hospitals. Catherine of Genoa (d. 1510) adopted a life of asceticism and religious devotion while married to her extravagant and unfaithful husband. After a series of misfortunes he underwent a religious conversion and the couple lived a chaste life until his death in 1497. Both husband and wife cared for the patients in the hospital of Pammatone in Genoa where Catherine showed considerable practical skill in running the establishment. Like other religious women, she saw her service to the needy as an integral part of her religious devotion.[36] Women like her accepted society as it was, with all its pain and violence, but were concerned to help those with whom they came into contact.

The effect of charitable work was felt in the woman's own community or locality. Religious influence might be limited to the locality or have a much wider impact. The mystic Juliana of Cornillon eventually influenced the whole Church through the feast of Corpus Christi. This was first adopted in her home area of Liège, and although the feast was proclaimed by Urban IV in 1264 and a special rite composed by St Thomas Aquinas, it did not become popular in the thirteenth century. With its further proclamation at the Council of Vienne, it spread over Europe and became a popular feast in the fourteenth and fifteenth centuries.[37] Judging by the circulation of their writings, other mystics had a more limited influence. Jacques de Vitry's *Life* of Mary of Oignies was to be found in monastic libraries, but did not have a wider circulation until the fourteenth century when parts were translated into French and Italian. Mechtild of Hackeborn's *Book of Gostlye Grace* is found fairly widely in continental Europe by about 1350, but there is no reference to it in England until the first half of the fifteenth century. *The Book of Margery Kempe* was unknown in England until 1934, although short extracts were printed at the beginning of the sixteenth century. The *Revelations* of Julian of Norwich survive in a shorter and a longer version; three manuscripts of the longer version survive, dating from the sixteenth and seventeenth centuries, and the shorter version is found in a medieval devotional manuscript. Political factors might limit a mystic's influence. Birgitta of Sweden did not become well known in France, partly because the University of Paris was hostile to her type of mystical writing, but also because she was thought to favour the English in the Hundred Years War and to support Rome in the Great Schism.[38]

Mystics probably considered it of greatest importance to serve and teach their own communities. The Helfta mystics gave spiritual counsel to their fellow nuns, as well as to clergy and lay people with whom they came into contact. They saw themselves as mediators and intercessors between Christ and the people around them. The nuns were especially anxious that the visions of Mechtild of Hackeborn and Gertrude the Great should be written down so as to provide teaching for those coming after them.[39] Women living in the world built up their own groups of male and female supporters for whom they were the inspiration. Catherine of Siena was regarded by her circle as 'mother'; it included a poet, the artist Andrea Vanni, and several men from the contemplative monastery of Lecceto, such as William Flete who was Catherine's spiritual director between 1367 and 1373. Angela of Foligno was considered to be the spiritual mother of her following.[40] Women were not only making use of their gender and sometimes their actual experience but were turning the customary household hierarchy upside down; normally, a man acted as head.

Religious influence over a small circle might however overlap with political involvement. Religious women in the Italian towns, which often suffered from war and faction, were an influence for peace. Clare of Montefalco is said to have mediated between Trevi and Montefalco.[41] Certain religious women became known as prophets, particularly after the Black Death. Prophecy had its dangers, as the prophetess might find herself accused of heresy by the Church and of treason by lay rulers. The Frenchwoman Constance de Rabastens supported the Roman pope, Urban VI, during the Great Schism and appealed to Gaston Phébus, Count of Foix, to save France. Nothing was heard of her after her imprisonment by the Inquisition at Toulouse.[42]

The two best known prophetesses of the second half of the fourteenth century, Catherine of Siena and Birgitta of Sweden, both faced questions as to their orthodoxy, Birgitta on her return journey from the Holy Land, and Catherine, a Dominican tertiary, at the general chapter of the order at Florence in 1374. Although both were vindicated, their reliance on God's will rather than on the authorised teaching of the Church made for problems. Both combined asceticism and mysticism with a political and religious role. Catherine was one of those who urged Pope Gregory XI to return to Rome from Avignon in 1377; after the outbreak of the Great Schism the following year, she was active in both her criticism and support of the Roman pope, Urban VI. She also made strenuous efforts both by visit and letter to secure peace in Italy, hoping that eventually a crusade might be launched. During her time in Rome from 1349 until her death in 1373, Birgitta also pressed for the return of the pope from Avignon. Urban V returned temporarily in 1367, but Birgitta did not live to see the permanent return. According to Birgitta, Christ told her to go to Rome to see the return of pope and emperor; both entered St Peter's together in 1368. Birgitta wanted the pope in Rome to take the lead in the reform of the Church; God's anger had to be appeased by reform, otherwise Christians would suffer divine punishment. Such prophetic statements regarding the Church were not found among the religious women of the fifteenth century.[43]

The careers and activities of women like Catherine and Birgitta raise the question of the empowerment of religious women. Were they able as a result of their lives as mystics to exercise power to a greater degree than other women in the later Middle Ages? The evidence of their writings, together with saints' lives and canonisation proceedings, give the impression that the women were a powerful spiritual force. Yet there are problems in taking this material at its face value. The dates at which the lives were written, their purpose, and the bias of the author or, in canonisation proceedings, witnesses, all have to be taken into account. Few of the women were well educated and therefore they relied on dictating their accounts to a scribe, who was usually male. This meant the account might be altered to a greater or lesser degree and further changes might creep in when the work was translated or copied. The attitude of the Church has to be taken into consideration, since it wanted to ensure that visions were genuine and orthodox, and women's austerities and excesses might well have been regarded as suspect. Women's insistence on their divine instruction was sometimes received with scepticism.

All the women were subject to their spiritual directors and confessors, and their relationship with them is central to the question of empowerment. In some cases, the confessor developed a great sense of admiration, even when there was initial hostility. In others, the confessor can best be described as domineering. Some confessors were able to help the mystic to deepen her spiritual life and had the political skills to ensure that her visions were accepted. It was in those instances where the woman was largely free to develop her spiritual gifts that she can be said to be really empowered, and this empowerment could be facilitated by her director. A few examples can be taken to illustrate the variety of relationships. That between Jacques de Vitry and Mary of Oignies was mutually beneficial; he gave her spiritual advice, while she became the inspiration for his preaching. Elizabeth of Hungary's confessor was the severe Conrad of Marburg, who may have induced her guilt over the sources of her husband's wealth. Umiliana dei Cerchi progressed from concentration on the works of mercy to contemplation of the sufferings of Christ under the influence of her Franciscan director. The skills of Alfonso of Jaen were instrumental in ensuring the acceptance of the mysticism of Birgitta of Sweden.[44]

When Angela of Foligno had a vision of Christ in the church at Assisi and screamed and cried out, her confessor, a Franciscan friar, told her never to come back to Assisi. Later, at Foligno, he asked her to describe her experiences, and the *Memorial* was compiled between 1292 and 1296, much of it ostensibly in Angela's own words. The friar wanted to hear her account because he was afraid that she was prompted by an evil spirit, although he came to believe that the visions were inspired by God. The *Memorial* was approved by Cardinal Giacomo Colonna in 1296 or 1297.[45]

Relationships with confessors varied but, provided that the woman's visions were considered to be orthodox, she was recognised as having an exceptional gift and as being an inspiration to other Christians. In this sense, she could be regarded as powerful. It might take time, however, before her power was accepted, even in her home area. Margery Kempe caused resentment and alienation in her home town of Kings Lynn with her long bouts of sobbing, and one friar refused to have her present at his sermons. Possibly certain women were too well known in their own localities to be easily accepted as religious women; it was not until nearly the end of her life that Margery Kempe was admitted to the Trinity guild at Kings Lynn. Dorothea of Montau's move to Marienwerder may have enhanced her reputation because she was far less well known than at Montau and Gdansk.[46]

Sanctity

For religious women to achieve more than a local reputation, their sanctity had to be authorised by the Church, which then fostered their cult across Christendom. By 1200, the process of canonisation was in the hands of the papacy, and not all of those who were regarded as holy in their own region became saints. Yet what is notable about the later Middle Ages is the increasing number of women who were canonised. They were still fewer in number than men, but they constituted a larger proportion of saints than had been the case earlier. Out of their sample of 864 saints between 1000 and 1700, Donald Weinstein and Rudolph Bell found that 151 were women, a proportion of 17.5 per cent. A remarkable contrast emerged between the twelfth and thirteenth centuries, with 11.8 per cent of the twelfth-century saints being women, as against 22.6 per cent in the thirteenth; this proportion was maintained in the fourteenth and fifteenth centuries, with figures of 23.4 per cent and 27.7 per cent respectively. Of the 349 saints canonised between 1200 and 1500, 84 were women, many of them lay-women, including servants. For a man or woman to be canonised, close relations with the papacy and nearness to Rome or Avignon were an advantage: 75 per cent of the processes concerned Italy, France and the British Isles, and no saints were recognised from the Low Countries, Iberia and north Germany. Certain women who were highly regarded in their own locality were canonised only centuries after their deaths, such as Margaret of Cortona in 1728 and Clare of Montefalco in 1881.[47]

The figures indicate that the wider opportunities for women to lead religious lives in the later Middle Ages were mirrored in the canonisations. In the early seventeenth century, Urban VIII decreed that the saint had to be orthodox in doctrine, live a life of virtue, and intercede miraculously after death.[48] These qualities were looked for in the medieval period. Because women did not pursue an active ministry, the life of virtue, seen in terms of poverty, chastity, asceticism and charity, was seen as particularly important, as was the performance of miracles. Canonisation and sanctity have to be linked with lay as well as clerical attitudes and expectations, as it was the people of a locality who would be anxious to foster the cult of their local saint. Certain regional patterns emerge. The later Middle Ages have been described as the age of the north Italian urban saint, and the influence of both towns and friars was of great significance not only in the women's religious lives but in their cults after their deaths.[49] Many of the women belonged to the mendicant third orders, and friars acted as directors, confessors and biographers. Catherine of Siena was typical: she became a Dominican tertiary in her teens, and her director and biographer was the Dominican Raymond of Capua who later became Master-General of the Dominicans.

In view of the intense local feeling in the towns of north and central Italy, urban authorities were anxious to foster the cults of men and women whom they regarded as powerful local patrons offering supernatural protection. In addition to her international reputation, Catherine came to be viewed as the principal saint produced by Siena and was canonised by the Sienese pope, Pius II, in 1461. The Fatinelli patrician family of Lucca fostered the cult of Zita and, although she was not officially canonised in the Middle Ages, they built a chapel in 1321 in the church of San Frediano with an altar dedicated to her; the family continued to be buried in the chapel into the fifteenth century, and her cult was spread by the friars.[50]

Although urban saints are found elsewhere in Europe, they were by no means as concentrated as in northern Italy. This was partly because the towns were for the most part smaller and less numerous, and did not have the same level of civic independence and patriotism. Instead, the political emphasis was on the lordship and the kingdom, and it was the king or lord who would press for canonisation. Dorothea of Montau has parallels with the north Italian saints, as well as with German nuns, in her urban background, austere life, affective piety and strong ties with her spiritual director, but although proceedings were opened, she was not canonised in spite of her cult in the Baltic region. She was a rarity in north Germany, and there seems to have been no pressure from the authorities to get her made a saint.[51]

Dynastic saints are found in eastern Europe, where several women from the royal houses of Hungary and Bohemia were canonised. Their piety and way of life were similar to those of religious women elsewhere, with the emphasis placed on asceticism and renunciation and religious devotion coupled with service to the community. These elements were coupled with the concept of the sanctity of the powerful which was much more often found in early medieval Europe. In Bohemia, Agnes of Prague, daughter of Ottokar I, was an early Poor Clare; she did not become a saint but was termed *beata* or blessed. The male and female saints of the Arpad dynasty of Hungary go back to the eleventh-century King Stephen. Elizabeth of Hungary was canonised four years after her death in 1231. Her niece Margaret, daughter of Bela IV, became a Dominican nun in a convent built for her near Buda by her mother; the house had an altar dedicated to St Elizabeth where the nuns made their vows. Canonisation proceedings took place for Margaret in 1276 and her cult spread from Hungary to south and central Italy in the time of the Angevin kings, who continued to venerate Arpadian saints. Other members of the Arpad dynasty became known as *beatae*, including Elizabeth, daughter of Stephen V, and Elizabeth, daughter of Andrew III, who became a Dominican nun at Töss.[52]

For people living in the later Middle Ages, it is likely that a local holy person, reputed for living a religious life and working miracles after death, was as important as an intercessor with the divine as one who had been officially canonised. André Vauchez has shown that local sanctity long continued to be important.[53] In looking at mysticism and sanctity, some regional patterns are apparent: the aristocratic emphasis in eastern Europe, the German mysticism strongly influenced by the Dominicans, and the importance of urban women in northern and central Italy, the Low Countries and the Rhineland. At the same time, the forms which religious life took are broadly similar north and south of the Alps. Although the devotions of men and women followed the same lines, gender differences were apparent in the religious life. Girls were more likely to experience a religious vocation at an early age than to have a sudden conversion as a teenager.[54] Women in several cases had to obey their family's wishes over marriage and carry out obligations to children and parents before they could adopt the religious life. Their austerities and devotion to the Eucharist often went further than men's. However much they might want to, women were unable to lead an active life of preaching. Yet they were able to carry out their own form of ministry through prayer and personal example, and the holy life lived by nuns, beguines, tertiaries and recluses had a direct impact on the lay people around them.

Notes

1 *Acta Sanctorum*, April vol. III (Paris and Rome, 1866), pp. 868–72; R. Voaden, 'All girls together: community, gender and vision at Helfta', in D. Watt (ed.), *Medieval Women in their Communities* (Cardiff, 1997), pp. 76–7; C.W. Atkinson, '"Precious balsam in a fragile glass": the ideology of virginity in the later Middle Ages', *JFH* 8 (1983), pp. 140–1; R.M. Bell, *Holy Anorexia* (Chicago, 1985), pp. 22–53.

2 S.B. Meech and H.E. Allen (eds), *The Book of Margery Kempe* (EETS original series 212, 1940), pp. 23–5; Angela of Foligno, *Memorial*, (ed.) C. Mazzoni and (trans.) J. Cirignano (Woodbridge, 1999), pp. 1–2, 83–4; R. Kieckhefer, *Unquiet Souls. Fourteenth-Century Saints and their Religious Milieu* (Chicago, 1984), pp. 22–33; J.B. Holloway (ed.), *St Bride and her Book. Birgitta of Sweden's Revelations* (Woodbridge, 1997), pp. 1–5; B. Morris, *St Birgitta of Sweden* (Woodbridge, 1999), pp. 40–6.

3 E. Menestò, 'The apostolic canonization proceedings of Clare of Montefalco, 1318–19', in D. Bornstein and R. Rusconi (eds), *Women and Religion in Medieval and Renaissance Italy* (Chicago, 1996), p. 119.

4 Voaden, 'All girls together', pp. 75–7; L. Eckenstein, *Woman under Monasticism* (Cambridge, 1896), pp. 328–30, 347–53.

5 C.W. Bynum, 'Religious women in the later Middle Ages', in J. Raitt (ed.), *Christian Spirituality. High Middle Ages and Reformation* (London, 1987), p. 131.

6 C.M. Mooney (ed.), *Gendered Voices. Medieval Saints and their Interpreters* (Philadelphia, 1999), pp. 1–15.

7 Kieckhefer, *Unquiet Souls*, pp. 44, 46.

8 *Acta Sanctorum*, April vol. III, pp. 872–4.

9 C.W. Bynum, *Holy Feast and Holy Fast* (Berkeley, California, 1987), pp. 207, 211–17, 239–42.

10 Holloway (ed.), *St Bride and her Book*, p. 6; R. Blumenfeld-Kosinski (ed.), *The Writings of Margaret of Oingt Medieval Prioress and Mystic* (Woodbridge, 1997), p. 49.

11 *Acta Sanctorum*, April vol. III, pp. 903–5; *Acta Sanctorum*, June vol. V (Paris and Rome, 1867), pp. 548, 552; Thomas of Celano, *Legenda Sanctae Clarae Virginis*, (ed.) F. Pennacchi (Assisi, 1910), pp. 25–7; E. Amt (ed.), *Women's Lives in Medieval Europe. A Sourcebook* (New York and London, 1993), p. 238; Bynum, *Holy Feast and Holy Fast*, pp. 165–70; Bell, *Holy Anorexia*, pp. 22–53; S. Noffke (ed.), *The Letters of St Catherine of Siena*, 2 vols (Tempe, Arizona, 2000–1), I, pp. 159–61.

12 Blumenfeld-Kosinski (ed.), *Writings of Margaret of Oingt*, pp. 50, 56.

13 Bell, *Holy Anorexia*, pp. xii, 22–53, 84–113; Bynum, *Holy Feast and Holy Fast*, pp. 197–207.

14 Bynum, *Holy Feast and Holy Fast*, pp. 143, 168; Angela of Foligno, *Memorial*, pp. 44, 50, 56.

15 Book of Genesis, chapter 3, verse 16.

16 Sister Bartolomea Riccoboni, *Life and Death in a Venetian Convent*, (ed. and trans.) D. Bornstein (Chicago, 2000), pp. 66, 67, 69–70; Julian of Norwich, *Revelations of Divine Love*, (ed.) C. Wolters (Harmondsworth, 1966), pp. 63–6; W. Simons and J.E. Ziegler, 'Phenomenal religion in the thirteenth century and its image: Elisabeth of Spalbeek and the Passion cult', in W.J. Sheils and D. Wood (eds), *Women in the Church* (Studies in Church History 27, Oxford, 1990), pp. 117–26.

17 Angela of Foligno, *Memorial*, pp. 11–13, 23–5, 67–70; Meech and Allen (eds), *The Book of Margery Kempe*, pp. 11–13; Julian of Norwich, *Revelations of Divine Love*, pp. 185–6; F. Beer, *Women and Mystical Experience in the Middle Ages* (Woodbridge, 1992), p. 149.

18 Meech and Allen (eds), *The Book of Margery Kempe*, pp. 198, 209; Holloway (ed.), *St Bride and her Book*, pp. 119–21; Bynum, *Holy Feast and Holy Fast*, p. 133; C. Klapisch-Zuber, *Women, Family and Ritual in Renaissance Italy*, (trans.) L.G. Cochrane (Chicago, 1985), p. 325; U. Rublack, 'Female spirituality and the infant Jesus in late medieval Dominican convents', in R.W. Scribner and T. Johnson (eds), *Popular Religion in Germany and Central Europe, 1400–1800* (Basingstoke, 1996), pp. 16–37.

19 R. Kieckhefer, 'Major currents in late medieval devotion', in Raitt (ed.), *Christian Spirituality*, pp. 83–9.

20 Angela of Foligno, *Memorial*, p. 52; Julian of Norwich, *Revelations of Divine Love*, pp. 65, 87–90, 92–3.

21 Menestò, 'The canonization proceedings of Clare of Montefalco', pp. 104–29; Angela of Foligno, *Memorial*, pp. 112, 114–17. The emblems of the Passion were the cross, the scourge and the pillar to which Christ was tied during the scourging, the crown of thorns, the nails, the lance which pierced Christ's side, and the rod with the sponge with which Christ was offered a drink of vinegar.

22 Kieckhefer, *Unquiet Souls*, p. 30.

23 Blumenfeld-Kosinski (ed.), *Writings of Margaret of Oingt*, pp. 55–7; Angela of Foligno, *Memorial*, pp. 61, 109.

24 Angela of Foligno, *Memorial*, pp. 47, 113; Bynum, *Holy Feast and Holy Fast*, pp. 161–3.

25 Angela of Foligno, *Memorial*, pp. 41, 50; A.B. Mulder-Bakker, 'Ivetta of Huy: *mater et magistra*', in A.B. Mulder-Bakker (ed.), *Sanctity and Motherhood.*

Essays on Holy Mothers in the Middle Ages (New York, 1995), p. 241; Julian of Norwich, *Revelations of Divine Love*, pp. 164–7.

26 *Acta Sanctorum*, April vol. III, p. 891; Meech and Allen (eds), *The Book of Margery Kempe*, pp. 86–9; Angela of Foligno, *Memorial*, pp. 59–60; E.A. Petroff (ed.), *Medieval Women's Visionary Literature* (Oxford, 1986), pp. 195–200; A.M. Haas, 'Schools of late medieval mysticism', in Raitt (ed.), *Christian Spirituality*, p. 167; Bynum, *Holy Feast and Holy Fast*, pp. 153–60.

27 Holloway (ed.), *St Bride and her Book*, pp. 31–3.

28 Beer, *Women and Mystical Experience*, pp. 151–6; Bynum, *Holy Feast and Holy Fast*, pp. 265–7; Julian of Norwich, *Revelations of Divine Love*, pp. 151–73.

29 Breastmilk was thought at the time to be a form of the blood which nourished the baby in the womb.

30 Haas, 'Schools of late medieval mysticism', pp. 156–8; Paul Lee, *Nunneries, Learning and Spirituality in Late Medieval English Society. The Dominican Priory of Dartford* (Woodbridge, 2001), pp. 150–2; U. Rublack, 'Female spirituality and the infant Jesus', pp. 16–37; A. Minnis and R, Voaden (eds), *Medieval Holy Women in the Christian Tradition c. 1100–c. 1500* (Turnhout, 2010), pp. 105–31.

31 Eckenstein, *Woman under Monasticism*, pp. 328–53; Beer, *Women and Mystical Experience*, pp. 78–108; C.W. Bynum, *Jesus as Mother. Studies in the Spirituality of the High Middle Ages* (Berkeley, California, 1982), pp. 172–246; Voaden, 'Community, gender and vision at Helfta', pp. 72–91; Petroff (ed.), *Medieval Women's Visionary Literature*, pp. 212–30. The works of the mystics have been translated into English: Mechtild of Magdeburg, *The Flowing Light of the Divinity*, Susan Clark (ed.), C.M. Galvani (trans.) (New York, 1991); Mechtild of Hackeborn, *The Book of Gostlye Grace*, T.A. Halligan (ed.), (Toronto, 1979); Gertrude the Great, *The Herald of God's Loving Kindness*, (ed. and trans.) Alexandra Barratt (Kalamazoo, Michigan, 1991).

32 Kieckhefer, *Unquiet Souls*, pp. 10–15.

33 Beer, *Women and Mystical Experience*, pp. 85–9; Holloway (ed.), *St Bride and her Book*, pp. 61–3, 90–6; Bynum, *Holy Feast and Holy Fast*, p. 269.

34 Angela of Foligno, *Memorial*, p. 53; *Acta Sanctorum*, April vol. III, p. 901.

35 *Acta Sanctorum*, April vol. III, pp. 502–14, 955–6; D.H. Farmer, *Oxford Dictionary of Saints* (Oxford, 1997), pp. 159–60, 525–6; Bynum, *Holy Feast and Holy Fast*, pp. 135–6, 170; In England, Zita was known as Sitha.

36 *Acta Sanctorum*, September vol. V, pp. 123–95; Bynum, *Holy Feast and Holy Fast*, pp. 181–5; S.A. Epstein, *Genoa and the Genoese, 958–1528* (Chapel Hill, North Carolina, 1996), pp. 304–9.

37 M. Rubin, *Corpus Christi. The Eucharist in Late Medieval Culture* (Cambridge, 1991), pp. 169–85.

38 A. Vauchez, *Saints, prophètes et visionnaires. Le pouvoir surnaturel au moyen âge* (Paris, 1999), pp. 162–74, 175, 187; R. Voaden, 'The company she keeps: Mechtild of Hackeborn in late-medieval devotional compilations', in R. Voaden (ed.), *Prophets Abroad. The Reception of Continental Holy Women in Late-Medieval England* (Woodbridge, 1996), pp. 65–7; B.A. Windeatt (trans.), *The Book of Margery Kempe* (Harmondsworth, 1985), p. 9; Julian of Norwich, *Revelations of Divine Love*, pp. 13–14.

39 Bynum, *Jesus as Mother*, pp. 178–81.

40 A. Zumkeller, 'The spirituality of the Augustinians', in Raitt (ed.), *Christian Spirituality*, p. 68; Bynum, *Holy Feast and Holy Fast*, pp. 170–1; *Acta Sanctorum*, April vol. III, p. 936; J. Hook, *Siena. A City and its History* (London, 1979), pp. 123–4; Angela of Foligno, *Memorial*, p. 3.

41 Menestò, 'The canonization proceedings of Clare of Montefalco', p. 119.

42 A. Vauchez, *Les laïcs au moyen âge. Pratiques et expériences religieuses* (Paris, 1987), pp. 278–9.

43 Ibid., pp. 266–7, 275; Vauchez, *Saints, prophètes et visionnaires*, pp. 125–8; Haas, 'Schools of late medieval mysticism', p. 167; Farmer, *Oxford Dictionary of Saints*, pp. 74–5, 92–3; *Acta Sanctorum*, April vol. III, pp. 931–6; Noffke (ed.), *Letters of St Catherine of Siena*, I, pp. 60–3, 79–81, 98–102, 122–39, 147–54, 204–10, 244–51; Hook, *Siena*, pp. 139–42; D. Watt, *Secretaries of God. Women Prophets in Late Medieval and Early Modern England* (Woodbridge, 1997), pp. 21–3, 26; Morris, *St Birgitta of Sweden*, pp. 113–17.

44 Vauchez, *Saints, prophètes et visionnaires*, pp. 175–88; Vauchez, *Les laïcs au moyen âge*, pp. 197–201; Bynum, *Holy Feast and Holy Fast*, p. 135; R. Voaden, *God's Words, Women's Voices. The Discernment of Spirits in the Writing of Late-Medieval Women Visionaries* (Woodbridge, 1999), pp. 78–93.

45 Angela of Foligno, *Memorial*, pp. 2–3, 11–13, 37–43, 67–8.

46 Meech and Allen (eds), *The Book of Margery Kempe*, pp. 139–42, 147–52; J. Wilson, 'Communities of dissent: the secular and ecclesiastical communities of Margery Kempe's Book', in Watt (ed.), *Medieval Women in their Communities*, pp. 155–85; Kieckhefer, *Unquiet Souls*, p. 31.

47 D. Weinstein and R.M. Bell, *Saints and Society. The Two Worlds of Western Christendom, 1000–1700* (Chicago, 1982), pp. 220–1; A. Vauchez, *La sainteté en occident aux derniers siècles du moyen âge* (Rome, 1981), pp. 316–19; Bynum, 'Religious women in the later Middle Ages', pp. 127–8; M. Goodich, '*Ancilla dei*: the servant as saint in the late Middle Ages', in J. Kirshner and S.F. Wemple (eds), *Women of the Medieval World. Essays in honor of John H. Mundy* (Oxford, 1985), pp. 119–32.

48 Weinstein and Bell, *Saints and Society*, p. 141.

49 Ibid., pp. 168–71.

50 Vauchez, *La sainteté en occident*, pp. 246, 281–2.

51 Ibid., p. 427; Kieckhefer, *Unquiet Souls*, pp. 32–3.

52 Vauchez, *Saints, prophètes et visionnaires*, pp. 69–74. Margaret of Hungary was canonised in 1943.

53 Vauchez, *La sainteté en occident*, p. 185.

54 Weinstein and Bell, *Saints and Society*, pp. 19–65.

13 Laywomen and charity

The number of laywomen living a life of religious devotion and piety in the later Middle Ages blurred the distinction between the lay and religious worlds. The charity practised by nuns, beguines, penitents and saints overlapped with that of the housewife living in village or town. Religious precepts formed an integral part of a woman's upbringing, and from an early age girls were taught that love of one's neighbour, as epitomised in active help, complemented love of God which was expressed in worship and prayer. Whether girls married or entered the religious life, their early education made for similar attitudes towards the poor and meant that laywomen's activities had strong similarities to those of the religious.

During the Middle Ages, charity had a much wider definition than at the present day. The emphasis on practical help for the living was very much to the fore, but charity implied a reciprocal act, the material help being reciprocated by prayers. Everyone was expected to know the Seven Corporal Acts of Mercy which provided a basic guide to one's duty towards one's neighbour and which all could practise to some degree. These comprised the obligations to give food to the hungry, drink to the thirsty, clothing to the naked, and shelter to strangers, to visit the sick and those in prison, and to bury the dead. The duty of providing for the poor and the great importance attached to their prayers underpinned many of the acts of charity in the later Middle Ages. Many of the poor were lay people, but gifts to the religious poor also counted as charity, whether they were made to monks, nuns and friars, to beguines and penitents, or to a hospital or almshouse. A number of chantry foundations contained a charitable element, such as the provision of education. Money for public works on roads and bridges also came under the heading of charity.

Charity met very real needs, although there is no means of assessing the actual degree of relief or the attitude of more than a minority of the European population. Motivation of donors cannot be assessed and it is likely that they were driven by desire for reputation and prestige, the need for remembrance and fear of the poor, as well as by religious concern for their neighbour. The evidence points to acts of charity being carried out by men and women of every social status. Women had different opportunities to exercise charity from men because of their control of the household, and there are parallels between the actions of rich and poor in spite of their contrasting resources. At a time when urban and royal governments were increasingly concerned with the preservation of order, it was mainly left to individuals, parishes and endowed institutions to provide relief for the poor.

Looking at charity from the point of view of the recipient, the question arises as to whether women were in special need. It was taken for granted that poverty was part of the natural social order, but a distinction has to be drawn between permanent destitution and temporary need resulting from illness, disability, unemployment, old age, famine or war. Women were particularly vulnerable at the time of childbirth and when they had young children, as well as when they were old. Relief to widows and orphans, and to the defenceless, was sanctioned by biblical teaching. The variety of needs was reflected in the policies adopted by the Orsanmichele in Florence in the fourteenth century with the application of selective rather than indiscriminate charity, and the decision to help poor families with large numbers of children, women in childbed and widows. The company of the Neri in Florence in 1360 cared for the sick and women in childbed, as well as carrying out their work for pilgrims and travellers.[1] The desire to support families in temporary need encouraged social stability. Yet the targeting of particular groups meant that others went unaided: disabled men, for instance, were rarely mentioned, and the needs of women should not overshadow those existing elsewhere in society.[2]

Charity to religious men and women, in the form of new foundations and grants of property, were mainly made by the better-off in society. By the thirteenth century, the great age of monastic expansion was over. Some new foundations were established, such as Blanche of Castile's foundation of the abbey of Maubuisson for Cistercian nuns, but they were few in number compared with the twelfth century.[3] Moreover, the coming of the friars directed patronage into new channels. The principal patrons of monastic houses were members of the nobility who also came to patronise the newer forms of religious life. Connections between noble families and individual monastic houses were maintained through confirmations of their property, some grants and bequests, and burials. Members of the nobility still valued the link with a monastic house and the prayers and commemoration which were offered. The Benedictine abbey of Tewkesbury continued to be the mausoleum of the Clare earls of Gloucester and their wives and of the Despenser family in the later Middle Ages. Elizabeth de Burgh maintained connections with the Clare family houses on her lands and also founded a Franciscan priory at Walsingham.[4] The presence of kindred who were religious might dictate gifts or bequests to a particular house. In 1495 Cecily, Duchess of York, bequeathed two crimson and gold copes to the Bridgettine house at Syon, as well as making personal bequests to two granddaughters, Anne, who was the prioress of Syon, and Bridget, a nun at Dartford.[5]

Some houses were founded in the later Middle Ages with the intention of becoming the family's religious centre. The first Cistercian house in the Tyrol was founded at Stams by Count Meinhard II of Gorz-Tyrol and his wife Elizabeth of Bavaria around 1273, the church being consecrated eleven years later. Elizabeth had previously been married to Conrad IV (d. 1254) and local tradition has drawn a link between Stams and the last rulers of the Hohenstaufen dynasty. However, it is likely that the house was intended as a mausoleum for Meinhard's family; the bones of his ancestors were transferred there and the church became the burial place of himself and his wife and their descendants. In the fifteenth century, members of the Habsburg family were buried there.[6]

The nobility also patronised the friars, but mendicant patronage embraced a far wider range of men and women, including gentry and townspeople as well as nobles. Women played a major role, either alongside their husbands or as widows. Gifts ranged from the establishment of new priories to grants of property, furnishings and money, the sums involved varying from the substantial to the very small. Just as members of the nobility valued the prayers of monks and nuns, so many people set a high value on the prayers of mendicant men and women. Patrons were influenced by family connections, locality and personal preferences. Religious and family factors lay behind the foundation of the house of Corpus Domini at Mantua around 1416 by Paola Malatesta, wife of Gianfrancesco Gonzaga. Paola petitioned Pope Martin V to allow the Poor Clares to follow the Observant Rule, and in 1420 she used her power to change the route of the Corpus Christi procession so that it would stop at the nunnery. She herself entered Corpus Domini after her husband's death, as did her daughter Cecilia and other members of the Gonzaga family.[7]

Marie de Saint Pol, Countess of Pembroke, had a strong personal preference for the Minoresses. She established a house for them at Denny in Cambridgeshire, receiving royal and papal permission to transfer the Minoresses of Waterbeach to Denny, a move which encountered opposition at Waterbeach but which was largely complete by the early 1350s. She secured papal privileges for the abbey for which she supplied new buildings, including a residence for herself within the complex. Her attachment to the Minoresses is apparent in her will in which she said that she wanted to be buried in the choir of the abbey church wearing the nun's habit.[8]

Most patrons among the nobility and townspeople made much smaller gifts, but the patronage across Europe testifies to the popularity of the friars. This popularity and the sense of civic patriotism and family feeling help to explain the growth of houses in the Italian towns. At Santa Maria di Monteluce at Perugia, the principal benefactors in the fifteenth century came from the elite of the town itself, many of the nuns coming from wealthy urban families. In the German towns, property and money were given to the friars by wealthy burghers and their wives and widows. At Cologne, Rika, widow of Philip Cleingedank, gave the Dominicans a house and property near the town in the mid-thirteenth century; Agnes Cleingedank bequeathed money to both the Franciscans and Dominicans, while Richmudis Birklin left the Franciscans and Dominicans one-sixth each of her property on the Hafengasse. In England, bequests were often made to the friars of the locality. Katherine Peverel left money to the friars of Sussex, just as she did to the monks and nuns of the county. Isabel atte Mere of the market town of Sudbury in Suffolk left £1 each to the friars of Clare and Sudbury, in addition to two bequests to individual friars and two to nuns at Malling in Kent. Other forms of religious life were also patronised. As well as remembering religious houses, Beatrice Lady Roos left bequests to the anchoresses of Leake and Nun Appleton in Yorkshire.[9]

The benefit which all patrons hoped to receive from religious houses comprised intercessions on their behalf, often after their deaths, to enable them to pass more quickly through purgatory. A two-way relationship existed, with prayers offered on one side and material support on the other. For the well-off, it was possible to secure indulgences which enabled the recipient to have a closer relationship with the religious house. In 1333, Marie de St Pol was allowed to enter nunneries with a retinue of six matrons once a year, and in 1342 her confessor was allowed to give permission to the religious to eat meat at her table. Lay people were received into confraternity by religious houses. Marie de St Pol wanted all the houses where she had been received to be informed of her death, and each was to be given one of her relics, vestments or images for the greater remembrance of her soul.[10]

Provision for education was also considered a work of charity, and the growth of the universities was fostered by the foundation of colleges to house students, with both women and men acting as patrons. Grammar schools were also established. Joan of Champagne, wife of Philip IV of France, established the College of Navarre in the University of Paris at a time when a number of other colleges were being founded. Marie de St Pol intended to have a French presence at Pembroke College, Cambridge, founded by her in 1347, but this did not materialise, and neither did her plan nine years later to establish a college in the University of Paris, because of the Hundred Years War. Marie's great friend, Elizabeth de Burgh, founded Clare College at Cambridge in the 1330s, and in the mid-fifteenth century Queens' College was initiated by Margaret of Anjou, although her successor, Elizabeth Woodville, described herself as the true foundress. At Oxford, in 1284–5 Devorguilla de Balliol carried out her husband's intention to establish Balliol College.[11] Such foundations presupposed wealth and generosity and a long-term commitment in time, since the acquisition of both property and royal and papal privileges took many years. The patronage combined a concern to meet the need for trained administrators with a desire to perpetuate family prestige and the pious wish to achieve salvation. The foundations can be regarded in the guise of chantries, since the inmates were expected to pray for their founders and benefactors. Devorguilla made her foundation for the salvation of herself and her husband, her parents and ancestors, and her children and successors; according to the statutes, three requiem masses were to be celebrated every year. It is likely that the women had some say in the college statutes and this would explain the reference to French students at Pembroke College, Cambridge.

The need for hospitals for the sick, disabled and aged became more urgent with the growth of towns from the twelfth century. Foundations were made by royalty, nobility and townspeople, and by men, women and married couples. Mahaut, Countess of Artois, built the hospital at Hesdin between 1321 and 1323. In addition to the main room for the sick, the complex included a chapel, a kitchen and a room for women in childbirth. The staff comprised a chaplain and mistress, five female and two male servants, a doctor on a yearly salary, and a midwife. Many people made small bequests to hospitals in their wills. Garsende de Boutenac in 1236 left 10 *sous* each to the four hospitals for the poor in Narbonne, 20 *sous* to the house of Holy Trinity, and 10 *sous* each to the alms of St Just and St Paul. At Genoa, the hospitals of St John and the leper colony at Capo Fari attracted bequests from people of all social levels. Some hospitals besides Hesdin included special care for women, the Hôtel-Dieu at Paris having a special lying-in room with a midwife in attendance, and the paupers' hospital at Narbonne having a women's ward.[12] The hospitals were run by religious orders or by beguines and, as in other religious foundations, prayers were offered for founders and benefactors. Not all hospitals had sufficient endowments to be able to survive in the long term, and many small foundations had a relatively short life. Nevertheless, most large towns had a network of hospitals of various types and sizes, about sixty existing in Paris in the early fourteenth century, twelve in Toulouse and Narbonne, fifteen in Cordoba and thirty in Florence. The hospitals at Ghent in the fourteenth century included orphanages, a leper hospital outside the town, and hospitals for the sick, the blind, and for old women, travellers and reformed prostitutes.[13]

Social charity came to be regarded as of growing importance in the fourteenth and fifteenth centuries, and women were alive to the needs of their own localities. Many of their foundations were almshouses for the poor and old. In 1348, a widow of the Cavalcanti family of Florence wanted her house to be turned into a hospital for the poor, while money from the sale of most of her estate was to be used to purchase clothing, sheets and blankets for the hospital of Santa Maria Nuova and the Society of the Misericordia in the contado. Nearly thirty years later, a Florentine widow, Filippa, daughter of Jacopo di Ser Cambio, charged her heir to sell property to finance the building of a hospital within two months; if he failed to do this, her estate was to pass to the hospital of Santa Maria Nuova. Similar action was taken by women in other Italian towns. Margaret, Lady Hungerford established an almshouse at Heytesbury in Wiltshire in 1472 for a chaplain, twelve poor men and one woman, laying down requirements for prayers as well as providing for the support of the inmates.[14] The disparity between the numbers of men and women is found in other English foundations.

The emphasis on social charity took in not only the needs of the poor but also those of people who had fallen on hard times. In the will of Elizabeth de Burgh of 1355, she bequeathed the residue of her goods to poor men and women religious, poor gentlewomen burdened with children, poor scholars, merchants and prisoners; she wanted to help poor people keep up their households, to support poor parish churches, and provide for the repair of bridges and roads, and other works of charity for the salvation of her soul.[15] The list appears comprehensive but betrays a desire to support people of the gentle social group rather than to give indiscriminate aid to those who were destitute. Testators often specified the poor of their own localities or their own estates. In 1434, Joan Beauchamp, Lady Abergavenny, left £40 for poor prisoners and £100 for the repair of weak bridges and bad roads, but otherwise specified the poor of her own lordships, leaving them £133 6s 8d in money, £100 to be distributed in kind and £100 for the marriage of poor girls. Similar concerns for the locality are found lower down the social scale. Margaret Wareyn of Long Melford in Suffolk wanted a weekly distribution to twelve of Melford's neediest poor as long as her bequest of £6 13s 4d lasted.[16]

Testators probably felt that they were performing an important act of charity in helping poor people to stand on their own feet. In Florence, aid was given to citizens' families who had fallen on hard times. At Siena, the thirteenth- and early fourteenth-century practice of making a large number of religious bequests changed to an emphasis on the provision of dowries in the late fourteenth and fifteenth centuries. The size of bequests varied, but the girls were expected to be of good character. Dowry inflation in Italian towns made it difficult for some girls to find marriage partners. Marriage and the family were considered the bedrock of society, and mortality during the plague led to concern about the level of population and the need for children, a point emphasised by Bernardino of Siena in his sermons. Bequests of dowry funds became increasingly important in Florence, Arezzo, Perugia and Pisa from the later fourteenth century. On a much more lavish scale, Mahaut, Countess of Artois, left 1,000 *livres* in her will for dowries for girls who might be unable to find a husband because of poverty.[17]

Medieval women, along with their husbands, fathers and sons, provided for men and women religious and for particular groups in need. They also showed concern for those at the bottom of the social scale, whether this was due to unemployment, disability, old age, or war and devastation, although the effect on the overall problem of poverty was probably small. Both the religious and the lay elite distributed alms to the very poor in a variety of ways. All great households gave food and alms to the poor. On a daily basis, the leftovers of meals were collected by the almoner of the household and distributed. Some noblewomen personally gave away food from their own table, as did Elizabeth of Hungary. Others distributed food on anniversaries and special feast days. Throughout her widowhood, Elizabeth de Burgh regularly distributed bread and herrings to the poor on 12 March, the anniversary of the death of her third husband, and in the last years of her life was making regular payments of 1 penny each to poor people at a number of her manors. All women of the elite practised casual almsgiving, but this was rarely recorded. Elizabeth de Burgh's chamber account of 1351–2, however, listed her giving in her chapel, and to friars and the poor, including one-off gifts such as 6s 8d to seven men going to the Holy Land. Mahaut, Countess of Artois, gave food, bedding and money to the hospitals and Poor Tables of Artois and set aside 500 *livres* a year for clothing and shoes for the poor, insisting that the distribution should be made before the winter and that the same recipients should not be chosen two years running. Almsgiving was also called for at times of disaster, as when Countess Mahaut provided alms in Calais during the harsh winter of 1306 and made a special distribution during the great freeze of 1321–2. The countess's casual almsgiving was extensive and recipients included wounded soldiers, workers, pilgrims, poor brides, women in childbed and the families of those killed in her service.[18]

The practice of offering hospitality to religious, pilgrims and strangers was widespread, as recorded in the household book of Dame Alice de Bryene. Some households contained poor inmates. Katherine de Norwich fed thirteen poor people in her household, the number present at the Last Supper, while Beatrice Lady Roos bequeathed 6s 8d each to seven poor old men of her household. Maundy Thursday was regularly celebrated by washing the feet of the poor and by almsgiving. In 1388, Mary de Bohun, Countess of Derby, distributed eighteen russet gowns and hoods to eighteen poor women and gave them 9 shillings in alms; the number probably corresponded to Mary's age.[19]

The final distribution to the poor by a member of the elite was made at death, with payments and clothing given to poor mourners in return for prayers. Provision for these payments was regularly made in late medieval wills. Margaret Adhémar of Monteil in 1363 wanted her executors to be responsible for giving alms to the poor of Christ at her burial. Three years later, Matilda de Vere, Countess of Oxford, left £40 to be distributed to the poor on the day of her funeral.[20] There is clearly a discrepancy between what the elite spent on charity and the sums they expended on conspicuous consumption and display. It is easy to say that they should have spent more on the poor, a criticism which has been levelled at the well-off down the ages. Yet it has to be borne in mind that they were aiming to relieve distress, not trying to eradicate poverty. From their point of view, the poor were a permanent part of society and the wealthy had the duty to help them in return for prayers. Few of the elite were concerned with international charity; both Elizabeth de Burgh and Mahaut of Artois made contributions to the crusade, but it was rare to find others doing so.[21] Nobility and patricians were primarily concerned with their own locality, and their desire for stability and order went alongside their charitable giving.

The majority of the poor were relieved within their own community and family networks. Families were regarded as responsible for their kindred, servants and dependants and it is likely that both husband and wife had a role to play in providing help. Taking examples from Bohemia, in 1505 Wenceslas the draper settled his whole estate on his wife on condition that his brother should live with her, earn his living there and help her; if they failed to live together amicably, she should pay the sum of money due to him. In 1460, a widow gave her estate to two of her daughters and provided that they should care for their invalid sister. A butcher in 1499 bequeathed his house and property to his son on condition that he gave his mother fitting support until her death.[22]

Similar provision is likely to have been made all over Europe, but migration often led to the break-up of the family and it was therefore not always possible to look to kin for support. In a sample from manorial courts in East Anglia, about half the pensioners negotiated arrangements with their children before the Black Death, but less than a quarter afterwards. The answer lay in making a retirement contract with someone outside the family, as when a couple in Gressenhall, Norfolk, in 1455 handed over most of their property to a presumably younger couple, keeping two rooms, a little land and part of the barn for themselves, together with a cow, pig, cock and eight hens.[23]

Poor relief was mainly provided by the parish and the guild and was administered by leading men of the community. Women presumably had a role through their contributions to the parish and to guild dues, but on the whole these went unrecorded. The Poor Table next to the church with the purpose of distributing alms to the poor was found in the Low Countries and the Holy Roman Empire. At Ghent the Holy Ghost Tables in the fourteenth century distributed food, shoes and fuel, and relied for their income on private donations. In the Low Countries, the organisation was often in the hands of town officials, or they might be supervised by the local lord such as Countess Mahaut. A similar system operated in southern France and Spain, and in north and central Italy.[24] The Florentine parish provided alms, free burial and free or subsidised accommodation. Within the parish of San Frediano, the Compagnia delle Brucciate was established in 1323 when its statutes were approved by the church authorities and the men and women of the parish; it aimed to succour the living and the dead, giving alms to the sick and to women in childbed, and providing help with funerals. Between 1362 and 1376, women received 76 per cent of the alms together with help over housing; there was a large number of destitute widows after the Black Death.[25]

It is likely that charity was performed by women in the community but that this was done on an informal, neighbourly basis and was rarely recorded. Inevitably, some women would be more charitable than others and make more skilful use of their brewing and cooking abilities. How far they concentrated on 'deserving' or 'undeserving' poor is impossible to say, but some English manorial courts were taking this distinction into consideration from the 1460s. Many families in town and country fell into difficulties from time to time, and it was the responsibility of neighbours to tide them over. In England, help was provided by church-ales, also known as help-ales. The church-ale is generally thought of as a means of raising funds for the parish church, but it was also used to help a family in need, whether the couple was newly married or the family ran into a crisis in middle or old age. With the church-ale, an enjoyable and sociable event was combined with charity.[26] The importance of private charity and neighbourly help was probably felt in villages and towns across Europe, and gave women a vital role to play.

The nature of women's lives enabled them to know their communities and where the real needs lay. The evidence for female networks is often found in wills which point to women living together for mutual support or relying on a maidservant or friends and neighbours. Such networks within the community were less usual among men. The contrast can be seen in fifteenth-century Norfolk where 36.7 per cent of women's wills left legacies to unrelated women, as against 17 per cent of men's wills.[27] These legatees received personal possessions which women were far more likely than men to name in their wills. Whether women were concerned to provide a remembrance for their friends and servants to thank them for past help or to meet future need is impossible to say. Marion Fenkele of Stowmarket, Suffolk, was probably providing for her servant's old age when she left her 6s 8d, the cottage where she was living, two bushels each of wheat and malt, and a parcel of land. It is more difficult to interpret the will of Alice Drawswerd of a nearby village who bequeathed a cloak, a green gown, a blue tunic and a bushel of wheat to four individual women.[28]

Venetian women operated within the parish, building up relationships based on personal patronage, while their husbands operated in a wider political sphere within the state. Women visited their neighbours and were present at births and deaths and so built up their networks of contacts. They also made bequests in their wills, as women did in England. Close relationships developed between women and their servants, and also between patrician women and *popolano* women living nearby. Some patrician women took responsibility for those around them and left money for *popolano* dowries and trousseaux; a number of *popolano* women appointed a patrician as executrix of their wills.[29]

Charity in the later Middle Ages was an essential part of religious practice and for the majority focused on the local community, just as worship centred on the parish church. Although charity was considered obligatory for all, among women a contrast emerged between the elite and the rest of the population. The elite women, in their grants to religious foundations, social charity and relief of the poor, acted similarly to the men of their families. Women below the elite were unable to administer public charity, whether in the parish or the guild, because this political role was taken by men. They concentrated on informal, neighbourly activity. Less is known of lifetime giving than of testamentary bequests, and lack of evidence makes it impossible to draw a full picture. It is likely that all women preferred to help the 'deserving' poor; in the later Middle Ages there was widespread fear and dislike of idle vagabonds, although this attitude became more deeply entrenched in the early modern period. Many medieval women took need seriously and, for the salvation of their souls and love of their neighbours, and probably also with the desire to promote peace in their communities, attempted to alleviate the distress of the poor.

Notes

1 J. Henderson, *Piety and Charity in Late Medieval Florence* (Oxford, 1994), pp. 233, 260–70, 288, 321–31, 341; B. Pullan, 'Support and redeem: charity and poor relief in Italian cities from the fourteenth to the seventeenth century', *Continuity and Change* 3 (1988), p. 183.

2 This point was made by Sharon Farmer at the Gender and Medieval Studies Conference at the University of York, January 2001.

3 M.H. Caviness, 'Anchoress, abbess, and queen: donors and patrons or intercessors and matrons', in J.H. McCash (ed.), *The Cultural Patronage of Medieval Women* (Athens, Georgia, 1996), pp. 136–8.

4 J. Nichols, *A Collection of All the Wills of the Kings and Queens of England* (London, 1780), pp. 32–3; *Calendar of Patent Rolls, 1345–8* (London, 1903), p. 255; ibid. *1348–50* (London, 1905), p. 7; British Library, London, Cotton MS Nero E vii, fos 160–1.

5 J.G. Nichols and J. Bruce (eds), *Wills from Doctors' Commons* (Camden Society old series 83, 1863), pp. 2–3.

6 K-U. Jäschke, 'From famous empresses to unspectacular queens: the Romano-German Empire to Margaret of Brabant, d. 1311', in A.J. Duggan (ed.), *Queens and Queenship in Medieval Europe* (Woodbridge, 1997), pp. 105–7.

7 J.M. Wood, *Women, Art and Spirituality. The Poor Clares of Early Modern Italy* (Cambridge, 1996), pp. 89–96.

8 A.F.C. Bourdillon, *The Order of Minoresses in England* (Manchester, 1926), pp. 19–22; H. Jenkinson, 'Mary de Sancto Paulo, foundress of Pembroke College, Cambridge', *Archaeologia* 66 (1915), pp. 419–22, 432–3. The Minoresses were Poor Clares who followed the Isabella Rule.

9 Wood, *Women, Art and Spirituality*, pp. 103–4; J.B. Freed, *The Friars and German Society in the Thirteenth Century* (Cambridge, Massachusetts, 1977), p. 95; Lambeth Palace Library, London, Register of Simon Sudbury, fo. 90; Borthwick Institute of Historical Research, York, archiepiscopal register 18, fos 357v–358v; J.C. Ward (ed. and trans.), *Women of the English Nobility and Gentry 1066–1500* (Manchester, 1995), pp. 224–30; P. Northeast (ed.), *Wills of the Archdeaconry of Sudbury, 1439–61* (Suffolk Records Society 44, 2001), p. 203.

10 *Calendar of Entries in the Papal Registers relating to Great Britain and Ireland, Papal Letters, 1305–42* (London, 1895), pp. 393, 413; *Papal Letters, 1342–62* (London, 1897), pp. 68, 226; Jenkinson, 'Mary de Sancto Paulo', p. 434.

11 J. Strayer, *The Reign of Philip the Fair* (Princeton, 1980), p. 67; J.C. Ward, *English Noblewomen in the Later Middle Ages* (London, 1992), pp. 156–60; Jenkinson, 'Mary de Sancto Paulo', pp. 411, 422–4, 433; A.C. Chibnall, *Richard de Badew and the University of Cambridge, 1315–40* (Cambridge, 1963), pp. 16–17, 37–41; D.R. Leader, *A History of the University of Cambridge. I, The University to 1546* (Cambridge, 1988), pp. 82–4; J.I. Catto (ed.), *The Early Oxford Schools* (Oxford, 1984), pp. 205, 240, 244–5, 275–9, 282–3, 292–3,

299; H.E. Salter (ed.), *The Oxford Deeds of Balliol College* (Oxford Historical Society 64, 1913), pp. 1–4, 277–83.

12 J-M. Richard, *Mahaut comtesse d'Artois et de Bourgogne* (Paris, 1887), pp. 263–5; J. Caille, *Hôpitaux et charité publique à Narbonne au moyen âge* (Toulouse, 1978), p. 144; C. Rawcliffe, *Medicine and Society in Later Medieval England* (Stroud, 1995), p. 204; S. Epstein, *Wills and Wealth in Medieval Genoa, 1150–1250* (Cambridge, Massachusetts, 1984), pp. 175–9; M. Mollat, *The Poor in the Middle Ages. An Essay in Social History*, (trans.) A. Goldhammer (New Haven, Connecticut, 1986), p. 149.

13 Mollat, *Poor*, pp. 146–53; D. Nicholas, *The Metamorphosis of a Medieval City. Ghent in the Age of the Arteveldes, 1302–90* (Lincoln, Nebraska, 1987), pp. 42–4.

14 S.K. Cohn, Jr. *The Cult of Remembrance and the Black Death* (Baltimore, 1992), pp. 58–9; W. Dugdale, J. Caley, H. Ellis and B. Bandinel (eds), *Monasticon Anglicanum*, 6 vols (London, 1817–30), VI, pp. 725–6; Ward (ed. and trans.), *Women of the English Nobility and Gentry*, pp. 204–6.

15 Nichols, *Collection of All the Wills*, pp. 40–1.

16 E.F. Jacob (ed.), *The Register of Henry Chichele, Archbishop of Canterbury, 1414–43*, 4 vols (Canterbury and York Society 42, 45–7, 1937–47), II, p. 536; Northeast (ed.), *Wills of the Archdeaconry of Sudbury*, p. 326.

17 R.C. Trexler, 'Charity and the defense of urban elites in the Italian communes', in R.C. Trexler, *Dependence in Context in Renaissance Florence* (New York, 1994), pp. 61–111; S.K. Cohn, Jr., *Death and Property in Siena, 1205–1800* (Baltimore, 1988), pp. 54–6, 85; Cohn, *Cult of Remembrance*, pp. 65–7; Richard, *Mahaut comtesse d'Artois*, p. 97; D. Herlihy, *Women, Family and Society in Medieval Europe* (Providence, Rhode Island, 1995), pp. 174–92.

18 The National Archives, London, E101/93/4, m. 14; E101/93/12, m. 1, 4d; E101/93/18, m. 2, 8d; E101/93/20, m. 18d. The men going to the Holy Land were from Tregrug, alias Llangibby, Monmouthshire, one of Elizabeth's manors in her lordship of Usk. Richard, *Mahaut comtesse d'Artois*, pp. 90–7.

19 V.B. Redstone (ed.) and M.K. Dale (trans.), *The Household Book of Dame Alice de Bryene, 1412–13* (Suffolk Institute of Archaeology and Natural History, Ipswich, 1931); British Library, London, Additional Roll 63207; The National Archives, London, DL28/1/2, fos 20v, 26r; Ward (ed. and trans.), *Women of the English Nobility and Gentry*, p. 228.

20 A. Jacotin, *Preuves de la maison de Polignac*, 5 vols (Paris, 1898–1906), IV, p. 239; G.M. Benton, 'Essex wills at Canterbury', *Transactions of the Essex Archaeological Society* new series 21 (1933–7), p. 263.

21 Nichols, *Collection of All the Wills*, p. 29; Richard, *Mahaut comtesse d'Artois*, p. 98.

22 J. Klassen, 'Household composition in medieval Bohemia', *JMH* 16 (1990), pp. 64–9.

23 E. Clark, 'Some aspects of social security in medieval England', *JFH* 7 (1982), pp. 315, 319.

24 Mollat, *Poor*, pp. 135–45; Nicholas, *Metamorphosis of a Medieval City*, p. 42.

25 J. Henderson, 'The parish and the poor in Florence at the time of the Black Death: the case of San Frediano', *Continuity and Change* 3 (1988), pp. 247–72; I. Chabot, 'Widowhood and poverty in late medieval Florence', ibid., pp. 291–311.

26 J.M. Bennett, 'Conviviality and charity in medieval and early modern England', *PandP* 134 (1992), pp. 19–41; M.K. McIntosh, 'Local responses to the poor in late medieval and Tudor England', *Continuity and Change* 3 (1988), pp. 210–25; M.K. McIntosh, *Controlling Misbehavior in England, 1370–1600* (Cambridge, 1998), p. 83.

27 P. Maddern, 'Friends of the dead: executors, wills and family strategy in fifteenth-century Norfolk', in R.E. Archer and S. Walker (eds), *Rulers and Ruled in Late Medieval England. Essays presented to Gerald Harriss* (London, 1995), p. 166; the sample comprised 306 men's wills and 63 women's.
28 Northeast (ed.), *Wills of the Archdeaconry of Sudbury*, pp. 130, 146–7.
29 D. Romano, *Patricians and Popolani. The Social Foundations of the Venetian Renaissance State* (Baltimore, 1987), pp. 120, 131–9.

14 Lay beliefs and religious practice

Charity comprised an indispensable religious duty, but was only one of many religious practices which pervaded everyday life. The sacraments of the Church served as rites of passage: baptism administered soon after birth, confirmation during childhood, marriage, ordination if a boy became a priest and extreme unction, the anointing just before death. The other two sacraments, penance and Mass, were available throughout life, and confession before receiving communion at Easter was prescribed at the Fourth Lateran Council of 1215.[1] The Mass lay at the centre of religious practice, Masses being offered for both the living and the dead. In a society where death often struck suddenly and unexpectedly, Masses and prayers to enable the soul to pass more quickly through purgatory were regarded by most people as essential. As with many of the religious women, devotional attention focused on the Passion and Crucifixion of Christ, with the Virgin Mary and the saints being regarded as intercessors. Religious activity merged with social and political concerns, and social gatherings and celebrations were an integral part of the Church's activity. As in the case of charity, worship of God was set alongside concern for one's neighbour.

These beliefs and activities were found among men and women, and among nobles, townspeople and peasants in the later medieval world. The degree of piety in individuals and society obviously cannot be assessed, even among elite groups where the existence of wills and other material throws considerable light on religious practices. It is likely that there was considerable variety and that to some extent this depended on age and circumstances. Families such as the Pastons thought religious observance important in order to achieve success in life.[2] Others were deeply pious. Anticlericalism is likely to have had an impact on attitudes to the Church's practices. There are some signs of scepticism, although not of atheism. There has been considerable argument among historians as to the extent of superstition, as opposed to well-informed religious faith. This involves a subjective judgement as definitions of superstition vary widely, but it is clear that not all the Church's teaching was accepted automatically and growth of local cults might easily transcend what the Church regarded as the limits of orthodoxy.

Many communities indulged in a mixture of orthodox practice and customs viewed by the Church as suspect. In the diocese of Nantes, the white clothes, impregnated with holy oil, which a baby wore at baptism were believed to possess magical power. At Montaillou, Catholic beliefs and practice existed alongside heresy and superstition. Doubts were expressed about Christ's miracles at Soria in Castile, as well as about his descent into Hell and his resurrection, and one woman thought that Christianity was not the only route to salvation. Scepticism was expressed over devotion to the Virgin Mary and the saints around Turin in the 1370s and 1380s.[3]

In an age when a family's livelihood was often at the mercy of the weather and natural forces, religious practice and magic might well overlap. Rogationtide processions to ask God's blessing on the crops were an important occasion in the Church's year. The dramas enacted at Easter and other festivals might be linked in some people's minds with magic. In Germany, candles blessed at Candlemas, palms blessed on Palm Sunday and herbs at the Assumption of the Virgin Mary were sometimes used for protective magic. Water blessed on St Blaise's day was thought to be good for horses and cattle, and the practice was forbidden in the diocese of Passau in 1470, although allowed elsewhere.[4] In considering religious practices, it is important not to assume that deep piety was the norm. It was in fact difficult to draw the line between ceremonies accepted by the Church and others which grew up within the community.

Religious practice and the household

In looking at women's practices, it is apparent that there was considerable overlap with their everyday duties and family responsibilities. At the same time, they exercised a degree of freedom as individuals in their devotions and in the way these were carried out. Men as heads of the household were responsible for the religious well-being of the inmates, but women's responsibilities for family and servants gave them a special religious role.[5] Women were responsible for the upbringing of their children, and in addition to religious teaching, children assimilated morality and belief from their mother's example. Writers of didactic treatises, such as the knight of La Tour-Landry, underlined the need for women to be pious and to have received their religious and moral grounding at home during their childhood. Prayer, worship, fasting and charity were all part of their education. In addition to attending mass, private devotion took place at home, and women of the elite made use of their psalters and books of hours, as well as religious objects, such as relics of the true cross and rosaries. Everyday life was affected by the feasts and fasts of the Church's year, and it was the woman's responsibility to ensure that these were observed and the right food served at table. Women's religious responsibilities within the household gave them a social and an individual role, since they provided for the needs of family, visitors and servants while fostering their own devotion and piety.

Noble households had their own private chapels where services were held for family, officials and servants. Licences for oratories and private chapels, granted by the bishop, were widespread among the nobility, gentry and elite townspeople. When a widow was head of the household, she had a particular responsibility for ensuring that worship was fittingly carried out. Elizabeth de Burgh made offerings on behalf of herself and her household in her private chapel at great festivals, as when 12s 8d was given at three Masses on Christmas Day, 1351. Private chapels were richly furnished with altar vessels, service books, images and candles; the chapel furnishings of Marie de St Pol, Countess of Pembroke, included gold chalices and images of St Peter and St Andrew. Additional religious privileges were secured by papal indulgence, as when Catherine, Countess of Salisbury, in 1347 was allowed to have Mass celebrated before daybreak.[6]

The household took on an even stronger religious aura if it was headed by a vowess. Vows of chastity might be taken by a man or woman or by a married couple, but for women, becoming a vowess entailed a special ceremony of receiving the mantle, veil and ring from the bishop. This had parallels with the profession of a nun, although the vowess lived in the world and often continued to run her own household. Many women who became vowesses were widows, and worldly motives intermingled with religious in their decision to take the vow. The vowess was freed from pressure to remarry and had a free hand to deal with property; some husbands insisted in their wills that property would come to the widow only if she remained unmarried. In 1421, William Lynne died leaving five young children and left property to his wife if she remained unmarried; she took the vow of chastity less than three months after his death.[7]

The daily life of a late fifteenth-century vowess of the high nobility is described in the household rules of Cecily, Duchess of York, mother of Edward IV and Richard III. The duchess rose at seven o'clock, said matins with her chaplain and heard a Low Mass in her chamber. She then had breakfast. The morning was spent in chapel. At dinner, she listened to a religious reading from Walter Hilton's *Epistle on the Mixed Life*, the *Life of Christ* attributed to Bonaventure, the *Golden Legend*, or the works of Mechtild of Hackeborn, Catherine of Siena or Birgitta of Sweden. After dinner, she spent an hour giving audience to people who had business with her. After a short nap, she spent the time until evensong in prayer. She took a drink of wine or ale before saying evensong with her chaplain and hearing it sung in chapel. At supper she talked over the reading heard at dinner with those who were with her. She spent the evening with her gentlewomen. One hour before bedtime she had a drink of wine and spent time in private prayer before going to bed at eight o'clock. She combined the religious life with running her household and conducting business, the mixture of the active and contemplative life as advocated by Walter Hilton. Several of her books and religious possessions were mentioned in her will, including several gold rosaries, one of them made of gold and enamel, with a gold cross and jet scallop shell, the emblem of St James of Compostela.[8]

Public worship

The household constituted an important centre for religious instruction and devotion, but women at all social levels attended public worship in parish and monastic churches, attended sermons and went on pilgrimages, and many belonged to guilds and confraternities. In these settings, individual devotion combined with concerns for family and community. For men and women of the later Middle Ages, worship comprised Mass in the parish church which met the needs of both community and individual. The Church laid down that Christians should attend Mass on Sundays and feast days, although not all did so. The service was in Latin and celebrated by the priest in the chancel at the east end of the church, while the laity usually stood in the nave, and men and women were segregated. Few were able to follow the Latin, and books existed to guide the laity through the service and to prepare them for it, such as the *Lay Folks' Mass Book*, probably dating from the late twelfth or early thirteenth century.[9]

Attitudes of the laity to the service were rarely recorded in the Middle Ages. According to a comment by an Observant Dominican in the 1480s, young men and women flocked to Mass, vespers and compline at the church of Santi Giovanni e Paolo in Venice on feast days, not to hear the service but to listen to the music and singing. Worshippers might be disturbed by talking in the congregation or by rowdy children who had been brought by their mothers. Some did not attend the whole service.[10] When the Lollard Margery Baxter questioned Joan Clyfland about what she did in church, Joan answered that on entering the church she genuflected in front of the crucifix, said the Pater Noster five times in honour of the cross and the Ave Maria five times in honour of the Virgin Mary. In answer to further questions, she said that she believed that the host after consecration by the priest was the true body of Christ in the form of bread. Margery poured scorn on Joan's actions and beliefs, but the answers epitomised the teaching of the Roman Church.[11] Even though they could not understand the Mass, the congregation was expected to engage in a corporate act of worship. They participated in the priest's sacrifice when members of the laity offered candles, bread, wine and alms at the altar, joined in the sharing of the *pax* (or kiss of peace) and adored the host when it was elevated after consecration. At the end of the Mass, the blessed bread was distributed to the congregation.[12]

The evidence of catechisms, sermons and collections of *exempla* makes it likely that lay people had at least a rudimentary grasp of the doctrine and moral teaching of the Church. The parish church itself, with its paintings, images and stained glass, provided pictorial teaching of the birth and death of Christ, the Last Judgement and the saints. The catechism, written by Jean Gerson in 1429 and very popular in the fifteenth century, shows that lay people were expected to know the Pater Noster and the Ave Maria. The Apostles' Creed, summarising the central doctrines of the Church, was given in a French translation. The seven sacraments were listed, but the only explanations given concerned penance and ordination. Ethical teaching was summarised in the lists of the seven deadly sins, the seven virtues, the ten commandments, the seven gifts of the Holy Spirit, the eight beatitudes of the Sermon on the Mount, and the works of mercy.[13]

Thirteenth-century *exempla* collections from the Rhineland, Low Countries, France and Ireland provide stories of women in church and conversations about religious and moral practice. Of the sacraments, most attention was paid to confession. Berthold of Regensburg considered that women attended church and sermons more often than men and were more eager to pray. The Church's teaching was spread by sermons throughout the later Middle Ages, some of which were specifically addressed to women, such as the *ad status* sermons of Humbert of Romans. These sermons combined religious and moral teaching which was set in the context of the listeners' everyday lives, as when Humbert exhorted the townswoman not to put love of her house before love of God. Sermons by St Bernardino of Siena focused on the Christian implications of marriage, motherhood and family; he criticised men's refusal to marry and the practice of birth control. According to the paintings of his open air sermons, he attracted large audiences of men and women who were segregated from each other.[14] Women's attendance at sermons as well as Mass gave them instruction about their religion and a knowledge of how they were expected to conduct their lives. Further teaching was given at confession. In Florence and Fiesole, women were to confess in the daytime in the main body of the church where they and the priest could be seen but not overheard. Confessions were not to be held in the choir or behind the altar, and it was laid down in 1517 that the last-minute rush to confess on the Wednesday before Easter was to stop.[15]

Although marriage was regarded as a sacrament, it did not have to take place in a church. The Church, however, taught that marriages should be conducted in public and it is probable that an increasing number were celebrated at the parish church by the end of the Middle Ages.[16] In one respect, married women's experience in church was different from men's, in that they underwent the ceremony of churching after the birth of a child. The service normally took place about a month after childbirth as a way of giving thanks for the birth. It was not compulsory, but many women appear to have made use of it. The priest met the mother at the church door, recited the prayers of thanksgiving, sprinkled the woman with holy water and took her into Mass, thus symbolically bringing her back to her place in the community. The ceremony was often followed by a celebratory feast.[17]

At baptism, women served alongside men as godparents. The diocese of Lisieux in 1321 limited their number to two godfathers and one godmother for a boy and two godmothers and one godfather for a girl. Too many godparents might give rise to problems over spiritual affinity when the child's marriage came to be arranged. Godparents in fifteenth-century England were expected to instruct their godchildren, oversee their physical well-being and bring them to confirmation. Some helped their godchildren at marriage when they set up their own households and often remembered them in wills; Agnes Umfrey of Edlesborough, in her will of 1484, left 4 pence each to her godchildren.[18]

Devotion to the Passion and Death of Jesus and to the saints is apparent in many aspects of the life of the medieval church. Amédée de Saluces, *vicomtesse de Polignac*, arranged for the establishment of chapels in five churches for reverence of the Passion and especially of the five wounds of Christ, and for the redemption of her own and her parents' souls, as well as those of her friends and benefactors.[19] Parish churches usually had images and paintings of a number of saints, some of whom had their lights maintained by a guild dedicated to them. The church itself was dedicated to one or more saints. Medieval people regarded saints as intercessors on their behalf and also as having the power to respond to particular prayers and sometimes to effect healing. In addition to her devotion to the Virgin Mary, Queen Isabeau of Bavaria showed a devotion to St John the Baptist's shrine at Amiens where she first met her husband Charles VI, and to St Margaret of Antioch, the patron saint of pregnant women. She probably also had a devotion to St Michael, who was credited with the king's recovery from madness in 1394, and the following year she named her seventh child Michelle.[20]

Saints' days were times of religious and social celebration, as were the new cults which evolved in the later Middle Ages, notably the feast of Corpus Christi. Processions were organised and plays and pageants staged based on the story of man's redemption. Yet although women can be assumed to have been present at the celebrations, it was in the role of spectators or insignificant participants. The Corpus Christi procession at Würzburg in 1381 was made up of clergy, masters and apprentices from the guilds and representatives of the eight quarters of the town. The route of the procession linked the various parts of the town, ecclesiastical and lay. Women took part in Corpus Christi processions in the later fifteenth century, divided into the unmarried, married, widows and religious, and were usually placed at the rear.[21]

In addition to worship and the sacraments, many women were involved in the running and maintenance of their parish churches. The festivals of the ritual year required preparation as well as participation. Women brought to the church the skills used in their own homes, cleaning the church before festivals, decorating it and washing altar linen.[22] These tasks emphasised their subordination but were essential to the maintenance of the church. Women's support of their parish churches is apparent in their wills; the elite were less likely to look to their parish churches, but other women made gifts to the church and its priests. At Norwich, which had forty-six parish churches in the 1520s, 95 per cent of the will-making laity made a bequest to at least one parish church between 1370 and 1532; most frequently, bequests were made to the high altar and for the church's upkeep. In her will of 1516, Margery Dogett left 2 shillings to the high altar of the parish church of St Michael at Plea where she was to be buried, 3s 4d for church repairs, and her best coverlet to lie before the high altar. She left bequests of a few pence each to the church lights, including the lamp before the high altar, and the lights of St Michael, the Virgin Mary, St Anne, St Nicholas and St Christopher, thus underlining the importance attached to devotion to the saints. Margery's will can be compared with that of 1277 of Guillemette, wife of the knight Pierre de Bonnay. She wanted to be buried in the church of Bonay, near Besançon, and left 100 *sous* to the parish priest for alms, 5 *sous* to another priest there, and 10 *sous* to the fabric of the church. In 1361, Jacquette Venyeu, wife of a Besançon shoemaker, left 15 *sous* to the parish priest of the church of St Mary Magdalen and 10 *sous* for the church's procession. Similarly Venetian women relied on their parish churches for mass and confession, although they also attended sermons in the churches of the friars.[23]

Guilds and confraternities

The later Middle Ages saw a great growth of guilds and confraternities. The guilds took a variety of forms. Craft guilds were primarily concerned with work but had their religious, social and charitable side. Other guilds were founded primarily for religious purposes and ranged in size from small parish fraternities to large urban guilds which attracted members from a large area. All types of guild focused their religious concern on particular cults and on prayer for the living and the dead, with obligatory attendance at funerals and anniversary requiem masses to aid the passage of the soul through purgatory. Religious was combined with social activity, notably feasting and drinking. Many women belonged to guilds, although arrangements for membership varied widely.

In England, membership was normally open to men and women, and many joined as married couples. A married couple founded the guild of St Christopher in March (Cambridgeshire) in the later fifteenth century, and thirty-eight (63 per cent) of the 1389 guild statutes for Cambridgeshire mentioned women members who sometimes had specific duties within the guild, as in Holy Trinity church in Cambridge where the wives were responsible for looking after the light of the Virgin Mary.[24] In the late fifteenth century, there appears to have been a growth of women's guilds in England which worshipped and socialised together and raised money for the church. A guild of maidens is mentioned at Bodmin in Cornwall in 1469, and a guild of wives three years later, while St Olave's, Southwark, had a guild of wives in 1466, dedicated to St Anne, and St Ewen's, Bristol, a guild of maidens in 1465, dedicated to the Virgin Mary.[25] Worship and prayer centred on the members of the guild, living and dead. At Helston in Cornwall in 1517, every brother and sister was to come to church on the Saturday after Trinity Sunday, hear the dirge at the Trinity altar and say a psalter of the Virgin Mary for all the lives and souls of those who were to be prayed for by the guild.[26] Such an occasion was usually followed by a social get-together. The guild of Holy Trinity at Coventry had nobility and gentry as well as town citizens among its members. In 1533, after the anniversary Mass of the former mayor, Nicholas Burwey, and his wife, those present met to enjoy wine, ale, cheese, cakes and comfits; 4 shillings was given in alms to the poor. With the London parish guilds, the recreational element received greater emphasis by the late fifteenth century, as compared with the stress on burial, intercession and lights earlier.[27]

The English guilds gave women a religious outlet and an identity within the community, and catered for all social levels except the very poor. They also gave some opportunity for them to exercise leadership and organisational skills. Although guilds are found before the Black Death, the great expansion in numbers took place after about 1350, possibly partly as a response to the plague itself and the need to ensure burial and commemoration, partly as a result of greater wealth and higher standards of living among members of the peasantry and the urban workforce, and partly due to the need for mutual support in an age of movement and migration. Women's importance within the guilds, however, should not be overrated. Just as it was rare for a woman to be churchwarden in her parish church, so it was unusual for women to hold office in a guild. There is no evidence of this in the parish guilds of London. Very occasionally, female wardens were appointed in the Cornish guilds, and some of the Cambridgeshire guilds in 1389 stated that the sisters took part in decision making.[28]

Similarly, women are found in guilds in continental Europe, where the need for group support was equally felt. In the Avignon region, fraternities increased between about 1350 and 1420, and over one-third of the male and female testators at Avignon between 1420 and 1500 left bequests to at least one guild.[29] Most guilds in France admitted both men and women, but some of the entry fees were high. Members were expected to attend the funerals of members and services on the patronal festival, when High Mass was followed by a feast. A few confraternities laid down a form of daily observance. At Châlons-sur-Marne, each member was to repeat the Pater Noster and Ave Maria seven times each day in honour of the seven gifts of the Holy Spirit, say grace at dinner and supper, and take communion at Easter, Pentecost and Christmas. Women were also members of confraternities in Spain. The great expansion at Zamora began about 1480, and there were 150 guilds by the second half of the sixteenth century. Few excluded women, but they had only an organisational role in female confraternities.[30]

Confraternities might change in form over time, as seen in the Italian commune of San Sepolcro. Here, the fraternity of San Bartolomeo was established in the second half of the thirteenth century to commemorate the dead and provide charity for the poor; it also had a political and civic role. At its height, it had a membership of over 1,000 men and women. Taking a sample of 176 women who entered in 1274–5, 67 per cent were married women, a further 10 per cent widows, 11 per cent unmarried daughters and

6 per cent servants. Membership reflected all levels of communal society except the very poor. It was not essential to have resources in order to join – one-third of the women entrants made no promise to give money or grain each year. From the 1280s, membership dropped and by the mid-fourteenth century the fraternity had changed into a small female charitable institution, under male administrators. The main reason for the change seems to have been the emergence of *Laudesi* and flagellant confraternities which were limited to a male membership.[31] The opportunities which were open to women in the thirteenth century no longer remained available in the fourteenth and fifteenth. Women were in a better position in Venice, although they were not admitted to membership of the *scuole* (fraternities) on the same basis as men; they were, however, able to have their own organisation under the supervision of the *scuola*.[32]

Pilgrimage

In addition to their religious practice at home and in church, men and women had the opportunity to show their devotion by going on pilgrimage. Pilgrimages were undertaken by all social groups, by married couples as well as by lay and religious women, just as the prioress and the wife of Bath joined Chaucer's Canterbury pilgrims. The woman might want to show her devotion to a particular saint, she might hope for a miracle cure for herself or another, she might be carrying out the wishes of a dead husband or relative, or she might be enjoying a break from everyday routine. Women pilgrims visited both local shrines and the great pilgrimage centres, such as Jerusalem, Rome and Santiago de Compostela, undeterred by hostile comments from churchmen.

The largest number of pilgrims visited local shrines. In addition, women made bequests of clothing and jewellery to particular shrines. The shrine of the Virgin Mary at Walsingham attracted English pilgrims between the thirteenth and early sixteenth centuries and was easily reached by pilgrims from the eastern counties. In her will of 1440, Isabel Turnour of Sudbury in Suffolk made bequests to her daughter on the condition that she should go to Walsingham in order to fulfil her mother's vow. Nicholas Culpeper in 1434 left money to his wife to carry out his pilgrimages to Canterbury and Walsingham. The shrine at Walsingham was famous for its cures. During her husband's illness, probably in 1443, Margaret Paston promised to go there on pilgrimage, and her mother-in-law promised to present a wax image of the same weight as her son. Isabeau of Bavaria made local pilgrimages every summer and autumn while she was in her twenties, particularly favouring the shrines at Chartres, Saint-Sanctin, Maubuisson and Pontoise. In south-east France, the tomb of Delphine de Sabran became a place of pilgrimage – although Delphine was not officially canonised – with paralytics, epileptics and the blind seeking cures. Another local cult was centred on the tomb of Dorothea of Montau, again a woman who was not officially canonised, and this mainly attracted Germans and Poles from the Baltic region.[33]

Many women journeyed to more distant shrines, some with their husbands, others alone. Some made several long-distance journeys, such as St Birgitta of Sweden who visited Santiago de Compostela, Rome and the Holy Land. In the mid-fifteenth century, Sister Eugenia di Tommaso da Treviso was denounced by a priest and left her convent of Le Murate at Florence to go to Rome to clear her name. She dressed as a man and proceeded on pilgrimage to Jerusalem where she established a hospice and remained for thirty-four years before returning to Le Murate via Portugal.[34] Many women, such as Dorothea of Montau, visited Rome, but in the fourteenth century they were excluded from particular chapels in the churches of St Peter and St John Lateran. Whether this was due to misogyny or to fears that they might be crushed in the crowds is not clear. The shrine of St James at Santiago also attracted large numbers of women from Galicia in north-west Spain and from many other parts of Europe in spring and autumn. Elizabeth Luttrell accompanied her husband there in 1361, their ship carrying twenty-four men and women and twenty-four horses. St Isabel, queen of Portugal, made the pilgrimage in 1325.[35]

Margery Kempe was an inveterate traveller and journeyed further than most people. Her pilgrimages highlight problems which many women must have faced. In addition to her travels within England, Margery visited the Holy Land in 1413, returning home two years later and taking in Rome and Assisi on the return journey. In 1417 she was at Santiago, and in 1433 in Germany, having escorted her German daughter-in-law home after her son's death. She made this last trip as a widow, the others as a wife but on her own, and this made her vulnerable. Her journey to the Holy Land took her by sea to Flanders and then overland to Constance, Bologna and Venice, and from there by sea. According to her own account, the company she was with perpetually fell out with her; they were perturbed by her religious intensity, her weeping and her refusal to eat meat. Her account of the Holy Land concentrated on her spiritual experience, although she described where she went during her three weeks in Jerusalem, and also her visits to Bethlehem, Bethany and the River Jordan. Her difficulties with her companions continued; they were unwilling for her to accompany them to the River Jordan, and refused to help her up the mountain near Jericho where Jesus had fasted for forty days and been tempted by the devil. She was abandoned once the whole party was back in Venice.[36]

Margery made her way to Assisi with the help of a poor Irish hunchback named Richard. There they joined the wealthy party of Margaret Florentyne, who had come on pilgrimage to Assisi and was returning to Rome. In Rome, Margery ran into further trouble from her former companions. She spent her time in the shrines and also serving a poor old woman, as directed by her confessor. She was destitute once she had given away her and Richard's money. However, she again met Margaret Florentyne, who gave her food and money, and she received other charity. When Margery found herself in need, she begged from door to door.[37] She again met Richard on her pilgrimage to Santiago and paid him what she owed him. At her embarkation port of Bristol, she alienated people with her shrieking and crying, and some did not want her on board ship, although they were pleasant to her once they reached Spain. She spent a fortnight there before returning.[38]

Margery made her last overseas pilgrimage when she was an old woman. After spending a few weeks in Gdansk, she visited the shrine of the holy blood at Wilsnack. She then went to Aachen and after a number of difficulties returned to England. This journey brings out the problems facing a woman travelling on her own. Margery hoped to return from Aachen with a London widow who had come with a large retinue, but the widow left Aachen so quickly that Margery was unable to overtake her; when she caught her up, the widow refused to have her in her party. Two Londoners were unwilling to allow her to accompany them so in the end she journeyed to Calais with a friar.[39] Margery's experiences bring out the need for a woman pilgrim to be able to get on with her companions, as the dangers of travelling in company were not as great as travelling alone. A woman pilgrim also needed money and above all a strong constitution.

Death and commemoration

Many lives were cut short unexpectedly in the later Middle Ages, and the concern to speed the passage of the soul through purgatory was found across Europe. Men and women wanted to make provision for burial, requiem masses and remembrance. North of the Alps, some historians have seen the Black Death as ushering in an era of gloom and pessimism, and this may have contributed in some places to changes in practice over deathbed wishes and commemoration. At the same time, changes of attitude may have been caused by social disruption, war and economic change. In his study of the Avignon region, Jacques Chiffoleau placed greater emphasis on social change, urbanisation and migration.[40] S.K. Cohn, Jr. found change at Siena setting in before the Black Death. The steady increase in the number of pious bequests in the thirteenth and early fourteenth centuries was followed by decline in the years before the plague until about 1363; the fifteenth century saw an increase in the value but not the number of such bequests. Siena's structure of pious giving was similar to that of other towns in Tuscany and Umbria in the fifteenth century.[41] The changes may have been due to new religious and cultural ideas on death and salvation.

Much of the information about death comes from wills. These provide a detailed picture of final wishes, the funeral, provision for requiem masses and commemoration in this world. Yet wills have their limitations, and practices of will-making varied. The number of wills is smaller for women than for men and it is more usual to have the wills of widows than wives because of the husband's control over his wife's property. In some places, married women's wills are more numerous; in Venice, for example, pregnant women usually made their wills before childbirth.[42] The social grouping of women will-makers also varied. In England, it was the women who had possessions to leave who increasingly made wills in the later Middle Ages – wills are not found for the poor members of society either in town or country – while in Mediterranean regions, wills are found for women lower down the social scale. At Genoa by 1250 even people of limited means made a will, provided that they could pay the notary.[43] Relatively little information survives of individuals' religious giving during their lifetime, and having to use the will on its own gives a skewed picture of the person's outlook. Where evidence survives of lifetime giving, a much more rounded picture of the individual's attitude emerges. Finally, it is rare to have information as to whether the will was carried out, because of lack of resources or the dilatoriness of those responsible.

Looking at death from the woman's point of view, the primary consideration was where and with whom she was to be buried. Three options were available. She could be buried with her husband, with her natal family or on her own. In the Avignon region, about half the male testators wanted to be buried with father or ancestors, a little over a quarter wanted burial with their wives, and a little under a quarter wanted to be buried with their dead children. Women opted for burial with their husbands more than with their parents. In both Genoa and Venice, women were divided between their marital and natal families. In England, the practice of husband and wife being buried together was widespread but not universal. Marie de St Pol, dying over fifty years after she was widowed, preferred burial with the nuns at Denny rather than with her husband at Westminster.[44]

The majority of the population were buried in the cemetery of their parish church or, if they were well off, inside the church. Even when husband and wife chose to be buried in the same place, they were not necessarily buried together. At Avignon, a mercer and his wife who were buried in the church of Notre-Dame-la-principale chose interment in front of different altars. The coming of the friars extended the choice of burial places, although this tended to be an option for the wealthier, and in the Avignon region attracted a few more women than men. The wife of a grocer chose burial in the Franciscan church with her parents rather than in St Peter's church with her husband. The countess of Besançon in 1271 chose to be buried in the Dominican cemetery next to her first husband if she died in or near the city. Nearly 200 years later, Jeannette, wife of the notary Pierre Euvrard, chose the Carmelite church in Besançon where her father was buried.[45]

Family mausolea were the privilege of the elite. Some families created or continued to use burial places in monasteries; others chose a mendicant church. The Polignac family had their tomb in the centre of the choir of the Dominican church of Le Puy; in her will of 1473, Amédée de Saluces, wife of Armand, *vicomte* de Polignac, wanted to be buried in her husband's family tomb and to have 500 Masses celebrated on the day of her funeral.

In contrast, Anne, Countess Stafford (d. 1439), continued to patronise the priory of Augustinian canons at Lanthony with which her natal ancestors had long been connected. The family burial centre might be moved; in 1377, the lord of Viens moved the family tomb from the church at Viens to the Franciscan church at Apt so as to rejoin his ancestor, Mabel de Simiane, lady of Castillon and Viens, who had a great reputation for sanctity and who had known Elzéar de Sabran.[46]

Funerals varied widely in elaboration and expense, partly reflecting the social status of the deceased and partly contemporary ideas as to what was appropriate. In the period between 1150 and 1250 at Genoa, the mean cost of funerals worked out at about 3 *lire*, with 100 *lire* being the largest sum expended. The Pisan, Adalasia, widow of Alberto from Vecchiano, specified that 8 *lire* were to be spent on her funeral and on anniversary masses a week and month later. In the Lyonnais, funerals became more elaborate and expensive from the late fourteenth century, with processions included in town funerals, an increase in the number of priests present, and a growth in requiem masses which testators wanted within a year of their deaths. Ten times the number of masses were laid down about 1500 by inhabitants of Lyons as compared with those living in villages.[47]

Many testators liked to settle the details of their funerals in their wills. In a joint will drawn up at Avignon in 1466, a husband and wife stated that they wanted to be buried in the Carmelite convent. Their bodies were to be clothed in a white cloak and shoes, and two funeral sheets, one of silk and one of cloth of gold, were to cover the bier. The letters of indulgence which they had obtained were to be placed on the bier on four red and two green cushions. After the funeral, the sheets and cushions were bequeathed to the Carmelites. Jeannette, wife of Pierre Euvrard of Besançon, wanted processions of Dominicans, Franciscans and Carmelites to accompany her body and to carry out the funeral ceremonies at the Carmelite church.[48] Other wills prescribed simple funerals. In England around 1400 both orthodox Christians and Lollards emphasised contempt for the body and feelings of unworthiness. In her will of 1391, Margaret Courtenay, Countess of Devon, wanted to be buried beside her husband in Exeter cathedral, and specified that only two candles, weighing five pounds each, were to be lit, one at her head and one at her feet. Elizabeth de Juliers, Countess of Kent, wanted her funeral in 1411 to be conducted without worldly display.[49]

For most, the funeral and commemoration were a matter for family, friends and neighbours. For noblewomen and queens, they had greater public significance. A splendid noble funeral not only underlined the importance of the deceased but made a social statement underpinning the proper social order and the importance of hierarchy. For the queen, the funeral could be linked with her wedding and coronation as an event reinforcing the legitimacy of monarchy. The journey of Eleanor of Castile, wife of Edward I, from Lincoln to Westminster drew attention to the presence and power of the Crown. The imagery used at queens' funerals evoked their importance as queen and as wife and mother; it was through the queen's motherhood that the dynastic line continued. These images paralleled those of the Virgin Mary as mother and intercessor. In addition, it was possible for the queen to take an individual line. Eleanor of Castile may well have ordered her tomb in advance, as many did in the Middle Ages, and its heraldry depicted her in her own right, with her natal arms of Castile and Leon, her marital arms of England, and her own arms as countess of Ponthieu. It is likely that she was influenced by royal burial practice at the convent of Las Huelgas at Burgos.[50] The combination of dynastic, social and individual statements was most apparent among queens, but also applied to women of the nobility.

The importance of prayers and requiem Masses was felt across Europe. The presence of the poor at the funeral was regarded as of great importance, since the prayers of the poor were considered to be of great value to the deceased. In the Lyonnais, Genoa and elsewhere, testators wanted the poor to be there. Eleanor de Bohun, Duchess of Gloucester, wanted fifteen god-fearing men, chosen because of their age or poverty, to stand round her bier, holding torches and praying for her and her husband, and for all the living and the dead and for all Christians. They were supplied with clothing and shoes, and other wills specified a small payment. Wills also provided for a general distribution of alms to the poor at the funeral, and Elizabeth Lady FitzHugh wanted the uninvited poor and others to be fed, according to what her executors thought reasonable.[51]

The number of anniversary Masses escalated among the elite in the four-teenth and fifteenth centuries, while the less well-off made what provision they could afford and relied on their membership of guilds. The practice of celebrating Masses not only for family and friends but also for all Christians meant that everyone might be included. Provision ranged from establishing an anniversary Mass, to be celebrated at the weekly, monthly or yearly anniversary of death, to the foundation of a chantry, endowed with money or land, where Mass might be celebrated for the named people for a set time or for ever. Only the elite could afford a chantry. The decision as to where the services were to take place reflected family connections and the churches' reputation, and commemorations were established in parish churches, monasteries and cathedrals.

There was great variety of provision. Between 1150 and 1250 most Genoese testators who could afford a funeral were able to fund Masses for a week or a month. John and Alice Codrynton of Gloucestershire estab-lished a perpetual chantry in 1469 in the Dominican house at Bristol where a daily Mass was to be celebrated for the benefit of their souls, those of their ancestors and all the faithful departed, with additional services on their anniversaries. The women of the Polignac family in the fourteenth and fifte-enth centuries made frequent use of the Dominican friars of Le Puy for their requiem Masses, the *Vicomtesse* Mascaronne de Montaigut-Listenois specifying four Masses a week in 1410 and wanting commemoration for herself and her parents. Margaret Adhémar of Monteil, who was buried at

Solignac in the tomb of her first husband and was a member of the confraternity there, relied mainly on the confraternity for commemoration. A widow of the magnate Sismundi family of Pisa in 1392 left 30 florins to the Franciscans of Pisa to celebrate 1,000 Masses for her soul.[52]

Within a town, some people inevitably were able to spend more than others, but the widespread belief in the importance of anniversary Masses was found among all will-making groups. In Norwich in the late Middle Ages between one-third and two-fifths of the male and female testators left money either for a set number of Masses or Masses for a specific time, usually between one and four years. Many asked for the Masses to be for all the faithful departed and not just for family and friends. A number of perpetual chantries were also founded by both men and women. Lettice Payn established two chantries in 1313 which were later united because of inadequate endowments. Two women of the Norfolk gentry, whose families had interests in the city, founded chantries in the cathedral, Denise de Tye around 1375 and Elizabeth Clere in 1478. Elizabeth asked for the priest to say extra prayers in addition to the daily Mass, and the congregation could obtain an indulgence by saying the Pater Noster and the Ave Maria during Mass, for the souls of herself, her husband and all Christians.[53]

Testators thus provided for the future of the soul, but many women of the elite wanted to be remembered by the world they had left. To some extent this could be done through possessions bequeathed to the Church, but the names of donors would be forgotten over time. The provision of a tomb or family chapel made memorial more permanent and encouraged those who saw them to say a prayer for the soul of the deceased. Surviving monuments bear witness to the quality of craftsmanship, at least some of it commissioned before death. The commissions of women such as Mahaut, Countess of Artois, and Marie de St Pol bear witness to the desire that both they and their families should be remembered.[54]

Laywomen's religious practice displayed concerns for both this world and the next. Religious practice permeated their daily lives, and although degrees of piety undoubtedly varied, there was no way in which the religious aspects of life could be evaded. The sacraments of the Church were available to all, rich and poor. Beliefs and cults varied across Europe; superstition and magic were present, and not only among the poorest of society. At the same time, there was a universality in the influence which the Church exercised. The woman has to be seen as an individual believer, but her individuality and power of choice are less visible than the part which family and community played in her religious life. As in other areas of activity, her responsibilities to both tended to override her identity as a person in her own right, and this applied not only to orthodox religion but to heresy as well.

Notes

1 R.N. Swanson, *Church and Society in Late Medieval England* (Oxford, 1989), p. 277, considers that most people did not receive confirmation and it was not

thought necessary before receiving communion. Children went to confession when they reached years of discretion, the age being set at eight in the diocese of Bourges and fourteen at Avignon in the first half of the fourteenth century; P. Adam, *La vie paroissiale en France au quatorzième siècle* (Paris, 1964), pp. 107–11.

2 C. Richmond, 'Religion and the fifteenth-century English gentleman', in R.B. Dobson (ed.), *The Church, Politics and Patronage in the Fifteenth Century* (Gloucester, 1984), pp. 193–208.

3 Adam, *Vie paroissiale*, pp. 273–4; E. Le Roy Ladurie, *Montaillou, Village Occitan de 1294 à 1324* (Paris, 1978), pp. 501–22; John Edwards, 'Religious faith and doubt in late medieval Spain: Soria c. 1450–1500', *PandP* 120 (1988), pp. 5, 13–23.

4 A. Vauchez, *Les laïcs au moyen âge. Pratiques et expériences religieuses* (Paris, 1987), pp. 145–55; R.W. Scribner, *Popular Culture and Popular Movements in Reformation Germany* (London, 1987), pp. 17–47.

5 D.M. Webb, 'Woman and home: the domestic setting of late medieval spirituality', in W.J. Sheils and D. Wood (eds), *Women in the Church* (Studies in Church History 27, Oxford, 1990), pp. 159–73; N. Orme, 'Children and the church in medieval England', *Journal of Ecclesiastical History* 45 (1994), pp. 566–8.

6 R.N. Swanson (ed. and trans.), *Catholic England. Faith, Religion and Observance before the Reformation* (Manchester, 1993), p. 169; London, E101/93/12, m. 2; H. Jenkinson, 'Mary de Sancto Paulo, foundress of The National Archives, Pembroke College, Cambridge', *Archaeologia* 66 (1915), p. 433; *Calendar of Entries in the Papal Registers relating to Great Britain and Ireland. Papal Letters, 1342–62* (London, 1897), p. 251.

7 Swanson, *Church and Society*, p. 271; Swanson (ed. and trans.), *Catholic England*, pp. 173–4; M.C. Erler, 'Three fifteenth-century vowesses', in C.M. Barron and A.F. Sutton (eds), *Medieval London Widows 1300–1500* (London, 1994), pp. 167–9.

8 *A Collection of Ordinances and Regulations for the Government of the Royal Household* (London, 1790), p. 37; J.C. Ward (ed. and trans.), *Women of the English Nobility and Gentry 1066–1500* (Manchester, 1995), p. 217; C.A.J. Armstrong, 'The piety of Cicely, duchess of York: a study in late medieval culture', in C.A.J. Armstrong, *England, France and Burgundy in the Fifteenth Century* (London, 1983), pp. 135–56; Swanson (ed. and trans.), *Catholic England*, p. 107; J.G. Nichols and J. Bruce (eds), *Wills from Doctors' Commons* (Camden Society old series 83, 1863), p. 6.

9 M. Aston, 'Segregation in church', in Sheils and Wood (eds), *Women in the Church*, pp. 237–94; Swanson (ed. and trans.), *Catholic England*, pp. 78–91; T.F. Simmons (ed.), *The Lay Folks' Mass Book* (EETS original series 71, 1879), pp. 2–60, 122–7.

10 D. Chambers and B. Pullan (eds), *Venice. A Documentary History, 1450–1630* (Oxford, 1992), pp. 198–9; Adam, *Vie paroissiale*, pp. 246–54.

11 N. Tanner (ed.), *Heresy Trials in the Diocese of Norwich, 1428–31* (Camden Society fourth series 20, 1977), pp. 44–5.

12 J. Bossy, 'The mass as a social institution 1200–1700', *PandP* 100 (1983), pp. 32–56; V. Reinburg, 'Liturgy and the laity in late medieval and Reformation France', *Sixteenth Century Journal* 23 (1992), pp. 526–47.

13 B. Hamilton, *Religion in the Medieval West* (London, 1986), pp. 109–10, 132–8; Gerson entitled his catechism, the *ABC des simples gens*. The seven deadly sins comprised pride, envy, anger, sloth, avarice, gluttony and lechery; the three theological virtues were love, hope and faith; and the four cardinal virtues were prudence, temperance, courage and justice.

14 P. Biller, 'The common woman in the western church in the thirteenth and early fourteenth centuries', in Sheils and Wood (eds), *Women in the Church*, pp. 127–40; D. Herlihy, *Women, Family and Society in Medieval Europe* (Providence, Rhode Island, 1995), pp. 188–91; S.K. Cohn, Jr. *Death and Property in Siena, 1205–1800* (Baltimore, 1988), pp. 83–5.

15 R.C. Trexler, *Synodal Law in Florence and Fiesole, 1306–1518* (Rome, 1971), pp. 62–4.

16 See earlier, pp. 34–5.

17 Hamilton, *Religion in the Medieval West*, p. 113; Adam, *Vie paroissiale*, pp. 105–6.

18 Adam, *Vie paroissiale*, pp. 104–5; Orme, 'Children and the Church in medieval England', p. 564; P.J.P. Goldberg (ed. and trans.), *Women in England c. 1275–1525* (Manchester, 1995), p. 281; R. Lutton, 'Godparenthood, kinship and piety in Tenterden, England, 1449–1537', in I. Davis, M. Müller and S. Rees Jones (eds), *Love, Marriage and Family Ties in the Later Middle Ages* (Turnhout, 2003), pp. 221–33.

19 A. Jacotin, *Preuves de la maison de Polignac*, 5 vols (Paris, 1898–1906), II, pp. 318–19.

20 R. Gibbons, 'The piety of Isabeau of Bavaria, queen of France, 1385–1422', in D.E.S. Dunn (ed.), *Courts, Counties and the Capital in the Later Middle Ages* (Stroud, 1996), pp. 218–21.

21 C. Zika, 'Hosts, processions and pilgrimages: controlling the sacred in fifteenth-century Germany', *PandP* 118 (1988), pp. 38–43.

22 K.L. French, 'Maidens' lights and wives' stores: women's parish guilds in late medieval England', *Sixteenth Century Journal* 29 (1998), pp. 401–2.

23 N.P. Tanner, *The Church in Late Medieval Norwich 1370–1532* (Toronto, 1984), pp. 2, 126–7, 230; U. Robert, *Testaments de l'officialité de Besançon 1265–1500*, 2 vols (Paris, 1902–7), I, pp. 275–6, 430–1; D. Romano, *Patricians and Popolani. The Social Foundations of the Venetian Renaissance State* (Baltimore, 1987), pp. 98, 131–9.

24 V.R. Bainbridge, *Gilds in the Medieval Countryside. Social and Religious Change in Cambridgeshire c. 1350–1558* (Woodbridge, 1996), pp. 46–8.

25 French, 'Maidens' lights and wives' stores', pp. 399–425.

26 J. Mattingly, 'The medieval parish guilds of Cornwall', *Journal of the Royal Institution of Cornwall* new series 10 part 3 (1989), p. 300.

27 G. Templeman (ed.), *The Records of the Guild of the Holy Trinity, St Mary, St John the Baptist and St Katherine of Coventry*, 2 vols (Dugdale Society 13, 19, 1935–44), II, p. 153; C.M. Barron, 'The parish fraternities of medieval London', in C.M. Barron and C. Harper-Bill (eds), *The Church in Pre-Reformation Society. Essays in honour of F.R.H. Du Boulay* (Woodbridge, 1985), pp. 25–8.

28 There was a woman churchwarden at Yatton, Somerset, in 1496; Bishop Hobhouse (ed.), *Churchwardens' Accounts of Croscombe, Pilton, Yatton, Tintinhull, Morebath and St Michael's Bath, 1349–1560* (Somerset Record Society 4, 1890), pp. 79, 120; Barron, 'The parish fraternities of medieval London', pp. 23–4, 31–2; Mattingly, 'The medieval parish guilds of Cornwall', pp. 296–7; Bainbridge, *Gilds in the Medieval Countryside*, pp. 104–5, 132, 141; K.L. French, 'Women in the late medieval English parish', in M.C. Erler and M. Kowaleski (eds), *Gendering the Master Narrative. Women and Power in the Middle Ages* (Ithaca and London, 2003), pp. 156–73.

29 J. Chiffoleau, *La comptabilité de l'au-delà. Les hommes, la mort et la religion dans la région d'Avignon à la fin du moyen âge, vers 1320–vers 1480* (Rome, 1980), p. 273. A total of 648 men and women out of 1,737 testators made a grant to a guild.

30 Adam, *Vie paroissiale*, pp. 16–19, 35–65; M. Flynn, *Sacred Charity. Confraternities and Social Welfare in Spain, 1400–1700* (Basingstoke, 1989), pp. 15–16, 33–4.

31 J.R. Banker, *Death in the Community. Memorialization and Confraternities in an Italian Commune in the Late Middle Ages* (Athens, Georgia, 1988), pp. 40, 47–54, 64–87, 111, 131, 146–7.

32 Romano, *Patricians and Popolani*, pp. 106–12.

33 P. Northeast (ed.), *Wills of the Archdeaconry of Sudbury, 1439–61* (Suffolk Records Society 44, 2001), pp. 65–6; E.F. Jacob (ed.), *The Register of Henry Chichele, Archbishop of Canterbury, 1414–43*, 4 vols (Canterbury and York Society 42, 45–7, 1937–47), II, pp. 539–40; N. Davis (ed.), *Paston Letters and Papers*, 2 vols (Oxford, 1971, 1976), I, pp. 217–19; Gibbons, 'The piety of Isabeau of Bavaria', pp. 213–14; Chiffoleau, *La comptabilité de l'au-delà*, pp. 123, 144, 378–9; R. Kieckhefer, *Unquiet Souls. Fourteenth-Century Saints and their Religious Milieu* (Chicago, 1984), p. 33; D. Webb, *Pilgrimage in Medieval England* (London, 2000), p. 197.

34 K.J.P. Lowe, 'Female strategies for success in a male-ordered world: the Benedictine convent of Le Murate in Florence in the fifteenth and early sixteenth centuries', in Sheils and Wood (eds), *Women in the Church*, pp. 215–16.

35 J. Sumption, *Pilgrimage. An Image of Mediaeval Religion* (London, 1975), pp. 262–3; H.C. Maxwell Lyte, *Dunster and its Lords, 1066–1881* (Exeter, 1882), p. 45; Ward (ed. and trans.), *Women of the English Nobility and Gentry*, p. 219; M.G. Vazquez, 'Women and pilgrimage in medieval Galicia', in C.A. Gonzalez-Paz (ed.), *Women and Pilgrimage in Medieval Galicia* (Farnham, 2015), pp. 29–42.

36 S.B. Meech and H.E. Allen (eds), *The Book of Margery Kempe* (EETS original series 212, 1940), pp. 60–78.

37 Ibid., pp. 74–103.

38 Ibid., pp. 103–11.

39 Ibid. pp. 223–43; Sumption, *Pilgrimage*, pp. 282–4.

40 J. Delumeau, *La peur en Occident* (Paris, 1978), pp. 98–142; Chiffoleau, *La comptabilité de l'au-delà*, pp. 91–105, 186–202.

41 Cohn, *Death and Property in Siena*, pp. 38–47; S.K. Cohn, Jr. *The Cult of Remembrance and the Black Death* (Baltimore, 1992), p. 79.

42 S. Chojnacki, 'Dowries and kinsmen in early Renaissance Venice', *Journal of Interdisciplinary History* 5 (1974–5), p. 579.

43 S. Epstein, *Wills and Wealth in Medieval Genoa, 1150–1250* (Cambridge, Massachusetts, 1984), p. 44.

44 Chiffoleau, *La comptabilité de l'au-delà*, pp. 183–4; Epstein, *Wills and Wealth in Medieval Genoa*, pp. 146–7; Romano, *Patricians and Popolani*, pp. 114–15, 262; Jenkinson, 'Mary de Sancto Paulo', pp. 432–3.

45 Chiffoleau, *La comptabilité de l'au-delà*, pp. 184, 262; Robert, *Testaments de l'officialité de Besançon*, I, pp. 271–2; II, p. 153.

46 Jacotin, *Preuves de la maison de Polignac*, II, p. 318; J. Nichols, *A Collection of All the Wills of the Kings and Queens of England* (London, 1780), p. 278; Chiffoleau, *La comptabilité de l'au-delà*, p. 182.

47 Epstein, *Wills and Wealth in Medieval Genoa*, p. 152; Cohn, *The Cult of Remembrance*, p. 123; M-T. Lorcin, *Vivre et mourir en Lyonnais à la fin du moyen âge* (Paris, 1981), pp. 135–45.

48 Chiffoleau, *La comptabilité de l'au-delà*, p. 133; Robert, *Testaments de l'officialité de Besançon*, II, pp. 153–4.

49 N.H. Nicolas, *Testamenta Vetusta*, 2 vols (London, 1826), I, pp. 127–8; Nichols, *Collection of All the Wills*, p. 212.

50 J.C. Parsons, '"Never was a body buried in England with such solemnity and honour": the burials and posthumous commemorations of English queens to 1500', in A.J. Duggan (ed.), *Queens and Queenship in Medieval Europe* (Woodbridge, 1997), pp. 322–37.

51 Epstein, *Wills and Wealth in Medieval Genoa*, pp. 159–60; Lorcin, *Vivre et mourir en Lyonnais*, p. 154; Nichols, *Collection of All the Wills*, pp. 178, 225; R.L. Storey (ed.), *The Register of Thomas Langley Bishop of Durham, 1406–37*, 6 vols (Surtees Society, 164, 166, 169–70, 177, 182, 1956–70), III, pp. 62–4.

52 Epstein, *Wills and Wealth in Medieval Genoa*, p. 154; Swanson (ed. and trans.), *Catholic England*, pp. 231–3; Jacotin, *Preuves de la maison de Polignac*, II, p. 202; IV, pp. 239–40; Cohn, *The Cult of Remembrance*, pp. 81–4.

53 N.P. Tanner, *The Church in Late Medieval Norwich 1370–1532* (Toronto, 1984), pp. 92–6, 100–6; *Calendar of Patent Rolls, 1313–17* (London, 1898), p. 31.

54 See earlier, pp. 156–9, 236–8.

15 Women, heresy and witchcraft

Although the majority of the population in medieval Europe followed the tenets of the Roman Church, heresy flourished at different times in the later Middle Ages in particular regions, implicating families and communities as well as the individual believer. The Church displayed a lively fear of heresy. From the twelfth century, with its upsurge of popular religious movements, it was faced with a number of fringe and heretical groups aspiring to follow the apostolic life. Some, like the Humiliati and the Franciscans, were incorporated into the Church by Innocent III. Others, such as the Waldensians and the Cathars, were judged heretical and the papacy and local ecclesiastical authorities did their best to suppress them. Heresy remained a problem for the Church in the fourteenth and fifteenth centuries, with the rise of the Hussites in Bohemia and the Lollards in England.

Not every part of Europe was affected by heresy, and some of the cults were highly localised. In 1300 in Milan, the bones of a woman called Guglielma (d. 1281) were disinterred and burnt because her followers believed that she personified the Holy Spirit. They also believed that one of the women amongst them would become pope and be attended by female cardinals and that this would mark the dawn of a new age.[1] Other groups were much more widespread and posed a serious challenge to the Church. The Waldensians spread from Lyons into southern France, Italy and Germany, and at the end of the Middle Ages were particularly associated with the Alpine regions of Dauphiné and Piedmont. The Cathars were first recorded in the Rhineland, but soon came to be primarily associated with Languedoc and the towns of northern and central Italy; by the early fourteenth century, they were restricted to fringe areas such as the Pyrenees. The Hussites and Lollards were found almost wholly in Bohemia and England respectively, and both continued into the Reformation period.

The part played by women in these heretical movements has given rise to considerable discussion. It has been suggested that women were drawn to heresy because it gave them a wider role and greater influence than was allowed by the medieval Church. Heresy provided opportunities for preaching and ministry at a time when even abbesses were finding that their preaching to their fellow nuns was being increasingly restricted. Yet at the same time opportunities for women to live a religious life within the Church were growing, and many women found fulfilment within the Church. Recent research has found that female heretics pursuing an active ministry were the exception rather than the rule. The idea that women were subordinate to men in the social hierarchy applied among orthodox and heretics alike, as did the concept that the woman's life centred on her household. It was in the context of family and household that women exercised their greatest influence.

In assessing this influence and the attraction which heresy had for women, the nature of the evidence has to be taken into consideration. In the regions where the Church was concerned to suppress heresy, considerable information was amassed on the women involved. The Church was concerned with the individual heretic and therefore the women had to answer for themselves; however, there is no way of telling whether they were convinced heretics or simply echoing their husbands' beliefs. Individual examinations provide a vivid picture of heresy, as E. Le Roy Ladurie found in the case of Montaillou. Yet these examinations have to be carefully assessed, since the Church was working to a set agenda and had particular questions to follow up. The examinations are essentially of suspects and do not give the full story of the man or woman being interrogated. Without the examinations, information on heresy would be much more limited, but contemporary attitudes of both Church and society have to be borne in mind.

Waldensians and Cathars

Although the Church was anxious to draw the line between heresy and orthodoxy, this was not so easily done in practice. As has been seen with nuns, beguines and penitents, women were attracted by the popular preachers of the twelfth and early thirteenth centuries, and were drawn to both the Waldensians and Cathars for similar reasons. Poverty and asceticism were regarded as integral to the apostolic life and were at the heart of both heresies. Valdes in the 1170s renounced the fortune which he had made as a merchant in Lyons and took up a life of poverty and preaching. He sold his goods once he had provided for his wife and dowered his two daughters so that they could enter the abbey of Fontevrault.[2] He was condemned by the Church for his emphasis on having the Scriptures in the vernacular and for his unauthorised preaching.

Valdes attracted both men and women. According to Stephen of Bourbon, who was undoubtedly a hostile witness, he sent his illiterate followers out to preach in the villages, and the preachers included women. The trial of heretics at Trier in 1231, held by Conrad of Marburg, indicates that the heretics' ideas on the Mass were very different from those of the Roman Church. It was said at the trial that the host could be consecrated anywhere by a man or woman and that the priest's ordination was unnecessary. It would therefore appear that women played a significant role among the Waldensians.

However, the information does not come from Waldensian sources and it is unknown how many women either preached or celebrated Mass. In view of society's attitudes towards women, it is likely that the number was small and probably restricted to the early years of the movement.[3]

Even in the early years there is evidence that Waldensian women were living in small communities like the beguines and penitents. A group of Sisters probably had a house at Castelnaudary about 1206 where they lived a life of prayer and wore distinctive dress. Further evidence is found in the 1240s when it appears that the Brothers were more numerous and led an active preaching ministry; preaching by the Sisters mainly took place in private houses. Information around 1300 refers to Sisters and Brothers living together in communities, and Sisters were referred to in Piedmont in 1530. Persecution probably drove such communities underground in the fourteenth and fifteenth centuries, but evidence from Strasbourg around 1400 suggests that they continued to exist.[4]

In the late Middle Ages, Waldensians were living in the mountain regions of Dauphiné and Piedmont. In this peasant society, the women's role has to be set in the context of the family. It appears to have been expected in the Dauphiné that Waldensians would marry within the sect. The accusation that they did not observe the rules over consanguinity and did not regard fornication as a sin could be mirrored in orthodox peasant communities in other parts of Europe, as could the importance attached to betrothal. Although on the whole they disapproved of the Catholic clergy, Waldensians attended Mass and Easter communion. However, they had their own pastors who preached to them, heard confessions and gave absolution. Within this framework, women had a role as individual believers and as dispensers of hospitality. When Catherine Ripert was looking after livestock on the high Alpine pastures, she met a pastor, but did not have the chance to make her confession. Pastors lodged in the houses of Gabriel Orsel and Gabriel Vincent, and the wife and mother respectively were unable to persuade their menfolk to make a confession.[5] Such statements point to women being active Waldensians within the family.

From the Church's point of view, the Cathars presented a much more serious threat than the Waldensians because of their dualist beliefs, their organisation, and their support, notably in Languedoc (where they are often known as Albigensians and where there is more abundant information) and in the towns of north and central Italy. The example of poverty and asceticism set by the Cathar Perfecti appealed to contemporary society, notwithstanding their dualist doctrine that the material world was evil and that good was to be found only in the spiritual sphere. The heresy has been seen as providing women with the greatest opportunities for independent action since women are found not only as believers but also as Perfecti who had the right to administer the Cathar sacrament of the *consolamentum*. More recently, the importance of the women's role has been questioned on the basis of a statistical analysis of Inquisition material.[6] Moreover, as with the Waldensians, change was likely to occur over time, from the years around 1200 when the heresy was at its height, through the years of Simon de Montfort's crusade and persecution by the Inquisition, to the time when the heresy was largely confined to the Pyrenees. Looking at the social context, this was the time when Roman law was growing in importance in these regions and when women's rights to inheritance and dower were becoming increasingly limited.

Both men and women became Cathar believers in large numbers, especially in the heartland of the heresy in Languedoc, the region around Toulouse, Carcassonne, Albi and Foix. As believers they lived their lives within their families and received the sacrament of the *consolamentum* only on their deathbeds. The actual number of believers is unknown, but it is likely that a sizeable proportion were women. In the inquiry of 1245–6 for the region between Toulouse and Carcassonne, which was planned to bring in all men and women over the age of puberty, 31.8 per cent of the witnesses and 26.8 per cent of those who said that they had been believers were women. These figures may well have been underestimates. As with the women of the Dauphiné, the women's role centred on their families and households, and it has been suggested that their importance in providing hospitality grew as persecution mounted in the 1230s and 1240s and the Perfect found it increasingly difficult to find safe refuges.[7]

The role of women among the Perfect has attracted greater attention. A man or woman became a member of the Perfect by receiving the *consolamentum*, and from that time until death was entitled to receive the *melioramentum* or special greeting from believers, and to administer the *consolamentum*. The Perfect abstained from sexual relationships and from any food, such as meat, dairy products and eggs, which resulted from copulation. Cathar bishops and deacons were chosen from the Perfect. The way of life of the Perfect, with its fasting, poverty and asceticism, gave them a high reputation among their followers, as has been seen among those with similar lifestyles elsewhere. Their beliefs, however, were in radical contrast to those of the orthodox mystics who meditated on the sufferings of the human Christ; for the Cathars, Christ was a spirit and not a man, since everything in the material world was evil.

Women were to be found among the Perfect in considerable numbers, several receiving the *consolamentum* when they were widowed. In the inquiry of 1245–6, 44.2 per cent of the Perfect were women, 318 out of a total of 719, although by then their numbers were declining. An inquiry in Florence in the 1240s uncovered fifty-three Perfecti, of whom at least twenty-three were women. The Perfect in Languedoc included women from leading noble families. Blanche de Laurac received the *consolamentum* in 1209 after the death of her husband, her daughter Mabilia receiving it at the same time; Blanche's son and four daughters were all Cathars. Esclarmonde, sister of the count of Foix, was widowed around 1202 and received the *consolamentum* two years later at Fanjeaux along with three other women.[8]

Did these women engage in an active ministry of preaching? The woman who comes most readily to mind is Esclarmonde de Foix, who was present at the public debate between Catholics and Cathars at Pamiers in 1207. She was told by a Catholic monk that she had no right to speak on such an occasion and would be better employed getting on with her spinning. On the whole, it appears that male Perfecti agreed with him. Women were not appointed Cathar bishops and deacons, and it is likely that this was something which would never have been tolerated by society. It was rare for women to preach or to administer the *consolamentum*, although with the establishment of the Inquisition in 1234 and the fall in male Perfect activity, women did more travelling round the country. One woman Perfect at Orvieto in central Italy was found administering the *consolamentum*.[9]

Most of the women Perfecti of Languedoc lived a life comparable to that of nuns and beguines in communities established for them or in their own homes. Family networks were important. Raymond-Roger, Count of Foix, appointed his wife Philippa as head of the house at Dun and his sister Esclarmonde as head at Pamiers. These houses came under the ultimate control of the male Cathar hierarchy.[10] Within this framework, the women Perfecti had the opportunity to be Cathar activists. Just as Jacques de Vitry saw the importance of Mary of Oignies as an example of orthodox life, so the women Perfecti can be seen as examples in their own locality and as a means of attracting further Cathar believers. The houses became a base for both teaching and hospitality, and the influence of a woman Perfect who was also a member of the nobility should not be underestimated. According to a deposition made by her grandson, Bernard-Oth of Niort, in 1246, Blanche de Laurac lived in a community of the Perfect which was visited by the local deacon and by other Cathars. Knights and nobles of the area were invited to sermons and all of them gave the Perfect the ritual greeting and asked for their blessing before departure.[11]

The houses also played an important part in the education of children. Some girls in the houses of the Perfect received the *consolamentum* as young as the age of nine, although this was not invariably the case. Dulcia spent a year with Brunissende, another Perfect of Laurac, and then had a two-year trial with a view to receiving the sacrament, but she was thought to be too young to take the step. Arnaude, later the wife of Arnaud de Frémiac, was forced to take the sacrament as a child by her uncle, but was later converted to orthodoxy by St Dominic. Girls who received a Cathar education and then married spread the heresy in their locality and among their children. Guiraude, daughter of Blanche de Laurac and a Perfect, together with her brother Aymeric put the town of Lavaur in a state of defence against Simon de Montfort and the crusaders; on the town's surrender in 1211, both were put to death. Another daughter, Esclarmonde, married the lord of Niort and probably brought heresy into the area. She brought up all her children as heretics, although her husband did not favour them; her eldest son, Bernard-Oth, spent four or five years as a child with his grandmother. Esclarmonde became a Perfect, probably after the death of her husband, and she and her eldest son submitted to Louis IX in 1240. The mother's influence can also be seen with Furneria, wife of Guillaume-Roger de Mirepoix, who left home to become a Perfect and later persuaded her daughter to follow her example.[12] St Dominic's foundation of a nunnery at Prouille challenged Catharism on its own terms, providing for women and girls in a way which would have an impact outside the convent walls. The house was a mission centre to the surrounding region.

In theory, women Perfecti had greater powers than women in the Roman church, but in practice their role was more limited. They certainly exercised influence within their own localities, and the spread of Catharism was due to women as well as men. Many of their activities ran parallel to those of religious women in the Roman Church, and therefore the question arises as to why they became Perfect heretics. Enthusiasm for a poor and ascetic way of life provides part of the explanation, and the attraction of the example of the Perfect can be compared with that of St Francis, St Clare, Mary of Oignies and others. In Languedoc, the Cathars offered the best opportunity to live an ascetic life. Few nunneries had been established in the Cathar heartland and there were none on the lands of the count of Toulouse, east of the River Garonne. It was only in the thirteenth century that the number of nunneries grew.[13] Moreover, the experience of women such as the daughters of Blanche de Laurac underlines the importance of family networks, which were both powerful and extensive. As in other aspects of women's lives, the family group exerted strong influence from birth to death.

In their heyday, before Simon de Montfort's crusade of 1209–18 and persecution by the Inquisition from 1234, the Cathars drew support from all social groups. Changes were becoming noticeable from the 1240s and by the time that Jacques Fournier, Bishop of Pamiers, was investigating Montaillou in the Pyrenees in the early fourteenth century, the situation was radically different. No women were then numbered among the Perfect and the women accused of heresy were rather to be counted among the believers. Yet although families can be described as Catholic or Cathar, there was no rigid division of beliefs, and the same person could follow tenets of both orthodoxy and heresy. Beatrice de Planissoles, whose first husband was lord of Montaillou, was Cathar and orthodox at different points in her life. She also had various superstitious beliefs; she kept her daughter's first menstrual blood to use as a future love potion, and her grandsons' umbilical cords to help her win her lawsuits. Her orthodox practices did not save her from punishment as a heretic and she was condemned to wear the double yellow cross.

The family and household constituted the centre of women's activity and it was here that they exerted influence. A small colony of heretics settled in Catalonia where Raymonde Piquier was the mistress of the Perfect Guillaume Bélibaste. Women householders, such as Alazais Rives, the sister of Prades Tavernier who was a Perfect, gave hospitality to the heretics. Intermarriage took place between heretics, and religious differences within a family led to trouble. Emersende Marty, a Cathar, planned to murder her Catholic daughter, Jeanne Befayt, who had been converted while in Catalonia and who is known to have attacked her mother while they lived together. Mengarde Clergue sent food parcels to the Montaillou heretics who were in prison. She spread her heretical ideas in conversation with village women, as when she described the Perfect as blessed and holy during a delousing session with Raymonde Guilhou. Her son, Pierre Clergue, the parish priest, buried her body before the altar of the Virgin Mary in Montaillou church, another instance of the religious cross-currents in the village.[14]

Hussites and Lollards

The Hussites took their inspiration from the academic and popular preacher, John Hus, who was put to death at the Council of Constance in 1415. He condemned Church abuses and emphasised the authority of the Bible and frequent communion; although orthodox on the doctrine of transubstantiation, he came to advocate communion in both kinds for the laity. Hussitism grew rapidly after his death and developed as a political, military and national movement which the Church was unable to repress. Women undoubtedly supported the movement, but information on their role is limited. The reports that they preached in Prague and that, among the radicals, they consecrated the bread and wine at the Eucharist have to be treated with caution. Some women formed small groups to live a religious life and also provided patronage. Thomas of Štítný moved to Prague with his daughter in 1373 and spent the rest of his life translating and writing devotional works. His daughter joined a community of women living near the Bethlehem chapel where sermons in Czech were preached twice every Sunday and feast day. The women's way of life was similar to that of the beguines. Catherine of Vraba endowed a group of twelve women who had decided to follow the religious life. She also provided an endowment in 1402 for Czech sermons in Prague cathedral every feast day and three times a week in Advent and Lent.[15] Such provision was in the tradition of popular vernacular preaching in Bohemia.

Certain noble families in Poland became Hussites and protected the heretics in their localities. A number of women were active in the movement. Helena Krzywosądzka was one of those who arranged meetings with heretical priests and brought up their children to be Hussites; two of Helena's sons were heretics and she rejected another son who was orthodox. In Pakość in 1441, the wife of the lord of the town, Anna Maternina, and three other women abjured their heresy before the archbishop of Gniezno; all had received communion in both kinds. Some husbands may have compelled their wives to adopt Hussitism. Abraham Zbąski became a Hussite and recanted in 1440; after his death two years later, his wife, mother and daughter were examined by the Church and claimed that they had been forced to become heretics. There is no way of knowing whether their claim was true.[16]

There was a close relationship between the Hussites and John Wycliffe (d. 1384) and the Lollards in England. The heresy ceased to be a political threat after the collapse of the Oldcastle rebellion in 1414. Yet the number of heresy trials in the late fifteenth and early sixteenth centuries indicates that pockets of heresy probably continued to exist throughout the fifteenth century in several large towns and certain parts of the countryside. It was in such a local context that women were influential, and women supporters were to be found among the gentry and urban elite, as well as at craftsman and artisan levels.

As with other heresies, women may also have played a religious role. The evidence for women priests and preachers is problematical, although such roles were acceptable in theory as agreeing with Lollard beliefs. Stories circulated of girls celebrating the Eucharist, but these cannot be proved. The omission of the words of consecration, specifically mentioned in some cases, would be in accord with the Lollard denial of transubstantiation. Certain Lollards specifically attributed priestly powers to women. Walter Brut, who recanted in 1393, based his arguments on women's administration of baptism and therefore argued for their ability to administer extreme unction, give absolution and consecrate the host. He also accepted that women might preach. However, he saw women as exercising their priesthood only in the absence of those who had been ordained. William White in 1428 believed that all pious men and women had the right to forgive sins, and it has to be borne in mind that Lollards wanted no intermediary between themselves and God.[17] In the Church's sense of the term, it appears unlikely that there were women priests among the Lollards. During the Norwich heresy investigations of 1428–31, John Godsell, parchment maker of Ditchingham, believed that any pious man or woman was a priest. His words were echoed by his wife Sibyl.[18]

As far as women Lollards among the gentry are concerned, the difficulty lies in identifying them. Few of these women were examined by the Church authorities and the use of wills gives rise to problems of interpretation. Apart from the denial of transubsantiation, there was no clear dividing-line between orthodoxy and heresy, and the desire for simplicity and contempt for the body are found on both sides.[19] It appears probable that Anne Latimer, widow of the Lollard knight Sir Thomas Latimer, held Lollard beliefs; in her will, she placed particular emphasis on charity to the poor, and she made no provision for prayers for her soul. The widow of another Lollard knight, Alice Sturry (d. 1414), appears to have been orthodox in her piety, providing for Masses for her soul and making bequests to religious houses.[20] Women Lollards among the gentry were able to exercise influence in both household and locality, protecting known heretics, exercising patronage in local churches and carrying out their duties of hospitality and charity.

Lollards were also found among men and women of urban elites. The involvement of artisans and craftsmen has long been known, but Lollardy among people of higher status has become apparent in more recent research. The inquiries into heresy at Colchester in 1527–8 show that a number of women of the elite were implicated; Margaret Cowbridge and Catherine Swayne were widows of bailiffs and part of a tight-knit social network, linked by ties of marriage as well as godparent relationships going back to the early sixteenth century. A similar phenomenon has been found at Coventry where Alice Rowley played an exceptionally prominent role. While most of the women exerted influence on their households and acquaintances, Alice Rowley was a prominent member of a group of women Lollards. She was the widow of a mercer and became most active in Lollardy as a widow. She was literate and a book-owner, and the inquiry into heresy in 1511 revealed that she preached and taught in groups of men and women. She admitted her heresy in 1511–12 and was sentenced to perform penance. Her history after 1512 is unknown.[21]

The evidence for women Lollards in the lower social groups comes mainly from the heresy trials and the examinations reveal how they supported heretics in the course of their daily lives. The investigators were concerned to discover the women's beliefs, and the refusal to accept transubstantiation, hostility to the institutional Church and opposition to pilgrimages, saints' cults and images were widespread. In her abjuration, Hawise Mone of Loddon in Norfolk stated that she had believed that the sacraments of baptism, confirmation and extreme unction were unnecessary; confession should be made only to God, and the priest had no power at Mass to transform bread into the body of Christ. The sacrament of marriage did not need to be solemnised in Church, nor by a special form of words as the Church insisted. She regarded the pope as Antichrist. Tithes might be withheld and Church property confiscated. Fasting was unnecessary. Pilgrimages served only to make priests rich and innkeepers and ostlers merry and proud. She regarded every good man and woman as a priest, and prayer should be made direct to God.[22]

The investigations make it clear that it was the women's family and household role, and not their individual beliefs, that made them influential among the Lollards. Many Lollards married each other and kinship links helped in the spread of the sect and its consolidation in particular parts of England, such as the Chilterns, Kent and Norfolk.[23] In the Norwich trials of 1428–31, several of the heretics were married couples, such as Sibyl and John Godsell, Hawise and Thomas Mone and Matilda and Richard Fletcher. Husband and wife combined in receiving heretics and holding schools for heresy in their homes. This was especially important with a sect which relied on the meeting of house-groups. Hawise Mone admitted that she had harboured nineteen named heretics and many others; the list included four priests, headed by William White, who was a leading Lollard teacher in the area. She also admitted that schools of heresy had been held in her house and she herself had learned many of her beliefs there. Similar accusations were made against her husband, who was a shoemaker.[24]

Whether Hawise and her husband learned the heresies orally or could read Lollard books is not clear; both claimed not to be able to read when they made their abjurations.[25] Lollard meetings included the reading of texts, and Margery Baxter invited Joan Clyfland to come to her room at night to hear her husband read the law of Christ, possibly the English Bible. Margery considered her husband to be the best teacher of Christianity, and she also had a high opinion of William White, whom she thought of as a great saint. She had kept him concealed in her house and carried his books from Yarmouth to her home village of Martham. Margery passed his teaching on to other women, and it is likely that other Lollard wives did the same. Margery was convinced of her own prospects of salvation. She said that she would never go on pilgrimage to 'Falsyngham' or anywhere else. Crucifixes and images, in her view, were fashioned by lewd carpenters and painters.[26]

In receiving heretics, women carried out their customary function of hospitality, and the Lollard belief that the fasts laid down by the Church need not be observed had its implications for housekeeping. It was also a way in which the heretic could be discovered. Margery Baxter saw no need to fast, and when Joan Clyfland's servant saw Margery soon after Ash Wednesday, she found a piece of salt pork being boiled over the fire. Isabella Davy ate young doves in Lent. John Burell alleged that Hawise Mone and three men broke the Lenten fast on Easter Saturday by eating a quarter of cold pork. It was difficult for these women to keep their activities secret in the living conditions of the later Middle Ages.[27]

As a result of contemporary ideas on the weakness of women, churchmen often believed that they were more active than was really the case. There is no doubt that women were attracted to heresy in certain parts of Europe, and a few preached and administered sacraments. Yet constraints on public life for women applied all over Europe, and the role of most women heretics was rooted in their family and neighbourhood. The decision to become a heretic in the first place may often have been influenced by family considerations. The woman's position within her household enabled her to influence children, servants and visitors. She had the opportunity to spread heresy among friends and neighbours. Her influence was likely to be greater if she was a woman of standing, but the wife of a peasant or craftsman could help to spread heresy in a village or market town. The part that these women played was not dramatic, but it contributed to the tenacity of heretical beliefs into the sixteenth century.

Witchcraft

There was a close connection between heresy and witchcraft in the minds of churchmen, some of whom considered that all those who practised magic were heretics. From the thirteenth century, the Church saw all forms of magic, whether beneficent or harmful, as inspired by the devil, and in 1398 the University of Paris condemned all witchcraft as heretical.[28] Although the main task of the Inquisition was to suppress heresy, from the thirteenth century onwards it also heard cases involving magic. Cases of witchcraft were also heard by local ecclesiastical and secular courts. There is no doubt that magic was widely practised and it appears increasingly in the records of the fourteenth and fifteenth centuries. It was widely held that devils were powerful in human affairs and that witchcraft was performed with their help. Some trials brought out dramatic evidence of diabolism, the worship of the devil or the recognition of him as one's lord, often at a witches' sabbath, but the confessions of such activities may well have been imposed on the suspect by the inquisitor. Many trials were concerned with sorcery, or maleficent magic, and apart from the political trials of the reign of Philip the Fair in France, were primarily centred on the events and disasters of daily life.

The frequency of witch trials increased during the later Middle Ages. Figures remained relatively low in the fourteenth century, but there was a sharp acceleration after about 1430, especially in France, Germany and Switzerland. Trials were especially numerous between 1455 and 1460, and 1480 and 1485. To some extent, the increase is due to the survival of judicial records and the wider use of inquisitorial procedure. Whether the increase can be linked to plague and migration is uncertain, although social friction could well be a cause. What is clear is that by the end of the Middle Ages there was a growing fear of magic and greater stress on diabolic rituals in treatises written after about 1450. The growing concern over witchcraft was epitomised by the publication in 1486 of *Malleus Maleficarum* (The Hammer of Witches) by the Dominican friars and inquisitors, Henry Kramer and Joseph Sprenger.[29]

Although the witch in fairy tales is often portrayed as an old woman, medieval witches were both men and women, and their age was rarely specified. There was probably an overlap with those women who practised herbal medicine; in 1485, a woman in Innsbruck was accused of making her servant ill while preparing a remedy for a customer.[30] Over much of Europe, women were charged with causing disease and bodily harm, often by means of a potion or a wax image. Dorothea Hindremstein of Lucerne in 1454 was accused of making a neighbour's child ill after a quarrel. Love potions were in considerable demand. A woman at Todi in Italy in 1428 provided one for a woman to cook for her husband in order to put an end to his domestic violence, and it was said to have put him into a frenzy of infatuation for three days. Magic was also performed on livestock and the weather. In 1459 Catherine Simon of Andermatt was said to have made a pact with the devil leading to avalanches, deaths of livestock and illness.[31] In all these cases, events arose which people were unable to explain, and it was easy to put the blame on magic and witches. Women on their own who had a bad reputation within their communities were especially vulnerable to accusations of witchcraft. Occasionally, mass hysteria broke out. After an epidemic at

Marmande in 1453, the town authorities questioned a woman suspected of causing it. Not content with this, the mob seized ten or eleven other women and the next day, not observing the proper judicial process, subjected them to torture. Two died, while five confessed and were burnt at the stake. The authorities were reprimanded by the king for not maintaining law and order, but by then the women were dead.[32] Such events point to the witch craze of the early modern period.

With the coming of the Reformation in the sixteenth century, the Roman Church ceased to have a universal hold on the inhabitants of Europe, and the growth of Protestantism brought changes as far as women were concerned. Protestants did not extol the state of virginity and the opportunities for women to live a religious life narrowed sharply. In Protestant areas, women were no longer able to embrace the vocation of nun, beguine or recluse. Such a way of life remained possible in Catholic areas, but fewer women were canonised than in the later Middle Ages. As far as marriage was concerned, the position of the wife as subject to her husband continued in all parts of Europe, and the male head of the household became a more patriarchal figure in the course of the sixteenth century. The passive role of women continued to be regarded as the norm until recent times.

Notes

1 M. Lambert, *Medieval Heresy. Popular Movements from Bogomil to Hus* (London, 1977), p. 193; S.E. Wessley, 'The thirteenth-century Guglielmites: salvation through women', in D. Baker (ed.), *Medieval Women* (Studies in Church History subsidia 1, Oxford, 1978), pp. 289–303.

2 W.L. Wakefield and A.P. Evans (eds and trans.), *Heresies of the Middle Ages* (New York, 1969), pp. 200–2.

3 Ibid., pp. 209, 268; Lambert, *Medieval Heresy*, pp. 72, 158, 163; P. Biller, *The Waldenses, 1170–1530. Between a Religious Order and a Church* (Aldershot, 2001), pp. 127–33.

4 Biller, *Waldenses*, pp. 135–54.

5 E. Cameron, *The Reformation of the Heretics. The Waldenses of the Alps, 1480–1580* (Oxford, 1984), pp. 78, 87, 93, 104–13.

6 R. Abels and E. Harrison, 'The participation of women in Languedocian Catharism', *Medieval Studies* 41 (1979), pp. 215–51.

7 Ibid., pp. 221, 241–3.

8 Ibid., pp. 225, 237; Lambert, *Medieval Heresy*, p. 137; C. Lansing, *Power and Purity. Cathar Heresy in Medieval Italy* (Oxford, 1998), p. 118; E. Griffe, *Le Languedoc cathare de 1190 à 1210* (Paris, 1971), pp. 109, 116–17; E. Griffe, *Le Languedoc cathare au temps de la croisade* (Paris, 1973), p. 202.

9 L. Paterson, *The World of the Troubadours. Medieval Occitan Society c. 1100–c. 1300* (Cambridge, 1993), p. 249; the identification of Esclarmonde is not absolutely certain, as it may have been her sister who was present. Abels and Harrison, 'Participation of women', pp. 226–7, 236–7; Lansing, *Power and Purity*, pp. 117–18.

10 Abels and Harrison, 'Participation of women', pp. 228–33.

11 Griffe, *Le Languedoc cathare de 1190 à 1210*, pp. 109–12.

12 Ibid., pp. 54–5, 81, 109–12, 119, 148–9, 179; Griffe, *Le Languedoc cathare au temps de la croisade*, pp. 29–30, 219–20; Abels and Harrison, 'Participation of women', pp. 231–2.

13 Paterson, *World of the Troubadours*, pp. 244–5.

14 E. Le Roy Ladurie, *Montaillou, Village occitan de 1294 à 1324* (Paris, 1978), pp. 55, 60–2, 86, 97, 143–8, 241, 279, 470–2, 501–22.

15 J.M. Klassen, *The Nobility and the Making of the Hussite Revolution* (New York, 1978), p. 87.

16 P. Kras, 'Hussitism and the Polish Nobility', in M. Aston and C. Richmond (eds), *Lollardy and the Gentry in the Later Middle Ages* (Stroud, 1997), pp. 187–93.

17 M. Aston, 'Lollard women priests?', *Journal of Ecclesiastical History* 31 (1980), pp. 444–52, 459–61, and reprinted in M. Aston, *Lollards and Reformers* (London, 1984), pp. 52–9, 62–5.

18 N.P. Tanner (ed.), *Heresy Trials in the Diocese of Norwich, 1428–31* (Camden Society fourth series 20, London, 1977), pp. 61, 67.

19 J.A.F. Thomson, 'Orthodox religion and the origins of Lollardy', *History* 74 (1989), pp. 44–7.

20 The National Archives, London, Prob. 11/3 Marche, fo. 18v; E.F. Jacob (ed.), *The Register of Henry Chichele, Archbishop of Canterbury, 1414–43*, 4 vols (Canterbury and York Society 42, 45–7, 1937–47), II, pp. 7–10; J.C. Ward (ed. and trans.), *Women of the English Nobility and Gentry 1066–1500* (Manchester, 1995), pp. 226–7; K.B. McFarlane, *Lancastrian Kings and Lollard Knights* (Oxford, 1972), p. 214; J.A.F. Thomson, 'Knightly piety and the margins of Lollardy', in Aston and Richmond (eds), *Lollardy and the Gentry*, p. 101.

21 R.G. Davies, 'Lollardy and locality', *TRHS* sixth series 1 (1991), pp. 204–5; J.C. Ward, 'The Reformation in Colchester, 1528–58', *Essex Archaeology and History* 15 (1983), pp. 84–5; S. McSheffrey, *Gender and Heresy. Women and Men in Lollard Communities, 1420–1530* (Philadelphia, 1995), pp. 12, 21, 29–31, 33–6, 44–5, 58, 70, 123–4. The two bailiffs at Colchester, elected each year, headed the government of the town.

22 Tanner (ed.), *Norwich Heresy Trials*, pp. 140–2; a translation is found in R.N. Swanson (ed. and trans.), *Catholic England* (Manchester, 1993), pp. 270–4.

23 Davies, 'Lollardy and locality', p. 195.

24 Tanner (ed.), *Norwich Heresy Trials*, pp. 59, 66, 84, 130, 138, 140, 175, 179; M. Aston, 'William White's Lollard followers', in Aston, *Lollards and Reformers*, pp. 71–99.

25 Aston, 'William White's Lollard followers', pp. 97–8; Tanner (ed.), *Norwich Heresy Trials*, pp. 139, 178.

26 Tanner (ed.), *Norwich Heresy Trials*, pp. 41, 43; depositions against Margery Baxter are translated in P.J.P. Goldberg (ed. and trans.), *Women in England c. 1275–1525* (Manchester, 1995), pp. 290–5. Margery was referring to the shrine of the Virgin Mary at Walsingham in Norfolk.

27 Tanner (ed.), *Norwich Heresy Trials*, pp. 46, 49–50, 64, 75.

28 B. Hamilton, *Religion in the Medieval West* (London, 1986), pp. 164–7.

29 R. Kieckhefer, *European Witch Trials. Their Foundations in Popular and Learned Culture, 1300–1500* (London, 1976), pp. 10–23; R. Kieckhefer, *Magic in the Middle Ages* (Cambridge, 1989), pp. 183, 190, 193–6.

30 Kieckhefer, *European Witch Trials*, p. 56.

31 Ibid., pp. 24–5, 31, 58.

32 Ibid., pp. 24, 55.

Conclusion

The history of women in the later Middle Ages reveals that their reputation as weak and irrational beings was misplaced. Despite the restrictions of patriarchy, subordination and living under the authority of father or husband, many were able to make the most of their lives. Their circumstances and experience were extremely varied, but within the communities in which they lived they had influence as wives, mothers, friends and neighbours. Noblewomen and queens exerted greater power, especially as mothers and widows, influencing political developments at regional and national level. Religious women similarly made their mark on society, and some of the saints and mystics retain their influence to the present day.

Certain experiences transcend chronological and geographical boundaries. The life cycle for women down the ages has moved from childhood to marriage, motherhood and widowhood. Childbearing has taken up a large part of women's adult lives. These biological factors have to be set alongside cultural considerations, and once this is done the distinctiveness of the later Middle Ages becomes apparent. The Church's doctrine on the formation and nature of marriage had a direct impact on the lives of men and women all over Christendom, who found that they were expected to make a lifelong commitment to their partners. The consent of the partners, according to the Church, should be exchanged at a public ceremony, in the presence of the local community and with the approbation of the parents concerned. Financial arrangements for the marriage were a secular concern and, although the dowry was an essential feature of marriage all over Europe, the woman's rights to dower from her husband and a share in her parents' inheritance depended on the law, which differed even over small areas. There came to be considerable diversity over property arrangements as well as over the ages at which marriage was contracted.

Family structures also showed regional variation, with the extended family being more prevalent in southern Europe and the nuclear family further north. It was within the family that most women lived out their lives, both the Church and the law regarding women as subject to their fathers and husbands. The concept of the family covered more than husband, wife, children and other relatives; rather it stood for the whole household, comprising servants, retainers, apprentices and other inmates. The wife was responsible for running the household and this gave her the opportunity to use her influence inside and outside the home. Her caring role extended over servants, kindred, neighbours and the poor. It was taken for granted that marriage would be followed by motherhood and that women of all social groups, from queens to the poor, would take charge of babies and young children and be responsible for the upbringing of their daughters until they married or embarked on the religious life. Mothers gave their daughters a primarily religious and moral education, but also taught them social, domestic and craft skills in order to fit them for their future station in life. These duties have a history well beyond the Middle Ages, and in some respects were still applicable in the twentieth century.

Motherhood had wider implications for noblewomen and queens, since in certain parts of Europe it gave them the opportunity to exercise political power as guardians or regents for their sons. Women such as Blanche of Castile in France and Margaret of Denmark in Scandinavia were strong and effective rulers. Queen Isabella of Castile, wife of Ferdinand of Aragon, was one of the few medieval women who ruled in her own right. Particularly in northern Europe, women had the right to inherit feudal lordships and this gave them a position of regional power, as is apparent with Mahaut, Countess of Artois. By the end of the Middle Ages, however, women's rights of succession had diminished and women found themselves excluded from the inheritances which earlier they would have enjoyed.

Whatever social group they belonged to, women's lives centred on their households. As well as acting as wife, mother and housekeeper, women among the peasantry or living in the towns often contributed to the financial well-being of the family. These women worked in partnership with their husbands, taking responsibility for livestock or poultry, or working at the husband's craft. They embarked on supplementary occupations which could be carried out within the household, such as brewing ale in England. More important was their role in petty retailing, and women retailers are found in all parts of Europe into the early modern period.

Women's paid employment was mainly in low-grade work, such as washing and spinning. Yet in the thirteenth and fourteenth centuries women worked in a wide range of crafts, and the women's guilds of Paris, and of Cologne in the fifteenth century, catered for the luxury market. However, this did not apply all over Europe, and few women in the Italian towns made their mark in the crafts. A small number of European women reached entrepreneurial status, often building on the work of their husbands or other family connections. The concept of a 'golden age' for women after the Black Death was true of certain towns where there was greater employment in expanding industries and a favourable legal situation for women, but often recession and war made for contraction in a wide range of trades. The growth of guilds in the fifteenth century led to increasing restrictions on women's employment, as found in England and Germany, and again this situation continued into the early modern period.

Medieval governments regarded the household as the basic unit within the community and this was reflected in the householder's responsibility for the good behaviour of his household and his duty to pay taxes. Yet with extensive movement of population and migration during the later Middle Ages, families became uprooted and both men and women found themselves marginal and vulnerable if they were on their own. Beggars and prostitutes were likely to find themselves harshly dealt with by the authorities. Prostitution was condemned by the Church, by Louis IX in the thirteenth century, and increasingly at the end of the Middle Ages, but there were also moves to license this marginal group with the establishment of municipal brothels in Spain, Italy, Germany and southern France. The desire to control those living outside respectable households was uppermost in the minds of rulers.

The religious life displays continuity with the early Middle Ages. The Roman Church intensified its hold over Europe between the thirteenth and fifteenth centuries. Its doctrines and recommended ways of life gave a universality to both men's and women's experience. For some women, however, conflict developed between their inner convictions and the control which the Church wished to exert. The popular religious movements of the twelfth and thirteenth centuries saw women engaging in new forms of the religious life, laying emphasis on poverty and renunciation and going back to the way of life of Jesus and the apostles. These movements affected many parts of Europe, notably Italy, Germany and the Low Countries, with the rise of the women mendicants and beguines. The Church felt that there was a danger that these women were out of control, and this led to the suppression of many of the beguines after 1311 and the use of the mendicant third orders to contain religious women.

Some women escaped control, and the thirteenth and fourteenth centuries were a great age for female mystics and saints. These were women who convinced their directors and confessors that they received their revelations direct from God. They had an influential part to play in counselling their communities and some, such as St Catherine of Siena, extended their activities to a larger political stage. Women like Catherine could not be ignored in local and papal politics, any more than Joan of Arc could be at the court of Charles VII.

Orthodox laywomen found that their control of the household gave them a key role in religious instruction, devotion and charity. Whether they were pious or not, their worship in parish church or guild brought them into close touch with their neighbours. Women's networks of friends and acquaintances were common, and since women rarely held public office, were their means of exerting influence and exercising charity. Religion was intertwined with daily life, and devotion to saints was often closely linked with the problems of illness and need which they encountered. In their commemoration of the dead, they remembered their husbands, parents, ancestors and friends, and included all Christians in their prayers. Women visualised themselves as belonging to the community of the dead as well as the living.

The prevalence of heresy in certain regions is a reminder that not all agreed with the doctrines and practices of the Roman Church. It has often been thought that heresy was particularly attractive to women, giving them a more active role than that sanctioned by the Church. Yet evidence among both the Cathars and Lollards indicates that men were normally the active heretics. Women Perfecti were certainly found among the Cathars, but they lived in their households or convents, carrying out the duties of hospitality and education which were expected of European women. Household tasks were similarly carried out by women Waldensians and Lollards. These duties might enable them to spread heretical ideas but did not give them organisational power within the group.

There is little doubt that the position of women was weaker in 1500 than in 1200. Women had fewer rights over property, were increasingly restricted over employment, and religious women were under the control of the Church. Yet they continued to exercise influence through their families and households, just as Christine de Pizan advocated in her advice to the wise princess. In an age when life for everyone was often both short and hard, they made the most of the present and looked forward to securing the best provision they could for the future of their children.

Further reading

Many of the recent works on the Middle Ages contain chapters on women or integrate their discussion of women and men. Works specifically on women cover either the whole of Europe or particular areas or themes. Women and gender are discussed by J.M. Bennett and R.M. Karras (eds), *The Oxford Handbook of Women and Gender in Medieval Europe* (Oxford, 2013); M. Schaus (ed.), *Women and Gender in Medieval Europe. An Encyclopedia* (London, 2006); and P. Stafford and A.B. Mulder-Bakker (eds), *Gendering the Middle Ages* (Oxford, 2001). Masculinity is analysed in D.M. Hadley (ed.), *Masculinity in Medieval Europe* (London, 1999). G. Duby and M. Perrot (eds), *A History of Women in the West*, 5 vols (Cambridge, Massachusetts, 1992–4), cover women's history from ancient to modern times; volume II, C. Klapisch-Zuber (ed.), *Silences of the Middle Ages*, discusses the medieval period; S. Shahar, *The Fourth Estate. A History of Women in the Middle Ages*, (trans.) C. Galai (London, 1983), covers the period from the early twelfth to the early fifteenth century. J.M. Bennett and A.M. Froide (eds), *Singlewomen in the European Past 1250–1800* (Philadelphia, 1999), take the history of women on their own, as does C. Beattie, *Medieval Single Women. The Politics of Social Classification in Late Medieval England* (Oxford, 2007). J.M. Bennett, *Medieval Women in Modern Perspective* (American Historical Association, Washington, 2000), examines concepts of continuity and change.

There are a number of recent histories of medieval women in England, such as H. Leyser, *Medieval Women. A Social History of Women in England 450–1500* (London, 1995) and H.M. Jewell, *Women in Medieval England* (Manchester, 1996); M.E. Mate, *Women in Medieval English Society* (Cambridge, 1999); and J. Ward, *Women in England in the Middle Ages* (London, 2006). P.J.P. Goldberg (ed.), *Women in Medieval English Society* (Stroud, 1997), contains essays on the social aspects of women's lives. The archaeological dimension is considered by R. Gilchrist, *Medieval Life. Archaeology and the Life Course* (Woodbridge, 2012).

Volumes of essays, covering a wide range of women's experiences, incorporate recent views and research. Among the most important are M. Erler and M. Kowaleski (eds), *Women and Power in the Middle Ages*

(Athens, Georgia, 1988), and M. Erler and M. Kowaleski (eds), *Gendering the Master Narrative. Women and Power in the Middle Ages* (Ithaca and London, 2003).

A number of collections of sources has been published and these include G. Brucker (ed.), *The Society of Renaissance Florence. A Documentary Study* (New York, 1971); E. Amt (ed.), *Women's Lives in Medieval Europe. A Sourcebook* (New York and London, 1993); P.J.P. Goldberg (ed. and trans.), *Women in England c. 1275–1525* (Manchester, 1995); and P. Skinner and E. Van Houts (trans. and eds), *Medieval Writings on Secular Women* (London, 2011).

Laywomen

Women, patriarchy and gender are analysed in Bennett and Karras (eds), *Women and Gender in Medieval Europe*. A wide selection of sources on how women were viewed in the Middle Ages is given in A. Blamires (ed.), *Woman Defamed and Woman Defended* (Oxford, 1992). Medical ideas are discussed in C. Rawcliffe, *Medicine and Society in Later Medieval England* (Stroud, 1995). Ways in which ideas changed over the twelfth century are examined in P.S. Gold, *The Lady and the Virgin. Image, Attitude and Experience in Twelfth-Century France* (Chicago, 1985). Rape is discussed by K. Gravdal, *Ravishing Maidens. Writing Rape in Medieval French Literature and Law* (Philadelphia, 1991); G. Ruggiero, *The Boundaries of Eros. Sex, Crime and Sexuality in Renaissance Venice* (Oxford, 1985); and C. Dunn, *Stolen Women in Medieval England: Rape, Abduction and Adultery, 1100–1500* (Cambridge, 2013).

The overall legal position of women according to canon, civil and customary law is investigated in *Recueils de la Société Jean Bodin* 12 (1962), pp. 59–445. Aspects of the law as it affected women are considered in N.J. Menuge (ed.), *Medieval Women and the Law* (Woodbridge, 2000); T. Kuehn, *Law, Family and Women: Towards a Legal Anthropology of Renaissance Italy* (Chicago, 1991); and C. Beattie and M.F. Stevens (eds), *Married Women and the Law in Premodern North-West Europe* (Woodbridge, 2013). The evolution of the dowry is discussed by D.O. Hughes, 'From brideprice to dowry', *JFH* 3 (1978), pp. 262–96. The issues of dowry, property and inheritance are considered in a large number of works, including M.C. Gerbet, *La noblesse dans le royaume de Castille. Etude sur ses structures sociales en Estrémadure, 1454–1516* (Paris, 1979); S.P. Bensch, *Barcelona and its Rulers, 1096–1291* (Cambridge, 1995); M-T. Caron, *La noblesse dans le Duché de Bourgogne 1315–1477* (Lille, 1987); T. Evergates, *Feudal Society in the Bailliage of Troyes under the Counts of Champagne* (Baltimore, 1975); P. Lock, *The Franks in the Aegean* (London, 1995); and J. Hudson, *Land, Law and Lordship in Anglo-Norman England* (Oxford, 1994).

Upbringing

Interest in the history of childhood was stimulated by P. Ariès, *L'Enfant et la vie familiale sous l'Ancien Régime* (Paris, 1960). His views are disputed by S. Shahar, *Childhood in the Middle Ages* (London, 1990), and J.T. Rosenthal (ed.), *Essays on Medieval Childhood* (Donington, 2007). The life cycle is discussed by D. Youngs, *The Life Cycle in Western Europe, c. 1300–c. 1500* (Manchester, 2006). Works on childhood include D. Alexandre-Bidon and D. Lett, *Les enfants au moyen âge* (Paris, 1997); C. Klapisch-Zuber, *Women, Family and Ritual in Renaissance Italy*, (trans.) L.G. Cochrane (Chicago, 1985); B. Hanawalt, *Growing Up in Medieval London. The Experience of Childhood in History* (Oxford, 1993); and K.J. Lewis, N.J. Menuge and K.M. Phillips (eds), *Young Medieval Women* (Stroud, 1999); N. Orme, *From Childhood to Chivalry. The Education of the English Kings and Aristocracy 1066–1530* (London, 1984); N. Orme, *Medieval Children* (New Haven, Connecticut, 2001); K.M. Phillips, *Medieval Maidens. Young Women and Gender in England, 1270–1540* (Manchester, 2003); and L.J. Wilkinson (ed.), *A Cultural History of Childhood and Family in the Middle Ages* (New York, 2010).

The relationship between mother and child is explored in C. Leyser and L. Smith (eds), *Motherhood, Religion and Society, 400–1400. Essays presented to Henrietta* Leyser (Farnham, 2011). The experience of adolescent service is discussed by P.J.P. Goldberg, *Women, Work and Life Cycle in a Medieval Economy: Women in York and Yorkshire c. 1300–1520* (Oxford, 1992), and by K. Eisenbichler (ed.), *The Premodern Teenager. Youth in Society 1150–1650* (Toronto, 2002). The experience of orphans is discussed by P. Gavitt, *Charity and Children in Renaissance Florence. The Ospedale degli Innocenti 1410–1536* (Ann Arbor, Michigan, 1990).

Marriage

Overviews of medieval marriage are provided by G. Duby, *The Knight, the Lady and the Priest. The Making of Modern Marriage in Medieval France*, (trans.) B. Bray (Harmondsworth, 1983); J. Goody, *The Development of the Family and Marriage in Europe* (Cambridge, 1983); and C.N.L. Brooke, *The Medieval Idea of Marriage* (Oxford, 1989). Michael Sheehan's articles on the canon law of marriage have been published in *Marriage, Family and Law in Medieval Europe* (Toronto, 1996). Essays on migration are included in P. Horden (ed.), *Freedom of Movement in the Middle Ages. Proceedings of the 2003 Harlaxton Symposium* (Donington, 2007). Two collections of sources provide a comprehensive overview: C. McCarthy (ed.), *Love, Sex and Marriage in the Middle Ages. A Sourcebook* (London, 2004); and J. Murray (ed.), *Love, Marriage and Family in the Middle Ages* (Peterborough, Ontario, 2001).

Sexuality is discussed in J-L. Flandrin, *Sex in the Western World. The Development of Attitudes and Behaviour*, (trans.) S. Collins (Chur, 1991);

J.A. Brundage, *Law, Sex and Christian Society in Medieval Europe* (Chicago, 1987); and V.L. Bullough and J.A. Brundage (eds), *Handbook of Medieval Sexuality* (New York, 1996). Marital problems which came before the Church courts are examined in R.H. Helmholz, *Marriage Litigation in Medieval England* (Cambridge, 1974).

There is a considerable literature on the formation of marriage in particular parts of Europe and only a selection can be given here. For England, see Goldberg, *Women, Work and Life Cycle*, and Z. Razi, *Life, Marriage and Death in a Medieval Parish. Economy, Society and Demography in Halesowen 1270–1400* (Cambridge, 1980); and S. McSheffrey, *Marriage, Sex and Civic Culture in Late Medieval London* (Philadelphia, 2006). For Italy, Klapisch-Zuber, *Women, Family and Ritual*; and T. Dean and K.J.P. Lowe (eds), *Marriage in Italy 1300–1650* (Cambridge, 1998). For Spain, Bensch, *Barcelona and its Rulers*; H. Dillard, *Daughters of the Reconquest. Women in Castilian Town Society, 1100–1300* (Cambridge, 1984); and J. Guiral-Hadziiossif, *Valence, port méditerranéen au quinzième siècle* (Paris, 1986). For France, R. Boutruche, *La crise d'une société. Seigneurs et paysans du bordelais pendant la guerre de cent ans* (Paris, 1947); and M-T. Lorcin, *Vivre et mourir en Lyonnais à la fin du moyen âge* (Paris, 1981). For the Low Countries, M.C. Howell, *The Marriage Exchange. Property, Social Place and Gender in Cities of the Low Countries, 1300–1550* (Chicago, 1998). For the Balkans, S.M. Stuard, *A State of Deference: Ragusa/ Dubrovnik in the Medieval Centuries* (Philadelphia, 1992); and for Ireland, A. Cosgrove (ed.), *Marriage in Ireland* (Dublin, 1985).

Women and family; The house and household

An overview is provided by A. Burguière, C. Klapisch-Zuber, M. Segalen and F. Zonabend (eds), *Histoire de la Famille*, 2 vols (Paris, 1986). Two volumes of essays discuss family life: S. Roush and C.L. Baskins (eds), *The Medieval Marriage Scene. Prudence, Passion, Policy* (Tempe, Arizona, 2005); and I. Davis, M. Müller and S. Rees Jones (eds), *Love, Marriage and Family Ties in the Later Middle Ages* (Turnhout, 2003). A detailed analysis of late medieval Tuscany is found in D. Herlihy and C. Klapisch-Zuber, *Tuscans and their Families. A Study of the Florentine Catasto of 1427* (New Haven, Connecticut, 1985). Peasant families are discussed in W. Rösener, *Peasants in the Middle Ages*, (trans.) A. Stützer (Cambridge, 1992); E. Le Roy Ladurie, *The French Peasantry 1450–1660*, (trans.) A. Sheridan (Aldershot, 1987); R. Fossier, *Peasant Life in the Medieval West*, (trans.) J. Vale (Oxford, 1988); and B.A. Hanawalt, *The Ties that Bound. Peasant Families in Medieval England* (Oxford, 1986). An in-depth village study is provided by E. Le Roy Ladurie, *Montaillou. Cathars and Catholics in a French Village 1294–1324*, (trans.) B. Bray (London, 1978) or by the revised French edition, *Montaillou, Village Occitan de 1294 à 1324* (Paris, 1982). Urban families are discussed in B.A. Hanawalt, *The Wealth of Wives.*

Women, Law and Economy in Late Medieval London (Oxford, 1997); Klapisch-Zuber, *Women, Family and Ritual*; D. Romano, *Patricians and Popolani. The Social Foundations of the Venetian Renaissance State* (Baltimore, 1987); and by D. Nicholas, *The Domestic Life of a Medieval City: Women, Children and the Family in Fourteenth-Century Ghent* (Lincoln, Nebraska, 1985).

The growing interest in household, housing and domesticity is shown in C. Beattie, A. Maslakovic and S. Rees Jones (eds), *The Medieval Household in Christian Europe, c. 850–c. 1550* (Turnhout, 2013); J. Wogan-Browne, R. Voaden, A. Diamond, A. Hutchison, C. Meale and L. Johnson (eds), *Medieval Women: Texts and Contexts in Late Medieval Britain. Essays for Felicity Riddy* (Turnhout, 2000); and M. Kowaleski and P.J.P. Goldberg (eds), *Medieval Domesticity. Home, Housing and Household in Medieval England* (Cambridge, 2008).

For childbirth and motherhood, see J.C. Parsons and B. Wheeler (eds), *Medieval Mothering* (New York, 1996); and J.M. Musacchio, *The Art and Ritual of Childbirth in Renaissance Italy* (New Haven, Connecticut, 1999). For medical care, see Rawcliffe, *Medicine and Society*. Conditions of daily life are discussed by C. Dyer, *Standards of Living in the Later Middle Ages* (Cambridge, 1989); M. Carlin and J.T. Rosenthal (eds), *Food and Eating in Medieval Europe* (London, 1998); and I. Origo, *The Merchant of Prato*. (Harmondsworth, 1992).

Women and work in rural areas; Townswomen and work

A number of books consider women's work in the European context. There are several volumes of collected essays, such as Bennett and Froide (eds), *Singlewomen in the European Past*; Beattie and Stevens (eds), *Married Women and the Law*: B.A. Hanawalt (ed.), *Women and Work in Preindustrial Europe* (Bloomington, Indiana, 1986); C. Dolan (ed.), *Travail et travailleurs en Europe au moyen âge et au début des temps modernes* (Toronto, 1991); and C.M. Barron and A.F. Sutton (eds), *Medieval London Widows 1300–1500* (London, 1994). Individually authored works include E. Uitz, *Women in the Medieval Town*, (trans.) S. Marnie (London, 1990); D. Herlihy, *Opera Muliebria. Women and Work in Medieval Europe* (New York, 1990); and M. Howell, *Women, Production and Patriarchy in Late Medieval Cities* (Chicago, 1986), which looks at Leiden and Cologne in their general context; Howell, *The Marriage Exchange*, analyses the situation at Douai.

For England, work in the countryside and in retailing is considered by R.H. Hilton, *The English Peasantry in the Later Middle Ages* (Oxford, 1975), and *Class Conflict and the Crisis of Feudalism* (London, 1985); J.M. Bennett, *Women in the Medieval English Countryside. Gender and Household in Brigstock before the Plague* (Oxford, 1987), and *Ale, Beer and Brewsters in England* (Oxford, 1996); and S. Bardsley, 'Women's work reconsidered: gender and wage differentiation in late medieval England', *PandP*, no. 165 (1999), pp. 3–29, and ibid. no. 173 (2001), pp. 191–202. Urban work is discussed in Goldberg, *Women, Work and Life Cycle*; H. Swanson, *Medieval Artisans. An Urban Class in Late Medieval England* (Oxford, 1989); L. Charles and L. Duffin (eds), *Women and Work in Pre-Industrial England* (London, 1985); and in M.K. McIntosh, *Working Women in English Society, 1300–1620* (Cambridge, 2005).

The situation in Venice is examined by D. Romano in *Patricians and Popolani* and in *Housecraft and Statecraft. Domestic Service in Renaissance Venice, 1400–1600* (Baltimore, 1996), and in Genoa by S.A. Epstein, *Genoa and the Genoese, 958–1528* (Chapel Hill, North Carolina, 1996). Merry E. Wiesner, *Working Women in Renaissance Germany* (New Brunswick, New Jersey, 1986), covers the late medieval as well as the early modern period. The women's guilds in Cologne are considered in detail by M. Wensky, *Die Stellung der Frau in der stadtkölnischen Wirtschaft im Spätmittelalter* (Cologne, 1980). The situation in Ghent is discussed by D. Nicholas, *Domestic Life of a Medieval City*. Several works discuss women's work in Spain, such as *L'Artisan dans la Péninsule Ibérique* (Nice, 1993); Dillard, *Daughters of the Reconquest*; Guiral-Hadziiossif, *Valence*; and C. Carrère, *Barcelone, centre économique à l'époque des difficultés, 1380–1462*, 2 vols (Paris, 1967).

Women's role in medical care is examined by M. Green, 'Women's medical practice and health care in medieval Europe', *Signs* 14 (1988–9), pp. 434–73; M. Green, *Women's Healthcare in the Medieval West* (Aldershot, 2000); M. Green (ed. and trans.), *The Trotula. A Medieval Compendium of Women's Medicine* (Philadelphia, 2001); M. Green, *Making Women's Medicine Masculine. The Rise of Male Authority in Premodern Gynaecology* (Oxford, 2008); K. Park, *Doctors and Medicine in Early Renaissance Florence* (Princeton, 1985); D. Jacquart, *Le milieu médical en France du douzième au quinzième siécle* (Geneva, 1981); L. Granshaw and R. Porter (eds), *The Hospital in History* (London, 1989); and by Rawcliffe, *Medicine and Society*.

Considerable research has been done on later medieval prostitution, as in L.L. Otis, *Prostitution in Medieval Society. The History of an Urban Institution in Languedoc* (Chicago, 1985); B. Geremek, *The Margins of Society in Late Medieval Paris*, (trans.) J. Birrell (Cambridge, 1987); J. Rossiaud, *Medieval Prostitution*, (trans. L.G. Cochrane) (Oxford, 1988); R.M. Karras, *Common Women. Prostitution and Sexuality in Medieval England* (Oxford, 1996); P. Schuster, *Das Frauenhaus. Städtische Bordelle in Deutschland, 1350–1600* (Paderborn, 1992); and R.C. Trexler, 'La prostitution florentine au quinzième siècle', *Annales ESC* 36 (1981), pp. 983–1015.

Note L'Artisan dan la Péninsule Ibérique had no editor and has to be accessed by title.

Ethnic minorities: Jews, Muslims and slaves

Growing interest in this subject has sparked off a growth in publications. Jewish family life and work are discussed in J.R. Baskin (ed.), *Jewish Women in Historical Perspective* (2nd edition, Detroit, 1998); E. Baumgarten, *Mothers and Children. Jewish Family Life in Medieval Europe* (Princeton, 2004); C. Cluse (ed.), *The Jews of Europe in the Middle Ages* (Turnhout, 2004); A. Grossman, *Pious and Rebellious. Jewish Women in Medieval Europe* (Waltham, Mass., 2004); and P. Skinner (ed.), *The Jews in Medieval Britain. Historical, Literary and Archaeological Perspectives* (Woodbridge, 2003).

R.L. Winer, *Women, Wealth and Community in Perpignan, c. 1250–1300* (Aldershot, 2006) examines gender in the context of the Jewish, Muslim and Christian religions in the town. Muslims are discussed in M.D. Meyerson, *The Muslims of Valencia in the Age of Ferdinand and Isabel: Between Coexistence and Crusade* (Berkeley, 1991); and D. Nirenberg, *Communities of Violence. Persecution of Minorities in the Middle Ages* (Princeton, 1996).

Slavery in medieval Europe is analysed in J. Heers, *Esclaves et domestiques au moyen âge dans le monde méditerranéen* (Paris, 1981); and S.A. Epstein, *Genoa and the Genoese, 958–1528* (Chapel Hill, North Carolina, 1996).

Women and power: Noblewomen and queens

Several overall surveys have been published in the 1990s: J.C. Parsons (ed.), *Medieval Queenship* (Stroud, 1994); Parsons and Wheeler (eds), *Medieval Mothering*; A.J. Duggan (ed.), *Queens and Queenship in Medieval Europe* (Woodbridge, 1997); A.J. Duggan (ed.), *Nobles and Nobility in Medieval Europe* (Woodbridge, 2000); and J.C. Ward, *English Noblewomen in the Later Middle Ages* (London, 1992). English source material can be found in J.C. Ward, *Women of the English Nobility and Gentry 1066–1500* (Manchester, 1995).

Biographies of noblewomen include J-M. Richard, *Mahaut comtesse d'Artois et de Bourgogne* (Paris, 1887); D. Eichberger, A.M. Legaré and W. Hüsken (eds), *Women at the Burgundian Court: Presence and Influence* (Turnhout, 2010); C. Weightman, *Margaret of York Duchess of Burgundy 1446–1503* (Stroud, 1989); and M.K. Jones and M.G. Underwood, *The King's Mother. Lady Margaret Beaufort, Countess of Richmond and Derby* (Cambridge, 1992).

Biographies of queens include M. Howell, *Eleanor of Provence. Queenship in Thirteenth-Century England* (Oxford, 1998); J.C. Parsons, *Eleanor of Castile. Queen and Society in Thirteenth-Century England* (New York, 1995); M. Shadis, *Berenguela of Castile (1180–1246) and Political Women in the High Middle Ages* (Basingstoke and New York, 2009); J. Bianchini, *The Queen's Hand. Power and Authority in the Reign of Berenguela of Castile* (Philadelphia, 2012); T. Earenfight, *The King's Other Body. Maria of Castile and the Crown of Aragon* (Philadelphia, 2010); and P.K. Liss, *Isabel the Queen. Life and Times* (Oxford, 1992).

Laywomen and the arts

Most of the works in the previous section include chapters on patronage of the arts. A number of monographs focus on patronage, including J.H. McCash (ed.), *The Cultural Patronage of Medieval Women* (Athens, Georgia, 1996); C.E. King, *Renaissance Women Patrons. Wives and Widows in Italy c. 1300–1550* (Manchester, 1998); J.M. Wood, *Women, Art and Spirituality. The Poor Clares of Early Modern Italy* (Cambridge, 1996); and A.M. Morganstern, *Gothic Tombs of Kinship in France, the Low Countries and England* (Philadelphia, 2000). The patronage of Isabella d'Este is discussed in Julia Cartwright, *Isabella d'Este, Marchioness of Mantua, 1474–1539. A Study of the Renaissance*, 2 vols (London, 1903).

Books and book ownership are discussed by S.G. Bell, 'Medieval women book owners: arbiters of lay piety and ambassadors of culture', in Erler and Kowaleski (eds), *Women and Power in the Middle Ages*, (Athens, Georgia, 1988), pp. 149–87; J. Backhouse, *Books of Hours* (London, 1985); M.M. Manion and B.J. Muir (eds), *The Art of the Book. Its Place in Medieval Worship* (Exeter, 1998); C.M. Meale (ed.), *Women and Literature in Britain, 1150–1500* (Cambridge, 1993); L. Smith and J.H.M. Taylor (eds), *Women, the Book and the Worldly* (Woodbridge, 1995); and L. Smith and J.H.M. Taylor (eds), *Women, the Book and the Godly* (Woodbridge, 1995).

Troubadours are discussed by L.M. Paterson, *The World of the Troubadours. Medieval Occitan Society, c. 1100–c. 1300* (Cambridge, 1993); W.D. Paden (ed.), *The Voice of the Trobairitz. Perspectives on the Women Troubadours* (Philadelphia, 1989); and S. Gaunt and S. Kay (eds), *The Troubadours. An Introduction* (Cambridge, 1999).

Christine de Pizan's life and work are discussed by C.C. Willard, *Christine de Pizan. Her Life and Works* (New York, 1984), and a selection of her works in translation can be found in C.C. Willard (ed.), *The Writings of Christine de Pizan* (New York, 1994).

Religious women

Many of the works on religious women discuss nuns, beguines, penitents, mystics and saints, and only a selection can be given here: D. Bornstein and R. Rusconi (eds), *Women and Religion in Medieval and Renaissance Italy* (Chicago, 1996); *La femme dans la vie religieuse du Languedoc* (Toulouse, 1988); F.J. Griffiths and J. Hotchin (eds), *Partners in Spirit. Women, Men and Religious Life in Germany, 1100–1500* (Turnhout, 2014); A. Minnis and R. Voaden (eds), *Medieval Holy Women in the Christian Tradition c. 1100–c. 1500* (Turnhout, 2010); A.B. Mulder-Bakker (ed.), *Sanctity and Motherhood. Essays on Holy Mothers in the Middle Ages* (New York, 1995); M. Parisse (ed.), *Les religieuses en France au treizième siècle* (Nancy, 1985); J. Raitt (ed.), *Christian Spirituality. High Middle Ages and Reformation* (London, 1987); P. Ranft, *Women and the Religious Life in Premodern Europe* (Basingstoke, 1996); A. Vauchez, *Les laïcs au moyen âge. Pratiques et expériences religieuses* (Paris, 1987); and A. Vauchez, *Saints, prophètes et visionnaires. Le pouvoir surnaturel au moyen âge* (Paris, 1999).

The attitudes of religious women to food are discussed by C.W. Bynum, *Holy Feast and Holy Fast* (Berkeley, California, 1987). The background to devotion to the Eucharist is discussed by M. Rubin, *Corpus Christi. The Eucharist in Late Medieval Culture* (Cambridge, 1991). A wide selection of source material is included in E.A. Petroff (ed.), *Medieval Women's Visionary Literature* (Oxford, 1986).

Note La femme dans la vie religieuse du Languedoc has no editor and has to be accessed by title.

Religious life: Nuns and nunneries

An overview is found in M. Parisse, *Les nonnes au moyen âge* (Le Puy, 1983). Studies of nuns and nunneries in various parts of Europe include S. Thompson, *Women Religious. The Founding of English Nunneries after the Norman Conquest* (Oxford, 1991); M. Oliva, *The Convent and the Community in Late Medieval England. Female Monasteries in the Diocese of Norwich, 1350–1540* (Woodbridge, 1998); P.D. Johnson, *Equal in Monastic Profession. Religious Women in Medieval France* (Chicago, 1991); P. Linehan, *The Ladies of Zamora* (Manchester, 1997); J.L. Meacham; A.I. Beach, C.R. Berman and L.M. Bitel (eds), *Sacred Communities, Shared Devotions. Gender, Material Culture and Monasticism in Late Medieval Germany* (Turnhout, 2014); and R. Trexler, 'Le célibat à la fin du Moyen Age: les religieuses de Florence', *Annales ESC* 27 (1972), pp. 1329–50. The significance of the layout of nunneries is discussed by R. Gilchrist, *Gender and Material Culture. The Archaeology of Religious Women* (London, 1994).

Religious life: Beguines, penitents and recluses

Several monographs have been published on the beguines, including D. Phillips, *Beguines in Medieval Strasburg. A Study of the Social Aspect of Beguine Life* (Stanford, California, 1941); E.W. McDonnell, *The Beguines and Beghards in Medieval Culture* (New Brunswick, New York, 1954); J-C. Schmitt, *Mort d'une hérésie. L'Eglise et les clercs face aux béguines et aux béghards du Rhin supérieur du quatorzième au quinzième siècle* (Paris, 1978); and W. Simons, *Cities of Ladies. Beguine Communities in the Medieval Low Countries, 1200–1565* (Philadelphia, 2001). Recluses are discussed in A.K. Warren, *Anchorites and their Patrons in Medieval England* (Berkeley, California, 1985); A.B. Mulder-Bakker, *The Rise of the Urban Recluse in Medieval Europe* (Philadelphia, 2005); and L.H. McAvoy, *Medieval Anchoritisms. Gender, Space and the Solitary Life* (Woodbridge, 2011).

Mystics and saints

A useful work of reference is D.H. Farmer, *Oxford Dictionary of Saints* (Oxford, 1997). General surveys of the saints include A. Vauchez, *Sainthood in the Middle Ages*, (trans.) J. Birrell (Cambridge, 1997); D.M. Weinstein and R.M. Bell, *Saints and Society. The Two Worlds of Western Christendom, 1000–1700* (Chicago, 1982); R.M. Bell, *Holy Anorexia* (Chicago, 1985); and R. Kieckhefer, *Unquiet Souls. Fourteenth-Century Saints and their Religious Milieu* (Chicago, 1984).

Medieval mysticism is discussed by C.W. Bynum, *Jesus as Mother. Studies in the Spirituality of the High Middle Ages* (Berkeley, California, 1982); F. Beer, *Women and Mystical Experience in the Middle Ages* (Woodbridge, 1992); C.M. Mooney (ed.), *Gendered Voices. Medieval Saints and their Interpreters* (Philadelphia, 1999); R. Voaden, *God's Words, Women's Voices. The Discernment of Spirits in the Writing of Late-Medieval Women Visionaries* (Woodbridge, 1999), and R. Voaden (ed.), *Prophets Abroad. The Reception of Continental Holy Women in Late-Medieval England* (Woodbridge, 1996); and D. Watt, *Secretaries of God. Women Prophets in Late Medieval and Early Modern England* (Woodbridge, 1997). Monographs on the women mystics include C.W. Atkinson, *Mystic and Pilgrim. The Book and the World of Margery Kempe* (Ithaca, New York, 1983); and Bridget Morris, *St Birgitta of Sweden* (Woodbridge, 1999).

Laywomen and charity; Lay beliefs and religious practice

Works on the poor include M. Mollat, *The Poor in the Middle Ages. An Essay in Social History*, (trans.) A. Goldhammer (New Haven, Connecticut, 1986); J. Henderson, *Piety and Charity in Late Medieval Florence* (Oxford, 1994); and S. Farmer, *Surviving Poverty in Medieval Paris* (Ithaca and London, 2002).

A background survey of medieval religion is provided by B. Hamilton, *Religion in the Medieval West* (London, 1986). The significance of the Mass is discussed by J. Bossy, 'The Mass as a social institution 1200–1700', *PandP* 100 (1983) pp. 29–61. Source material for England is given in R.N. Swanson (ed. and trans.), *Catholic England. Faith, Religion and Observance before the Reformation* (Manchester, 1993).

Studies of religious life within the parish can be found in E. Le Roy Ladurie, *Montaillou*; P. Adam, *La vie paroissiale en France au quatorzième siècle* (Paris, 1964); V. Bainbridge, *Gilds in the Medieval Countryside. Social and Religious Change in Cambridgeshire c. 1350–1558* (Woodbridge, 1996); K.L. French, *The Good Women of the Parish: Gender and Religion after the Black Death* (Philadelphia, 2008); R.W. Scribner, *Popular Culture and Popular Movements in Reformation Germany* (London, 1987); Vauchez, *Les laïcs au moyen âge*; and Romano, *Patricians and Populani*. Guilds are discussed by Bainbridge, *Gilds in the Medieval Countryside.*

Pilgrimage is discussed by J. Sumption, *Pilgrimage. An Image of Mediaeval Religion* (London, 1975) and D. Webb, *Pilgrimage in Medieval England* (London, 2000).

Death and commemoration are discussed in a large number of works, including J. Chiffoleau, *La comptabilité de l'au-delà. Les hommes, la mort et la religion dans la région d'Avignon à la fin du moyen âge* (Rome, 1980); S.K. Cohn, Jr. *Death and Property in Siena, 1205–1800* (Baltimore, 1988) and *The Cult of Remembrance and the Black Death* (Baltimore, 1992); J.R. Banker, *Death in the Community. Memorialization and Confraternities in an Italian Commune in the Late Middle Ages* (Athens, Georgia, 1988); and S. Epstein, *Wills and Wealth in Medieval Genoa, 1150–1250* (Cambridge, Massachusetts, 1984); Lorcin, *Vivre et mourir en Lyonnais*.

Women, heresy and witchcraft

Medieval heresies are surveyed by M. Lambert, *Medieval Heresy. Popular Movements from Bogomil to Hus* (London, 1977). The Waldenses are discussed by E. Cameron, *The Reformation of the Heretics. The Waldenses of the Alps, 1480–1580* (Oxford, 1984); E. Cameron, *Waldenses. Rejections of Holy Church in Medieval Europe* (Oxford, 2001); and P. Biller, *The Waldenses, 1170–1530. Between a Religious Order and a Church* (Aldershot, 2001). Women and the Cathars are examined by E. Griffe, *Le Languedoc cathare de 1190 à 1210* (Paris, 1971); E. Griffe, *Le Languedoc cathare au temps de la croisade* (Paris, 1973); R. Abels and E. Harrison, 'The participation of women in Languedocian Catharism', *Medieval Studies* 41 (1979), pp. 215–51; C. Lansing, *Power and Purity. Cathar Heresy in Medieval Italy* (Oxford, 1998); E. Le Roy Ladurie, *Montaillou*; C. Sparks, *Heresy, Inquisition and Life Cycle in Medieval Languedoc* (Woodbridge, 2014). Works on Lollardy include S. McSheffrey, *Gender and Heresy. Women and Men in Lollard Communities, 1420–1530* (Philadelphia, 1995); M. Aston and C. Richmond (eds), *Lollardy and the Gentry in the Later Middle Ages* (Stroud, 1997); and R. Lutton, *Lollardy and Orthodox Religion in Pre-Reformation England: Reconstructing Piety* (Woodbridge, 2011).

Witchcraft is discussed in J.B. Russell, *Witchcraft in the Middle Ages* (Ithaca, New York, 1972); R. Kieckhefer, *European Witch Trials. Their Foundations in Popular and Learned Culture, 1300–1500* (London, 1976); and R. Kieckhefer, *Magic in the Middle Ages* (Cambridge, 1989).

Index